*Social*

*Foundations*

*of*

*Educational*

*Guidance*

# Social Foundations of Educational Guidance

CARL WEINBERG
UNIVERSITY OF CALIFORNIA, LOS ANGELES

*With Contributions by* DAVID NASATIR
UNIVERSITY OF CALIFORNIA, BERKELEY

*and*

WILLIAM LEWIS SPEIZMAN *and*
PETER McHUGH
COLUMBIA UNIVERSITY

THE FREE PRESS, NEW YORK
COLLIER-MACMILLAN LIMITED, LONDON

# PREFACE

ALTHOUGH many see the relevance of sociological knowledge to the work of the counselor, few perceive this knowledge as more than an additional abstract tool. It may well be that, should a new role such as the clinical sociologist emerge out of the long-range regrouping of thinking about counseling and guidance, a similar relevance will be delegated to psychological knowledge. This would be unfortunate. The problems of guidance are both personal and structural, and focusing upon one aspect to the exclusion of the other would be as disastrous as attempting to field a baseball team with offensive skills and no defense.

The arguments put forward in this book to encourage the inclusion of a sociological perspective in the training and work of the counselor may at times seem exaggerated. It may even seem that I have assumed that counselors and educators of counselors are completely ignorant of the role sociological knowledge can play in their task. For this, although I do not wish to take anything back, I still apologize. I feel that the state of both theoretical and applied knowledge about the sociological dimensions in guidance is so inadequate that I am forced to err on the side of overstatement.

My strongest motive for writing this book is my perception of the ongoing activities of educational guidance as an attempt to bale out a

v

leaky boat with a teaspoon. As the hole becomes larger, the teaspoon will appear even smaller. Guidance must, it seems to me, evolve quickly into a group- rather than an individual-oriented process. I would make the same argument for psychotherapy, but that is the subject of another treatise. The discipline that contains the greatest amount of systematically organized knowledge about group life, and particularly group life in institutions, is sociology. The next step is obvious.

Persons who have been most influential in structuring my thinking about educational functions such as guidance are C. Wayne Gordon of UCLA and Peter McHugh of Columbia University. Dr. McHugh's assistance in reviewing the manuscript and making valuable suggestions was considerable. His responsibility for the final product, however, ended after his suggestions to me. The weaknesses in conception and execution are totally assumed by me and may, in part, be a function of the fact that there were some suggestions which I did not accept.

Lee Weinberg, very much a relation, a university counselor, shared with me her insights into the dynamics of counseling within educational institutions. Her support of many of the important theoretical positions contained in the manuscript is acknowledged, both from the standpoint of advancing the theoretical arguments, as well as from that of reducing the personal conflict that would have accrued from disagreement.

CARL WEINBERG

# CONTENTS

*Social*

*Foundations*

*of*

*Educational*

*Guidance*

# A SOCIOLOGICAL
# POINT OF VIEW

EDUCATIONAL GUIDANCE is a philosophy, a function, a role, and an activity. As a philosophy, guidance is a programmatic conception of the way the educational institution should be related to students. As a function, guidance is a designated set of responsibilities that the school feels it can and should legitimately assume. As a role or set of roles, guidance can be perceived as containing structured positions that carry the obligation of dispensing the school's responsibility in this area. As an activity, guidance is a number of things role occupants do to and for students that are held to be consistent with the philosophy, the function, and the role.

The goals of guidance may be abstract and loosely prescriptive such as "helping students adjust to their school environment," or they may be concrete and directing such as "providing each student occupational and educational data in order for him to make a career decision." Goals are frequently determined by the realistic assessment of each school or district's capacity for accomplishing them. Thus, what is desirable and what is possible become the interacting mechanisms for structuring a guidance program.

Under the general rubric of educational guidance, persons administer intelligence, personality, and achievement tests; they collect vocational-interest data and information about occupations and institutions of higher learning; they group students according to some principle and interview them and their parents, together and separately, providing accumulated data to both; they advise students and teachers, make suggestions to school principals, and engage in psychological counseling. They may also visit homes, contact social agencies, work cooperatively with child guidance clinics, sponsor parent group conferences, and even go so far as coordinating expressive therapy, such as art and music, or have installed a steam room with showers and call it hydrotherapy.

In its most discoverable form, educational guidance is a conglomerate of notions and practices that have become routinized differently in different schools.

This book is a collection of essays about the way in which we may view sociologically the guidance enterprise in its varied aspects. It is hoped that the value of such an endeavor will become clear as the separate papers attempt to integrate the sociological perspective with the educational enterprise. At its motivational base, however, this book was written in order to argue that because guidance practices and individual counseling occur within a framework of collectivities, bureaucracy, and institutionalization, sociological knowledge and methodology are critical to the working understandings of guidance personnel. When the school counselor or the guidance-oriented teacher approaches a pupil problem, he is faced with two environments, one that is idiosyncratic to the individual, the other a social system that is common to the student group. Certainly teachers and counselors are not prone to ignore many demographic variables, but this is the least important contribution that sociology can make to an analysis of the guidance function. More important are the facts of social process, role interaction, leadership styles, intensity and frequency of interaction of peers, integrative functions of the school, and perception of expectations in small-group processes.

As this book does not intend to talk about the guidance function in any ideal sense, the question of what constitutes desirable guidance goals or ways of implementing these goals is not directly relevant. However, the kinds of analyses that follow in the subsequent chapters are frequently prescriptive in the sense that implications for both goals and methods may be logically deduced. The approach is sociological. This restricts us to a consideration of what is, and this "what is" is simply a regrouping of guidance phenomena into analytic schemes, models, and typologies using important sociological concepts and translating these concepts back again into meaningful educational terminology.

Put another way, the purpose of this work is to extend the understanding of the guidance function beyond that which a purely psychological approach, or an approach founded on the accrued intuition of school administrators, presently allows.

Certain characteristics of the guidance function operate within frameworks that have been important concerns to the discipline of sociology, although these frameworks have not necessarily been explored in educational contexts. The school is an important social institution, important to society in fulfilling its traditional and modern purposes. Socialization, integration, allocation to occupational roles, the development of commitments to perform in these roles are some of these purposes. The school is also important to families in the context of such manifest expectations as status validation, occupational mobility, and even entertainment (basketball games, school plays) in towns where the high school is the dominant recreational and entertainment agency. And the school is important to students who are required to make some satisfactory adaptation to institutionalized expectations. Guidance, at this point in time, has emerged as a sub-institution and is required to service some aspects of these social purposes, while at the same time, theoretically, mediating between the instrumental demands of the society and the differential qualities of individual students who are to be funneled into the larger mass.

In what sense, then, is guidance an institution? Despite extensive contributions by academic scholars and people on the firing line, where guidance programs and practices are continually being evaluated, guidance, like its brother functions, teaching and administration, has become relatively stable. That is, new persons entering the field of guidance and occupying a counselor role typically perform their functions in the same ways that they were performed by their predecessors. Routines around important social functions are the most difficult to abrogate, and individuals do not ordinarily change institutions. Culture makes only small concessions over long periods of time and these grudgingly. What people did is what people do. Variations occur only when certain functions and needs become obsolete and others emerge to take their place. New functions, however, become as stabilized as the old and in a relatively short period of time. With its bureaucratic norms, sanctions, and taboos, Madison Avenue advertising has become as highly routinized as were the earlier forms of shopping in the rural community, with the large-company catalogue and the predictability and dependability of local artisans.

The school, being highly dependent upon public support and good will, has rarely permitted itself the luxury of endangering this support. The accounts (by scholars and researchers) of difficulties involved in gaining access to schools for the purpose of initiating experimental changes or investigating practices are legion. The school will change when society clearly recognizes the need for this change, but until cues are clear and support predictable, the traditions will be maintained.

As institutions change, as eventually they will, new roles frequently emerge to carry some part of the burden incurred by the change. An audio-visual specialist is now a must for a modern secondary school just as an advertising executive is a must for the modern politician and political party. Projection of an image in an age of mass visual media is as crucial to the function of getting elected as a guidance counselor is to the function of individualizing instruction. The role of guidance counselor has emerged out of a new conception of the function of the school; this role has been legitimated in the sense that routines, training, status, position within the educational bureaucracy, certification, and a set of responsibilities have all been established, thereby guaranteeing the relative permanence of the role.

Sociology is concerned with groups, institutions, and roles within them. The contribution that sociology has already made to our understanding of the formal organization, bureaucratic functioning, the role of informal groups within institutions, and occupations is considerable, but it is only a beginning and for the most part unapplied. Sociologically we know little about the school, its administrators and teachers, and next to nothing about the guidance process or the guidance counselor. The reasons for this gap in our socioeducational knowledge may be a function of what has been going on within the discipline of sociology itself.

It has not been until relatively recently, at least in comparison with the development of psychology as a method of investigation, that sociology has turned with confidence to empirical research. Through the first part of the twentieth century, the fathers of American sociology (Ward, Sumner, Small, and Cooley) were concentrating their efforts on building systems of thought that would contribute some basic guidelines for the development of sociological theory. The history of the period was reflected in the theories of these men. Their concerns were deeply embedded in the social unrest and injustices that characterized a society in transition from a rural to an urban economy. In some cases their theses supported the social state of things whereas in others their theories argued an applied-science view. Sociology, to some of the foundation builders, was to be a useful tool in the amelioration of social problems. Through the latter part of the 1920s and into the 1930s, prompted by a reaction to what had characterized sociology theretofore, the University of Chicago led an expedition into the field to get the facts. The atheoretical new scientists, led by such men as Robert Park and Ernest Burgess, embarked upon a program of data collecting that was to add a new arm to the sociological venture. What still remained, however, was for the two parts of the body, theory and fact, to get together.

Not until the late thirties and early forties was this accomplished. But this getting together only revealed the inadequacy of the tools and techniques that sociology had to use in order to demonstrate the validity of its theories. Being limited in this way, sociologists realistically confined their endeavors to small theoretical areas, such as child training, ecological characteristics of communities, and voting habits. The complexity involved in the study of major societal institutions was still beyond their scope. Not until the fifties and sixties have we had any sophisticated sociological concepts applied to major areas such as the family, the church, and the school. With the development of sophisticated tools and techniques, accompanied by a staggering increase in the number of Ph.D.'s produced by various departments of sociology, sociological analysis has emerged as a reliable perspective for coming to grips with actual theoretical problems, particularly of the sort with which the guidance counselor must be concerned..

A second factor that has come from the discipline itself to retard its interest in making a contribution to educational theory has been the apparent lack of concern that sociology has shown for making contributions to the solution of social or educational problems at an ameliorative level. Having been so long associated, at least in line with the contribution of its founding fathers, with the business of social work, a concentrated effort has pervaded the ethos of the discipline in the direction of establishing itself as a basic science. Only in the light of gaining confidence in itself has the field begun to realize that contributions to its body of knowledge may be gained by work in laboratories such as educational institutions, where applied interests might also be served.

Education, on the other hand, has not taken a particular fancy to the field of sociology. A required course in the sociology of education for prospective teachers is a rarity even today, and this would seem particularly relevant. A strong foundation in the field of sociology for teacher trainees must be considered a distant possibility at best, but some signs are encouraging.

Institutions of higher education are now, more than ever before, recruiting to their schools and departments of education, psychologists, sociologists, and anthropologists to assist in a national program to translate knowledge uncovered in their separate disciplines into meaningful educational terms. The skills of these individuals are largely incorporated into the research interests of institutions, but as a group they have yet to make a dent in the officially designated programs of teacher, counselor, or administrator certification. Psychology, as a theoretical discipline, had done the most to ensure its place in the educational enterprise, and because of its long association with the field of education, it has been able to dictate a place for itself in the organization of formal requirements. Sociology and anthropology have yet to secure recognition for themselves in the educational program on any consistent or extensive basis.

One fact remains functional as a major deterrent to the incorporation of sociological analysis into official educational programs of colleges and universities. This is that state departments of education do not change their philosophies of what constitutes an adequate instructional program at the same speed that colleges and universities do. Something on the order of a cultural lag occurs, a situation that forces educators to be forever attempting to resolve their theoretical commitments to what constitutes a valuable program in a framework not amenable to such programs, at least not as long as such a program does not ensure the accreditation of its graduates. Such accreditation is still, in most places, in the hands of legislators, and until it is placed within the jurisdiction of the agency which creates and executes the programs (the school), this kind of lag will continue.

The role of the guidance counselor is functional to the school as an institution and to the society, and as such it is a fertile and legitimate area for sociological scrutiny. In the same sense, the role of sociological analysis is functional to the training of guidance counselors, but as this demand does not seem to be forthcoming from counselor training institutions, the impetus for sociologists to begin serious work in this area on any extensive basis is not encouraged. The cycle that leads to academic impotence and professional lag is and has been in motion for some time.

Willis Dugan clearly spelled out the emphasis that has traditionally formulated the character of a guidance counselor training program in an article in the Summer 1962 edition of *Counselor Education and Supervision*. It is his contention, and a correct one if certification requirements for counseling credentials may be taken as an indication of what is expected, that techniques of counseling rather than fundamental knowledge of the nature of the counselee constitute the major focus of programs throughout the nation. It is apparent that Mr. Dugan's concern with the nature of the counselee is clearly with the social and cultural as well as the psychological nature of the individual.

As has been suggested, psychological foundations have not been ignored in guidance training, but this is a matter of a gradual firming up of a relationship that has long existed. Training programs call upon psychological materials and skills partly because they are relevant and partly because they are present in the educational setting and tradition. Guidance counselors have been traditionally accustomed to associating their task generally with that of the clinical psychologist, adding this dimension to vocational counseling, and more often than not, their training is along these lines. Only recently, in the wake of a movement towards self-inspection of the field of guidance, accompanied by a simultaneous increase in sociological interest in education and problems of adolescents, has the profession begun to take account of the social forces that contribute to the school and career orientations of youth. This ferment may be observed at institutions of higher learning, but there is no indication that policy makers, members of boards of education, and state legislators, those who propose certification requirements, are ready to extend the dimensions of training to the sociocultural areas.

Before concluding this Introduction, a few more words about the meaning of guidance, the referent of the following chapters, are necessary. There will be observed a shift in reference, sometimes back and forth, when the concept of guidance is applied. On some occasions, we will be dealing with sheer practices that are engaged in under the formal rubric of guidance. At other times, we will be relating ideas and facts to guidance as an educational philosophy, a way of defining educational goals and methods in general. It is hoped that the reference and context will be constantly made obvious to the reader. Confusion is most likely to appear in those areas where guidance techniques are formally and informally applied in activities that are not considered by the administration of the school to be the responsibility of the guidance counselor. Such a situation, as discussed in some detail in Chapter 1, arises from the guidance responsibilities of the Federal government where it has attempted to initiate with the schools coordinated programs for the uplifting of culturally disadvantaged youngsters. Here there are both a pervading philosophy and applied programs involving schools and school teachers as well as pupils. To dispel confusion between formal function and other practices falling within a guidance philosophy is simply a matter, at this time, of deciphering the differences between standard educational practices and special innovations on these practices based upon emerging needs. The formalization of these needs into ordered routines and programs then follows.

In Chapter 1, "Guidance and Social Change," discussion focuses on the emergence of the guidance philosophy as an instrumental reaction to social change. It views the school as responding to new definitions of man's function in society and to new needs that large segments of that society require to have fulfilled as a prerequisite to adequate social functioning. The point of view presented in this chapter is one that sees social institutions as interactional and as shifting in specific emphases in response to changes in one another. The focus is clearly on how segments of the guidance philosophy emerged and eventually congealed around educational practices that took on a formal character, even though formal roles such as vocational advisor or guidance counselor may not have been present in the educational bureaucracy.

Chapter 2, "Social Explanations for Student Problems," discusses the kinds of data that teachers and counselors use in order to make guidance decisions about individuals that they intend to teach or counsel. The emphasis here is on the differentiation of knowledge that becomes crucial to the kinds of definitions of pupils and their problems and the kinds of hypotheses about solutions that teachers and counselors make. The assumption is that certain facts appear to counselors (or to teachers acting in a quasiguidance capacity) to be more relevant than other facts. The question of relevance is ordinarily resolved in the direction of what counselors are trained to look for. The typical direction is suggested by a preliminary investigation, presented in the chapter, on counselor preferences for the source of pupil difficulty. These data argue the necessity of discussing the alternatives in more depth, both as a way of showing the contribution that sociology may make to a more complete analysis of individual student problems and as a way of posing the logical validity of sociological interpretations of what might seem to be highly idiosyncratic acts presumably based on the unique psychological makeup of individuals. Attacking facts in this manner is certainly not new to sociology, but unfortunately the contributions of early sociologists did not have a serious impact on educational thinking at the time when the guidance function began to inspect fields of knowledge in order to establish training and practice.

Chapter 3, "The Application of Sociological Analysis to Educational Guidance," presents an overview of the kind of significant research, theories, and methods already part of the sociological literature that may be an important increment to the kinds of knowledge that guidance counselors and teachers already use. This sociological addition to their knowledge might help them make more sophisticated judgments in diagnosing individual problems. If we theoretically assume that the function of the guidance program within a school is more than one-to-one counseling, that it contains the possibility of manipulating the whole social system in ways that can avoid many adaptive difficulties for many students, then the kind of knowledge discussed in Chapter 3 would appear to be invaluable. Important work in such areas as demography, the adolescent subculture, formal organizations, stratification, and social mobility are discussed briefly, and the usefulness of each area to the working knowledge of the guidance counselor is suggested.

Chapter 4, "The Functions and Dysfunctions of Guidance," examines the manifest as well as the latent social functions of educational guidance. It attempts to analyze the way bureaucratic roles interact and to assess the consequences of this interaction in terms of task differentiation, professionalism, and the adaptation of the school to the implicit goals set for it by the society.

Sometimes the motivational techniques employed by teachers to accomplish specific goals set in motion a network of social forces that were not predicted to occur when the technique was initiated. This does not mean, however, that the forces could not have been predicted if the teachers had thought about long-range behavioral outcomes. A poignant example of these unanticipated, unconceived consequences of educational methodology occurs when competition is employed as a motivational technique within the classroom. Students compete with each other for honors, grades, popularity, and the attention and sometimes affection of the teacher. Teachers and administrators may gain maximum mileage from perpetuating the competitive ethos, in that most students are willing, although perhaps not eager, to join the race. The cost of finding oneself in a daily race may be high for the winners, but the cost in frustration and anomie for the losers is even higher. Unintended consequences of any process whose goals may be valid but that produces conditions detrimental to persons involved in the specific interactional system are the dysfunction of which we speak. The guidance function as well as specific guidance techniques are analyzed with this in mind.

Chapter 5, "Social Research in Educational Guidance," reviews the research and the more prominent statements that suggest directions for research on the social aspects of guidance and counseling. In this chapter we consider as well as evaluate what has been done and its significance, and we also suggest variations on completed themes. Much of the discussion focuses upon the notion of professionalism in counseling and the empirical questions that need to be answered in relation to this. Various perspectives of social role, role identification and perception, and role conflict are evaluated. One study, "The Educational Decision Makers," is discussed at some length as an excellent example not only of social research into this problem but also of the levels of analysis that we may approach with available methodology.

Chapter 6, "The Educational Counseling Situation As a Social System," seeks to represent, theoretically and hypothetically, the sociological perspective for analyzing decision making in the counseling interaction. It is an attempt to make the social-systems approach to the study of educational functions meaningful. This approach is one that classifies persons and behavior in conceptual categories (systems, roles, and interaction categories) and relates these categories to one another. Educational life is thus structured in a particular way, a way that is useful for understanding and manipulating persons and activities. Concepts and categories are ways of directing our attention to certain phenomena and specific interpretations of those phenomena. The concepts may be sociological, like those employed in this chapter, or they reflect another perspective for ordering and directing our attention. If our interest were the analysis of student creativity, we would bring to bear on the problem certain concepts that are explanatory of artistic dimensions. Using student art work as our guide, we could talk about and seek examples of spatial arrangement, linear description, use of color, or communication of feeling. Art products may also be utilized to evaluate dimensions of personality, e.g., rigidity or inventiveness. If our concern were with this, a new set of organizing concepts would be necessary to direct our observation. Here we would seek qualities that would distinguish persons on the basis of such dimensions as aggressiveness, inhibition, morbidity, self-depreciation, or frustration. Using the same art products but a sociological set of organizing categories, our attention could be directed to expressions of social feelings such as role identification, integration, stereotyping, and peer-group role taking.

The social-systems model of analysis provides us with the kinds of classifications that order our thinking about the complex dynamics of institutional life. The representative concepts that do this for us in sociology structure the exposition of Chapter 6. The development of a typology using this mode of analysis is presented as an operational example.

Chapter 7, "Social Typing and Educational Guidance," examines the function of social typing in society and in education. It looks at the social mechanisms that effect the kinds of typing that occur and suggests the consequences of this typing for interaction. Ultimately the discussion seeks to establish a basis for understanding the way in which counselor-counselee interaction is frequently hampered by stereotypes that they may apply to each other.

In Chapter 8, "Toward Research on Guidance: A Study of the Elements of Social Interaction," the authors, without resorting to external or antecedent structures, focus upon the transaction observed between two persons in a counseling situation. They analyze the the expectations of each member of the interaction, the behavior by which each intends to realize them, and how he resolves discrepancies between his expectations and the way things actually turn out in his dealing with the other. In their discussion of research on guidance as interaction process, the authors suggest some ways that it is possible to derive the presuppositions of each member of the interaction about the other. They also suggest ways to assess how each uses the behavior of the other during the interview to validate or invalidate these presuppositions. They attempt, ultimately, in terms of a specific methodological approach, to propose ways that the two worlds of presupposition and imputation, taken together, affect the interaction and produce the results.

Chapter 9, "The Social Context of Academic Failure," is contributed by David Nasatir of the Survey Research Center at Berkeley. He looks at the American university as an environment that influences students in predictable ways, independently of their personal inclinations and abilities. It is these latter characteristics that predominantly influence the thinking of school counselors in their predictions of student success. Although counselors typically establish profiles of American colleges and universities, they seldom focus upon the kind of dynamics of social life, typical of all or most universities, that Dr. Nasatir chooses to explore. This paper should add conceptual substance to the kinds of cautionary advice that counselors supply to students individually and, if group college counseling should emerge as a prominent guidance activity, to the curriculum of group sessions.

If there is to be a genuine difference between educational guidance and counseling psychology, this difference is reflected in the way guidance corporates and utilizes a wide number of ideas from the social sciences. It appears that any clear split between the two orientations will show up in this way, and it may be that these distinctions are already observable in the conceptual apparatus of working counselors. At the same time, ideas and work that relate educational guidance to social science are not apparent in the literature and not heavily weighted in training programs.

It is hoped that this book will help to open the door for the incorporation of sociological analysis and research into the guidance enterprise at the training, practice, and research levels. There is no wish on the part of the author to suggest that psychology and administration, as bodies of knowledge, do not make a crucial contribution to the philosophy and practice of educational guidance. But three heads, if each can make a case for itself, are better than two, and indeed four are better than three. Guidance operates constantly in the area of values, ethics, goals, the nature of man and reality, and the purpose of existence. There is little doubt that an existentialist philosopher, for example, could not write a treatise on the guidance endeavor arguing convincingly that his philosophy could provide a whole new basis for the practice of guidance.

As education becomes more of a discipline than it currently is, and it inevitably must, the systems of thought and the contributions of research from several areas of academic inquiry will help to accomplish this goal. The case for sociology is contained herein. Other cases may be forthcoming and make a greater contribution than has been made here, but we must begin.

# CHAPTER 1

# GUIDANCE AND SOCIAL CHANGE

THIS CHAPTER is not intended in any sense as a history, although we resort at times to discussions of environments that were characteristic of separate stages of American social history. These are intended as examples of the mechanisms of social change. Historical events do shape values, but our concern is principally with the values that changed rather than the events that changed them.

Educational guidance, as a philosophy and as a set of integrated activities, has evolved through time to its present appearance. In the process, events, values, and institutions were and are in continual interaction with each other. Out of this interaction there emerged social necessities that required the attention of the school. The social dynamics or processes by which these necessities became manifest and are linked to establishment of guidance definitions and functions constitute the focus of the chapter.

Social change has occurred in several ways and each of these will be indicated. Brief mention should be made at the beginning, however, that although an attempt will be made to draw lines of cause and response, we are not concerned directly with the sources of the major causes of social change. We will, for example, discuss the major ecological changes that occurred in the United States during the latter part of the nineteenth century. We could logically suggest that the concentration of industrial complexes would explain these population shifts, but we do not intend to delve into the forces that brought about the Industrial Revolution. We shall, however, examine the industrialization of America as this can explain institutional change. In the same way, when we begin to trace the impact of the civil rights movement upon the schools, we shall not be concerned with the history of segregation in America. Rather, we are concerned with the meaning of these events for American society and ultimately for educational innovation.

The approach in this chapter will be to outline the character of each of the factors we shall propose as explanations for educational change. Then, under each topic, the events, evolutions, and revolutions that have occurred in response to the onset of these conditions will be considered. Those changes that may legitimately be related to guidance innovations will focus the discussion and serve as a guide for our attempt to draw lines between a complex network of social phenomena.

## SOURCES OF SOCIAL CHANGE

Any categorization of social phenomena that is to be used in the sense of separate causes is fraught with problems if we are concerned with distinguishing primary from secondary causes or major from minor causes. It is frequently the case that we may interpret $A$ as a cause of $B$ and $B$ as a cause of $C$, and therefore conclude that $A$ has caused $C$. For example, the Industrial Revolution was responsible for urbanization, and urbanization was responsible for social disorganization (crime, delinquency, alcoholism), which in turn was responsible for the social justice movement that led to welfare legislation. It is of little substantive use, from this kind of analysis, to say that the Industrial Revolution was responsible for welfare legislation.

Classical theories of social change will not bear upon the kind of analysis conducted here. For instance, Spencer's conception of a society evolving gradually through differentiation of functions and the ordering of the same to a Nirvana devoid of conflict, or a Marxian conception of a world ordered and changed by economic organization and class conflict, are too broad for our purposes. These theorists have contributed concepts, however, such as the Marxian notion of class and Weber's concept of status, that will be utilized in the analysis. Nor are we concerned with selecting a linear theory (Spencer, Comte, Weber) over a cyclical one (Spengler, Toynbee). We will, however, consider the process of change through specific mechanisms that are a part of a social history.

Sociology lives only tangentially with untestable social philosophy and feeds almost exclusively on independent microscopic factors that explain some facet of social change. Although broad considerations such as those advanced by Spencer, Marx, Max Weber, and Talcott Parsons are useful in understanding the macroscopic dimensions of social change, a microscopic approach to specific innovations appears to be the most manageable when searching for explanatory factors that are clear and testable. At this level of analysis, the chapter proceeds, assuming that every proposition about cause and response may be put into the form of a conceptual hypothesis that may or may not be explored empirically. For example, if we should suggest that an increase in professionals in a given community will affect the knowledge of school counselors about American colleges and universities, then we may demonstrate this by comparing counselors in such communities with those who operate in communities populated primarily by industrial workers.

It seems necessary to draw as many direct lines as possible, although all important variables, even though they may appear to be secondary causes, will be considered independently of the conditions that might explain them. The following areas of social change will be designated as the major sources of educational innovation:

1. Demographic shifts.
2. Shifts in status characteristics.
3. Interinstitutional interaction.
4. The scientific revolution.
5. Social movements and events.

## Demographic Shifts

The meaning of a redistribution of population characteristics and concentration may best be seen in an analysis of the consequences of the Industrial Revolution. Such a discussion is not only important as an example, but it also describes the mechanisms by which educational innovation is shaped. That is, if an institution is to retain its character as being intrinsically related in form and purpose to the needs of the people who created and maintained it, then innovation is essential.

### INDUSTRIALIZATION AND URBANIZATION

The Industrial Revolution was more an evolution than a revolution. It represented a gradual process whereby new technology caught up with old demands. Productivity and efficient mechanization for the growth of this productivity were responses to the new social order that had its roots in the emergence of an artisan class. The artisans of Puritan New England, motivated by an ethic of social elevation and buttressed by the fortuitous geography that gave rise to the opportunities presented by natural harbors, sufficient forests to stimulate shipbuilding, and proximity to an ocean, began to make an appreciable dent in the pluralistic economic order. These persons formed the first American middle class. Throughout the Eastern part of the United States, and spreading into the Midwest, the spirit of enterprise accelerated, ultimately concentrating its productive initiative in localized geographical areas that became population centers. Cities began to rise from the seeds of industrial imagination. Within the mass society, the Jeffersonian ideal of equal educational opportunities was transposed more meaningfully into a necessity for education to make democracy work. Education was a necessity if one was to find a place in the industrial order. The school began to conceive of its function more in terms of how many students it could serve, within the boundaries of available funds and personnel, rather than in terms of what quality it could manufacture. This was to pose a special challenge to those who wished to go beyond equal opportunity and toward differentiation of the masses.

The stage for the first truly significant social change, affecting the schools on a grand scale, was set. The interaction of demand and response on an institutional level occurred. The school and the economic order, at one simple level of analysis, developed a compatible mutual exchange process with human talent for support and occupational outlets for trained workmen and those educated in commercial skills.

But the transformation of the school was a product of infinitely more complex motivations than that of making it a training ground for industry. The school was suddenly placed in the position of having to play a role in the amelioration of the many disruptive problems of urbanization. The shift from a rural to an urban society meant, at the grass roots level, a new way of life for millions. It meant, in sociological language, structural changes in role relationships at a family and community level. It meant the establishment of a new set of rules to live or survive by and the development of impersonal norms to regulate the interaction of an anonymous society.

Rural society was personalized. Individuals were known as individuals by their teachers, their clergy, their merchants, and their peers. Urban society was depersonalized. Population density required entirely new ways of defining others. That is, in the absence of antecedent biographical knowledge and in the presence of impossible conditions for getting to know many people well, persons began to differentiate each other by easily discernible symbols: occupations, possessions, statuses in a hierarchy of an occupation, language and nationality characteristics. Society began to react to labels; in fact, the attainment of certain labels provided the motivation for most urban residents. This condition is not unlike our contemporary urban scene. Not one person in ten knows the name of his mailman, his milkman, or his telephone repairman, but he recognizes uniforms and trucks without concentration. Today, this represents an established pattern of human interaction; but to the first immigrants to the cities it required a struggle to abandon their traditional patterns and live comfortably with new ones. Obviously, this created a legion of social problems to which the school, as the primary agency of socialization for the new society fell heir.

The most crucial area for our examination of this revision of values lies in the family structure. In rural society, the American family assumed a host of functions that were later to be abandoned to other agencies. The family was a self-contained, productive unit producing for itself food, shelter, and clothing. It was the primary agency of socialization in that it taught and sanctioned religious and social doctrine. It was the principle educative agency, teaching reading and writing when considered necessary, but primarily educating the children to perform the role of adults. It emphasized the agricultural or artisan skills for male succession to the work of the father and the domestic skills required of women to the work of the mother. Furthermore, the family was the main agency of recreation, when there was time for it.

In the urban society, familial succession was not possible in the earlier sense. Therefore, education could no longer remain in the hands of the parents if persons were to learn the social and occupational skills necessary for urban life. Population density made it economically feasible for religious institutions to build and retain a congregation. Religious training was conveniently taken out of the hands of the family, where time was not available to undertake it. Recreation shifted from the home to diverse community agencies: the church, the school, and neighborhood centers. The childhood peer group quickly found it could exert sufficient imagination to generate its own recreational activities. Finally, since both parents frequently worked, the home could not conveniently supervise the children. Thus, what some still refer to as the "baby-sitting" function of education became an additional task for the schools.

In the midst of this transfer of functions, a number of social problems found fertile ground. Increasing population density led to a degeneration of living conditions, crime and delinquency flourished, and prostitution, gambling, and a host of other "evils" characterized the conception of the city. Horatio Alger threw his country boy, pure and incorruptible, into page after page of pernicious urban influences. The rags to riches theme was no more true than the gold-paved streets were a reality for the European immigrant. The myth of a den of iniquity was both a reality and an image to those who viewed the city. To add to the confusion, Eastern political ward bosses found themselves immersed in the machinations of social, industrial, and educational controversy. Social reformers like Jane Addams and social philosophers like William Graham Sumner and Charles Ward were spilling out their criticisms and their analyses. In the midst of all this confusion, the school was seeking to find the limits of its responsibility.

The value that encompassed and rationalized the new order to its members was one of instrumentality. This was a view that saw a shift from reciprocity in social interaction to a utilitarian conception of others, an attitude that schools to this day have difficulty in abrogating.

What has often been referred to as the vocational guidance movement, accompanying the shift from rural to urban occupational training, is more simply and realistically understood as the vocational education movement. To specify a guidance function would be to argue an underlying philosophy of individualized evaluation for vocational choice. The implementation of vocational curricula, when this could be accomplished, was intended as a realistic reaction to the demands of a ballooning industrial configuration. Only in the sense that, during the process of training, individuals with demonstrated technical proficiency were isolated and allocated to skilled occupations, could we conceive of this movement as perfoming a guidance function. Still, it was a beginning. Allocation of various individuals to suitable occupations, once implicit, could and would be made explicit. The concern for the child in an age and at a place that was replete with social reformers was to lay the groundwork for another guidance purpose. Ultimately the school was to conceive of its function as providing an environment devoid of the iniquities and temptations of slum living and, therefore, conducive to individual self-fulfillment.

The shift from a rural to an urban ecology produced a condition that was ultimately to lead to the necessity for differentiating a large, though relatively homogeneous, population. The urban circumstance saw the development of education on a community basis. As neighborhoods developed along ethnic and socioeconomic lines, a single neighborhood could easily require one or more schools. Whereas the rural school contained several grade levels in one classroom, the urban school could have several classes of the same grade level. The sheer weight of numbers required that the school take action to break these groups up into manageable units based upon abilities and aspirations. Some individuals had to assume the responsibility of thinking about the best ways to accomplish this. Therefore, a function was necessary to isolate the individuals who had certain characteristics in common. Our earliest attempts as a primitive form of individual guidance emerged out this necessity. Moreover, the concentration of individuals with similar capacities and interests led to a response in the direction of specialization. A teacher was no longer a generalist for all grades and ages; she was expected to make a choice of age and grade level and to direct her training accordingly.

Industrialization and its consequences for urban organization produced important changes in the structure of the school. It influenced the role of education in general and of individual schools in particular; it caused a change in the role prerequisites of teachers, and it caused a qualitatively different kind of pupil-teacher interaction. The nature of this interaction was such that both teachers and pupils were required to regulate their behavior in terms of impersonal rules and values. Finally, industrialization led to bureaucratization of the school. In large urban educational complexes, where division of labor and authority was the only feasible response to the problem of size, classification of jobs became differentiated in terms of function and power. The specialization that was to change some of the functions of the teacher and much of her style was more consequential at the level of althority, where entirely new responsibilities neede to be designated. Although the responsibility for individualizing instruction was neither formalized nor assumed by all educational functionaries, the structure for the implementation of this process was established in the system.

## IMMIGRATION

An important function of the school during the last part of the nineteenth and first part of the twentieth centuries was to service a diverse population, in the sense of providing a uniformity of skills and understandings, so that immigrants could function as workers and citizens. Once uniformity was accomplished in the sense of socialization, differentiation in the sense of occupational allocation could be achieved. Population increase was important, but ethnic differences within that population were more crucial to the formulation of new and different functions within the school.

The reaction of the school to this particular challenge was geared along the line of teaching language skills and training persons for industrial occupations. Many immigrants came to the United States with skills that they could transfer to American needs. Most, however, came either with skills that were unsuitable to American urban demand or from rural areas where no industrial know-how had been developed.

This circumstance closely paralleled the vocational education beginnings and was, to some extent, responsible for its becoming an important function of American education. Also related was the fact that persons from diverse national backgrounds needed to be evaluated and advised as to appropriate training. In a crude fashion, vocational guidance was encouraged to make some formal attempt to routinize its function in order to handle this problem created by the population changes.

Industrialization, urbanization, and immigration constitute the realities that account for the major demographic shifts in American society. Such shifts have presented the schools with demands not only to expand their facilities but to do so in accordance with recognizable differences within the population that has shifted. The importance of focusing upon individual differences is evident in any system of education that proposes to accommodate large undifferentiated masses.

## POPULATION EXPLOSION

One reality that will concern our historians of the future is the inevitable fact that our resources will be challenged by the sheer weight of our numbers. A fundamental task of scholars concerned with this will be to explain the consequences of a population explosion. Moreover, the job facing public officials will be one of manipulating the limited natural and artificial resources so that the masses may be served.

Our concern is the effect that such a demographic change will have upon the educational institution. The task is to speculate upon the kind of functional adaptation that education will have to make in response to such an effect. The questions that our guidance counselors are already beginning to consider are

1. What can we do with average students who cannot get into college because of the overcrowding? Eventually, the question will be, what can we do with the good students who cannot enter college? How do we advise these people?

2. How can we structure the classrooms so as to overcome the many neurotic problems that emerge, and will increase, in a mass society that is becoming more massive?

Guidance counselors, who have served and will continue to serve in the capacity of vocational, educational, and clinical consultants to students, may ultimately find themselves playing a larger role—advising all educational functionaries how best to handle the combination of functions on an organized and, perhaps, mass-assembly basis.

AGE

Ordinarily the number of human beings of a given age who co-exist in a society remains relatively stable except for the variations that occur as persons begin to live longer. The increase in the number of septua- and octogenarians is not particularly significant with educational innovation except insofar as the distribution of persons of various ages shows up in the logistics for a given community. In the San Fernando Valley section of Los Angeles, the average age is considerably less than that of residents of most other communities in the Los Angeles complex. The Valley emerged as the logical place for young parents to begin raising their families. The land was cheaper and so were the homes, particularly in relation to the inflated costs of property in the city proper. Most aspiring family men assume that some day they will be in a position to move "over the hill," but in the early years of family raising the San Fernando Valley is their home.

The effect upon the schools in the Valley of the existence of a larger percentage of young people than would be found in the general population has taken many forms. Of major concern to most of the parents of school-age children has been the problem of overcrowding and the subsequent adaptations such as double sessions and large classes. On the other hand, in a community where education is generally a concern of most of the residents, because most of them have children in school, a condition exists favorable to the support for progressive teaching, heavy expenditures for teaching materials, and building and staffing in line with modern needs. The Valley school district, however, is not autonomous but is, rather, tied to the interests and wishes of the rest of the city. The general point is that when communities do represent the age characteristics of the San Fernando Valley, and when they do possess independence (unlike the Valley) from neighboring districts, important innovations are bound to occur. In terms of our concern with the guidance function, we may assert that when communities are dominated by residents who are parents of children in schools, the attitudes toward mental health are generally more positive. Further, it is not uncommon to observe that there are several times the number of persons serving in the capacity of guidance counselors than in neighboring districts.

Historically, the important client for the guidance counselor was the high school adolescent who needed preparation for taking his role as a member of the industrial order. The existence of, and needs presented by, this particular age group has set the tone for the training of counselors during most of the twentieth century to date and is still strongly in evidence. As the distribution of adolescents who intend to go on to college continues to increase, although the focus may remain upon the same age bracket, the content of the counseling sessions will be required to change. This is certainly the case already and is destined to become more so. The structure of the counseling function now resolves around clinical diagnosis more than in the past, even for students who do not exhibit disruptive behaviors. If we were to predict the organization of pupil personnel services of the future, our best bet might be to suggest a vocational advisor, a college advisor, and a clinician. If a new compulsory education law is enacted and the age limit revised upwards, as well might be the case, the responsibilities of the guidance office will certainly be such that new adaptations will have to be made. Out of just such contingencies, innovation in education in general and in guidance in particular evolves.

## RACE AND NATIONALITY

There does not appear to be existing evidence that can tell us anything specific about the way the guidance function changes as the racial composition of communities changes. This problem has primarily stimulated interest where American Negro, Mexican, and Puerto Rican invasion has occurred to reshape the characteristics of communities. We can, however, make certain speculations based upon what we suspect the school as a whole has done to accommodate the ability and interest differences that are related to race or nationality.

Existing data on social mobility indicate that the basis for innovation in instruction and guidance is that educational aspirations are differentially distributed according to race and nationality. The opportunity structure in American society has never operated to the advantage of Negroes, Mexicans, or Puerto Ricans, and as a result, the motivation for educational attainment in these groups is not great.

The effect of neighborhood change in which non-white minority groups constitute an overwhelming majority in the school has led to some fairly routine innovations, some of which, unfortunately, appear to be not in the best tradition of the guidance philosophy. The school counselor in schools where ethnic turnover has occurred has often been forced to play the role of disciplinarian along with other school administrators. It is clearly the belief of most functionaries in schools in interstitial or disadvantaged neighborhoods that the problem of control has become a responsibility more urgent and more time-consuming than teaching. This situation is consistent with other general notions about the problems that students encounter whose value systems are not particularly conducive to attaining the rewards of the educational enterprise.

In secondary schools where non-whites are in the majority, the guidance function has logically routinized its patterns predominantly around vocational guidance, job seeking, and placement. The combined problem of maintaining discipline and finding jobs for dropouts and semiskilled trainees has left little time for the important responsibility of talent seeking and helping potentially successful students. As other social changes begin to penetrate the educational conscience, such a task as discovering outlets for talented but disadvantaged members of ethnic groups may become a formalized function of the guidance services. This eventuality would result not from the sheer demographic redistribution of the population, based upon ethnic qualities, but from the social movements that seek a wider application of social and educational justice. Although the mental health of students is certainly an intrinsic concern of the school counseling ethic, it would seem at present almost superficial, certainly premature, in the face of widespread discontent and disorganization, lack of job opportunities and educational motivation, and a scarcity of personnel for the guidance enterprise, to mobilize and attack the problems of individual neurosis.

## Shifts in Status Characteristics

In this particular section of the general discussion of guidance and social change, our unit of analysis is the school, the guidance functions, and the community. We are not primarily concerned here, although we are elsewhere, with discussing the social context of the changing distributions of status characteristics. Technological innovations have influenced directly the changing face of the American occupational structure and, to a large extent, the distribution of income. But these technological changes do not account for the microscopic innovations that occur in some community schools and not in others. For these we must look to the community itself. Technological innovations do account for the wide effects upon the larger society, however, and we will discuss them in another section. More explicitly, what is being indicated is that changes occur in different communities at different rates of speed, and schools react to these changes in different ways. For example, some schools are more sensitive to the redistribution of ethnic characteristics within their population than other schools. Whereas one school will immediately seek funding to facilitate a changing curricular emphasis, another school will continue to play out its traditional role, emphasizing activities that scholars will argue are completely nonfunctional for certain kinds of students.

Perhaps the difference in response may be associated not specifically with the changing characteristics of a community but with the way in which these characteristics find expression in political action. School administrators recognize that within certain ethnic communities alienation of the inhabitants does not erupt into political awareness. A feeling of powerlessness is characteristic, at least until the emergence of segmented activist groups within these communities, of those whom we see as disenfranchised socially. These same administrators recognize further that the configuration of certain other status characteristics is predictive of a politically active and concerned community. It is this kind of interaction that may best explain educational change. We may argue with some evidence[1] that the amount and type of counseling in secondary schools varies with the type of community and the characteristics of persons within that community.

We cannot always clearly explain the form that educational innovations will take until diligent and penetrating investigations have inspected these innovations. This is because certain innovations occur latently and without benefit of formal planning. These innovations may be the more important consequences of a shift in the distribution of status characteristics within a community, more important, that is, in the sense of explaining the changing image of the guidance function. They remain latent and only informally engage the efforts of the school and guidance counselors because status is a term that has realistically come to imply invidious distinctions. Any actions per-

---

1. Cicourel, Kitsuse, Weinberg, and Skager. For details of the research, consult Chap. 5.

petrated by the school to maintain these distinctions would obviously not be regarded openly as consistent with formal educational purposes.

## CLASS, STATUS, SITUS, AND FUNCTION

The discussion of status characteristics involves an understanding that a society may be differentiated by a number of criteria that position persons on a ladder of economic advantage. What Karl Marx[2] originally called social class and what Max Weber[3] revised to include class, status, and power, so as to include the noneconomic symbols of position such as style of life, access to education, and so forth, are conceptual designations that assume the meaningful division of a population. This division is meaningful in the sense that a person's social position is more than an objective designation of social scientists. Social position is also a social psychological reality in that it has important consequences for attitudes and behavior. Political behavior, religious participation, racial intolerance, attitudes toward sex, aspirations, recreational styles, and certain forms of deviant behavior may be linked to social position.

The major determinants of a person's social class have traditionally been occupation, income, and education. Each of these is strongly related to the others and all relate similarly to other variables such as those mentioned in the previous paragraph. American society has in recent years closed status ranks to the point that the notion of a mass society is generally applicable. The rise of the working class through the effective efforts of unions and the availability, due to general affluence as well as to installment buying, of most of the symbols of status such as cars and television sets have forced social scientists to rely upon a simple dichotomy of working and middle classes as a realistic division of the status ladder. Although the very poor and the very rich are certainly present, the distribution of status characteristics now approximates a normal curve, and it is toward the 90 per

2. Karl Marx, "Karl Marx's Theory of Social Class," in *Class, Status, and Power,* ed. by R. Bendix and S. Lipset, The Free Press, New York, 1966, pp. 26–34.

3. Marx Weber, from H. Gerth and C. Wright Mills, *On Max Weber,* Oxford University Press, Inc., New York, 1958.

cent that the bulk of our educational concerns and experiments are directed.

In looking at the distribution of status characteristics at the community level, certain assumptions are made and certain cautions are indicated. One assumption is that within the urban society persons of similar status occupy the same residential areas. This is important insofar as residential areas usually feed a community school. A second assumption is that members of a single community have like interests, expectations, aspirations, and attitudes. The analysis of the interaction of the school as a social institution and the community as a social type proceeds on this basis. An important caution is suggested by the sociological work of Hatt[4] and of Morris and Murphy[5] on social situs. The latter work attempts to bring to the mind of the social scientist the idea that although certain occupations may be considered similar insofar as educational requirements and income are the same, there may be other important differences. Situs categories are those that incorporate a differentially evaluated range of similar occupations such as professional, business, and service. In this way scientific technicians would not be ranked with librarians although the previously used gross categorization would incorporate both.

This suggests that any evaluation of the interaction of schools and communities based upon the distribution of status characteristics needs to take into account this meaningful distinction. We are suggesting that the influence of a community containing a large portion of businessmen and bankers would be qualitatively different from that of a community with a preponderance of scientists and engineers, even though all groups have relatively the same status. The influence of voluntary associations upon educational decisions requires the same analytical cautions. We do not advance our knowledge of the impact of groups upon institutions very far if we treat status as a unidimensional category. It is more important to be able to assess the kinds

---

4. Paul Hatt, "Occupation and Social Stratification," *American Journal of Sociology*, May 1950, pp. 533–543.

5. Richard Morris and Raymond Murphy, "Occupational Situs, Subjective Class Identification, and Political Affiliation," *American Sociological Review*, Vol. 26, 3, pp. 383–392.

of occupations that dominate a particular voluntary association than the amount of status each occupation holds. The John Birch Society, for example, contains more professionals than would be found in a random sample from the total population. This is also true, however, of the League of Women Voters, a fairly liberal organization. The point is that one would want to question the kinds of professions that contribute membership to liberal or conservative organizations. It is unlikely, for example, that the John Birch Society would have a great many university professors proportionate to the number of businessmen. In the same example, education level may be generally associated with membership in the Birch Society, and the education level may be higher than in the general population, containing a large percentage of college graduates. The status argument is only one way of evaluating such information. Another way, for example, to examine the association with education would be to question whether members majored in philosophy or business administration. This point is emphasized to suggest that the status as well as the nonstatus components of education, occupation, and income are useful in the analysis of the interaction of communities and schools.

The interaction of status characteristics of communities and schools is ordinarily viewed as an interchange between expectations of community members and school response. It has been suggested that the kind of response is affected by the way status characteristics associate with political potency and influence. From another point of view, the status characteristics of communities may be associated with conditions affecting the vocational choices of students. At the simplest level of analysis, it is possible to argue that students from a middle class community are socialized to aspire to high status occupations that are usually specific and reflected by models in the community. Children from low status communities are less likely to interact with professional models, on the one hand, or to be socialized to expect a great deal out of education, on the other.

Many communities may be described in terms of one dominant function that explains their existence and to which the components of status may be related. Large and small communities may be designated in the same way. These functions ordinarily account for the kind of jobs, income, and education levels of the residents. Atlantic City, New Jersey, for example, is a resort community. Most of the residents depend upon summer trade as the major source of income. Occupations, income, and forms and levels of education are highly influenced by this fact. In the same way a fishing community such as San Pedro, on the southern coastal border of Los Angeles, would predictably contain certain other distributions of education and educational types. These distributions, independent of the specific functions, influence the kind of schools and the kind of guidance that communities have. Within large urban areas, disadvantaged communities function as focal points for transients, the unemployed, and those on relief, who require inexpensive housing. Many communities spring up overnight to accommodate workers of specific industries, such as textiles, that have increasingly moved their production centers from the North to the South. Contemporary suburbia and "Commutersville" function to accommodate the prestige needs of adults and the clean neighborhood and educational requirements that parents demand for raising their children.

## CHANGING NEIGHBORHOODS

When neighborhoods change in the sense of a redistribution of status characteristics, they also change in one of two other ways. Either the property values decrease and persons of small means populate the area, or in rare instances, urban renewal changes the appearance and, consequently, the cost of living in a community that had at one time many of the characteristics of a slum or semislum. Infrequently we find a mix when industries enter the suburbs. The school must make adjustments to revised population characteristics. School counselors whose specialization is college information and clinical diagnosis have little function in a community where vocational information and the prevention of talent loss are the pervasive guidance purposes. Childhood neurosis is not typically a preoccupation of the poor, and surviving the compulsory educational range is not usually a problem for children of professionals or semiprofessionals.

Sometimes functions change and occupational types change, although the population remains stable. Vocational guidance is sensitive to the possibility that careers at the skilled-workman level are impermanent. The anthracite coal-mining industry in Pennsylvania, for instance, disappeared before a replacing industry was available. Although occupational characteristics of the community may change because of job retraining and replacement, the status characteristics of industry remain the same. Nevertheless, the guidance task shifts in response, and the institution of the school adapts its programs to changing occupational demands. In one location in Pennsylvania, after prolonged status as a depressed area, a skiing boom suddenly transformed the outlook of many thousands of residents. With small, low-interest business loans, whole communities began to look toward entrepreneurial careers. Resorts require restaurants, hotel and cabin managers, food suppliers, bartenders, liquor dealers, clothing salesmen and buyers, and small storekeepers for various products. Secondary schools began to change their guidance approach in the light of the new inevitability that most of the graduates who did not go on to college would become a part of the local industry. Even ski instruction became a part of the curriculum.

Changing neighborhoods mean, to administrators, teachers, and counselors, a challenge to their capacity to enforce discipline, prevent disorganizations, and hold the status quo until new programs may be routinized to the point where their besieged ship reaches quiet waters. Counselors find that one of their major responsibilities lies in grouping students in such a way that the few high achievers will not be held back by the others. A second major responsibility resides in a province previously assumed by disciplinarians. There may have been just too many disturbed and disturbing students for one vice-principal and a principal. Counselors often assume this responsibility after psychologists, recruited on one-shot occasions, have verified that some students were too disturbed in one way or another to benefit from standard programs.

As some neighborhoods settle into clearly defined minority-group ghettos despite a high rate of transiency, the school counselor finds himself faced with responsibilities that would legitimately fall to the skills of trained social workers. The disruptions of traditional organization, a breakdown in morale, a high rate of teacher turnover, the absence of adequately trained psychological counselors and social workers, and the ever-increasing number of pupils make the job of individualized instruction based upon an adequate knowledge of the individuals a difficult task. The consequence often appears to be a mass-production assembly line based upon the principle of maintaining order and social sanity. Certain institutionalized subfunctions emerge, based upon necessity but little invention. Social-adjustment classes are organized in many schools run, for the most part, by firm disciplinarians whose "adjustment" activities fall short of good counseling techniques. New teachers are frequently assigned to small groups of students whose segregation into small classes was based upon the fact that their IQ's approached the moron level.

The conditions today may be changing, but the eyes of an involved public, acutely aware that children of the poverty ghettos deserve a better deal in the Great Society, are upon the schools. And along with this involvement, coupled with the resources of sensitive public protest, the effects of the civil rights movement and of Federal and state poverty programs are also being felt. The obvious inequality of having one guidance counselor in a black ghetto and a dozen in a golden ghetto will emerge as an important issue as the wheels of reformism are in motion. Educational innovation may spring from this awakened awareness. New techniques for counseling, group guidance with an eye to airing needs and grievances, individual testing with an eye on the linguistic and auditory difficulty produced by social conditions, family rehabilitation, work-study programs, and a legion of other techniques have emerged out of the impetus of the present. Education changes when society acknowledges the incongruity in function between the activities of its schools and the needs of its population.

## EMERGING COMMUNITIES—SUBURBANIZATION AND URBAN RENEWAL

Suburbanization represents an ecological evolution whereby persons of similar moderate to high socioeconomic statuses find themselves living in proximity to each other. Factors such as housing costs, the probability that one will be among people of like mind and values, and reputedly good schools draw middle class citizens to suburbia.

Urban renewal is another ecological evolution, the characteristics of which are in some senses similar to suburbanization but in another important sense are a reaction against the conditions of suburban living. The cost of returning to the renewed housing of central city is high, and it is primarily professionals who are attracted to such housing. These persons expect that their neighbors will have returned, like themselves, to reap the cultural and social benefits of central-city offerings. They suspect that the suburban communities from which they came are stifling and restrictive. They wish to escape the conformity that suburban visibility breeds and to activate their lives beyond the bridge parties, barbecues, and social incest of suburbia. One of their main problems is that central-city schools have not been renewed in the same sense that their own vision of central city has. However, they believe that they can solve this problem through private education, through supplementing their children's education with their own intellectual contributions, and by exposing them to the culture of the city.

Urban renewal is not, and may never be, the force that suburbanization is in effecting structural innovations within the schools. The population of those returning to the city is presently simply not sufficient to generate educational change. Suburbanization is a different story.

Suburban schools draw well-trained and tenured teachers and recruit psychologists, consulting psychiatrists, and the best-trained college advisors. The status of the community becomes the mechanism by which educational personnel restructure their tasks. In the stratification order of school counselors, the clinician ranks high, the vocational counselor low. A high status atmosphere produces high status adaptations in the school. Counselors in high status schools make their adaptations to their roles in the direction of a super sophistication. Routine tasks are enacted in ways that reflect the modus operandi of a clinician, and the recruitment of new counselors occurs in an atmosphere of professionalism where "vocational" types are viewed with the same disdain accorded hooky cops. At the same time, representations of status performance become legitimate by the selection process and by the stabilization of the guidance function around a guidance director. The guidance director, with the financial and moral support of the community, recruits specialists in guidance and counseling skills. The end result of status differentiation is always, and ultimately, specialization. Suburbia believes in specialists in the same way that wealthy patients find it hard to believe that they are getting adequate medical treatment from a general practitioner.

Another analytical factor, associated with status and related to the interaction of community characteristics and the schools, is the function of the community. The work of Getzells and Jackson suggests the necessity of exploring the ramifications of a more complex dynamic that may be associated with living in low status communities. This work suggests the important difference in consequence for vocational aspiration between being intelligent and being creative. The creative students in the Getzel's and Jackson study scored considerably below those designated as intelligent on standardized IQ tests. It was discovered that creative children expressed interest in a wider range of vocational choices, including many nonconventional choices, than did their intelligent counterparts. At the same time, creative children also related to a different set of "desirable" adult qualities. The implications of this work for our concerns are considerable. If we assume that the composite influence of low status communities retards the kind of motivation and aspiration correlated with IQ and school success, then we would expect a different set of vocational aspirations in these communities, particularly when we add to our consideration the fact that specific professional models are absent in the community.

One of the traditional vocational guidance functions of schools is involved with familiarizing students with the range of possible careers. Many schools, both junior and senior high, conduct some form of career day. Representative occupations from the community are presented to students in the form of talks by members of the community. If we acknowledge that occupational aspirations are differentially associated with different social types, we have laid one more foundation stone in the basis for innovation in our vocational programs. The distribution of status characteristics, particularly occupations, within communities should provide insights into the kinds of innovations that will occur. Such an activity as a career day will not reflect the assumption that a representative sample of typical careers is the best kind of program organization for schools in all types of communities.

## Interinstitutional Interaction

One of the more commonly observed responsibilities of the guidance office is to mediate between the conflicting loyalties of the school and the peer group. Many a counselor considers with a failing child and his parents the wisdom of membership in a high school fraternity or a gang. Because the peer group is not an institution in the pure sociological sense, other terms will be applied in the following analysis.

PTA's are only the formalized representation of the interaction of parents with the schools. The real interaction proceeds more in terms of an institutionalized public-relations game. One of the more difficult tasks that the school counselor may have to face is telling a doctor and his wife that their son would probably be happy and successful as a cabinetmaker and would be a predictable failure as a medical student. On the other hand, convincing low income parents who see very little value in higher education that their son should go to college is an equally difficult task.

The family and the peer group constitute the two major units with which the public school comes into frequent and meaningful contact. The church is decreasing as an important interactional institution in this sense. Our consideration of interinstitutional interaction is logically limited to these three: family, peer group, and school.

In Chapter 2, we deal at considerable length with the importance of considering the social context of psychological problems. The stronger point, which is also made, is that these problems not only require a look at the social context in which they occur but that the

social condition is responsible for the psychological condition. Moreover, what we are calling a psychological condition may frequently
be an example of the products of inadequate socialization. That is,
the learning that occurs as a result of a student's membership in a
family and a peer group does not concur in all cases with the goals
and values of educational personnel.

The American family, by necessity, has relinquished to the schools
certain traditional functions such as socialization, recreation, and instruction in reading, writing, and arithmetic. At the same time, the
average parent perceives that it is still his right as a parent and a
taxpayer in support of the schools to expect the school to serve his
children efficiently, morally, and enthusiastically. To this end, the
average parent is willing to advance his own understanding of the
uniqueness of his children in the cause of helping school personnel
adapt their techniques to his children's unique qualities. In this sense,
the family is requiring education to adopt a pupil-centered approach
to education, and innovations within the school are responsive to this
expectation.Through time these innovations become stabilized as thematic patterns of the school's approach to students.

Families, however, vary in the extent to which they interact with
the school as well as in the kind of interaction that takes place.
Working class families, in comparison with middle class families,
operate less as a pressure group for academic achievement and more
as a hypothetical partner in the school's attempts to ameliorate problems of student discipline. School social workers, who in many districts constitute the strongest arm of elementary guidance, spend much
of their time attempting to work through problems of family disorganization so that these problems do not represent permanent obstacles to educational progress.

The difficulties that children of lower class parents face—problems of broken homes, overcrowding, alcoholic parents, and the vast
range of demoralizing effects of poverty—have given rise to remedial
programs sponsored by governmental agencies. The evolution of this
attitude and implementing the programs themselves will be discussed
in greater detail later in this chapter. The point is made here only to
exemplify the ways in which institutions, in this case the family,

interact with the school to produce educational innovation, particularly along guidance or individual-centered lines.

Another example, taken from a stratum of American society, is the case of the only child of middle class parents. Through being spoiled or having had too much expected of him, he may develop overaggressive, sarcastic, or nervous habits that interfere with both his learning and his relationship with peers. This kind of student is not uncommon, and counselors are or should be looking toward the advancement of methods or techniques to remedy his difficulties.

## THE PEER GROUP

In an age that David Riesman[6] has characterized as "other-directed" and that many social observers have described as a time of conformity, the relationships of persons take on great explanatory power as determinants for behavior. The school, serving as an agency of this conformity, may indeed create conditions that restrict its own functioning in terms of many of the manifest goals of social adjustment and creativity. School children, who are socialized to avoid deviation, find reinforcing bonds of solidarity in the groups into which they are compressed.

The school obviously cannot provide all the institutional supports that young children and adolescents require. If they could, then peer groups would not emerge. Therefore, the function of the peer group must be distinct from that of the school, and in these distinctions often lie the components of institutional conflict.

The peer group has several functions not covered by membership in the family, the school, or the church. Although the peer group may assume some of the functions of other institutions and vice versa, the total configuration of these functions and meaning is completely unique. Ordinarily, two conceptions of a peer group are necessary. One is that of a collectivity of individuals who have some mutual purpose and who structure their relationships in face-to-face interaction in order to adapt to these purposes. A second conception,

---

6. David Riesman, *The Lonely Crowd,* Yale University Press, New Haven, Conn., 1950.

which has been applied to the analysis of the adolescent society and is useful for our analysis, is that of a subculture. Albert Cohen[7] called the group of adolescents with which he was concerned a delinquent subculture. He differentiated it from a delinquent gang or group in the sense that delinquents of many groups and gangs take on similar characteristics, although they avoid dependency upon mutual interactions. For example, surfers in San Diego take on many, if not most, of the characteristics of surfers in Los Angeles. In a more expanded sense, the rituals of dress, dance, and general posture toward the adult world characterize the adolescents from Miami to Seattle as members of a unique and distinct social entity.

The first major function of the peer group is association and identification. It offers a person membership and identification with those of similar characteristics of age or of interest. It also offers the growing child the security of numbers in a world that does not protect or ensure the support of its young on grounds of the child's own making. In this sense, it offers both independence and security. It offers mechanical solidarity in an organic system. The child takes this offer because of the widening difference between generations and because he wants available cues for behavior in a time of rapid social change. The second major function of the peer group is that it socializes the child to the relationships of his world about which his parents, teachers, and clergy know little. It provides in this way for the adoption and implementation of new roles (friend, leader, dater) that are not serviced by other affiliations. The group provides information and clarification about the expectations of peers that most young people find crucial to their daily interaction. Moreover, in groups that cross socioeconomic lines, peers reveal the values and modes of other levels, making social mobility easier.

Teachers and guidance counselors are constantly interacting with more than individuals. They are interacting with value systems and personalities molded by common denominators. As the peer group or subculture becomes more and more homogeneous and more demanding of loyalty, changes that accommodate this collective need will

---

7. Albert K. Cohen, *Delinquent Boys,* The Free Press, New York, 1955.

occur. Innovations within the school will become institutionalized around a set of predictable interactions between school norms and peer-group norms. The system of extracurricular activities is one example of an important educational innovation in this area. Student councils, representative committees, and perhaps, ultimately, arbitration activities are logical outcomes of this interinstitutional interaction.

## The Scientific Revolution

As the nineteenth century turned to the twentieth, scholars began to look at the problems of American society and American education with an intelligent and systematic eye. Urbanization was a reality whereas social reform was a random set of hopelessly limited but well-meaning parries against an impossibly complex set of human circumstances. From the analytic pens of men like Herbert Spencer, William Graham Sumner, Lester Ward, William James, G. Stanley Hall, Edward Thorndike, and John Dewey came the foundation works of the new scientism that was to reshape American education with profound consequences for the greater society.

Science became a concept and a reality in the early twentieth century. It was an ethic, a motivation, an interest, a method, and a technology. Automobiles and radio did not just happen, any more than washing machines and television have. Scientific technology became the theme of the times, and one came to expect anything. Industry was engaged in the business of making its products obsolete along with its machinery and, ultimately, its manpower. Automation has its roots in the industrial organization of the nineteenth century. The economy was geared for change, and experimentation was an institutionalized practice.

In another sphere, a world hidden by ivy-covered walls, another branch of science was crudely growing. The study of the human being and the study of human beings in groups was spreading behind the impetus of Freudian psychology and social philosophy. The human mind, the ultimate subject of educational speculation, was of consummate interest to an increasing circle of disciples of German and

English psychologists and social philosophers. They were concerned with the problems of contemporary society and with speculating about the possibility of averting social trends; at the same time, they were sowing the seeds for the scientific study of society. Sociology was to take forty years after Ward and Sumner to reach a tenuous maturity, but behavioral science was established early in the wave of the twentieth century's confidence in itself to discover the answers to almost all questions. These questions demanded, ultimately, the answer to what lies beyond the near reaches of outer space; though an unrelated concern as a specific question, this query is relevant to the attitudinal advance and acceptance of scientific thinking.

To explain the processes of social and educational change, the scientism of the twentieth century requires us to delve into two areas independently and then to bring these areas together. First, we need to consider the impact that the scientific revolution had upon society in general and to speculate upon the way in which the changed society influenced innovations in the school. Secondly, we must ask how the scientific spirit or method influenced the questions that education was to ask of itself, primarily those questions concerned with how to learn. We will next consider the kinds of skills, disciplines, and cognate tools that were instrumental in answering these questions. Fnially, we will discover that the first honest format for what we have referred to as the guidance movement in American education was the operational result of the combined and independent contributions of these two streams.

## THE TECHNICAL SOCIETY AND THE SCHOOLS

The technical society was a fast-paced society, a collection of individuals eager to be something and to do things. In the beginning, the technical society saw rainbows of discovery and itself riding them. As adolescents entered the world of work, there were several challenges: One was to discover what one's role could be in a highly technical urban society, another was to learn the skills involved in realizing a particular occupational goal, and a third, the most challenging and elusive goal of all, was to break away from the mob. The

fantasy heroes of the age—Ford, Edison, Marconi, Carnegie, Rocke-
feller, and numerous others—were models of this break from
anonymity.

As is the case in most mass societies, there were many who failed
these challenges and many who succeeded only to find great dis-
illusionment. There were also many who, for lack of intelligent
advice, made wrong life decisions and many who, because of the color
of their skin, their nationality, or their religion, found the goals
impossible of attainment even though they had the ability and the
motivation. Many of these conditions of failure and disappointment
persist into our own times. In addition, there were always those, as
we are discovering today happens in any technical society, who were
being displaced by automation.

To combat the depression and disorganization that flourishes under
these conditions, other occupations came into being, and their practitioners worked hard to develop skills. Vocational advisors, industrial
psychologists, personnel specialists in industry, social workers, mental
hygienists, and psychiatrists all contributed their efforts to find
remedial measures that they could administer wisely to the labor force.
Such measures include retraining or relocating, supporting crushed
egos and depressed personalities, rehabilitating alcoholics, and saving
families on the threshold of social and physical disorganization.

Preventive action, through some sort of osmosis and common-sense
acceptance, eventually fell into the already overburdened and confused
hands of education. The task of the school in the scientific age was
to differentiate the scientists from the technicians and these, in turn,
from the laborers. Further, its task was to advise the talented and
untalented, to indoctrinate students with a commitment to ambition,
and to be on the lookout for signs of maladjustment—symptoms,
that is, that suggested that a home was not conducive to productive
study or mental health—and then to make referrals to the proper
contributing agencies. Teachers had to become guidance oriented,
which was often the same thing as becoming progressive. Out of the
occupational complex, a liaison person came to be attached to the
school; out of the miasma of the slums, a social worker was indicated;
nervous disorders of the progeny of those who moved too fast, too

slow, or too deviantly in the structure called for a mental hygienist; and chronic disorders required psychiatric skills.

Attitudes that developed in response to the disorganizing as well as the stimulating effects of scientific change congealed as articulated social demands. These demands, in turn, provoked the establishment of new functions and roles withing the school. The call for specialists was an outgrowth of scientific innovation and the widespread acceptance and indeed expectation of a scientific approach to almost everything. Within the school the specialist was to be presented with the responsibility of comprehending the dynamics of scientific innovation, of healing the casualties, and of intelligently directing the future through those who would inherit it.

The scientific revolution, unlike other revolutions, appears to be linear, accumulative, and unending. The sources of its impact upon the schools arise from both external and internal dynamics. Industrial technology contains its counterpart in education, and both point to innovations in both the function and techniques of guidance.

## EXTERNAL SOURCES OF INNOVATION

The automation of industrial tasks, with the development of the computer, the corresponding new industrial tasks that the use of the computer made possible, and the emphasis upon a space technology and the many satellite activities supportive of this enterprise have all created a condition vastly more complex than the simple displacement of work opportunities for the lowly skilled. More important than the displacement of existing occupational categories has been the proliferation of new ones. The functional problem for education has become to develop training programs on the one hand and to motivate students to seek and become committed to them on the other. This task requires the accumulation of a body of information about opportunities, a job large enough to engage school counselors for a considerable portion of their time.

Colleges and universities were and are being required to mobilize their forces to train people to train people. The challenges to higher education are comparable to those imposed upon the high schools and junior colleges where new curriculum, materials, and personnel must be developed. To add to the burden and confusion, administrators are becoming sensitive to the probability that even the new jobs are becoming obsolete. Key punchers, for example, will soon be displaced by an elaborate system of translating raw data directly to cards or, in the case of large utility billing, directly from the meter to the bill.

The scientific revolution has, for the majority of members of our society, created a condition of abundance and affluence. The functional problem for education in response to this condition involves reducing the conflict among persons differentially suited to aspire to this affluence as well as motivating those who are growing up in a culture where everything is easy and available. The problem for the counselor is one of seeking a method for understanding and helping the increasing numbers of able but unachieving youngsters who would rather ignore academic responsibilities than give up the excitement of a legion of distracting social, political, and even psychedelic experiences.

The affluence of our society, coupled with the possibility and often the necessity of early retirement, has created an additional problem for education—the problem of leisure. Previously defined as a highly tangential responsibility, this problem has become an important area of speculation for those interested in the long-range view of education and society. The major hope for our times lies in the fact that if science has created a gap in the life cycle, it almost certainly has the knowledge to fill it.

## INTERNAL SOURCES OF INNOVATION

⋋ Educational change has been effected by the contributions of persons interested in the dynamics of the human personality. The circulation of simple notions about human behavior has evolved into a complex network of institutional structures. Freud's idea that all behavior is motivated may have been the single most important conception behind the routinization of guidance activities to understand the student. The scientific contributions of psychiatry and clinical psychology provided the theories upon which many of our counseling activities are based. These two disciplines also pointed to the dynamics of conflict and motivation that provide the basis for our data-collecting instruments such as interest inventories and personality tests.

Paralleling the explosion of scientific knowledge about personality was a rapidly developing interest in measurement. Psychometrics, with its concern about precision and providing data on unexplored but intuited qualities such as intelligence and ability, provided the instrumentation of the counselor's task that created, in large part, a good segment of his responsibility. The administration and interpretation of psychological tests consume a substantial portion of the counselor's time. Large independent research and development organizations such as Educational Testing Service near Princeton, New Jersey, have emerged in response to an increasing demand for and reliance upon the objectivity so important to the scientific ethos that has infiltrated education.

In the same way that computer technology created more tasks than it displaced, educational technology evolves at a faster rate than a trained work force can accomodate. The systems approach, conceived as a necessary structure for developing industrial hardware, has yet to make its most important contribution to education. This is not because the system is not ready; it is because education cannot keep pace with innovations directly earmarked for its use. A computer-based data bank that can provide counselors with immediate retrieval of information crucial to their function will probably be an operational reality within the next ten years. It is an available reality at the moment.

The scientific revolution has certainly created an environment that present problems for school counselors. It is also likely to provide the instruments to solve these problems. But machinery does not conceive of the rationale for its own structure. This must come from the considered analysis of theoreticians and practicing counselors. Innovations in education that will shape the future of the counseling function will evolve from the reciprocal contributions of educators and technicians.

## INTRAINSTITUTIONAL INTERACTION AND THE
## PROFESSIONAL REVOLUTION

The contributions of scientific technology and the application of the scientific method to the study of human behavior played a considerable role in bringing about the kinds of changes encouraged by the emerging guidance ethos. Some of the inventions and ideas came from industry and extraeducational sources and were incorporated into the developing discipline of education. Many of the inventions and ideas that changed the face of the educational system developed from the theories, research, and experience of educators themselves, and insofar as change may be a function of what we might view as a linear historical evolution within the field of education itself, we may perceive this as a professional revolution.

In the same way that law and medicine moved from a diffuse and undefined set of responsibilities within a general area to a highly professionalized and specific set of functions as a result of accumulated work and knowledge, education has evolved its own professional image. The contributions of a sequence of educational scholars and researchers have built the foundation upon which educational innovations in several areas are rationalized. Changes in the kind of personnel recruited and trained for educational tasks, changes in educational facilities have their logical antecedents in educational theory and invention. The survival of the current conventions are dependent upon the tests of their viability that are being made on an ongoing basis. Educational change is the inevitable outgrowth of a concerted effort to professionalize the methodology of teaching and learning. The outline that follows describes briefly the kinds of innovation that have occurred in line with education's desire to comply with a guidance philosophy and at the same time establish a more rigorous professional image than has been characteristic of its history.

PERSONNEL
    General Training
        Required work in psychology and measurement
        Required work in the social sciences

PERSONNEL (*cont.*)

        Group dynamics, T groups

        Specialization in age levels

        Varied experiences in student teaching (suburbs, midcity)

    Specialized training for new job categories

        Vocational advisor

        Counselor

        School psychologist

        School social worker

        Psychometrician

        Expert in the exceptional child

        Cooperating referral personnel

        Child guidance clinics

        Mental health clinics

        Dieticians

        Audio-visual specialist

        Physiotherapist

CURRICULUM

    Grouping

    Expressive activities—art, music

    Special education programs

    Life-adjustment courses

    Freedom in secondary curriculum choice

    Extracurricular activities

    Team teaching

    Nongraded schools

    Social-adjustment classes

    Group guidance classes

FACILITIES

    Building construction—better lighting, carpeting, more attractive, play areas, one floor, landscaping

    Recreational facilities

    Laboratories

    Audio-visual aids

## *Social Movements and Events*

The educational response to social movements with national visibility has had to take on greater formal character than was the case with the problems of changing neighborhoods. The mobilization of materials, personnel, and technology behind the advancing tanks of government interest and financial support has left behind, perhaps wisely, the feeble attempts at the local community and school to handle the educational problems of the poor.

The Birmingham bus boycott of 1954 was the first epochal event in a tortuous, complex, and still far from completed chain of events that was to firmly establish the Negro as a social and political force in the United States. The civil rights movement has led to the establishment of an awareness and an attitude among power figures in most American institutions such that, regardless of personal values, the Negro's condition and needs now play an operational role in the action philosophy of these institutions. American government, acting through its most public agencies, began to speak to the nation about its historical violation of the supposedly basic American principle of egalitarianism, and it has set in motion forces to attempt to set right this now glaring disjuncture in our evolution toward the American ideal.

"Brown vs. Topeka," the Supreme Court's far-reaching school desegregation decision of 1954, made the first significant official splash in the controversial waters, and the waves are as yet far from settled. Institutional change is a grudging and slow process, and many temporary setbacks were to be expected. Six years after the historic decision, school integration had not even been started in five Southern states, and only token integration had begun to appear throughout the country; the educational establishment began to gird itself for a long and arduous task. While school integration was being conceived as an important educational task, the civil rights movement made it apparent to the nation that real segregation was an ecological fact throughout the nation—in the Northern urban communities as well as in the deep South—and that this required urgent attention and action. Education's problem, given the fact of segregation, became how best to mobilize its efforts to ensure equal educational opportunity. The "conventional wisdom of education," a notion adopted by Bressler[8] from a phrase employed by Galbraith, has also contended that education's role was to be viewed as one of remedial action, and the existence of school segregation could certainly be viewed as a remedial problem.

Education's concern with the Negro involves a great deal more, however, than just a concern with implementing the 1954 court decision. It is directly concerned with the broad spectra of the Negro's place in American society. The Negro problem has never been exclusively one of color or, in the broad, commonly accepted sense, a problem of cultural differences. The culture of the American Negro is not African. If anything, it is the pervasive culture of poverty, rural in its beginnings insofar as beginnings stamp persons in a cultural mold, but usually urban in its present aspects. Color may be the manifest form by which mobility appears to be frustrated, but rural poverty expresses similar conditions for whites. The War on Poverty, as it was conceived and as its funds appear to be allocated, shows itself as a general attack on the obstacles to social mobility encountered by those classes described so vividly by Michael Harrington in *The Other America* and, concomitantly, on the basis for discrimination itself.[9]

Education's conventional wisdom at present, then, views itself as having a concrete errand with certain types of activities: Project Head Start training programs, busing, the Job Corps supplementing vocational guidance for those not in school attendance, job freezing to deter teachers from moving so facilely out of lower class schools, extensive research grants to probe the sources of "disadvantage," in the new catch-phrase, and to call to arms the culturally disadvantaged, Operation Uplift, Upward Bound, and a host of other Federal-school-

---

8. Marvin Bressler, "The Conventional Wisdom of Education and Sociology," in *Sociology and Contemporary Education,* ed. by Charles Page, Random House, Inc., New York, 1963.

9. Michael Harrington, *The Other America,* The Macmillan Company, New York, 1963.

community alliances to overcome specific conditions, perhaps long present, but not previously viewed as disadvantaging both the student and the nation. Social problems such as delinquency, drug addiction, schoolgirl pregnancy, dropouts, and the increased hostility towards eduaction that occurs as a result of unrealistic expectations on the part of both school functionaries and students appear to be still another set of responsibilities that the school must deal with in the absence of other relevant social agencies to handle them.

In the sixties, with the nation's realization of a real lack of social justice (contrary to its previous self-conception), there has been instituted a major, serious attempt by the Federal government to come to grips with the problem. With the psychological groundwork laid by the Kennedy Administration and the Johnson Administration's highly publicized War on Poverty well launched by the passage of the Economic Opportunity Act in August, 1964, a bewildering array of special programs and services oriented toward the disadvantaged has been instituted. Outlined briefly here are just a few of the major programs.

## PEACE CORPS

Instituted by Executive Order of President Kennedy on March 1, 1961, on a temporary basis and made an official program with the passage by Congress of the Act for the Peace Corps on September 22, 1961, the Peace Corps is the oldest major program and the first to really catch the imagination of the nation and particularly of its youth. By the middle of 1965, over 150,000 Americans had volunteered for Peace Corps service, and some 15,000 of these had served in forty-nine countries. They had served in an immense number of difficult tasks—most of them impossible to prepare for adequately—tailoring their talents, skills, and ingenuity to the local problems. Volunteers have served in the general areas of agriculture, rural and urban community action, physical, vocational, elementary, secondary, university, and adult education, and various aspects of health, public works, and public administration. The Peace Corps volunteers, while relatively few in number, have played a highly visible role in showing to a generally skeptical world the peace-loving side of American policy. So successful has the Corps been in terms of good public relations that some thirty other nations have since established their own voluntary service programs modeled on the Peace Corps.

Aside from the valuable aid to the United States image abroad and the undoubted help to those the volunteers are trying to aid, some members of the Corps and its staff have wondered if their work is not too small to effectively make a dent in the world's vast problems. But it is at least a beginning, and the Peace Corps is having another, less heralded effect, this time at home. Returned volunteers have significantly shown carry-over effects from their overseas experience in terms of a deep sense of commitment to true social justice. This, coupled with the know-how of two years of field experience, is bringing forth on the domestic scene a new breed of socially aware and experienced activists ready to continue at home to come to grips with the problems of America and the world.

## VOLUNTEERS IN SERVICE TO AMERICA

What the Peace Corps is attempting to do overseas, VISTA is attempting to do at home. An Office of Economic Opportunity program, it is one of a whole series of OEO-sponsored programs resulting from the Economic Opportunity Act of 1964. The act reflects this nation's admitting to itself and to the world that, in spite of being the richest and most powerful nation the world has ever known, it has allowed some thirty-five million Americans—a fifth of its people—to exist in, or near, poverty.

VISTA volunteers (in early 1966 there were some 2,000 on the job or in training, out of some 20,000 applicants) work in those areas where American poverty is most likely to be found—the rural backwoods and mountain areas, the city slums, the migrant workers' camps, and the Indian reservations. Again with few preconceived ideas of what would have to be done, the programs and methods have developed in response to the found needs and range from teaching basic sanitation and basic English to community organizing. There have been numerous administrative problems, often political ones in connection with volunteers serving under local agencies in the community to which they are assigned, but the overall effects of the first years of operation have been very promising.

## PROJECT HEAD START

Of all the domestic programs, Project Head Start has probably been that with the greatest favorable publicity. The idea of giving at least some of the one million poverty children who enter school each year the opportunity to pick up learning experiences previously denied them that will enable them to enter school on somewhat equal terms with their more fortunate peers has apparently appealed to the nation's benevolent instincts. It was originally planned for the first eight-week preschool session (in the summer of 1965) to help 100,000 children. However, the community response to the idea was huge, and finally some 560,000 children attended sessions that summer in 2,400 communities in all fifty states—over five times more than the original plan. Head Start now operates on a year-round basis with special large summer programs and a follow-through program. There has been little real criticism of the program from the public, which feels that anything done for the children is fine. But some criticism has come from the academic world in terms of evaluation. Partly as a result of the rapidity with which the program grew, some have felt there was insufficient evaluation of the program's effects to justify all the money being spent. With the stabilization resulting from time, these legitimate criticisms are being met, however, and Head Start is likely to remain one of the nation's most popular antipoverty programs.

## UPWARD BOUND

Whereas Head Start attempts to ensure that no child is condemned to failure by the accident of his birth, Upward Bound tries to do the same for those poverty youths already nearing college age. Its purpose is to motivate non-college-bound students toward college and to help them get there. Set up in a similar way but on a much smaller scale initially than Head Start (eighteen eight-week projects in the summer of 1965), it too is being expanded to a year-round program. It operates essentially as a talent hunt by which capable but unmotivated and poor junior and senior high school students are tracked down and attempts made to instill in them, through sessions on local college campuses, a desire to learn. Although the attitudes and habits of seventeen years cannot be easily changed, this ambitious but difficult program is nevertheless succeeding in placing many of its students in colleges, and its administrators are extremely pleased with its preliminary results.

## JOB CORPS

The Job Corps sets up training centers where out-of-work and out-of-school young men and women may live and learn the necessary skills to get a job, which the Corps helps them get. The Job Corps has probably had more trouble and adverse publicity than any other antipoverty project as a result of a number of riots within Job Corps centers. Where large numbers of frustrated and desperate young people are living together, this sort of problem, while unfortunate, is only to be expected. The fact is that the positive results of the Corps in starting a large number of down-and-out young people toward self-sufficiency have been very real, and the program is bound to survive its criticism and grow, because the need for it is very apparent: over 275,000 letters of interest in joining had been received by the program's offices by October of 1965.

## LEGAL SERVICES

In terms of national publicity, this program has been largely ignored, probably because it must perforce deal disparately with detailed individual cases and cannot easily give an overall impression of some bold, new, dynamic force. Still, in terms of all the new approaches and considerations of the poor's problems, the probably far-reaching effects of the program's successful enlistment of the nation's legal establishment will be many. The American Bar Association, the National Bar Association, and the National Legal Aid and

Defenders Association have each strongly supported the idea of legal aid for the poor. The uneducated and ill-informed poor have always been easily bilked by unscrupulous businesses, landlords, and the like. As a consequence, those least able to afford it often pay exorbitant prices for all their possessions as well as jail bail, and so on. A National Conference on Law and Poverty was held in Washington, D. C., in June of 1965 to discuss these problems, and the result was nineteen projects in sixteen cities by October of that year. The early results of these programs have shown great savings to the poor as a result of legal intervention on their behalf, and there is little doubt that the turning of the legal profession's attention to the injustices of poverty will be a major contribution in the fight against poverty.

## AMELIORATION PROGRAMS AND THE GUIDANCE FUNCTION

The programs outlined here are only a few of the myriad new ideas that the nation's War on Poverty has generated. There are also special programs for the elderly, for migrants, for Indians, special loans for adults, and a whole array of neighborhood and community projects. At this writing (late 1966), there are signs of some disaffection throughout the country with some aspects of the War on Poverty and cries to go slower and reevaluate. No doubt there will be changes made and stringent reevaluations done. But the important point is that almost nowhere in the American political spectrum is there a disavowal of the aims of the War on Poverty, only with some of its methods. A process of immense social change has been set in motion with the full consent of the country, and its potential effects on the moral, social, and economic faces of the United States are incalculable.

The schools have been effected by these programs of the Great Society, and in many ways have serviced their goals. At the same time the school is caught in the middle of some of the dilemmas of that society. In the midst of a constantly escalating war in Asia, the school serves as a draft agency. Schools differentiate between those who will go on for further education and those who are to be available for warfare. The evidence seems clear that Negroes are overrepresented in Viet Nam as a result of this selection process. Many moral and ethical questions have been raised about America's role in the Viet Nam War, but the guidance office's role in helping students understand their own relationship to that war and consequently their career plans has never been in doubt. The official role of the school and all its segments is to support the intent and thereby the morality of the nation as a whole, regardless of any ethical considerations. If students require counseling about such significant and troublesome questions as "to go or not to go" it is not unlikely that they will receive an objective dialogue. The social reality is that schools participate in programs that are supported by the national interest and avoid activities that, although consonant with the professional philosophy of counselors, are problematic with respect to public sentiment.

The problem for the guidance function of education, remedial and prescriptive, in a time of ballooning social concern, is one of identification with causes and inspection of responsibility. The guidance function may be ready to extend its self-conception to include, as legitimate guidance activities and organizations, the kinds of programs discussed in the preceding sections. Bureaucratic structures are capable of absorbing additional functions and roles as long as these too become bureaucratized, as they usually will. The goals of these anti-poverty organizations and activities are certainly guidance goals, and the techniques are legitimate guidance techniques. The only missing quality is the lack of traditional affiliation with the educational bureaucracy. This association, which has already begun, is bound to solidify, signifying the kind of wedding that is necessary to absolve the schools from some of the responsibility to solve the nation's problems.

## EDUCATION AS A VEHICLE FOR CHANGE

Although we may explain the conspicuous absence of public education from the role of shaping cultural innovation, we may nonetheless speculate upon the kind of role that this type of education and guidance would play in changing culture and social patterns if the institutions were not hampered by their institutionalized obligations.

Burton Clark has specified several ways in which higher education has made a contribution to the shaping of the modern world.[10] A consideration of these ways and an evaluation of why and how higher education can play this role in contrast to elementary and secondary education should present us with a clear picture of what could be done and the conditions under which lower education could play an active role.

Clark designates five areas in which colleges and universities serve as an active agent of cultural change and presents evidence that these roles are actually being played.

## 1. Higher Education Contributes Institutionalized Research

Technological innovation occurs here that affects the structure of industry, the distribution of population, the status of occupations, and even the tenor of international relations. Research in American universities in atomic energy, medicine, engineering, and mental health are several examples. What and how we eat may result from research conducted on food technology. At the same time that this research is being conducted, persons are being trained to carry on the research, either in the university or in industry itself.

## 2. Higher Education Supports Groups That Innovate in the Arts

Poets, writers, and artists in residence are common personages on university campuses, and those whom they teach and influence become a large segment of those who hope to keep the culture alive with their productions and artistic criticism. The university also trains the technicians for more recent artistic media such as the film and television. Drama, writing, and dance workshops are frequently annual

---

10. Burton Clark, *Educating the Expert Society,* Chandler Publishing Co., San Francisco, 1962, pp. 28–39.

affairs, and the university theater group often provides the community with its only opportunity to view the classics of drama.

### 3. Higher Education Liberalizes Attitudes

Data are available that imply that mere attendance at a college or university is likely to produce more tolerant and humanitarian attitudes, particularly toward social groups different from one's own. Clark talks about the tendency of college graduates to be more supportive of democratic norms than non-graduates. Sepcifically, it was found that as education increased, attitudes towards political nonconformists became more tolerant.

The recurrent consideration of controversial subject matter in college classrooms encourages students to review their attitudes and the factual bases for these attitudes. Introduction to the scientific method structures the approach that students come to take toward social and psychological issues, and those moralities founded upon dogma are seriously questioned. In this way a liberalization occurs, if not behaviorally, then attitudinally. As behavior is perceived both as human and as relative, moralistic judgments are held in abeyance even though a violation of long-held values does not occur for the person himself. This condition, in effect, influences shifts in the position and approach of religious institutions, the logic being that, in order to hold the affiliation of young adults today, the issues that may keep the church and its populace apart must be reviewed. This movement can be observed in practically every segment of religious institutional life.

#### THE DELIBERALIZATION OF ATTITUDES

There are a number of ways in which the liberalization of attitudes takes on a pattern opposite from the gross tendencies. This is also a direct consequence of higher education. Two patterns evolve that involve two kinds of persons, those who are upwardly socially mobile and those who come to have vested interests in the economy. Advanced education makes both of these situations possible.

*Upward Mobility.* There is some theory and evidence to suggest that as members of the lower social strata move upwards on the social ladder, their attitudes become more conservative.[11] Education, for these people, is perceived more as a vehicle for mobility, an occupational channel, than as a world of challenging ideas. Once mobility is attained through education, persons settle into status roles that carry expectations of responsibility and loyalty to the normative moral order. Because it is their first time at this level, their attitudes appear to be more rigid than those of members of the middle class who have come from middle class backgrounds. They are, in effect, more middle class than the middle class. Stabilization of a new status appears to these people to be a necessary pose, and they feel that if they do not represent themselves as upstanding and highly moral, their occupational mobility will be questioned by the great unknown significant other. A good case in point appears in the writing of Franklin Frazier[12] and of G. Franklin Edwards[13] where the development of a super middle class Americanism on the part of the Negro is discussed. The present writer has collected evidence of his own to show that those Negro students who appear destined for college training reveal attitudes toward social issues that are not only more conservative than those of nonmobile Negroes but even more conservative than those of white students' leaders who are destined for the same mobility.[14]

*Vested Interest.* Here the argument is more logical than empirical, but the plausibility of such a mechanism as vested interest influencing a conservative turn in social attitudes is sufficiently strong to warrant a statement. American doctors have a greater investment in the national economy than do college professors. Businessmen have a greater investment than teachers or social workers. Regardless of their ultimate occupational slots, college graduates who have majored in English, philosophy, history, or some branch of the behavioral sciences are more likely to have a weak investment in the economy than those

11. See L. Reissman, *Class in American Society,* The Free Press, New York, 1959, pp. 371–373.

12. E. Franklin Frazier, *Black Bourgeoisie,* The Free Press, New York, 1957.

13. G. Franklin Edwards, *The Negro Professional Class,* The Free Press, New York, 1959.

14. Carl Weinberg, "Social Attitudes of Negro and White Student Leaders," *Journal of Negro Education,* Spring 1966.

who have majored in business, engineering, accounting, or pre-law. It makes psychological sense to assume that someone struggling to maintain or attain economic stability will be less satisfied with the status quo than those who have already attained this stability, except in cases where conservatism itself is a force adopted by those hoping to insure mobility. Advanced education makes this stabilization more available and so contributes to the kind of complacency that seems to characterize social conservatism.

This discussion of the deliberalization of social attitudes as a result of higher education is an appendage to the Clark analysis. It contradicts in no way the major point that higher education does play a role in shaping the culture. It simply suggests that, in the area of attitudes, the influence of advanced education may be observed in polarized opinions.

Capitalism and industrialism in the United States have been strongly associated with individualism, which in turn is associated with conservatism. It is not difficult to understand, in this context, the actual social meaning of the counseling bromide, "Help others to help themselves." It suggests an attitude about individualism that few bureaucratic types would disclaim. The problem of this version of guidance is the problem of differentiation despite unequal starts and unequal opportunities. In many ways, the high satisfaction level of those with the greatest vested interest in the economy is the best predictor of what schools will or will not do in the area of influencing cultural change.

## 4. Higher Education Differentiates Culture

The differentiation of culture occurs at the career level, and its form is specialization. At its highest point of specialization social life bifurcates into what C. P. Snow[15] refers to as the two cultures, that of the scientist and that of the humanist. Burton Clark writes of specialization as follows:

---

15. C. P. Snow, *The Two Cultures*, Cambridge University Press, New York, 1965.

The specialization trend, which is irreversible, means that individuals are allocated to a widening spectrum of adult subcultures that are hooked to occupational subworlds. In this general process, the educational system initiates changes as well as reactions to changes forced upon it. Much impetus for further specialization comes from within the academy, for here if anywhere the specialized expert is at home and the process of fields giving rise to subfields continues endlessly.[16]

For many decades, the market for economic goods has dichotomized its prospective consumers into fairly gross categories, the well-to-do and the poor, the educated and the noneducated. In the years since the Second World War, with the upsurge and adamancy of the labor union, with millions of GI's taking advantage of the GI Bill to secure either higher education or vocational skills, and with a geometrically increasing college attendance (greater for females than males), the market has increasingly worked on the principle of the lowest common denominator of the masses. Most people, particularly with the advent of installment buying, can buy almost anything. In many senses, then, there has been an evolution toward the classless society, occurring as Marx predicted but certainly not in the way he predicted. To meet the pejorative connotation of mass equality, society has evolved another layer of status differentiation. If a person cannot be differentiated from the large bulk of society in what he can buy, in college attendance, or in his hobbies, as everybody has more free time and money to exploit it (witness the waiting lines on golf courses, the saturation of wilderness camping spots, and crowded tennis courts and fishing streams), then he must seek individuation in other areas. Higher education serves to accommodate this drive. Having completed an occupationally designed curriculum, having graduated and taken his place in the economic order, a person may turn back to the university to explore interests and inclinations. Painting and sculpture classes today cannot meet the public demand; university extension classes in every field service a host of those who want not only to continue their education but to begin it anew. Persons come to learn languages and then travel; they take courses in the humanities so as

---

16. Burton Clark, *op. cit.*, p. 39.

to be genuinely "educated" rather than occupationally schooled. With a greater sophistication in the traditional humanities, their participation in such groups as discussion groups, book-study groups, and social-protest groups takes on a greater self-realization function than in the past.

In some ways these activities are related to the purposelessness that housewives often attribute to their college training. If colleges were marriage marts only and had little effect on the nonacademically motivated female, then accepting one's role as wife and mother, living in a world of children whose demands call forth little use of the mind, would be easy. But for most women today this role is not easy, and the difficulty of accepting it is the source of much family disorganization and stress. Women want to be alive as individuals, alive in a world that stimulates the mind that they have discovered in themselves. The feminine mystique is crumbling, and any professor who teaches a general evening course finds his class crowded with women who want to be differentiated from other women, from a no longer noble class called "housewife." Higher education provides valuable access to that differentiation.

## 5. Higher Education Contributes to Cultural Diversity

Cultural diversity occurs through the variation in the character of American colleges and universities. Colleges differ on a host of grounds, and the ecological characteristics presumably form a general type such that graduates respond in ways related to these characteristics. When parents and counselors look into the subject of the right college for a given child, they are taking into consideration not only the personality of the child but also the personality of the college. What are the major factors that we expect to influence students in different ways? There are the size of the college, the geographical location, the reputation of the school and faculty, and the sponsorship (public or private, church-affiliated or nonsectarian). There are also the factors of specialization (teachers' college, liberal arts, technical-scientific, art college, theological school, and so on), and finally the degree of homogeneity of the student population, depending upon the school's "pull" from diverse geographical areas and social backgrounds.

These factors are presumably indicators of abstract but crucial characteristics of institutions of higher learning. Either independently or in combination they may say something about academic freedom, a student's freedom in his social and personal life, the atmosphere of personal versus impersonal relatedness, the availability of culture contact, the likelihood of encountering challenging controversial issues, and the availability of cultural, intellectual, and social life.

## Differential Capacities for Playing an Active Role in Cultural Change

What is there about the American college that it can serve these functions and public education cannot? First, the public school is tied to the community in an ongoing interactional dialogue that forces the school to be hypersensitive to the concerns of parents. The university does not interact with the community in this way. In actuality, where universities are located in small towns or semirural areas, a distinction and often hostility may occur, as in the "town and gown" phenomena.

The public schools are supported by local funds, and this fact gives the local authorities, usually persons totally untrained in the educational process, complete authority over the behavior of administrators and teachers. The university, on the other hand, receives its support from a variety of sources. Furthermore, in most cases the administration is so monolithic that sponsorship agencies confine their activities to budgetary matters and allow the administration of the university to lie in the hands of educators.

Second, at the college level the students are older, and society accepts the fact that, for the most part, they can now take care of themselves. On the other hand, school administrators take the position that they must be the guardians of the cognitive and moral input to children because they are so malleable and impressionable.

Third, attendance at the university is not compulsory, and anyone who does not like what is happening on the campus is free to leave. Public school students, on the other hand, are a captive audience who oblige those responsible for their welfare to be cautious in imposing activities that are not highly sanctioned by the culture at large.

Fourth, there is the question of differing philosophies of role. In the socialization of its students, the wisdom of public education holds guardedly to the notion of its responsibility to the traditional values and, thereby, to motivations of the traditional culture. The ethos of the university revolves around the development of a personality equipped to deal cognitively with either general or specialized phenomena. Universities seek to produce an attitude of inquiry based upon logical or empirical evidence and never to advance doctrinaire moral requirements for living. We speak here of an ethos. The fact that the many colleges and universities may not behave wholly in terms of this ethos does not negate its existence as a basic philosophy of purpose.

Finally, the faculties of American universities are professionalized to the point where any infringement of the right of academic freedom imposed on any one individual is a threat to the total profession. Any violation of this right may result, after careful assessment of the claim by representatives of the profession, in censure of the violating university's administration. Public school teachers seem to have been hindered in their attempts to professionalize because of some identification of necessary tactics with union behavior in general, an identification that tends to lower the self-esteem of the group. Whether they are actually hindered in this way or not is, of course, debatable. The only point to be made here is that teachers do not control any of the important dimensions of their occupational life, nor do they have any recourse against impingements from the outside on their freedom or dignity except personal surrender or flight.

The conclusion of this section is logically to suggest that none of the conditions present in the public schools need deter them from playing an active role in cultural change. The fact that students are younger does not preclude intelligent shaping of innovative capacities through advanced techniques. The concern for the reaction of the community is a dysfunctional assumption that may be partly myth, but even that part that is a real concern looms as a threat only because teachers and public education in general are, as yet, unready to assert their claims to specialized knowledge with which the layman has no right to tamper. The question of financial support is also equivocal because there are various ways of translating support into coercive action and also ways of resisting this action. Professionalization may be one way of resisting, and the controversial nature of that subject is currently alive in teaching circles everywhere.

## Guidance Functions for Cultural Change

If we should grant that school counselors and pupil personnel in public schools are amenable to playing a more active role in shaping culture and society and that their level of skill is adequate to this task, then our only problem is one of defining goals, eliminating constraints, and establishing ongoing techniques. Practically, the problems are large, involving all the considerations of restraint discussed earlier. Ideally, on the other hand, the only problems involved are academic and are eliminated by taking the step of attacking the issue. The restraints upon practice may, in part, be a function of a general absence of ideas to which persons may become committed. We are working in a time that enthusiastically embraces innovation. The new as well as the conventional wisdom of education is on our side, and we perform a distinct disservice to pupils, as well as to professional guidance workers, if we ignore the broad and engaging function of helping to shape the society in a way that will support the healthy individualism we want to promote in schools.

In general, the guidance function is one of helping to shape students and their environment in such a way as to increase the probability that they will make life choices congruent with their abilities and personality. In order to accomplish that, a subsidiary function revolves around helping students overcome barriers to educational and social progress in their daily life. At this point we need to consider the kind of world that these functions presume to be possible. It is a world that is occupationally as well as psychologically gratifying for the person. It is a world in which people can work, play, and love without neurotic anxieties, without self-created conflict, and without harming others either physically or psychologically. We all share this dream that requires more personal and social responsibility than a government, a church, or a school can possibly enforce.

To a very great extent, the kind of shaping of the individual that will produce this personal and social responsibility can only be accomplished at the level of education that appears to have the most difficulty innovating. Higher education may provide an active function in some areas because the students are presumably mature, but precisely because their students are not mature, the public schools have a clearer shot at molding the crucial elements of personality.

The social and personal problems of our time are many: The problems of mental health seem insoluble, occupational dissatisfaction is high,[17] prejudice and discrimination are rampant, frigidity and sexual impotence are partly responsible for excessive divorce rates, the pressures of living daily in a competitive "rat race" are increasing, a war and kill mentality seems easily engendered in the masses, there are riots in the street, and one television special labeled the average American "detached." It might easily have gone one step further and labeled him "alienated."

Even if our society is only half as seriously afflicted as this picture of it suggests, then either the guidance function in the schools has failed or it has never really begun. Let us presume the latter condition, for criticism on the grounds of failure would degenerate into a complaint about obstacles and this would not advance our case any further than we have gone. In order to take a giant step, we may have to conclude that the guidance function should be primarily preventive and only secondarily involved with individual problems. Rather than constantly asking ourselves the question, "Why does this child react so aggressively to educational personnel?" we might begin by asking the more applied, general question, "What structural

---

17. Consult the yearly job-satisfaction studies by H. A. Robinson and R. P. Conners in *The Personnel and Guidance Journal,* October 1963, pp. 136–142.

changes may we make within the school that would help to eliminate aggressive behavior?" The same questions may be asked about withdrawal, nervous anxiety, stereotypic attitudes, frustration that evolves into general disruptive behavior, and, on the secondary level, the observance of delinquent norms.

The approach, if we take the sociological view, is structural. That is, what organizational patterns, interactional modes, and role perceptions contribute to the shaping of adaptive patterns in students that lead to insecurity and unhappiness in adult life? What, for example, are the patterns by which allocation to occupational roles begins, how is commitment developed, how is aspiration infused, and how is it frustrated? In what ways does the school contribute to sexual inhibitions, to impersonal, self-defeating competitive striving? How do we turn the insecurity of childhood to an educational advantage that has dysfunctional consequences for the student? These questions will be considered in more detail as we look at the functions and dysfunctions of guidance in a later chapter. All that needs to be said now is that, given the goals of educational guidance and that the traditional role of education is passive, we must be consistently inquisitive about the ways in which the guidance function may play its most important role in affecting the general culture.

# CHAPTER 2

# SOCIAL EXPLANATIONS
# FOR STUDENT PROBLEMS

IN THE LAST PART of the nineteenth century, Emile Durk-
heim, a French sociologist, published *Suicide*.[1] This work represented
a major advance toward pushing sociological concepts into the field
as possessing explanatory potential for the source of individual problems. Durkheim and several of his followers, Levy-Bruhl, Charles
Blondel, and M. Halbwachs, developed theoretically and empirically
the notion that individual or highly idiosyncratic acts are tied to and
can be explained by cultural or social facts. The structure of group
life, to these men, ordered not only behavior but also the meanings
that persons attach to behavior and the feelings they have about what
they do. Levy-Bruhl developed a system of attaching social meanings
to individual acts by comparing the thought processes of primitive
with those of civilized peoples. Blondel extended this conception by
analyzing the way in which human feelings were attached to social
life. Halbwachs, in terms again of social determinism, showed the way
in which the structure of group life influenced the selective perceptions
that evolve as memory. This work proceeded in the face of a prevailing emphasis on psychological explanations and theories for human
behavior. The persistence of this emphasis and the difficulty of in-

---

1. Emile Durkheim, *Suicide*, The Free Press, New York, 1951.

stilling in educators a conceptual approach based upon social facts is a problem that contributes to retarding a necessary explosion of knowledge about the social aspects of educational counseling.

The evolution of conceptual emphases in the analysis and description of man and his environment is metaphorically expressed by John Seely:

Just as in the latter half of the nineteenth century a Darwinian tidal wave passed along the world, upheaving the depths of thought and feeling, and even religion, just so a psychoanalytic movement of the waters marked our entry upon this, our century. And, hardly less noticeable, so a sociological disturbance of seismic proportions marked the middle of the century we are now in.[2]

The accumulated knowledge about the function and interaction of institutions is building rapidly, as Seely indicates. It is both logical and necessary that sociological thinking become involved in the analysis of such small segments of institutional life as the basis of decision making in guidance interactions in schools. This chapter presents one approach to this problem area.

Typically, school counselors rely upon psychological facts to explain student problems. This assertion is based on the description of course requirements for school counselors mentioned in the Introduction and from a survey study conducted by the writer. This study was an attempt to assess, descriptively, the kinds of concepts that both professional counselors (all members of the American Personnel and Guidance Association) and graduate students in counseling and guidance programs preferred as preliminary hunches about the background of student problems. The format of the investigation was to present those who responded to the questionnaires with a number of case fragments involving student problems. The case fragments were chosen and presented in such a way that a great deal of information was missing, so that no clear-cut relationship between the source of the problem and the problem itself could be reached. At the same time, by easy inference, both social and psychological conditions could

---

2. John Seely, *The Americanization of the Unconscious,* International Science Press, New York, 1967, p. 79.

be perceived as a part of the history, so that one condition, the other, or neither could be chosen as representing the proclivity of the chooser. These case fragments are presented in the appendix to this chapter. In the fragments themselves may be perceived the germ of potential theoretical alternatives for the explanations of the students' problems.

Three cases, one representing an elementary school situation, a second representing a high school problem, and the third a college problem, will be presented and analyzed in detail later in this chapter. Sociological as well as psychological facts, concepts, and generalizations may be relevant to specific ages. At the same time, a sociological framework that exposes important dimensions of elementary school life would be substantively different when applied to either high school or college organizations. Through the analysis of specific problems and specific age and grade levels, those social and psychological facts and concepts that are useful in the exploration of problems of personal disorganization may be discussed.

## PROBLEM DEFINITION AND
## EDUCATIONAL ACTION

As will be illustrated in discussion of the three cases, the choice of a particular problem source will guide the process of amelioration. At the same time, the whole question of educational policy is raised when we speculate about patterns of remedial action. It is suggested later, in the chapter on educational functions, that decisions about where problems begin are often determined by the structures that are available to deal with the problem. When new functions appear and new roles are created, it may be that, in our zest to incorporate them into the educational enterprise, we act like a woman with her new dishwasher who runs it through its whole cycle with only a couple of dishes just to see the new toy in operation. The analogy is intended to suggest that problems that called forth one set of responses at one time might be submitted to new roles or inventions at another, simply to justify the expenditure of acquiring the new means of interpretation. For example, rather than switch a child from wood shop to another activity because he blocks when it comes to using tools, the answer may become therapy if the district has invested in a school psychologist or a part-time psychiatrist.

This discussion introduces the reader to the possibility that psychological facts seem to dominate guidance thinking simply because the inventions of psychology (therapy, interest inventories, psychometric grouping, personality tests, and so on) are most readily available to counselors. Before inventions are forthcoming, however, it is usually the case that ideas (conceived necessities) indicate their development. If the idea of grouping students according to some criteria dominates educational thinking, it is certain that some technique will evolve to aid this kind of organization. The opposite is also possible that new technology creates much of the ideology. We may suddenly decide that homogeneous grouping is undesirable because teaching machines are available to individualize instruction.

This chapter is intended to advance the potential applicability of a set of ideas and concepts to the counselor's task, ideas that may have been of intellectual interest to education but have seldom been translated into routine action patterns. Many of the ideas and concepts that will be discussed are posed as interpretive notions around specific problem areas and juxtaposed with traditional psychological or psychoanalytic ideas.

## GUIDANCE ORIENTATION SURVEY

The survey of guidance counselors and graduate students working for advanced degrees in educational guidance was conducted in order to tap the intellectual basis of decision making in guidance. Every person who offers advice or help to others has some theory, although he may not be able to articulate it as such, that guides his interaction. A theory, in this sense, is an orientation to segments of social life that predict behavior. The general behavior. The general notion of political conservatives that was discussed in the preceding chapter is a good example. Although a person may not be able to articulate a consistent set of ideas that supports his conservative orientation to social life, we may assume that accumulated experiences and contact with ideas have had the aggregate effect of causing him to believe that one course of action is wise and another foolish. These theories that guide a counselor's interaction are often simple sentiments about the truth of one idea over alternatives or about the meaningfulness of certain concepts in a context and the irrelevance of others. The intellectual basis of decision making is those ideas and concepts that people use to help order the contribution they make to a social arrangement in which offering help is the structural base of the interaction.

The choice of school counselors and graduate students as respondents was made out of a concern about the role of education and specifically the function of guidance in the amelioration of problems resulting from social disorganization. One view of guidance activities sees the counselor as responsible for ad hoc solutions to individual problems of students. These solutions involve resolving conflict, removing barriers to educational progress, and facilitating individual goals through providing students with useful information. In this chapter we are only concerned with conflict and with barriers to educational progress. Organized activities focused on educational and career planning are problematic in another way, involving questions about differentiation, status, and allocation. These are discussed in other chapters. Here we focus upon students in conflict with their school.

A second conception of the guidance function is one that is closely associated with the basic purpose of this analysis and, in many ways, of this book. This conception holds that the guidance enterprise is preventive, that counselors are responsible in some way for organizing activities and programs that will reduce the frequency of general problems of conflict. We are not talking about institutionalized control, although counselors often find themselves involved in the mechanics of this task. Such control is perceived as an educational device for rewarding conformity and punishing deviance. The kind of program we are discussing is not a system of rewards and punishments or the promise or threat of either. It is a system of approaching deviance as a specific case of a general phenomenon (i.e., approaching throwing a book or talking back to teachers as a specific case of the more general phenomenon of frustration in the classroom) and organizing personnel and materials so that the general phenomenon itself may be so ordered that problems will not emerge. It is the difference between establishing rules that prohibit truancy and restructuring attitudes toward education so that truancy will not be a response. These attitudes, for example, may frequently be couched in the general phenomenon of social class. We know that persons in different economic strata have different attitudes toward education as the vehicle for upward social mobility. Attitudes toward education are also a function of responses to differential status systems within the school. Failure to achieve mobility in this status system leads to a depreciation of the system itself. Preventive guidance would assume that because a large portion of problems of conflict emerge out of class differentiation and competing status systems, it is these areas that require the utilization of energy fully as much as the area of the acts themselves. Focusing upon general problems of social disorganization and upon social facts that conspire to produce conflict is one way to explain the contribution that guidance may make to equality of opportunity in education.

## Results of the Survey

Table 1 summarizes the responses of counselors and graduate students to the fifteen case fragments they were asked to analyze. The response categories were reduced from fifteen to eleven as some fragments were combined (they were construed as containing the same basic set of alternatives). Three kinds of responses were designated: sociological, psychological, and common sense. The response that was intended to characterize each category was developed with the help of professional sociologists and psychologists. The common-sense category incorporated the dimensions of folk wisdom and practical administration. Certain social and psychological notions have filtered into the vernacular of the man on the street. Expressions such as "attention seeker," "inferiority complex," and "broken home" are examples. The way in which these ideas were used in the response categories was such that a label rather than an interpretation prompted the choice. This indicated that the behavior was within the normal range and not a special case for counseling, or that the problem was so obvious that complex speculation was unnecessary. Another possible interpretation of the "common sense" response was that although a problem may have existed, it was irrelevant to the school's interest and should call forth no educational response.

Two purposes influenced the conduct of the survey. One was specifically to measure the extent to which sociological ideas influenced the decision-making process of school counselors. The second, and more basic, concern, which the current data only begin to explain, was to find out how school counselors organize their thoughts in the process of dealing with specific kinds of student problems. In the early stages of formulating the case fragments and responses, interviews were conducted with counselors individually and in groups in an informal manner because no hypotheses or classification systems were yet established. From these interviews the range of student problems (problems of conflict and disorganization rather than guidance administration problems) was revealed. The counselors were next asked about some of the specific problems they felt were representative of the kinds of cases they dealt with regularly. They were then asked to associate freely to the kinds of ideas, factors, and circumstances they felt were either typically associated with each problem area or were products of their training or general reading. One representative response to a case similar to Case 7, the case of John (see Appendix), went something like the following (reconstructed from the interviewer's notes):

The first word I think of, naturally, is overachiever. These kids are under a lot of pressure, usually from their parents. A lot of the parents in our school [a suburban high school] are like that. They push their kids unmercifully. I also think about how kids sublimate, especially kids like that, putting everything they've got into pleasing their parents when they should be out having a good time like most kids their age. The thing I usually do when they start to crack under the pressure is to try to get them to slow down, to try to get the parents to lay off a little bit. I also think, when kids like that get into trouble involving girls, that all that studying is hiding the fact that he is suppressing some pretty important feelings which are natural to boys his age. I wouldn't be surprised if parents who are pushing all the time are pretty stuffy when it comes to sex. The boy probably picked up a lot from them.

Between the accumulated counselor associations and the contributions of psychologist and sociologist colleagues, the material for the case fragments and for the responses was provided. The thematic concepts that posed the essential dichotomy of sociological and psychological responses are represented by the categories in the left-hand column of the table. The response frequencies and percentages representing orientations to problems are contained within the cells.

*A Methodological Problem in the Construction of the Response Categories.* Behavioral scientists who construct instruments to measure personality traits or social and political attitudes are sensitive to the problems of response set and social desirability. These considerations involve organizing the questions in such a way as to preclude the possibility of answers being affected by conditions unrelated to the actual content of the questions. When all questions are stated positively, such as "this is a good world in which to bring up children," rather "It is not a good world . . ." there may be a tendency to agree more often than when the questions are stated negatively, regardless of how one feels about them. The question of social desirability of items is one that asks a similar question, that is: Are all the questions equally weighted so that one doesn't sound better than the other regardless of the import of the content? If, for example, we wish to derive an occupational interest area and are looking to differentiate an outdoor occupation from a managerial bureaucratic type of role, and we ask the following questions: "Would you rather work with children in a mountain resort or work with adults in a stuffy office?" we would have obviously loaded the question. Such loading would direct the respondent's attention away from the distinction between outdoors and indoors or working with children or adults to the associated distinction between a pleasant and an unpleasant environment.

The present study faced a dilemma in this area insofar as the focus is precisely upon what seems most conceptually desirable and the actual content cannot be divorced from the attractiveness of the item itself. It is possible that the response patterns revealed in the data are a function of the fact that the sociological responses were intrinsically more appealing than the psychological responses or vice versa. To make the responses equally appealing through a process of validating this fact through the subjects who are to respond would be to effectively destroy the possibility of studying the fact of desirability itself. The criteria for knowing when the alternative responses are equally strong would be when the respondents split fifty-fifty, but in the process of improving one or the other response category to arrive at this even split, the possibility of discovering preferences, which is the actual theme of the survey, is precluded.

This survey must rely upon the contributions of those who chose the different concepts and the informal pre-test discussions as well as the best guess of the writer that the alternatives are equally weighted. The true worth of each response category must be evaluated on this basis alone.

Before proceeding with the interpretation of the data in the table, the results of one analysis that is not presented graphically deserve brief mention. Within the counselor and graduate student categories, differences in response patterns based upon personal characteristics of the subjects were evaluated. When differentiated by sex, age, geographical area of training, undergraduate major, and marital status, the professional counselors showed very slight and statistically insignificant differences in their proclivities for social versus psychological alternatives. Females and younger counselors (under forty) exhibited a slightly greater tendency to select sociological alternatives than did those over forty, but these differences were not large enough to warrant even a preliminary generalization. The conclusion of the investigator was that the role itself was the great equalizer. Persons learn the expectations of role enactment through the combined experiences of graduate training, reading similar materials, and interacting with other members of the field. The fact that the graduate students do not exhibit radically different patterns from the professionals supports the notion that one characteristic of graduate training is socialization to a professional role.

## The Sample

The professional sample consisted of seventy-nine currently active school counselors who were members of the American Personnel and Guidance Association. They were randomly selected from the rolls of the Association and represented all sections of the country. The actual response to the mailed questionnaires was 55 per cent of the total; by geography, age, and sex, this percentage was representative of the original sample. The graduate student sample consisted of the majority of counselor trainees in six different colleges (N = 102) selected for geographic disparity. Two colleges of the eight originally requested to participate in the study did not do so. The colleges were generally representative of the range of American universities with counselor training programs.

## Category Terms[3]

1. Sex identification vs. Role conflict
   Problem source one of a missing sex model in the home or incompatible expectations between school and classmates.

2. Defense mechanisms vs. Status
   Hitting students in class defined as a problem of frustration

---

3. Only the sociological and psychological alternatives are presented. Common sense alternatives were not presented, because decisions that problems did not exist or that the problem was out of the school's jurisdiction do not advance the interest of the chapter, which is focused upon the two competing approaches. Responses in these categories were ordinarily too slight to deal with as an important dimension.

Since some of items reflected a similar dichotomy, they were combined. This occurred in four cases, reducing the fifteen items to eleven categories. Discrepancies in N (numbers running above 102 in the table) occur as a result of the combining of categories.

leading to aggression or seeking status among peers by being the strongest.

3. Need to belong vs. Role playing
   Being identified as a class clown is a result of a personal need to belong and be loved by his classmates or choosing a social role that is both available and suitable.

4a. and 4b. Frustration-Aggression vs. Lower class socialization and Frustration-Aggression vs. Ethnic identification
   Aggressive behavior in the classroom as a result of failure feelings or behavior related to certain class and ethnic socialization patterns.

5. Need for affection vs. Inadequate role perception
   Inappropriate behavior toward female teacher on the part of a male high school student interpreted in terms of the need for affection on the part of a mother figure or in terms of inadequate socialization as to appropriate role behavior.

6. Psychosexual guilt vs. Middle class socialization
   Disturbing and disruptive sexual feelings in school defined as reaction-formation consequence of excessive desires, or the inhibitions associated with middle class morality.

7. Sublimation vs. Cultural disruption
   Overachieving and sexual problems associated with the problem of diverting normal sexual energy into socially acceptable channels (school achievement) or related to the problem of learning the rites of passage, from childhood to adulthood, without experiencing the necessary trauma of the nowhereland of adolescence.

8. Anxiety vs. Competition
   Psychosomatic illness on test days interpreted as an anxiety reaction associated with fear of rejection by parents or as a safe response to the dangers inherent in competing with peers.

9. Unconscious anger vs. Impersonal institutions
   Potential college failure associated with a need to express

anger toward parents who sent female student away from home or with a reaction against the impersonality of a monolithic university.

10. Repressed sexuality vs. Role ambiguity
Problems of a female student in a male-dominated field interpreted in terms of anxiety associated with an emerging femininity and a sibling rivalry with brothers in the same area in which she has been working or in terms of the confusion of the role itself with social expectations for the behavior of females.

11. Anxiety vs. Peer-group identification
Inability to persist as a member in chosen groups and curriculum interpreted as anxiety about inferiority projected on to others or as a case of the inability to survive in highly fluid social circumstances, where a cohesive group is desired.

## Findings

Graduate students show a slightly stronger proclivity toward sociological responses (3 per cent) than do the professional counselors when the total responses for all fifteen items are summed, although within-category examination reveals more precise differences. Category 1 (Sexual identity vs. Role conflict, the case of Edward—see Appendix to this chapter), shows a 10-per cent difference between the groups. Professional counselors appear to place a greater emphasis on the student's living situation, which was dominated by females, than do the graduate students, who find a greater appeal in the idea that Edward is caught between wanting to meet the expectations of the two units present in the classroom—the school, represented by the teacher, and the peer group, represented by his classmates.

In only two areas do the professional counselors show a greater tendency than the graduate students to prefer sociological explanations to psychological ones. Category 5 (Need for affection vs. Inadequate

## Table I—Responses

| | Counselors | | | | | | Students | | | | | |
|---|---|---|---|---|---|---|---|---|---|---|---|---|
| | SOC. | | PSYCH. | | CS | | SOC. | | PSYCH. | | CS | |
| | N | % | N | % | N | % | N | % | N | % | N | % |
| Sex ident. vs. Role conflict | 35 | 45 | 38 | 49 | 5 | 6 | 56 | 55 | 39 | 39 | 6 | 6 |
| Defense mech. vs. Status | 35 | 15 | 160 | 69 | 37 | 16 | 70 | 22 | 206 | 65 | 43 | 13 |
| Need to belong vs. Role playing | 24 | 31 | 52 | 67 | 2 | 2 | 32 | 31 | 69 | 68 | 1 | 1 |
| Frust. -Aggress. vs. L.C. socializ. + Frust. -Aggress. vs. Ethnic ident. | 70 | 45 | 81 | 53 | 3 | 2 | 98 | 50 | 93 | 47 | 6 | 3 |
| Need for affect. vs. Indequate role perception | 34 | 45 | 41 | 54 | 1 | 1 | 37 | 37 | 63 | 62 | 1 | 1 |
| Psychosex. guilt vs. M.C. socializ. | 21 | 27 | 48 | 62 | 9 | 11 | 33 | 33 | 54 | 53 | 14 | 14 |
| Sublimation vs. Cultural disruption | 26 | 17 | 118 | 77 | 10 | 6 | 47 | 23 | 126 | 63 | 28 | 14 |
| Anxiety vs. Competition | 20 | 25 | 53 | 69 | 4 | 6 | 31 | 31 | 61 | 59 | 10 | 10 |
| Unconscious Anger vs. Impersonal instit. | 58 | 75 | 8 | 10 | 12 | 15 | 75 | 74 | 10 | 10 | 16 | 16 |
| Repressed sexuality vs. Role ambiguity | 34 | 44 | 16 | 20 | 28 | 36 | 40 | 40 | 24 | 24 | 37 | 36 |
| Anxiety vs. Peer-grp. ident. | 10 | 13 | 67 | 86 | 1 | 1 | 15 | 15 | 80 | 78 | 7 | 7 |
| Total | 367 | 32 | 682 | 59 | 112 | 9 | 534 | 35 | 825 | 54 | 169 | 11 |

role perception, the case of Michael) shows counselors more willing than graduate students to accept the possibility that Michael does not completely understand the expectations for the student role. Nonetheless, the entire group still prefers the need-for-action thesis as the best description of the case. Category 10 (Repressed sexuality vs. Role ambiguity, the case of Ann) is the only case in which the common-sense explanation competes successfully with the other two. The notion of an inferiority complex, although considered rather an unsophisticated and incomplete explanatory mechanism in most psychological circles, still seems to carry some weight in the thinking of these counselors and graduate students. Upon close inspection it appears that both the common-sense and psychological explanations may be construed to carry important psychological implications. As such, the necessary comparison then becomes one of looking at the two groups to see which preferred the idea of role ambiguity more than the other. In this case, the professional counselors demonstrate a greater tendency to accept this alternative.

The two most significant concepts in the perceptual apparatus of the subjects of this survey appear to be defense mechanisms and anxiety. Where these psychological interpretations appear to apply to alternative explanations of student problems, there is relatively little chance of a sociological idea gaining much recognition. In two cases (Categories 4a and 4b), minority-group identification and poor economic circumstances, the current attention to the War on Poverty and to programs for the culturally deprived seems to have had an influence. The sociological idea with the greatest appeal to counselors as an explanation for student failure at the college level is the notion of an impersonal institution. This suggests that the recent Berkeley revolt over depersonalization and the spread of this kind of sensitivity to other monolithic universities may have a fundamental appeal as an explanatory mechanism for school failure.

The dichotomies presented in this discussion will be elaborated in a more general way later in the chapter. The next section will be devoted to the consequences of the selection of one or the other alternative as the probable basis for student problems.

## *ALTERNATIVE EXPLANATIONS AND*
## *ALTERNATIVE ACTION*

The following case analyses are provided in order to explore the process of data evaluation. The counselor is required by the precepts of his discipline to accumulate as much data about the individual as is available; at the same time, he must understand the meaning of his facts. When he looks at an intelligence score, he understands something about the student's ability to perform certain educational tasks. Because IQ and achievement tests are highly correlated, he also understands something about the student's educational progress to date. He wonders about the student's ability to take tests, and he thinks about problems of grouping involving intelligence levels. Experience and reading have taught him that the fact of coming from a broken home or being a lower class Negro or orphan has meaning related to educational progress. But these are simple facts that tell only small and often insignificant parts of a more complex story. In order to expand his consideration of these behaviors, he needs cohering concepts, concepts that have as much meaning if not more than these simple facts. Counselors do employ many concepts such as aggression, attention seeking, compensation, withdrawal, ego defense, and inadequate self-concept. The theories of Freud, Horney, Murray, Allport, Rogers, and others have contributed many concepts to the counselor's perspective of disruptive behavior. The analysis of the following cases will show that sociological conceptual thinking is also potentially relevant to the appraisal of student problems, both in terms of precision of diagnosis and in terms of remedial action.

The interpretations that follow the presentation of each case will be, of necessity, limited and quite probably incomplete. They are simply sample speculations, with no contention that any one suggestion is definite. We are working with fragments in much the same way that the respondents in the study did. Although we cannot specify their thought processes, the interpretations probably approximate the general modes of conceptual thinking that accompanied evaluation and consideration of the case fragments. There is evidence from the pre-testing of the Guidance Orientation Questionnaire that such thoughts as are supplied in the interpretations are representative of counselors' thinking when they are confronted with incomplete data.

In each case, following the two interpretations (psychological and sociological), a set of hypothetical recommendations for remedial action is proposed. This is done in order to indicate to the reader that one's orientation in conceptual interpretation is directly linked to consequent remedial activities. If we change the interpretation, we must turn to another source of remedial action.

## Case 3: The Case of Max

Max is the class clown. He's in the sixth grade in an upper middle class elementary school. Several times Max has been sent to the principal for disrupting the class. His teacher told his parents that Max would be doing better in school if he didn't make a joke of everything. Max has never excelled in any field of subject matter. He received only C's and D's in Physical Education but has never been in danger of failing any subjects.

### PSYCHOLOGICAL INTERPRETATION

Max makes fun of everything as a defense against not standing out in class. Making fun of things is a way of devaluating academic performance. If the work is not particularly important, then lack of success is not important. Another factor that could be operating is the sense of pressure so typical of highly competitive middle class students. Pressure has been known to make these students potentially neurotic. Max's clowning is a symptom of extreme anxiety in such a situation. A third factor could be that Max has a need to belong. He feels that joking will endear him to his classmates. He is willing to sacrifice his grades in order to fulfill this need.

In line with these three areas of interpretation, remedial action would involve the following: (1) Max must be given an experience in which he can stand out so that he will come to value the activity and ultimately all educational activities. In this way Max will have a better self-concept as he relates to the school. (2) Some effort should be made to explore the source of pressure. Parents are frequently the focal point for such pressure, expecting more than their children can deliver. If this is at all suspected, the parents should receive a communication and suggestions about how to decrease the manifestations of high expectations. If the classroom itself seems overly pressured, some consideration should be given to creating a less competitive environment. (3) Max must be given a sense of belonging. This may be accomplished by suggesting to the teacher that Max be integrated into some project on which several students are working and given some specific task within that project that suits his strongest skills so that the others will recognize his contribution to the joint effort.

## SOCIOLOGICAL INTERPRETATION

Being neither a class leader, class failure, nor an athlete, Max selects one of the few social roles available to him. The peer group seems to be for Max the most significant reference group in his life, outweighing the expectations of two competing institutions, the family and the school. Max is aware of these competing expectations and is experiencing a conflict because he is a participant in all three units. A related interpretation revolves around the social function of humor. Humor is an effective device for integrating group members and reducing tension implicit in social contexts.

Remedial action consistent with this interpretation would involve the establishment of some institutional activity that would permit Max's clown role to be played out within an acceptable framework. Another way of handling the same problem would be to sanction the behavior by not reinforcing it. These are psychological terms but have meaning in the formulation of social characteristics. Any social behavior diminishes when others in the group do not respond to it. The reason the behavior strikes students as tension-reducing and leads to supportive laughter is that the teacher defines and acts upon it as a violation of the institutional expectation. Increasing the flexibility of the teaching situation so that humor is not seen as disruptive would remove that element from the interaction. A common reason why some things are funny is that they are defined as being out of the ordinary, that there is some deviation from normal routines. Perhaps the transition from affective relatedness prevalent in the earlier grades to affective neutrality of the more academically oriented years could be made more gradual through structural innovations on the part of the administration.

For Max, and those like him who experience a conflict in role expectations, the school may attempt to provide appropriate outlets so that neither school nor family is affected adversely and the goals for each are served. Another example of the same principle would exist in a school where the student role is expected by the school and depreciated by the peer group. Volunteering information to teachers would be viewed as a kind of "rate-busting," putting a serious student in a similar role conflict to that experienced by Max. If communication and sharing of knowledge between teacher and students is deemed desirable by the teacher, then the technique of asking for volunteers increases the possibility of role conflict. Alternative techniques such as ordering response groups or mere requests for information should be considered. Recognizing the expectations of the student group is an important step toward reducing the possibility of role conflict. If the student group desires tension-reducing moments such as those provided by Max, there might be a way to organize the informal character of the group so that this occurs appropriately.

Expectations for behavior are class-linked. That is, the likelihood of perceived role conflict between home, school, and peer group is partly a function of the family's position in the social order. Many students, those who are grossly referred to as middle class, come from homes where the expectations for the child's behavior are congruent with the expectations of the school and where agemates are seldom in conflict with their parents. This pattern, of course, varies considerably when the student reaches late adolescence and beyond. Behavior that is viewed by the school as deviant may not be seen as deviant by the family or agemates of the student when he reaches that age. Therefore, cues for remedial action may partly lie in the definition of the behavioral act as being congruent or incongruent with the values of family and agemates.

We have employed the notion of social class in both the psychological and sociological interpretation of Max's problem. The important distinction is in the consequences of class position. The meaning of class to the psychological mode of interpreting behavior lies in the psychodynamics of family interaction. If students in middle class homes see their relationship with parents as performing for love and acceptance, and failure means the potential removal of affection, a neurotic intrapersonal dynamic has been set in motion. If, on the other hand, social class is linked to values and attitudes regarding the means for achieving cultural goals rather than to the issue of mental health versus neurosis, we center our attention on modes of social adaptation, deviance versus conformity.

## Case 7: The Case of John

John is a sixteen-year-old high school boy from an upper middle class family. He is an honor student despite a measured IQ of 94, and is a favorite of most of his teachers. One day he is apprehended in a back alley by the police and sent to juvenile court as a "peeping Tom." When he returns to school, he begins to withdraw from participation in class discussions and spends much more time alone than before. He comes to the counselor saying that he feels he needs to speak with somebody. He believes that everybody is now looking at him and talking about him behind his back. He thinks he might stop coming to school.

### PSYCHOLOGICAL INTERPRETATION

John has, for a long time, sublimated his basic sex drives by an overdedication to his studies. The expectations of middle class parents regarding both sex and study have reinforced the anxiety about the former and compensation about the latter. His subsequent withdrawal may be explained by guilt, and his paranoid symptoms are a function of the guilt projected outward. John is an "overachiever." This produces excessive strain. Having been apprehended by the police and put through a traumatic experience (particularly traumatic for a boy of his background), his subsequent adjustment reflects the earlier strain and trauma. He wants to escape, first through withdrawal, and then by entertaining thoughts of dropping out. He probably wants emotional support and encouragement to refrain from leaving school. He probably also perceives his teachers as withdrawing the affection that he experienced prior to his trauma.

Remedial activity would involve the reduction of tension and anxiety through discussions with the counselor in which he would be allowed to externalize all his fears and concerns. Teachers and others should be asked to give signs that he is still basically accepted. Consideration should be given to activities that would return him to the mainstream of student life. In order to decrease the feelings of guilt expressed in paranoid symptoms and withdrawal, the actual "deviant" act should be explored. He should be given some perspective about the knowledge and reaction of others through the basic acceptance (although not approval) of the counselor. Some consideration should be given to his interaction with his parents. Middle class notions about achievement and the "vulgarity" of sex in general are probably tied to his family environment. To the extent that John perceives the judgment of his parents carrying over into the evaluation of him in the school, certain propositions regarding his evaluation as a student should be communicated.

## SOCIOLOGICAL INTERPRETATION

John has probably not been integrated into a peer group where socialization about sexual activities is adequately accomplished. Having chosen the student role and exaggerated this, as evidenced by his outstanding achievement, John may have found little time for playing a significant role in the peer group. In this way he is encapsulated in the value system of the school and family. This in turn limits his capacity to take a role within the society of peers. Therefore, he cannot define his behavior in terms other than the institutionalized norms of the school and adult subculture, particularly the middle class adult subculture.

A more general cultural explanation would revolve around the way in which the ideals of sex are communicated in American society. John has been raised, probably somewhat in isolation from the reality of actual adult behavior, in a culture where the sex hero is the epitome of virility and potency. This is the John Wayne movie image, the athlete, the masculine idol. He has not learned that sexual interaction can be adequately attained by boys who do not possess the idealized qualities of the culture hero. Therefore, actual boy-girl interaction is a loaded situation for him, fraught with dangers of finding himself wanting. Vicarious experiences are less threatening and are an adaptation to sex that is associated with his class and his role within the school and family. Simply because of greater exposure to sexual interaction, this behavior would be less likely to occur with lower class males and those who are integrated into a significant peer reference group.

John could be encouraged to decrease his emphasis on his studies by a representative of the school. This would help to demonstrate that institutional expectations are not always intended unidimensionally. At the same time, some effort could be made to integrate John into the informal system of the school, the society of peers. The reality of interpersonal interaction would soon communicate to John that his "deviant" act is not so evil as he thinks, that others not only judge his behavior but also can understand the circumstances. Many deviant activities, at any rate those that will be considered deviant by John, are normal inclinations in adolescent males. The importance of the peer group as an agency of socialization should be recognized as paramount in the consideration of remedial or integrative action on the part of the counselor.

### Case 11: The Case of Michael

Michael, a B student in his junior year at a large university, is a joiner. In his two-and-one-half years at college, he has joined a dozen organizations ranging in nature from political to social to professional. Yet he never remains a member of any of these organizations for more than a month. He always renounces the organization and its purposes and agitatedly leaves the meeting, never to return. Michael is majoring in English, working toward a credential in secondary education. In the middle of one of his education classes, he stood up and said that he disagreed with everything the instructor was saying, that he couldn't take it anymore, and left the classroom. He came to the counseling center to inquire about another way of getting certification, but in the first discussion the other matters came out.

## PSYCHOLOGICAL INTERPRETATION

This pattern of Michael's reflects a sense of insecurity that is projected outward. Personal feelings of inferiority may be kept from being revealed to oneself or others if one questions the organization and its legitimacy rather than one's personal motives. If one does not stay in one place for very long, this kind of discovery may be avoided. This pattern further reflects a deep-seated frustration in Michael, the kind of feeling usually accompanied by aggression. Striking out against all organizations and affiliations would seem to reveal this. Such seemingly inappropriate and constant aggression would appear to signal a reaction-formation defense against the anxieties associated with self-contempt. Michael's basic anger, which is projected outward, is probably based on his relationship with his family. Guilt associated with anger toward persons on whom one is so totally dependent in the early years usually evolves into anger toward oneself. This in turn becomes directed inward, leading to depression, or outward, leading toward inappropriate aggression. The latter could apply to Michael.

Michael essentially needs to understand more about himself, his basic attitudes, proclivities, and educational and occupational interests. He should be persuaded to take a battery of ability, personality, and interest tests and then to explore the results in some detail with the counselor. He needs to see that his hostility is inappropriate and misplaced, and he should evaluate the basis of these feelings.

## SOCIOLOGICAL INTERPRETATION

Campus organizations are highly fluid and temporary. Members come and go. Michael is seeking an identification with a cohesive group and is concerned with a social identification in terms of some ideology that he is formulating. His aggression may be interpreted as social rebellion, linked to a set of values that are not being met within those organizations he chose for focusing his ideologies. His unwillingness to be associated with the education class is probably a variation on the same theme. It may be that he differentiates his formal associations and occupationally oriented classes in terms of either a social or an intellectual status.

Michael needs to explore his ideas and his occupational orientation in terms of those beliefs that motivate him. He should be given material about the activities and requirements of organizations that serve some special need such as VISTA or the Peace Corps. Michael's living situation should be evaluated in terms of ways of establishing a compatible reference group with whom he might associate on a more intensified and meaningful basis. It is also possible that since certain persons are excluded from leadership roles within campus organizations, Michael falls in this category. His behavior would be consistent with this possibility.

## Competing Approaches

The principal assumption of the research was that any act of deviancy on the part of a student contained two elements: the state of the personality at the time of the behavior and the social context within which the act was committed. Both have meaning for remedial action. These analyses of three cases expose the alternative meanings attached to the diagnosis of the source of the problem.

Let us suppose that we have a case of active aggression. A student hits other students, curses his teacher, destroys school property. For many children, this is not an abnormal way of acting out moments of frustration. Violence, in many segments of our social structure, is not an unfamiliar phenomenon. For many other children, however, shielded from all activities associated with the expression of strong emotion, violence is frightening and a highly abnormal way of dealing with frustration. The exhibition of aggression, then, may reveal something about the adaptive modes of different kinds of students, according not only to their personalities but also to the kinds of family and neighborhood experiences that have conditioned them to behave in typical ways (typical for their class, race, nationality). Furthermore, they do not view these typical ways as inappropriate.

Case 1 presented a fatherless boy, living with four females, going to school among working and lower class children, experiencing constant fighting, and frequently absenting himself from school. His principal educational activity was one of befriending the teacher, volunteering for jobs to help the teacher, and pushing himself forward as a willing and interested student. When asked what she felt was the most significant fact in this description, one counselor from an upper middle class school said that it was his living situation, the lack of a male in the home. When asked how this would explain his behavior, she answered that she thought his behavior in class was more like the kind of behavior she would expect of girls at that age. A male counselor in a predominantly Negro school felt that the most significant fact was the kind of school he attended. He said, "That boy has got to learn that making up to the teacher doesn't go over in that kind of school."

Sexual identity or inadequate socialization, need for affection or peer-group integration? The dimensions are clear, but the selection of one set of conceptual cues as the basis for remedial work often means that a second set is ignored. Sociologists are not typically committed to the idea that their interpretations should provide the only basis for social or individual action. One role of sociological inquiry, however, is to expose patterns of occupational activity. The basis for socialization to the selection of certain cues for group behavior is of interest and may reveal patterns that explain the basis for structural elements within institutions. This kind of analysis helps to explain the organization of counseling functions as they are translated into specific interaction goals and activities. The following sections discuss competing concepts rather than cases, although specific behavioral representations of conflict may easily be constructed to help the reader order his consideration of the dynamics of several kinds of conflict.

## FRUSTRATION-AGGRESSION VS. STATUS

Frustration-aggression is a notion popularized by Freud that holds that aggressive behavior should be evaluated in terms of frustrations within the personality. Destruction of school property is a behavioral act. Its meaning is dependent upon the proposition or theory that guides our interpretation. If we should subscribe to the frustration-aggression hypothesis, we must treat the destruction of property as the aggressive act and seek for the source of frustration that must have preceded it. Where we look for the source of this particular behavior is inextricably tied to our beliefs, a set of theories or ideas that we are persuaded are reliable.

Status refers to a stratified position within a group. Suppose, then, that we are tied to a conception of social behavior that sees all deviant or innovative acts as embodied in a struggle for status within the larger or smaller society. Our logical question then becomes, in what sense has the destructive act enhanced the status of the student? We recognize that many subcultures hold a set of norms not congruent with those of the major institutions. Within this subculture, the destructive act is evaluated differently than within the school itself. It may confer status upon the perpetrator. This is not unlike the case of Max, the class clown. His disruption of classroom activities was quite conceivably motivated by his desire for some kind of status within the group, not necessarily a function of hitting out against a system that was frustrating to him.

## DEFENSE MECHANISMS VS. DIFFERENTIAL SOCIALIZATION

Defense mechanisms, a set of ideas contributed by Sigmund and Anna Freud, implies that the ego utilizes certain unconscious techniques to reduce anxiety. Some of these techniques are repression, regression, and reaction formation. Constant temper tantrums thrown by a junior high student are the kind of behavior that challenges alternative explanations of the sort suggested in this section. Those who are cued to look for defense mechanisms in disruptive behavior would immediately focus upon an act of regression. The child is regressing to a pattern of behavior that was appropriate at an earlier stage in his psychosexual development. For this to occur, the situation must have been fraught with anxiety for the student because defense mechanisms emerge only when anxiety is present. Differential socialization refers to a condition wherein members of a group hold different expectations about their own behavior and the behavior of others. The degree of conflict produced by different sets of expectations varies according to the degree of commitment the two groups, or institutions, have to the core values of the Protestant Ethic.

As has been suggested earlier, externalized emotion as a way of dealing with frustration is differentially acceptable to different socio-economic, ethnic, and racial subgroups. The fact that more members of the lower class have police records than members of other classes is not only a function of greater need and lesser influence but is also attributable to weaker controls over feelings as well as different social modes of expression of feelings. Greater or lesser control is a function of socialization and is differently managed by the various groups.

Withdrawal is another defense mechanism; students who experience anxiety in dealing with a school classroom may reduce this anxiety by psychologically taking themselves out of the race. At the same time, we have accumulated considerable anthropological evidence that argues that certain ethnic groups are not competitive.[4] These alternative conceptions of a given behavior such as nonparticipation in group activities will influence the approach to remedial action. The American school is a competitive institution and those who are defined as successful are usually those who have been best socialized to compete for the rewards of the system. If we could detach ourselves from our cultural encapsulation, we might contend that it is the successful competitor who is most likely to require guidance, as he is the least likely to know himself. If there are such things as basic personality traits, the high achiever-high competitor is probably the one who has submerged these in the process of acquiring all the skills and attitudes for academic success.

---

4. It has been reported that this was the case among the Zuni by Ruth Benedict in *Patterns of Culture,* Houghton Mifflin Company, Boston, 1934.

## ADJUSTMENT VS. ADAPTATION

Adjustment is a concept used to indicate a process of bringing the personality into a congruent order with the life space, the specific environment impinging upon the self. Problems viewed clinically as adjustment problems are those in which the personality is seen as inadequately organized to cope with internalized demands upon the self. Adaptation, on the other hand, focuses upon the role rather than the personality. Adaptation problems are viewed as those in which some role conflict is present. The person is conceived as occupying one or more roles in one or more institutions. Conflict occurs when the expectations for the roles are incompatible.

Most of the problems of adjustment are seen as variations on one of several conceptual themes introduced by Sigmund Freud. One theme is associated with his conception of the organization of the personality. The notion of neurotic anxiety is perceived as a condition in which the person develops fears about basic instincts being out of control, causing him to commit some act he knows he should avoid. The fear is linked to his conception of the consequences of instinctual gratification. Neurotic anxiety emerges from conscience, a struggle between the uncontrolable segments of personality housed in the id and the socially instilled controls, the super-ego. This has considerable basis in reality to the child because the adult world does impress upon him the dangers of impulsive behavior and punishes him when he violates their constraints.

A second Freudian theme centers on the idea of stages of psycho-sexual development in which the natural process of growth is associated with a conception of emotional maturity. This has been significantly updated by Erikson[5] who sees emotional growth occurring beyond the fifth year, which was considered by Freud to represent a cut-off point beyond which all growth was a variation of the themes experienced earlier.

The accumulation of impulses associated with successful passage (this is indicated by the ego successfully displacing and sublimating

---

5. Erik Erikson, *Childhood and Society,* W. W. Norton & Company, Inc., New York, 1950.

the impulses of the pregenital stages) and their consequent organization into acceptable personality traits reveals the mature person. Conflict emerges in the personality when the pregenital impulses are not successfully displaced and sublimated.[6]

Problems of adjustment, utilizing this reference, are problems of personality defect, in which certain control mechanisms (the ego and super-ego) have not functioned adequately, leaving certain stages unsatisfactorily resolved. The unsuccessful resolution of the oedipal complex, for example, could evolve into a host of deviant behaviors associated with parental surrogates, particularly teachers.

Problems associated with adaptation will be discussed in relation to two themes that will be considered as representative of the sociological perspective. The ideas contributed by Freud in the discussion of adjustment were examples intended to help distinguish one kind of thinking from another. The ideas that follow are intended to provide a contrast necessary for understanding the potential contributions of separate disciplines to the evaluation of student problems.

The first idea involves the notion of role conflict. Sociologists and social psychologists have been pursuing research in this area for some time. Research findings are not relevant here, as we are only concerned with exposing conceptual frameworks for understanding competing approaches to the same behavioral phenomenon. Four categories of conflict have been advanced by way of ordering our thinking about role conflict. These distinctions are utilized again in Chapter 6.

Intersender role conflict involves a situation in which more than one member of the same institution is communicating an expectation to a person and these expectations are incompatible. An example from family life would be when the father expects his son to be an athlete and the mother wants him to be a musician.

Intrasender conflict occurs when the same person holds incompatible expectations for the behavior of another. An example of this in the school would be when the teacher communicates an expectation for students to explore themes in terms of their own innovation but

---

6. For a general survey of concepts introduced here, see Hall and Lindzey, *Theories of Personality,* John Wiley & Sons, Inc., New York, 1957, pp. 29–72.

grades on memorization. Many college students will recall instances of this bothersome dilemma.

Inter-role conflict, the most commonly explored of the four, refers to a situation in which a person receives incompatible cues for behavior from two or more institutions of which he is a member. A frequently discussed example of this is the conflict a student feels when caught between the desires of his peer reference group and the expectations of the school.

Self-role conflict refers to a circumstance in which institutional expectations for role performance are in conflict with the person's own identification of how the role should be enacted. Teachers, trained and socialized to operate in terms of student needs and differences, are often confronted with a school that expects highly routinized and ritualistic behavior.

Adaptation to the school is conceived, then, as a process of picking up expectations and weighing these against others. When the expectations of all groups and persons are congruent and compatible, conflict does not appear. Problems of adaptation in school are circumstances in which incompatible expectations appear. The resolution of this conflict may often occur in such a way that no matter which expectation is held to be paramount, the child is the loser.

The second perspective involves the notion of typical social modes. It grows out of the idea that persons in different relations to the goals and rewards of the social system establish patterned ways of relating to the important institutions of that system. The model is one provided by Robert Merton.[7] Utilizing the dimensions of cultural goals and institutional means, he represents the society as being differentiated in terms of choices of one of five possible adaptive modes (see Table II).

Merton argues that within every social system there are certain goals that the members have been influenced to esteem. In American society the goals are primarily economic. This does not mean that every member of the society needs to revere financial success. It only

---

7. Robert K. Merton, *Social Theory and Social Structure,* The Free Press, New York, 1956.

## Table II—Modes of Adaptation

| Mode | Cultural Goals | Institutionalized Means |
|------|:--------------:|:-----------------------:|
| Conformist | + | + |
| Innovator | + | — |
| Ritualist | — | + |
| Retreatist | — | — |
| Rebel | ∓ | ∓ |

means that the culture may be generally characterized as placing an emphasis on economic rewards. He says further that every society designates appropriate ways to attain these goals. In our society, one is expected to work for economic rewards and usually to work hard. The cultural hero is the man who has raised himself from the slums through hard work and ingenuity.

According to Merton's scheme, the act of being a conformist involves acceptance of both the mainstream goals and the acceptable means for attainment. The innovator mode accepts the value of the goals but rejects the established means. The ritualist mode rejects the goals as being either troublesome or unworthy but does not simultaneously reject the means as an acceptable social mode. The retreatist mode rejects both the goals and the means, and the rebel mode, while rejecting both, conceives an alternative set of goals and means.

Conformity, as an adaptive mode, represents the norm. Most students are conformists and as such experience little adaptive conflict. All other modes produce strain and in many ways are antithetical to guidance goals.

Problems of adaptation for the innovator mode involve a reliance upon illegitimate means for the attainment of culturally approved ends. Analysis of the problem itself within this framework would involve speculation upon the basis for rejecting traditional means. Either the innovator does not have access to the legitimate means or he is convinced that those like him who accept the institutionalized means will not attain their goals. Members of minority groups frequently described as disadvantaged are cognizant of social realities in the form of barriers to mobility, even if the larger society can demonstrate that there are exceptions.

The ritualist is the person who does not try very hard because he does not expect to be mobile with respect to status-linked goals. At the same time, he has been socialized to avoid conflict by not violating expectations for normative behavior. The good boy–bad student may frequently be an instance of this dynamic. "Don't rock the boat but don't try very hard because you'll either get knocked down or fail," may be a representative slogan for these persons. Guidance personnel, at least theoretically, will be as concerned about this adaptive mode as they are about the innovator. Many of these persons do not come to the attention of the counselor because many teachers are only concerned about those who are "troublesome."

The retreatist, represented in society by the hobo or hermit, an uncommon type in contemporary society, may be a more common type in the school. This is the student who is simply waiting to be a dropout. He places no faith in either the school's goals or the routine means. In this sense, being a dropout is not synonymous with being a failure, for in the dropout's terms, you cannot fail in a game in which you were not participating.

The rebel represents a type that may pose the greatest challenge to the intellectual mechanisms of education. Having lost all faith in the system and its goals, the rebel wants no part of them. But he aligns himself with others to establish for himself a new system with different goals and means. A student movement, having its roots in sociopolitical ideologies such as attitudes toward American war commitments, abortion, the illegal status of certain drugs, capital punishment, civil rights, and a host of other issues, may be more than a minor disruption in the society's ordered purposes and activities. Clinical work with those who fall into this adaptive mode could go far astray should it concentrate exclusively upon personality dynamics and ignore the attraction of ideas. More will be said on this point in the next section.


## REBELLION VS. RELIGION

Although a consideration of this topic is somewhat associated with the conception of the rebel as an adaptive mode, a separate section is dedicated to its discussion because it is more than an example. Rebelliousness in a social adaptation that is useful as a conceptualization for ordering our understanding of disruptive behavior. Used in this way, the idea is appropriate to the discussion of adjustment vs. adaptation. This section, however, looks at the substantive characteristics of contemporary student rebellion. The title for this section was taken from an expression employed by Timothy Leary in many of his speeches and writings.[8] Dr. Leary, a former Harvard psychologist and current proponent of the drug LSD, has used this expression to distinguish his psychedelic society from those political activists who stand in open conflict with the current strains in American political life. He also contends that his values and activities are not to be seen as born out of a desire to attack the major institutions but as a desire to be apart from them; the new values and activities, he further claims, have their own intrinsic legitimacy.

More than ever before, American high school and college students are forming a subculture of dissent. Viewed from the traditional perspective of rebellious students who come into open conflict with their institutions, these students are conceived as passing through a psychological stage typical of persons their age. This stage is one of resistance to normal social controls and rebelliousness born of a need for independence from traditional loyalties, family, church, and school. Historically, the pattern sees these young people kicking up their heels, throwing a few punches, relishing their fought-for individuality for a short time, and then returning to the fold. Defiance of authority frequently becomes a problem for the schools, particularly when large groups of students band together to protest what they feel to be inappropriate impingements on their rights to dress as they like, grow long hair or beards, and associate with whatever groups they choose.

The question is raised here as to whether or not we may continue to apply the same interpretations as in the past. If we take the position that those who defy institutional regulations or expectations are acting in terms of a singular need for engaging the establishment in a fight for independence, then we do not focus upon the issues of dis-

---

8. Timothy Leary, "Changes," *The City of San Francisco Oracle,* Vol. 1, No. 7.

sent. We do not assume that the issues themselves are what cohere the group and motivate the deviant activities. Rather, we focus upon the psychological dynamic as a struggle for independence from authority constraints. The form becomes irrelevant and is viewed as being only a matter of choosing whatever issues happen to be available at a given historical moment.

The validity of this interpretation might be empirically established through the accumulation of data relating the involved issues to conditions within the family. Does the child see himself as being in essential conflict with his parents? After all, if one does not take a position opposed to the values of one's parents, the credibility of the psychological argument diminishes. A second approach would be to seek for dimensions of conflict with other adult figures, particularly those in the school, in areas other than those reflected by the issues. A psychological conception of rebellion is one that assumes the ability to observe dynamics of personality conflict on grounds other than sociopolitical.

A sociological perspective would assume that the basic motivation of the group, the dynamic that coheres the members, is the ideology[9] itself. This implies a set of beliefs that are intrinsically meaningful to persons and not simply a set of antagonisms to the major institutions. A peace movement or a civil rights movement is not seen, then, as a reaction to a society's belief in war or segregation, although this might be the focus of the conflict. This interpretation, for example, would not view taking marijuana or LSD as an activity stimulated by the fact that these drugs are outlawed, whereas the more traditional evaluation of rebellion would. Rebellion, then, as Dr. Leary would argue, is an incorrect designation for the particular phenomena at issue. Religion, on the other hand, broadly conceived as a set of physical and metaphysical beliefs, accompanied by rituals that reaffirm the solidarity of the group, appears to be a more correct representation. Long hair, dress, marches, rallies, be-ins, certain kinds of

---

9. *Ideology* has two senses, as a set of beliefs and set of social rationalizations of position. The former meaning is intended.

music, all these constitute, in this sense, not acts of rebellion but ritualistic paraphernalia that establish the identity of the membership. We would not think of arguing that Mennonite beards or the white sheets of the Ku Klux Klan are in themselves symbols of rebellion. They are, rather, symbolic extensions of a set of beliefs that the members of a social group hold in common.

Religion would probably not be the term the sociologist would care to apply to contemporary student dissenters to represent the mechanism by which their behavior is motivated. Ideology, however, could emerge as a representative designation. The choice for educators, particularly counselors who are engaged in confronting students in conflict with the expectations of the school, is between unresolved dependency needs and ideas. If, in the struggle for independence, persons need to depend upon others for support, then membership in groups is explained by this need. The issues are secondary. If participation is based, rather, upon a commitment to some idea or set of ideas, then participation in protest groups cannot be summarily dismissed as a child's need for belonging or, to employ a more sophisticated concept, the need for affiliation.

## THE ADOLESCENT — PSYCHOSEXUAL VS. CULTURAL DISRUPTION

To Erik Erikson[10] and a host of others who subscribe to his conception of the adolescent, this problem is one of identity.

With the establishment of a good relationship to the world of skills and tools, and with the advent of sexual maturity, childhood proper comes to an end. Youth begins. But in puberty and adolescence all samenesses and continuities relied upon earlier are questioned again, because of a rapidity of body growth which equals that of early childhood and because of the entirely new addition of physical genital maturity. The growing and developing youths, faced with this physiological revolution within them, are now primarily concerned with what they appear to be in the eyes of others as compared with what they feel they are. . . . In their search for

---

10. Erik Erikson, *op. cit.,* pp. 227–228.

a new sense of continuity and sameness, adolescents have to refight many of the battles of earlier years, even though to do so they must artificially appoint perfectly well meaning people to play the role of enemies; and they are ever ready to install lasting idols and ideals as guardians of a final identity; here puberty rites "confirm" the inner design for life.

To Erikson, the opposite of identity is role diffusion, a situation in which young persons are unable to fit external circumstances and roles to the internal order of the personality. Deviant behavior is often perceived as the end product of a history of doubt as to one's psychosexual identity. To avoid the disruptive effects of not having achieved a satisfactory sense of identity, adolescents overidentify with the heroes of cliques and crowds. At the same time, according to Erikson, "adolescent love is an attempt to arrive at a definition of one's identity by projecting one's diffused ego images on one another and by seeing them thus reflected and gradually clarified."

This line of thinking focuses upon the individual, his need to identify, his history of sex-role identification, the stage of genital physiological change, and the way in which this inner state seeks release in special forms of social participation. The disrupted adolescent is a person who either does not know himself well enough to relate to society in ways consistent with his inclinations or cannot find those roles suitable to inclinations which he does recognize. The functional problem for the counselor becomes one of exploring the personality in relation to available roles within the relevant society. This approach is neither inconsistent with nor contradicting of the sociocultural approach that will be discussed later. It is only that the base from which analysis and ameliorative action begin is a different unit. Erikson does not ignore the dynamics of culture; it is just that he sees the organization of culture as the structure within which universal mechanisms within the personality must cope, defining the form of adaptation. The sociocultural view begins with the organization of society, focusing upon the mechanisms of stability and change, and explains individual adaptations in terms of the characteristics of the society, ignoring the special properties of individuals that may explain variations in adaptation. Variations such as deviance and conformity are explained in terms of differential relationships of persons to the society or the culture.

The discussion that follows at some length is intended to provide the basis for exemplifying the preventive role of the counselor. In the early part of the chapter we viewed the sociological approach as one that is necessary for conceiving some segments of the counselor's role as social reconstruction. The key to this reconstruction may be found in the following view of the dilemma of the contemporary American adolescent.

We may begin with a series of excerpts from Margaret Mead's *Coming of Age in Samoa*.[11]

The Samoan background which makes growing up so easy, so simple a matter, is the general casualness of the whole society. For Samoa is a place where nobody plays for very high stakes, no one pays very high prices, no one suffers for his convictions or fights to the death for special ends. . . . No one is hurried along in life or punished harshly for slowness of development.

Our children grow up to find a world of choices dazzling their unaccustomed eyes. . . . This is an unthinkable situation in primitive society not exposed to foreign influence.

Our young people are faced by a series of different groups which believe different things and advocate different practices, and to each of which some trusted friend or relative may belong. . . . And not only are our developing children faced by a series of groups advocating standards, but a more perplexing problem presents itself to them. Because our civilization is woven of so many diverse strands, the ideas which any one group accepts will be found to contain many contradictions. If she (the thoughtful girl) has philosophically accepted the fact that there are several standards among which she must choose, she may still preserve a childlike faith in the coherence of her chosen philosophy. Beyond the immediate choice which was so puzzling and hard to make, which perhaps involved her hurting her parents or alienating her friends, she expects peace. But she has not reckoned with the fact that each of the

---

11. Margaret Mead, *Coming of Age in Samoa*. Reprinted by permission of William Morrow and Co., Inc. Copyright © 1928, 1961 by Margaret Mead. Pp. 198–211.

philosophies with which she is confronted is itself but the half ripened fruit of compromise.

So for the explanation of the lack of poignancy in the choices of growing girls in Samoa, we must look to the temperament of the Samoan civilization, which discounts strong feelings. But for the explanation for the lack of conflict we must look principally to the difference between a simple homogeneous primitive civilization, a civilization which changes so slowly it appears static, and a motley diverse, heterogeneous modern civilization.

Samoa's lack of difficult situations, of conflicting choice, of situations in which fear or pain or anxiety are sharpened to a knife edge will probably account for a large part of the absence of psychological maladjustment.

Nevertheless, it is possible that there are factors in the early environment of the Samoan child which are particularly favorable to the establishment of nervous stability. . . . It is conceivable that the Samoan child is not only handled more gently by its culture but that it is also better equipped for those difficulties which it does meet.

This last statement is one of the more crucial points of Dr. Mead's argument. The integration of Samoan children is continuous in the sense of exposing children to those experiences that they will be called upon to participate in as adults. They become familiar with sex, birth, death, and work roles on a continuous basis. There is not a long period of being a child and then an abrupt expectation to behave as an adult.

In contrast to a kind of linear development observed in most primitive societies, a highly industrial society presents a gap for transition between childhood and adulthood that is permitted to go unbridged except for the random attempts of the adolescent himself to find a reasonable way of crossing over.

The difference between this approach and the psychosexual approach discussed earlier is a matter of which variable is held constant and which is left free to vary. In the first case, the society is the constant and the individual varies his adaptation. Operationally, the counseling process will be quite different, depending on the choice of interpretive assumptions. Let us conceive, in some detail, the preventive role of the counselor dealing with adolescent problems. To begin with, this counselor has chosen the sociocultural approach as the source of his speculations about ameliorative action. He assumes that problems of the adolescent are deeply imbedded in the kind of culture that surrounds him. He sees this culture as highly differentiated, formal, restrictive, and sophisticated to the point where basic feelings and experiences are shaped by bureaucratic life. Since bureaucratic life contains all the explicit and implicit roles for interaction, basic feelings and needs become institutionally locked into organizational routines. This is true in the life of the adolescent as well as the adult.

The counselor will then also take note of the fact that there is a disjuncture in the social growth process. This occurs at a time when the person is leaving childhood and is looking toward a future as an adult. If there has been little preparation on a fundamental level for finding a berth in the occupational structure, there is bound to be a good deal of anxiety accompanying an adolescent's projection into the future. This is very spuriously resolved in our culture by linking these persons to the goals of institutions, particularly in the school. That is, the child's growth process is projected and conceived almost exclusively in economic terms.

The counselor will also consider the attributes and experiences of nonindustrial peoples in order to see if any adaptation may be made in an industrial culture. He will think about those encounters that are universal, such as birth, death, and physiological functions (particularly sex), and about the adoption of responsibility in areas other than those prescribed by bureaucratic roles. He will then ask himself what experiences the school can provide that will help young people look toward the future without the kind of anxiety that leads to personal disorganization at the stage of adolescence. We may not be able to reduce the amount of ambiguity surrounding the projection of adolescents into the future, but we may be able to provide certain experiences that will increase tolerance for ambiguity. The same would hold for frustration, misfortune, or independence. Many adolescents perceive that the only way to establish a condition of independence is by running away from the constraints. Are there some experiences we can provide in this area that would lead adolescents to recognize that independence may be achieved without escaping? David Riesman[12] talks in some detail about the autonomous personality, a condition of reliance and integration with other members of the society but with the implicit reservation that the person is free to abstain from participation in activities that are in conflict with his ideologies.

Certain kinds of experiences could be offered in schools as a kind of preventative guidance activity that would approximate the conditions necessary for developing independent and autonomous qualities. The two major conditions for making these activities honestly meaningful are choice and the guarantee that, within reasonable limits, one's independent choices may be effected. Consider an activity that is a genuine example of participatory democracy, such as student government. For most students, the insignificance of their experiences with this activity in the past as developing in them a sense of autonomy and independence is a function of the limitations of choice and thereby of the possibility to effect changes. The struggle for independence symbolized by the Free Speech Movement is a protest by students against the myth of participation and contribution. These Berkeley students were rebelling against the fact that they had little control over structures that directly affected them. Perhaps these students were not ready to assume independence, having gained so little experience with it in their earlier education, but the kind of experience that they were struggling to attain would be an example of the kind of activity that could help students bridge the gap between childhood and adulthood.

The counselor will realize that in order to play an active role in establishing patterns and activities to prevent the disorganizing effects of passing through adolescence, certain traditional assumptions will have to be violated. The division of institutional labor has provided

---

12. David Riesman, *The Lonely Crowd,* Yale University Press, New Haven, Conn., 1950.

administrators of the school with a rationalization for their unwillingness to participate in controversial activities such as a sex-education
program. That certain functions are the responsibility of the family is
a cliché that supports an unfortunate contradiction. Schools have already assumed certain responsibilities in the area of socialization and
life preparation. It becomes self-defeating to adopt a functional responsibility and then cut yourself off from access to the mechanisms
that achieve it. Some redefinitions of institutional prerequisites must be
a first step. But, granting the possibility of manipulating the environment, what specific activities would aid the bridge-building process?

We have already mentioned a realistic sex-education program. The
development of an individual identity separate from dependency on
others would be necessary to avoid symbolic rebellion. This would
increase tolerance to misfortune, which has its greatest impact on those
who are highly dependent on what they lose, and provide directions
for assuming responsibilities that are congruent with personality traits.
Specific activities such as unstructured freedom hours, work or living
experiences in unfamiliar situations, a social-studies sequence that
treats moral relativism honestly in the evaluation of other cultures instead of focusing exclusively on different family or economic patterns
—these are some possibilities.

Responsibilities in the school are only allocated as part of the
ongoing institutional process. Students are given responsibilities but
are also given the expectations of the institution as a guideline to their
behavior. The counselor would need to conceive of other dimensions
of assuming responsibility that are tied to the uncertainties and
anxieties associated with this kind of adult behavior. Student-council
members may learn something about the process of decision making,
and the class secretary may experience a feeling of ego gratification
or status, but few student roles that assign responsibility are realistically linked to the kinds of life experiences the students are bound
to encounter. Responsibility to a mate, to children, to oneself, and to
others through fulfillment of the self is a conception of this problem
that is seldom deemed appropriate for educational programs. The
school's responsibility is considered dispatched when students are put

on the "right" track to occupational fulfillment, a narrow view of the challenge to institutional resources at best.

The counselor has many choices, most of which are fraught with the difficulty of changing institutional patterns and values, but if he is to play a preventive role in line with a conception of culture as the determinant of adolescent disjuncture, the disruption of these patterns and values is necessary.

## CONCLUSION

The individual and the society are two distinctly different units of cognitive analysis. If we change individuals, we may change the society; if we change the society, we will most assuredly change individuals. The task of education, conceived as a guidance education, is to consider the kind of activities that may best accomplish its goals. These activities may reflect an ad hoc remedial emphasis based upon an institutional drive to maintain conformity or stability, or they may reflect a reconstruction attitude intended to produce a stronger, more self-directed populace. The dynamics of change lie both within the individual and within the society. We may go either way in organizing our remedial functions. Students in conflict are not particularly concerned about the conceptual basis of our strategies, but professional counselors are. If we expand the cognitive material upon which counselors are trained to include the analysis of student problems from a social or cultural framework, we will have taken a step toward increasing the basis of professional organization and identity for school counselors. To say with Shakespeare, "The fault, Dear Brutus, is not in the stars,/But in ourselves, that we are underlings," is but a half truth. Some cultures evolve a generation of underlings, others a generation of masters. Our task is to conceive of a society that provides an atmosphere conducive of producing a generation that is master of its environment. To do this requires an evaluation of the environment that needs to be mastered. This environment, despite the regulative behavior of our major institutions, must be more than a linear ascent from childhood to economic and bureaucratic roles.

## APPENDIX TO CHAPTER 2: CASE FRAGMENTS

1. Edward, a fifth-grade student in a lower socioeconomic community, spends a lot of time visiting with the teacher. He constantly raises his hand to volunteer for jobs for the teacher and always wants to answer questions. The other boys in the class are very aggressive toward him; often he finds himself in fights which he neither wins nor cares to participate in. Edward lives with his mother, grandmother, and two older sisters; his father died when he was 2. Edward's absentee record is high.

2. Marcia, a third-grade girl, was sent to the principal because she struck two of her classmates on the school grounds during recess. This was the fourth time she had hit a student. In the classroom, she is very quiet and obedient. She is in the lowest reading group, and when it's her turn to read, she tells the teacher that she doesn't feel like reading. Marcia's father is a lawyer; her mother is a PTA officer. Marcia's older brother, now in junior high, was a model student.

3. Max is the class clown. He's in the sixth grade in an upper middle class elementary school. Several times Max has been sent to the principal for disrupting the class. His teacher told his parents that Max would be doing better in school if he didn't make a joke of everything. Max has never excelled in any field of subject matter. He received only C's and D's in Physical Education but has never been in danger of failing any subject.

4a. Calvin is a fourth-grade boy in a middle class elementary school. His family, however, is on relief. They live in a housing development. Calvin receives free lunch passes from the PTA fund set up for such cases. Although smaller than most of his classmates, Calvin constantly picks fights. He talks back to his teacher occasionally and has been sent to the principal several times for using curse words in class. Calvin's grades are very low. His papers, always handed in late, are marked down for being messy.

4b. Carlos is a twelve-year-old boy in the sixth grade. His parents are both Mexican-Americans who have been in the United States for three years. Carlos is one of the two Mexican-American boys in the class. His teachers have all written the same comment on his cumulative record: He will not work or cooperate with the teacher or classmates unless he is governed by a strong hand. In free play and expressive activities, he always runs around creating clamor and chaos.

5. Michael, a seventeen-year-old high school student, stays after class almost every day to talk to one of his female teachers. Sometimes he brings them small gifts. He asks them personal questions and, on several occasions has tried to date one of the younger teachers. In his classes he does poorly. He tells his teachers that he considers schoolwork petty and childish; he says he has more adult things on his mind. He is referred to the guidance counselor.

6. Jennie, a fourteen-year-old eighth grader in junior high school, goes to noon dances alone. When boys ask her to dance, she always refuses. In her classes, she always sits next to boys, but when they speak to her, she ignores them. The teacher notices that Jennie spends most of her time in class doodling in her notebook. While discussing her social life, Jennie states that she hates boys. When tests are given in class, Jennie does very badly.

7. John is a sixteen-year-old high school boy from an upper middle class family. He is an honor student, despite a measured IQ of 94, and is a favorite of most of his teachers. One day he is apprehended in a back alley by the police and sent to juvenile court as a "peeping Tom." When he returns to school, he begins to withdraw from participation in class discussions, and spends much more time alone than before. He comes to the counselor saying that he feels he needs to speak with somebody. He believes everybody is now looking at him and talking about him behind his back. He thinks he might stop coming to school.

8. Joan is a fifteen-year-old junior high school girl whose father is a medical doctor. For two years she has been developing serious stomach aches on the day of any test. The nurse has suggested that she speak with the guidance counselor.

9. Judy, a freshman at a large university, away from home for the first time, has been missing her early morning classes. She tells her dorm-mates that she just can't get up in the morning. She has done poorly on her exams and has told her instructors that she tries to study and understands what she reads, but can't stay awake while she is studying. Judy is told by her dorm counselor that it might be a good idea to speak to someone at the counseling service before she flunks out of school. Judy was an outstanding high school student.

10. Ann, a senior at a small college, is majoring in physics and has an A-minus average for three and one-half years. In the last half of her senior year, she comes to the counseling office and says that she cannot sleep, has become very nervous, is afraid to talk to anyone, afraid to

travel, and even is nervous about attending classes. Ann's father is a very successful engineer, and Ann's two brothers are both engineers. Ann is the only female in her class who is majoring in physics.

11. Michael, a B student in his junior year at a large university, is a joiner. In his two and one-half years at college, he has joined a dozen organizations ranging in nature from political to social to professional. Yet he never remains a member of any of these organizations for more than a month. He always renounces the organization and its purposes and agitatedly leaves the meeting, never to return. Michael is majoring in English, working toward a credential in secondary education. In the middle of one of his education classes, he stood up and said that he disagreed with everything the instructor was saying, that he couldn't take it any more, and left the classroom. He came to the counseling center to inquire about another way of getting certification, but in the first discussion, the other matters came out.

# CHAPTER 3

# THE APPLICATION OF SOCIOLOGICAL ANALYSIS TO EDUCATIONAL GUIDANCE

IN CHAPTER 2 we observed that guidance workers rely upon a good deal of psychological material in formulating initial hunches about the context of student problems. The psychological data that provide the academic referents for pupil personnel workers are not structured in their minds as they were in the texts and lectures of their student days. Nonetheless, considerable exposure to concepts such as personality, learning, developmental tasks, abnormal behavior, motivation, cognition, ego, id, super-ego, self, oedipal complex, regression, defense mechanisms, aggression, and withdrawal have conditioned much of their thinking.

Pupil personnel workers, chiefly school counselors and school psychologists, have had primarily an undergraduate program in either education or psychology. Many have had one or two courses in sociology, but most have been exposed only to limited introductory courses, and, as we have stated previously, very little in the way of graduate study in sociology has been encouraged. Such introductory work ordinarily does little more than expose students to the general categories of working interest to the sociologist. Such simple concepts as norms, roles, values, and groups may have been digested, but employing these concepts in the analysis of collectivities, of interactional frameworks, or of bureaucratic structures is probably beyond the experience or interest of school counselors and psychologists. These people have not been permitted the opportunity to see how sociological analysis and research may be effective procedures for dealing with real problems facing students, teachers, counselors, and administrators.

Sociological analysis has turned a systematic eye upon many issues that constitute logical facets of the counselor's interest. The student, or prospective counselee, is attempting to function in an environment that has been and will continue to be an area for social research. School counselors would not deny that the school is but one environment among many that shape the beliefs, attitudes, and adaptations of students, nor would they argue against the fact that the school itself constitutes a highly complex set of environments. But a counselor's knowledge of the interaction of institutions or of socially defined segments of the institutions is not nearly as important to him as what he considers to be the components of personality or how to change individual behavior. It would appear to be no more or less difficult to change collective behavior, but guidance counselors have not yet institutionalized a role prerequisite that prescribes this function. Yet it is recognized that students in general are constantly maneuvering to survive in a complex climate of forces that are frequently incompatible. These so-called forces may be discovered as clear regularities of unclear expectations. Once the structure of these forces becomes clear, it is then possible to reconstruct the institutional behaviors in such a way as to avoid the disjunctures and conflicts that occur as a result of students' receiving different kinds of socialization.

The substantive contribution of this chapter is to summarize the analytical procedures and the important engagements of sociologists, emphasizing facts and concepts as well as interacting variables that should be taken into account in any comprehensive analysis of student motives and conflicts. These should constitute a logical extension of the working knowledge of the school counselor. The chapter will also suggest the kinds of contributions sociology has made to the applied interests of educational guidance.

## SOCIOLOGICAL ANALYSIS AND
## THE RESEARCH ENTERPRISE

Sociological analysis, which is discussed in the following pages, uses a procedure that is probably unfamiliar to guidance workers who have not studied the techniques of social research. We have used the term *sociological analysis* in the title of the chapter, and we should take time in the beginning to discuss the relationship of analysis, as the term is used here, to the research enterprise. Counseling psychologists should recognize the general procedures that will be discussed. However, by examplifying various techniques with sociological concepts that are to be put to empirical scrutiny, a clearer comprehension and, therefore, a better evaluation of the function of sociological analysis in educational guidance may be achieved.

When we talk about such notions as family size, broken homes, or physical mobility in the section on demographic and ecological factors, we are saying that these factors hold some explanatory potential for the comprehension of certain forms of educational behavior. Our major tools in sociological analysis are such facts as these as well as concepts, with which we will deal briefly. All research proceeds on the basis of observables. Given a fact such as broken homes, it is possible, through observations, to conclude easily which homes are broken and which are intact. Suppose, on the other hand, that we have a hunch that it is not so much the physical brokenness of a home that influences school adaptation for children but a brokenness that is not so easily observed. We are suggesting a condition in which a state of disorganization exists in the home despite the fact that the parents are living together. It is frequently the situations most difficult to observe that may best explain the difficulties students have in school. We know that there are many children from one-parent families who are constantly experiencing difficulty. If sociology had stopped its inquiry into delinquency with the conclusion that there is a strong relationship between slum living and delinquent behavior, the discipline would have achieved no better than a mediocre standstill.

Just as there are good students from single-parent homes, we know that all slum children do not become delinquents. Actually most of them do not. All we may really say is that proportionally more delinquents come from slum areas than from suburban areas.

Anyone who has had a course in introductory statistics realizes that correlation is not causality, although the more relationships we derive, the closer we come to designing a study that will get at the roots of certain phenomena. To do this, we usually have to raise our theories about behavior from the level of observable facts to the level of concepts.

Proceeding with our concern about testing the impact of social rather than physical brokenness of homes upon student behavior, it is clear that we would have to translate social disorganization into some kind of observable indicators. This is a useful procedure in any form of analysis even if we do not intend to employ these indicators as factors in a research project. For example, what should counselors look for in order to expand the range of accumulated data that could be useful in analyzing student behavior? This emphasis on devising indicators by which abstract concepts may be assessed becomes even more helpful when counselors attempt to act upon the comments of teachers who have referred students for help. Such statements as, "Johnny is too aggressive," or "anxious," or "socially immature" cry out for explanation. What do these words really mean in terms of observables? Although the process of operationalization and the development of constructs may be familiar to counselors who have studied research procedures, a presentation of the process here may serve to emphasize its importance as well as to simplify the techniques. It is through such a discussion that pupil personnel workers may become encouraged to approach scientifically what is sometimes viewed as an intuitive task.

In research in the behavioral sciences we refer frequently to the term *construct*. A construct is a concept that has been utilized explicitly for the purpose of scientific research. Intelligence is one of our more common constructs in education. Previous to its being adopted, defined, and measured as a scientific quantity, intelligence was an abstraction referring very generally to the innate capacities of persons.

As a construct, intelligence refers to the original meaning but has added to it those specific properties designated by research scientists as useful for observing and measuring it. Ordinarily it appears that constructs spring spontaneously to the mind of the researcher, but analytically we may presume that several important steps in the evolution of constructs are necessary.

Concepts that are intended for use in research are given two kinds of definitions. One definition is in terms of nonobservables, and the other is in terms of what we may observe that reveals the meaning of the concept. The first type of definition is called by one author "*constitutive.*"[1] The second is an *operational* definition. According to Kerlinger, a constitutive definition

. . . is a definition that defines a construct with other constructs. . . . We can define "weight" by saying that it is the "heaviness of objects." Or we can define "anxiety" as "subjective fear." In both cases we have substituted one concept for another concept.[2]

An operational definition is one that communicates the meaning of a concept by indicating the procedures required to measure it. Measurement, in this sense, refers to the kind of specific observations that will point to, or indicate the existence of, the phenomena that we wish to specify. In educational research the most prominent operational definitions are scores on tests or questionnaires that derive from persons the quantity or qualities of possessed characteristics such as abilities, personality traits, and attitudes. Standard IQ, personality, and achievement tests supply scores that researchers are willing to accept as the only observable manifestations of abstract symbols such as intelligence, achievement, and personality. Making formerly unobservable abstractions observable is necessary to the work of scientific research, but it should be noted that the artificial means by which abstractions are operationalized is purely arbitrary. That is, the establishment of operational definitions to make concepts workable in a research context is a function of the researcher's best estimation of what may

---

1. Fred N. Kerlinger, *Foundations of Behavioral Research,* Holt, Rinehart, & Winston, Inc., New York, 1964.
2. *Ibid.,* pp. 33–34.

legitimately represent the abstractions. The establishment of given operational definitions at one point in time suffers from the limitation of the researcher's cognitive framework and the availability of instruments to measure the concepts. A cognitive framework is built as given phenomena become the subject of intensive investigation by many researchers. The availability of psychometric instruments increases by the same process. Old tests are discarded as new approaches to the study of a given phenomenon are circulated throughout the field of research.

It is crucial to recognize the limitations and arbitrariness of operational definitions. It is this understanding, more than anything else, that may help us to avoid the error of reification from which most applied programs, built upon research in the behavioral sciences, suffer. Reification is the process of assuming that scores or operational definitions are identical to the abstractions they are intended to represent. It is such a mistaken assumption that leads teachers to believe that scores on IQ tests are *really* equivalent, rather than indicative of or *logically* equivalent, to intelligence. Operational definitions are, to reiterate an important point, best conceived as *if-then* definitions. If I do this and something results, then my operational definition of that something is what I have done to make it result.

It is a serious barrier to improving communication in education to assume, as many do, that test results reveal precisely the existence of abstract qualities. Out of this mistaken confidence by educators has come a further obstruction to basic understanding, and that is the belief that tests can and do measure everything. An interesting commentary on this dilemma has appeared in an article by Rodney Skager.[3]

A request that came to a national testing organization some months ago had both a familiar ring and a new twist. Could we, a university admissions office asked, recommend a test of creativity in time for screening the students who had applied for admission the coming semester? Also (the new twist) since there were so many candidates, could we recommend a test that was machine-scorable?

---

3. Rodney W. Skager, "The Wonderful Machine-Scorable Creativity Test," *College Board Review*, Fall 1965, p. 32.

. . . As far as I know, not a single one exists that can lay any claim whatsoever to having captured a significant part of the attribute it claims to measure. . . . Any test whose title suggests it can assess creativity in the same way we measure intelligence (and I realize some of these tests are selling like hot dogs at a ball park) strikes me chiefly as a profitable combination of hucksterism and fantasy.

Dr. Skager's evaluation highlights the caution that is being suggested.

Another problem with operational definitions, besides that of reification, is that the indicators chosen to represent certain concepts are selected out of the orientation of the person selecting them. We are back again to some of the problems discussed in Chapter 2. If we wish to discover whether or not love makes the world go round, we will find that the truth of the hypothesis is highly related to how we define both love and the world going round. A clergyman would be apt to look for behavior that reflects a brotherly or spiritual love; an older woman might look for familial love, a young man for passionate love, a scholar for the love of learning.

What is being suggested is that we not only make decisions about student problems based upon conceptual orientations, but also classify certain behaviors as expected results of given conditions. In this way we are influenced to construct certain structures so as to avoid the undesirable outcomes. If a child is sleeping in class, we may frequently change his circumstance to one that is more interesting. At the same time, we construct classes and activities that we predict will keep students interested because we make the assumption that low interest level leads to nonparticipation. In other words, both the definition of a student problem, in this case sleeping in class, as withdrawal or nonparticipation, and the development of an activity, in this case involving the student more actively, occur in line with the teacher's or counselor's orientation to the behavior. If, for a given student, sleeping in class occurred because the child needed to supplement the family's income by delivering papers at 5 A.M., then changing the activity could be irrelevant. Psychological withdrawal is not the same as physical withdrawal or social withdrawal. The behavior itself does not always supply us with clues as to the kind of withdrawal we are observing, but additional data will. However, if we begin with one set of indicators rather than another, we are bound to come up with only those observations that are suggested by the indicators we choose. We could all predict the kind of diagnostic dialogue that would transpire between a stereotypical neurosurgeon and a psychiatrist about a psychotic patient. We would all agree that in this case a five-year psychoanalysis without benefit of a neurological workup would be presumptuous. Putting a child into counseling because he sleeps in class before finding out something about his home situation, which might require the services of a school social worker, would be the same kind of error of omission. Errors of omission of helpful knowledge, then, may be avoided by providing persons with as broad a range of relevant orientations as is necessary to prevent them from taking a myopic view of the institutional world of which they are a part.

The study of human behavior undertaken from the perspective of psychological models will utilize operational definitions that incorporate the orientations of the prominent paradigms in the discipline. Sociological research follows the same procedure. Paradigms are those theories that bind persons to a certain way of looking at the world, of studying it, and of explaining it. Training programs for teachers and counselors are based upon these paradigms as they are adapted to help order our understanding of educational phenomena. These paradigms reflect the accumulated research and writing of the persons who helped them evolve. The most influential ideas dealing with learning were generated out of the work of men like Freud, Thorndike, Watson, and Skinner.

The emphasis on operational definitions has been intended to communicate the importance as well as the cautions of using concepts in the evaluation of educational behavior. Facts such as broken homes are often inadequate explanations for the kind of behavior that counselors need to understand. Concepts, on the other hand, once we have given them concrete meaning, usually explain a larger range of phenomena more completely. The concept of deprivation, for example, is a more useful description in explaining certain behaviors than the fact of poverty. Persons may be poor without feeling deprived—for example, the millions of primitives on this earth.

Areas of sociological interest represent conceptual ways of looking at social life. These areas not only subsume a large number of independent facts, they also serve to organize the interests of sociology into inclusive and exclusive categories. Such concepts as social class, role conflict, social mobility, and social disorganization are representative. The kinds of data adduced in order to extend and explicate the paradigms of sociology having relevance to the work of the school counselor are summarized in the following pages.

## DEMOGRAPHIC AND ECOLOGICAL FACTORS AND INDIVIDUAL ADJUSTMENT

The size and structure of the family unit, the size and structure of the neighborhood or community, the organization and distribution of community resources, the occupational backgrounds and educational level of parents, ethnicity, and a number of other such variables have been shown to bear a relationship to such factors as delinquent behavior, school dropouts, career choice, scores on intelligence, achievement, and personality tests, school grades, participation in extracurricular activities or voluntary associations, and mental illness.

Sociologists, in work situations such as colleges and universities, departments of urban affairs and urban planning, and research divisions of national, state, and local government, are constantly attempting to identify demographic factors that will provide an explanatory base for social dynamics. The wisdom of certain vocational choices might hand on an understanding of complex trends in such areas as urban renewal, rural stability, and occupational status.

But these are more comprehensive concepts than the limited factors that educators typically use to identify conflicts. Too many misconceptions take the form of generalized beliefs when these factors are categorized too quickly as salient causes of the educational problems of youth. Broken homes, working mothers, slum living, father's occupation, and high physical mobility too frequently jump to the attention as "of course" kinds of explanations, while the specific relationships, actual conditions associated with living in a broken home or a slum, many untested, rest in the journals.

Communities have their peculiar distribution of social characteristics: race, religion, nationality, population density, political participation, functional geography (fishing village, resort town, community to house workers of emerging industries), age and sex distribution, socioeconomic status, transiency, and so on. Not only do these characteristics describe a community but the variations in each category can and have been shown to relate to a host of other kinds of variables: vote turn-out in mayoralty or school-bond elections,[4] number of suicides or mental breakdowns,[5, 6] police arrests,[7] and voting behavior in national elections,[8] to mention a few. Schools are communities that also differ in regard to these characteristics and others. Most teachers and counselors know and are quick to emphasize that when a school shifts in the racial composition of its students from Caucasian to Negro, the mean IQ scores go down. This fact in itself may cause the school to make certain adaptations such as increasing the number of industrial shops, assigning more teachers to social-adjustment rooms, or even sending missionaries out into the community to help Negro preschoolers get ready to compete with white students for learning competencies. These are responses that an institution makes to what it perceives the consequences of such changes will be. But what does a counselor or an administrator who has to deal with these disruptions of traditional routines, on both group and individual bases, know about the structure of the ethos of minority groups? What are the traditional roles that parents and children play? How do they relate to authority and with what kind of authority

4. W. G. Savard, "Influence of Voter Turnout on School Bond and Tax Elections," U.S. Department of Health, Education, and Welfare, 1961.

5. J. B. Gibbs, "Suicide," in *Contemporary Social Problems,* ed. by R. Merton and R. Nisbet, Harcourt, Brace & World, Inc., New York, 1961, pp. 222–250.

6. Hollingshead and Redlich, *Social Class and Mental Illness,* John Wiley & Sons, Inc., New York, 1958.

7. Donald Cressey, "Crime," in *Contemporary Social Problems,* ed. by R. Merton and R. Nisbet, Harcourt, Brace & World, Inc., New York, 1961, pp. 40–41.

8. Angus Campbell, Phillip Converse, Warren Muller, and Donald Stokes, *The American Voter,* John Wiley & Sons, Inc., New York, 1960.

are they most comfortable? Intensive sociological analysis has been conducted in the area of minority groups, employing such important constructs as marginality, anomie, female-model families, and status crystallization areas that pursue more significant explanations about the behavior of minority-group members than does the mere fact of color.

Field projects that attack the question of the relationship between these demographic variables and behavioral adaptations are constantly being conducted. Leighton's intensive analysis, based on a multidisciplinary approach, has suggested several important relationships between community factors and institutional adaptations.[9] The particular problem he investigated was how community organization was related to the mental health of the members of the community.

Sociological methodology may suggest designs to test the best techniques for racial, cultural, or socioeconomic integration in schools as well as in communities. Does the school require a sociologist to make converts within the counseling ranks, which he will not do, or does the school counselor, whose responsibility it is to be concerned with individual and group disruptions and, ideally, to suggest preventive measures, incorporate some of this knowledge into his task?

Factors antecedent or extrinsic to the school have gained recognition as motivating and impinging forces that influence the adjustment that individuals make to that institution. Counselors and teachers, using their daily experience with students, may provide insights about the consequences of demographic characteristics that will expand the conceptual apparatus of sociological analysis and lead to better theories and better research.

## ROLE EXPECTATIONS AND ROLE CONFLICT

Whether we are focusing upon the role of the student or the role of the counselor in the school, the problem of conflicting expectation is relevant to the work of the counselor. The question of how

---

9. A. H. Leighton, *My Name Is Legion,* Basic Books, Inc., Publishers, New York, 1959.

decisions are made in the face of such conflicting expectations has occupied the attention of sociological analysis. Samuel Stouffer,[10] Neal Gross,[11] and Melvin Seeman[12] have made significant beginnings in this area. The range of possible roles to be subjected to this kind of analysis is not near being exhausted. Of most significance in this regard would be an investigation into the conflicts in expectations held by students, administrators, parents, teachers, and counselors themselves about the role of the counselor and how the counselor typically resolves ostensibly incompatible demands.

Students live in a world of separate institutions, all of which demand from them a separate and often conflicting loyalty. The home, the school, the church, the peer group, and the economic system present a complex network of allegiances. When two or more come into conflict, a choice must be made. Sociological analysis is constantly attempting to isolate the factors that explain the direction of the choice. When the formal expectations of the school conflict with the informal expectations of the peer group, the conflict, in our time, has frequently resulted in decisions leading to deviation and delinquency. An understanding of the complex base of these supposedly incompatible forces could result in a restructuring of the expectations that would allow survival in both systems. Students can comply to the expectations of both the school and the peer group if the school, or the counselor, understands the social structure that produces the conflict.

Role conflict ordinarily involves more than the kind of structural conflict discussed so far. When loyalties to two or more separate institutions are in conflict in a given situation, we refer to this as a role-role conflict. On the other hand, there are those situations in which a personal conviction comes into conflict with a role expectation, and this we refer to as a self-role conflict. This kind of conflict

---

10. Samuel Stouffer, "An Analysis of Conflicting Social Norms," *American Sociological Review*, vol. 14, 1949, pp. 707ff.

11. Neal Gross, *Explorations in Role Analysis: Studies in the School Superintendency Role,* John Wiley & Sons, Inc., New York, 1958.

12. Melvin Seeman, "Role Conflict and Ambivalence in Leadership," *American Sociological Review*, vol. 18, 1953, pp. 373–380.

may frequently post a decision-making difficulty for the school counselor. The following example represents a typical self-role conflict for the school counselor.

One of the principal functions of the American school is to allocate individuals to productive social roles. The importance of the school to the American society is highly determined by this prerequisite. Consider, then, a situation in which a girl student wishes to pursue the highly precarious (in terms of financial security) career of a creative artist. While conducting a series of career-counseling sessions, the counselor becomes highly unsure about the wisdom of her continuing toward such an unstable goal, despite her intense engagement in creative work. He perceives that she might do well in a more stable and socially desirable occupation, such as being an art teacher or fashion designer. In the purest sense, the school counselor recognizes a responsibility both to individuals and to the manifest function of the school, but in this case, he may feel that providing the student with information and advice about the stable occupations could cause her to question her artistic ardor and to retreat. Let us suggest that the counselor holds a strong conviction about encouraging and supporting even the most unrealistic goals and is inclined to suggest that she does not compromise her inclinations and instead of going to college, should go out and learn to paint. But a school administrator, finding his most promising students taking off to see the world, to paint, to write, to sculpt, to compose, and not to represent the school in the college population, would be apt to react unfavorably to such encouragement, unless he espoused a new definition of the guidance function. The counselor's job may thus be in jeopardy unless the definition of his function is clear. The resolution of a conflict between encouraging social responsibility and encouraging self-fulfillment, resides in the consultation of the two systems, the school and the personality. Does the counselor play the public-relations game with middle class parents, or does he tell them frankly that it is unlikely that creative students will be content in bureaucratic roles? Does he challenge the teacher's authority when he is convinced that the child is a victim of an unrealistic and overly rigid teacher? These are questions that a counselor needs to think about, and familiarity with the sociological work on the resolution of role conflict provides a structure for the consideration of such questions.

Finally, the role of the student, discussed briefly in Chapter 2, as an alternative explanation for deviant behavior to that of neurosis, offers the counselor an analytic framework for assessing many student problems. Is being a bully a comfortable role or an expression of frustration?

## THE ADOLESCENT SUBCULTURE

Of considerable theoretical import, Albert Cohen's *Delinquent Boys*[13] concerned itself with exploring the nature of the values and attitudes of delinquent adolescents. Other authors such as James Coleman[14] and Albert Reiss[15] have also conducted research attempting to derive some consistent system of adolescent values that might stamp adolescents as a subculture. It seems clear from the work of these men that society is both more differentiated and more stratified along age lines than ever before and that the adolescent age group has emerged as a distinct and highly institutionalized subculture. Coleman's study suggests that the group of agemates with whom an individual interacts in educational institutions provides the most significant influence for his adaptation to the school. If academic success is most highly valued by this group, the large percentage of students will swing toward this emphasis. If athletic success is dominant in the value system of the peer group, then the school takes on this characteristic. If, as happens on occasion, delinquent norms pervade the ethos of the adolescent group, then this school becomes structured as a disciplinary organization more than other schools.

The adjustment or adaptation of youth to the institution of the

13. Albert K. Cohen, *Delinquent Boys,* The Free Press, New York, 1955.
14. James S. Coleman, *The Adolescent Society,* The Free Press, New York, 1961.
15. Albert J. Reiss and A. L. Rhodes, "Are Educational Goals of Conforming, Truant, and Delinquent Adolescents Influenced by Group Position in American Society?" *Journal of Negro Education,* vol. 28, pp. 252–267.

school has been shown by sociological investigation to hinge on the concept of status. The status system fostered by the school around such criteria as achievement, participation, and cooperation is not a system that will serve all students equally. Opportunity to attain status in the school is differentially distributed throughout the student population. Lacking one avenue for status in the adolescent subculture, many members set up a competing status system, one in which their chances for success are greater. As new status systems arise, whole sets of values become reorganized to support the system. Many of these values are contradictory to such success goals as education and occupational stability and are supportive of deviation.

Counselors should be the first to recognize the existence of what we could call a collective reaction formation. Lacking the ability to achieve status along criterion lines that include such expectations as industriousness, performance, cleanliness, morality, conformity, punctuality, and passivity, those who cannot succeed reverse these criteria so that laziness, refusal to perform and conform, vulgarity, disorganization, and aggression become important criteria for status in the group of school failures. A recent study by the author has indicated that hostile attitudes toward school and its expectations were greater for middle class deviants than for working class deviants. When the expectations for success are high, as they are in the middle class community, failure becomes a serious ego-deflating blow. Therefore, the reaction-formation mechanism of defense becomes an even more important technique for dealing with failure.[16]

It seems unlikely that counselors can escape the fact that much motivation for educational and career decisions is highly related to the nature of the subculture of which the counselee is a member. The phenomena of the dropout subculture, of high school and even junior high political and social activism involving such behavioral manifestations as underground newspapers, student protests, strikes and rallies, psychedelic experiences, and religious devotion to new cultural heroes, are of profound interest to sociology and education. A rumbling

---

16. Carl Weinberg, "Achievement and School Attitudes of Adolescent Boys as Related to Behavior and Occupational Status of Families," *Social Forces,* Feb. 1964, pp. 462–466.

of potentially earthquake dimensions has aroused anxiety in adult society in general and in educators specifically. Traditional structural controls, typical of viable formal organizations, appear to be impotent in the face of the kinds of unanticipated behavior that may be signifying a major adolescent revolution. Preliminary sociological inquiries like *It's Happening*[17] will be followed by more sophisticated conceptual analyses. Sociologists and anthropologists are looking to the current organization of culture and society for explanatory factors. The adolescent subculture as a loyalty-demanding phenomenon can control the actions of millions of agemates in such a way that traditional educational goals are made to appear meaningless. The role of educational guidance as an intervening agency may only be effective if an understanding of subcultures and institutions is part of the counselor's intellectual apparatus. If certain incompatibilities exist between the traditional structure of the school and the value structure of the adolescent subculture, the guidance role would seem to require a set of organization-manipulating activities rather than a one-to-one interchange between counselors and subculture members.

## INSTITUTIONAL CLIMATES AND PUPIL ADJUSTMENT

The notion that schools have personalities that are peculiarly their own and different from other schools is a recent one. Despite the fact that we do not presently possess adequate psychometric instruments to allow us to fit individual personalities to schools, several researchers in social psychology are working toward this end. Some literature is available that at least sets forth the framework within which school counselors may begin thinking when helping students make decisions about colleges. Counselors are constantly influencing student decisions about college choice by making a general assessment of the qualities of both student and college. But these decisions are based more on intuitive assessment than on actual data. Although

---

17. J. L. Simmonds and Barry Winograd, *It's Happening,* Marc Laird Publishers, Santa Barbara, 1967.

definitive data are not available, this is not an adequate reason for not being familiar with those investigations that clearly expose certain regularities in student adaptation to college.

For example, some research has been generated on the likelihood of students from rural high schools experiencing college success.[18] Rural high schools are quite distinct in many ways from urban high schools. The nature of the interaction is more personal, the student-teacher relationships are based upon more extensive familiarity with each other's background, and the vocational orientations of a large segment of the student population would be dissimilar to those orientations in urban schools. The 4H clubs and the personalities of these students are vastly different from the Hi-Y or Hot Rod clubs of urban schools. To extrapolate from this kind of knowledge, however, to some conclusion that students with rural high school backgrounds would not do well in large impersonal universities would be an intuitive guess. Hopefully, we do not intend to operate this way when more research is available. At present, we may be making logical mistakes of the following sort: (1) it may be inaccurate that the high school environment shapes the personality of the individual; (2) our understanding of the relationship between types of universities, based only upon demographic or ecological data, and their personalities may be false (Berkeley, for example, is not the same kind of institution as Minnesota despite their similar monolithic structures); (3) we may underestimate the capacity of some individuals to adapt to new environments; and (4) our knowledge of the factors related to survival in new academic environments may be inadequate.

Robert Pace[19] and Clark and Trow[20] have been working along

18. Payne, Raymond, "Development of Occupations and Migrant Expectations Choices among Urban, Small Town and Rural Adolescent Boys," *Rural Society*, vol. 21, June 1956, pp. 117–125.

Also, William Sewell, "Community of Residence and College Plans," *American Sociological Review*, vol. 29. no. 1, Feb. 1964, pp. 24–38.

19. C. Robert Pace, "Differences in Campus Atmosphere," in *Readings in the Social Psychology of Education*, ed. by W. W. Charters, Allyn & Bacon, Inc., Boston, 1963, p. 73.

20. B. Clark and M. Trow, "The Organizational Context," in *The Study of College Peer Groups*, ed. by Theodore M. Newcomb and Everett K. Wilson, Aldine Publishing Co., Chicago, Ill., 1966, pp. 17–70.

similar lines in attempting to assess the personality or styles of different colleges and universities. The notion of subcultural emphasis is crucial to their conceptual frameworks. Institutions of higher education may be characterized in terms of these subcultural emphases. Four such subcultures are the *academic,* in which the institution is perceived as emphasizing liberal arts studies; the *social,* in which the school emphasizes the social life of students in fraternities, frequent parties, athletics, and so on; the *occupational,* in which the major emphasis is on training for professional roles such as teaching, engineering, and nursing; and the *nonconformist,* in which activities and interests, political and intellectual, are emphasized in nonformal academic settings. A student's adaptation in high school to these four categories of emphasis may offer the best possible prediction as to where he will best fit. Even though the available data may not be conclusive, what is important at this level of analysis and decision making is the possibility of operating within theoretical frameworks that help us to order our thinking about practical problems.

Secondary and elementary schools also possess what we might call styles. Using a framework suggested by the writings of Talcott Parsons,[21] schools have been designated as *Three R's* or *Pattern Maintenance, Adaptive Occupational, Goal Attainment,* and *Integrative.*[22] Pattern-maintenance, or three-R schools or classrooms are those that emphasize the generalized learning of all things traditionally expected of students. The style is authoritarian because the content must be known since it is basic and traditional. Adaptive-occupational environments focus upon specialization. The system relates to the economic accent in the general situation facing the school. These environments are particularly responsive to both the society's and the community's demand for certain kinds of productivity. In the high school this would currently be a highly scientific or technical emphasis. Goal-attainment environments focus upon the production of collective action, on the mobilization of the resources rather than on the

---

21. Talcott Parsons, *The Social System,* The Free Press, New York, 1951.
22. H. Lamb, P. McHugh, and C. Weinberg, "Teacher Alienation," a report of the U.S. Office of Education.

resources themselves. Gratification for students occurs out of participation with others and from the results of that participation. Group
movement toward goals is stressed. Integrative environments are
concerned with the maintenance of some normative order in relations
between members. These schools or classrooms stress traditional
relationships such as citizenship, equality, freedom, and differences
and similarities between people.

Although shifting the emphasis from personality styles to social
styles, we may still observe our original focus, only now we need to
talk about individual social styles being congruent with the social
styles of organizations. Research on this framework is nearing completion, and although the data are not yet available, they should be made
known when they are, as they will be relevant to the ongoing thinking
about the problem of goodness of fit between persons and situations.
The conceptual categories of this research may be useful tools in
placing individuals within institutional contexts that are congruent
with their capacities for adaptation. Stern, Stein, and Bloom[23] suggested earlier that certain students do better with certain kinds of
professors, according to the style of the professor and the student's
capacity to adapt to this style. Many students, for example, prefer a
learning situation that is highly authoritarian, ritualized, rigorously outlined, and impersonal. Other students work better in situations that
are loosely structured, highly interactional in terms of discussion, and
very personal. The recent research has indicated the value of this
assumption.

It should be clear that any one element, whether we are dealing
with the personalities of social systems or with their social styles,
does not constitute the total emphasis of the system. All four categories, in both the Pace and Trow scheme and the one discussed
here, are present to some degree in every institutional context. But
there is always the question of priority among the categories, and it
may be hoped that the extent of emphasis on each category in any
given institution will be measured. Individual personality systems are

---

23. G. Stern, Morris Stein, and B. Bloom, *Methods in Personality Assessment,*
The Free Press, New York, 1956.

equally multidimensional, with certain qualities dominating. If we may begin to match persons with institutional frameworks, be it college, school, or classroom, on the basis of these emphases, we will have accomplished considerably more than we have to date.

If we were to apply the results of this kind of thinking and research to a given school setting, we would want to have a sufficient description of the style of every classroom within this school and in other schools as well. We could then classify each classroom and hope to be able to fit individuals into their most comfortable classroom environment. This task may well fall within the jurisdiction of the school counselor of the future, whose goals and functions may be designated by longer range, more preventive purposes.

## THE SOCIAL STRUCTURE OF THE SCHOOL AND CLASSROOM

Although teachers and counselors ordinarily look for cues to student problems in the phenomenological environment, that is, they attempt to see the school environment through the eyes of the student, an understanding of the way in which purely structural elements shape behavior is useful. Students are typically myopic in their perception of the environment that intrudes upon their daily lives. The fact that a low grade is attained in a particular course may have an effect upon the student, but the organization of the total grading system and how this helps to structure the overall plan of the formal organization is beyond his ken. The fact that a particular personality conflict erupts between teacher and student may be as much a function of the organization of power roles within the school as a result of incompatible personality traits.

Institutions have much in common, and the school is as legitimate an institution for sociological inquiry into formal organization as the church or the industrial bureaucracy. In order to communicate the components of social structures so that they can be applied to many institutional environments, several conceptions are useful. Standard sociological concepts such as norms, groups, values, sanctions, roles, and bureaucracy come to have special connotations within different institutional systems, and these will be discussed briefly in relation to schools. Other notions such as formal and informal organization, internal and external systems, and cultures and subcultures have been adduced to describe and classify complex organizations.

## Norms and Sanctions

Norms are expectations for behavior, and sanctions are the way members of the group behave in order to maintain conformity to these expectations. Institutions may have similar expectations for conformity, but they differ considerably in their tactics for rewarding conformity and punishing deviation. An examination of the kinds of sanctions applied by teachers, administrators, and peers could reveal a great deal of the source of student problems. The continued absence of a reinforcing smile, grade, or accolade, the abundant use of detentions, low grades, and overextensive assignments may reveal to the sociologist the patterns of educational sanctions. But the applied advantage of these sanctions to the guidance worker rests upon his ability to evaluate as well as to discriminate the patterns.

## Roles and Bureaucracy

A social role may be thought of statically as a position within a set of ordered positions or dynamically as a patterned sequence of learned actions or deeds performed in an interaction situation by a person holding the position. A bureaucracy is a formal organization, the most defining characteristics of which are a set of explicit rules explaining the character of the organization and a set of positions that have both role and status dimensions. To conceive of a school in these terms may raise many important questions functional to the understanding and amelioration of student problems. We may ask about the clarity and strength of rules regulating role behavior, we may begin to talk about role stress or conflict between roles, and, finally, we may even talk about the extent to which formal rules are dysfunctional to expressed organizational as well as individual goals.

## Groups and Values

A group is the sociological unit of analysis, but in a sense pertinent to our concerns, it is also a crucial determinant of individual behavior. The values that mark a group's ethos are predictive of the individual member's behavior. Educators are, or should be, aware of the strength of the group in enforcing the behavior of members, as well as of the important function it has of socializing members into its unique world of rights and expectations. They should also, in order to make sense out of behavior, be able to trace many specific acts to the value system of the group of which the student is a member.

## Formal and Informal Organization

Wayne Gordon, in *The Social System of the High School*[24] applied the notion of formal and informal organization to his analysis of a high school. His distinction was between the system of achievement and that of sociometrics. Formal and informal systems may be broadly conceived as those interactions involving regulated interactions in the former case and spontaneous interactions in the latter. By no means are we to conceive of spontaneity as connoting randomness or being accidental. The criteria for friendship patterns are usually clearly focused around socioeconomic and ability factors. However, as interaction patterns, they are not determined by explicit organizational regulations. To these dimensions, in order to assess the factors influencing student status within the system, Gordon postulated the distinct usefulness of the semiformal system. It is a structured system given legitimacy by the formal authority but conceived in order to

---

24. C. Wayne Gordon, *The Social System of the High School,* The Free Press, New York, 1957.

satisfy student desires. This was represented by the system of extra-curricular activities. By charting the position of all students with respect to all three systems (formal, semiformal, and informal), certain patterns of association emerged. Students who had similar grades and a similar amount of extracurricular participation tended to choose each other as friends. The importance of conceptual schemes such as the above to those involved in the applied interests of education lies in their ability to construct a manageable and understandable world out of a plethora of complex educational phenomena.

## Internal and External Systems

One last conceptualization that bears upon our efforts to view the school as a distinct social system is that provided by George Homans.[25] His notions of an internal and an external system are shown to be useful in understanding the dynamics of group behavior. He conceives of an external system as the elements "Sentiment, activity and interaction, . . . and of their inter-relations, so far as they (the elements) constitute a solution—not necessarily the only possible solution—of the problem: How shall the group survive in the environment?"[26] Put more simply, What do we as a group have to do in order to fulfill some designated function, some reason for our existence? The internal system he conceives as "group behavior that is an expression of the sentiments towards one another developed by members of the group in the course of their life together."[27] The important difference between Homan's formulation and that posited by Gordon lies in the interactional context of Homan's system, whereby the external system acts upon and is, in turn, acted upon by the internal sysem. What we must do as a school to develop educated and responsible citizens is conditioned in part by what the students will allow us to do to them. Any reformulation of formal policy that occurs as a result of a student movement, such as that which occurred

---

25. George Homans, *The Human Group,* Harcourt, Brace & World, Inc., New York, 1950.
26. *Ibid.*
27. *Ibid.,* p. 90.

at the Berkeley campus of the University of California, would be a prime example of this interaction. Conflict may occur when school authorities do not perceive or, perhaps, accept the existence of the internal system. Industry has created unions to enforce acceptance, and now students may have no way to show their dissatisfaction except through their own personal failure. Social systems do reveal the structural basis for conflict.

Sociological theories, models, and schemata have and are being adapted to a consideration of the social structure of the school. Wayne Gordon,[28] Talcott Parsons,[29] W. W. Charters, Jr., [30] George Spindler and Jules Henry,[31] the latter two from an anthropological perspective, have appeared in the socioeducational literature with themes on the subject. The social system of the school serving as the foundation for civic and occupational allocation would appear to be a relevant dimension of knowledge for those who stand in a crucial position with respect to this allocation.

## EDUCATION AND SOCIAL CLASS

It has been the concern of many writers that the educational institution has not been able to produce the kind of vertical mobility that an open and democratic society espouses. At a time when applied programs are being sponsored by the Federal government to incorporate action toward achieving this segment of the American ideal, it would appear particularly relevant that those persons involved have some idea as to the factors inhibiting mobility. If knowledge of the stratified nature of the American social order is available in quantity and if it were coupled with some facility in applying the sociological perspective, much wasted effort could be

---

28. Gordon, *op. cit.*

29. Talcott Parsons, "The School Class as a Social System," *Harvard Educational Review,* Fall 1959, pp. 297–318.

30. W. W. Charters, "The School as a Social System," *Review of Educational Research,* vol. 22, 1952, pp. 41–50.

31. George Spindler, *Education and Culture,* Holt, Rinehart & Winston, Inc., New York, 1963.

avoided. The gross assumptions of "value conflicts," "middle class teachers and lower class children," and "improving aspiration levels" as foci in remedial programs involve considerable meaning apart from the common-sense notions held by well-meaning workers in anti-poverty programs, Head Start, Operation Uplift, and other such projects.

We have evidence from sociological investigations that substantiate one major idea, and that is that children of the lower classes do not succeed in educational tasks, including intelligence tests, as frequently as do middle class children. We have no reliable evidence that any applied program can obviate a condition that is intrinsically related to the most fundamental aspects of the social structure. We might be able to venture a hypothesis that if we held constant and equal the economic advantages of every member of our society, school success would be differentiated, in time, on the basis of ability or perhaps of other factors, on which it is impossible now to speculate. But this is Utopian. We simply cannot treat a situation as changeable that has as many facets as social class unless we have some basis for explaining assumptions such as the theories of social change, particularly those theories advanced by persons like Marx and Weber, who address themselves to conditions of the economic order.

The classical and most often mentioned study of the interaction of social class and education was conducted by A. B. Hollingshead in 1949.[32] His hypothesis was that the class position of the parents of Elmtown High children would be related to the educational behavior of the students. His evidence, collected in the manner of a participant observer in the community, supported this hypothesis, showing specific benefits to those of high social-class rankings. The data also illustrated the point that children from the lower classes were conspicuously absent from the lists of those who could be expected to attain high status through education. The research by Warner, Havighurst, and Loeb[33] revealed similar findings, and the conclusion based upon their evidence was a concrete indictment of

---

32. A. B. Hollingshead, *Elmtown's Youth,* John Wiley & Sons, Inc. New York, 1949.

33. W. Lloyd Warner, R. J. Havighurst, and Martin Loeb, *Who Shall be Educated?* Harper & Row, Publishers, New York, 1944.

the educational system in its failure as a vehicle for the upward mobility of lower class youngsters.

The process by which these unegalitarian associations occur is a considerably more complex problem than the revealing of educational correlates of social class. The issues involved, however, are probably more important to analysis of social-class consequences than to the relationships themselves. Both Hollingshead and Warner imply that the educational system itself is biased against lower class children and tends to favor middle and upper class students with the rewards at its disposal. It is one issue to contend that lower class children do not have the cognitive and moral commitments to succeed educationally; it is quite another that questions the organization of education in favor of those with such commitments.

Probing into this process, Becker[34] attempted to discover the way Chicago school teachers observed, classified, and reacted to class-typed differences in the behavior of students. He looked for reactions in three categories: teaching, discipline, and moral acceptability. His conclusions were as follows:

TEACHING

1. The common attitude among teachers was that middle class students were easiest to teach.

2. This leads to differences in teaching techniques—more flashy demonstrations were used.

3. Teachers expect that the amount of work expected of them will vary according to the social-class composition of the school. They do not expect that they will need to work as much in lower class schools, so they don't.

DISCIPLINE

1. Middle class students are the most docile, easiest to control.

2. Upper class students are "neurotic" or "spoiled."

3. Lower class students are hostile, aggressive, frequent problems.

4. Teachers are more tense in controlling lower class students, afraid to let down, believe that they will lose class.

---

34. H. S. Becker, "Social Class Variation in Teacher-Pupil Relationship," *Journal of Educational Sociology,* vol. 25, 1952, p. 451.

## Moral Acceptability

1. Lower class students are offensive in terms of some deeply felt set of moral standards on the part of the teacher.

2. Lower class students have inadequate values in the areas of health, cleanliness, and sex.

3. Upper class students have some deficiencies in the areas of respect for elders, politeness, drinking, and smoking.

4. Slum children are most deeply offensive in almost every area of the "Protestant ethic."

As American society becomes more industrialized, more bureaucratized, and more urbanized, the interaction of educational and economic variables increases in complexity. Many things have happened in the last decade to force us to wonder how the research of Hollingshead, Warner, and Becker may be applied in our current concern with helping individuals overcome barriers to educational progress that are based upon personality and economic determinants. Technology is erasing lower class occupational channels, and whole segments of our society have been uplifted through the practices of American trade unions so that income differentials between the classes are becoming more and more undifferentiated. When we add to these considerations the fact that education has become the single most important criterion for mobility in a bureaucratic society, we are forced to reevaluate our situation.

Some reevaluation has already taken place in that we may observe large governmental concern with "the other American," although the general public attitude is such that few of the insights that Harrington[35] reveals are apparent in the public middle class mind. At the same time, students who are to become the teachers of the future are exhibiting, in many university settings, an increased social conscience. Teacher training in most colleges involves a consideration of social issues and an exploration of ameliorative actions. It may be that the earlier research reviewed here does not reveal a useful perspective for today's teachers and today's schools. The earlier

---

35. Michael Harrington, *The Other America,* Macmillan Company, New York, 1963.

socioeducational data that have been made available may not be in line with certain assumptions, relative to class, upon which contemporary applied programs are basing much of their work. Teachers may not hold conflicting values for students in a time of cultural relativism, the school may not be so rigidly structured as to impose the unidimensional set of middle class expectations that researchers used either to find or to manufacture, and in many ways teachers themselves may not be the middle class personalities that fit so nicely into our conceptual mold.

Another tenuous assumption, which seems to have emerged from earlier focus upon the family in the study of social class, is that because family determines the status of the child, it is the family that requires exploration and action in discovering and changing student orientation to the school. The function of the family in socializing children has decreased immensely from what it was in a rural society.[36] With the emergence of such a clearly defined adolescent subculture that manufacturers and the mass media consider it a distinct social market, the function of the family has decreased even more. With the massification of tastes as an outgrowth of two decades of general affluence, there has appeared in American society a general attitude that children should have the advantages that most workers feel were denied to them but that they have been experiencing in recent years. With the general social uplift, has come a widespread motivation to stabilize one's economic status, this time in terms of education rather than income. For an overwhelming majority of school children, their parents' aspirations are not a handicap. To perceive the sources of student problems in sociological terms requires a consideration of socializers other than the family, particularly the peer group and the teachers themselves.

The dimensions of social class are more complicated than our assumptions about the source of student problems or even culture

---

36. Though the family has decreased in influence, it is still the subject of a host of recent investigations, both in sociology and in education. See Glen Elder, "Family Structure and Educational Attainment," *American Sociological Review,* Feb. 1965. Also, R. E. Herriot and N. H. St John, *Social Class and the Urban School,* John Wiley & Sons, Inc., New York, 1966.

conflict appear to indicate. Familiarity with many of the notions generated in this sociological area can only lead to less presumptive actions than are currently being taken in the name of helping disadvantaged children.

## EDUCATION AND SOCIAL PROBLEMS

In recent years sociology has taken two approaches to the subject of social problems. Predominantly, an interest in a social problem was and is evaluated on the basis of the extent to which knowledge of a given problem may contribute generally to the literature of deviance or social disorganization. A second perspective sees the etiology of specific problems as a legitimate area of inquiry in itself. Forces that explain alcoholism, insofar as these are social, need not also explain drug addiction or crime.

Coterminous with this social-problems approach, within sociology there evolved also a reevaluation of the role of sociology in the amelioration of these problems. Applied sociology and action research ballooned with the increased availability of research money. This development could work to the advantage of education, particularly to the interests of pupil personnel workers as sociological inquiry uncovers factors that help to explain the structure of student deviation.

It would be incorrect to assert that sociology has become directly concerned with the solution of social problems in any manner that might overshadow a specific sociological interest. But sociologists are no longer repelled by the thought of their research being turned into applied programs. Perhaps they never really were, although a myth arose around this notion. It is only with the rigor of careful investigation, however, that legitimate sociological inquiry proceeds. For this reason, quick and easy answers, the kind that educators too often seek in order to resolve problems, are not forthcoming from sociologists as rapidly as the seriousness of social problems effecting education are being recognized. This may be a practical problem at the moment, but the best solutions are seldom those interpreted from the first attacks upon concepts such as delinquency, student rebellion, fadism, student drug addiction, dropouts, and teenage sex and marriage.

Most teachers and pupil personnel workers who are seriously engaged in relating instruction to individual dispositions and in seeking ways to overcome social detriments to the educational progress of large numbers of students are intuitively aware that certain factors are operative. They speak of the effects upon students of a broken home, a disorganized unbroken home, a working mother, poverty, large families, transiency, and the "degeneration" of moral standards. Nor are these people unfamiliar with publicized notions about the effects of racial discrimination, urban segregation of minority groups, international tensions, the portrayal of violence and orgiastic sex in the mass media, and the computerization of daily life. What, however, is the actual meaning of these phenomena to education? How do we explain the effects, what are they precisely, how does one factor interact with another? Are there multiple or single causes, and what are the forms of adaptation that emerge from a controled set of environmental conditions? More specifically, why is it that one boy from a broken home is a deviant whereas another is a valedictorian, and why do some boys from slum neighborhoods become delinquent although others do not?

These are the scientific questions that sociological analysis asks, and any attempt to professionalize that aspect of education that hopes to help students in trouble must be aware of this method of inquiry as well as of the accumulating knowledge in each area. For many years the discipline of sociology itself was willing to accept poverty, slum conditions, urban location, and family organization as correlates of such behavior as crime and delinquency. But as we have indicated, these in themselves are not causes and only explain a small portion of the behavior. The best works in this field of sociological inquiry are the attempts to explain the ways in which crime and delinquency occur regardless of urban area or family organization.

The scope of this chapter is not so broad as to intend any summarization of sociological investigation into the many social-problem areas. But this material is available and should be read by counselors and teachers. Those counselors who insist upon relying on psychological explanations for mental problems should be aware that sociologists are flocking to mental health centers, psychiatric wards of county hospitals, and mental hygiene clinics to explore the social basis of mental illness, an area that currently is as legitimately designated a social problem as any other. It is interesting, for example, to learn that persons of different social classes emerge with different neurotic patterns, and that the treatment of these persons can also be differentiated by class background.[37]

In the introduction to their comprehensive book, Robert Nisbet and Robert Merton[38] summarize the broad scope of the context of social problems. It is this global perspective that frames the ideas of of sociological scrutiny into smaller areas of social conflict. It is also this perspective that influences the disruptions that occur within education, suggesting that counselors need be at least aware of the effects within the school in the form of student problems of macroscopic patterns within the larger society.

Much of the history of modern Western society is the history of the dislocation or changed emphasis of traditional values. Many of the values that are characteristically Western developed from the matrix of Judeo-Christianity and were given their institutional setting during centuries in which the economic order was largely agrarian and in which the typical units of society were small and homogeneous. The rise of capitalism, religious individualism, and democracy has inevitably affected the character of traditional values. It has done so by altering, often transforming, the social contexts of the traditional values, and by spawning new values more directly related to the nature of the modern order. Such doctrines as critical rationalism and utilitarianism have taken their toll from the traditional values of the past. It is difficult for a set of values to maintain clear moral ascendancy when the presumed sanctity or divinity of its roots is challenged by the secular ideas of rationalism and science.

Modern history has frequently been an arena for conflicts between such values, on the one hand, as patriarchalism, religious corporatism, and fixed social status, and, on the other hand, individualism of faith and morals, self-interest in economic and political affairs, and a belief in the

---

37. A. B. Hollingshead and F. C. Redlich, *Social Class and Mental Illness,* John Wiley & Sons, Inc., New York, 1958.

38. Robert Merton and Robert Nisbet, *Contemporary Social Problems,* Harcourt, Brace & World, Inc., 1961, pp. 17–18.

right of all individuals to those things for which their individual talents and virtues qualify them. Such conflicts in values can be seen in many parts of the world today. We see it in India where ancient values of family and caste are being challenged on a widening front by the values of individualism, democracy, and the scientific-technological order. We also see this conflict in our own society; it often occurs when families come from the traditional culture of Eastern Europe, Latin America, or the Middle East and settle in the more impersonal and secular atmosphere of an American city. Anomie, with its implicit tensions of moral conflict, alienation, and meaninglessness, is a notable and persisting aspect of the whole history of man.

## SOCIAL MOBILITY THROUGH EDUCATIONAL GUIDANCE

The open society, the society that promises each individual access to the benefits his talent warrants, may be myth in reality, but it is not a myth in intent. Educational ideology is clear on this point. Facilitation of this goal is a problem both of attitude and technique. Both are subject to sociological scrutiny. We cannot change the attitudes that inhibit a broader based mobility plan unless we recognize their dimensions and their source. Further, we cannot innovate on techniques until we discover the characteristics of persons that are predictive of educational success and are equally capable of manipulation.

If we grant the validity of the overwhelming evidence that suggests an environmental, rather than physiological, determinant of academic success, we are only one step away from an innovative approach to discovering talent. Up to the present, education has attempted to develop abilities as these were forced upon the attention of the educator. We worked with what we could observe. We knew of no other determinants and had not made the effort to discover them. The reason we had not made the effort heretofore was that education has always been limited in its perspective of the kinds of data on school students that could be useful. A comprehensive data system, including facts and observation on every school student, developed out of a multitude of ideas regarding relevant data, and, taken from a multidiscipline approach, was a necessary step. Currently murmurings of this necessity and certain proposed activities that would make this system a reality are being heard in educational quarters.

The following statement appeared in the abstracts of papers delivered at the Fifty-Seventh Annual Meeting of the American Sociological Society:

Samuel A. Stouffer, late professor of Sociology and Director of the Laboratory of Social Relations at Harvard University and Past President of the American Sociological Association, conducted basic and applied research on the process of social mobility for over a decade prior to his death. . . . In the course of his basic research, Stouffer became deeply concerned over the denial of opportunity and waste of human talent which he saw in the great career sorting, much of which occurs in the elementary and secondary school years. In order to help school personnel—especially guidance counselors—in their efforts to reduce the individual and social loss involved, Stouffer developed a unique school guidance questionnaire machine reporting system.[39]

## CONCLUSION

Sociologists are interested in education. As social scientists, some are primarily interested in explaining general social processes through the vehicle of regularities in educational behavior. Institutions have many structures in common, and discoveries made in one are frequently generalized to others. The knowledge uncovered in this way may have value to sociology in implementing its body of knowledge about social life and also to education as insights into dynamics that have been problematic to practitioners. The more we know about something, regardless of the perspective that supplies the information, the more likely it is that we may make intelligent decisions about ways of organizing personnel and tasks to solve specific problems.

Sociologists are also concerned with the effect of education on society. As men who have deep convictions about social justice and

---

39. Paper delivered at the annual meeting of the American Sociological Association, September, 1962, by Paul Shea of Harvard University.

egalitarian principles, they are gratified, as was Professor Stouffer, to apply their special skills to inquiries that will solve specific problems directly for schools and indirectly for the society in which they live. Sociological analysis is a technique that is, in itself, committed to exposing regularities, not injustices. But in most school systems there is some suspicion on the part of school personnel that sociologists want to utilize their tools to reveal system weaknesses, particularly in sensitive areas such as race relations, delinquency, and social class, so that the members of the institution will be exposed and dismissed. This is not only untrue, it is irrelevant. Either a technique provides an investigation with information that, in the first analysis, is objectively descriptive, or it does not. In the second analysis, the information may be explanatory; that is, certain relationships between variables will obtain. The results of these inquiries appear in scholarly journals that the public never reads and at the same time are made available to school personnel, who may decide how to use the findings if and as they wish.

Some areas of sociological inquiry may not be particularly relevant to students of education, or if they are, they apply in very special contexts. Knowledge of the structure and function of political systems, labor movements, or religious systems, for example, has not been included in this discussion, but the reader may wish to extend the considerations put forth here in his own way, as his special inclinations direct. The topic areas were those thought most relevant to the activities of the school and were intended as examples of the way in which sociological analysis can and has revealed knowledge that could be valuable to educational organization.

# CHAPTER 4

# THE FUNCTIONS AND
# DYSFUNCTIONS OF GUIDANCE

FUNCTIONAL ANALYSIS is and has been the predominant theme guiding the analysis of social systems. It asks that we look at separate segments of the individual system—a role, a value, a traditional pattern of interaction—and ask the following question: How does each segment contribute to the maintenance or survival of that system? What, for example, is the value of testing, of assigning homework, or of detentions in contributing to the survival of an educational system?

In seeking the functional attributes of various factors, social scientists had for many years been content to explain functions in terms of the evaluation of manifest outcomes. Specific results of traditional patterns were only looked at in terms of what they were expected to accomplish. The function of testing as an evaluative technique would be analyzed specifically in terms of what the institution of the school expected to do with the results of tests. If tests were intended to differentiate students for the purposes of grouping or of separating the college from non-college material and differentiation did occur, then the testing was functional. If students were not differentiated, then the testing would soon lose its utility and be discarded in favor of other techniques. Simply put, the viability of any cultural or system item is considered dependent upon the extent to which it serves a manifest function. A recognition of the concept of latent function can do much to change this attitude.

Anthropologists, among others, have been able to observe the extension of cultural traits and patterns beyond the point at which they appear to be functional to the structure of the group or system. In many investigations the functional analytic approach appears to be useless as no manifest function may be attached to certain behavioral patterns. An Indian rain dance, for example, may be quickly analyzed in terms of the attributable purpose of inducing rain and later discovered to be totally nonfunctional. It is even unlikely that the Indian participants believe any longer that they can influence the weather. An alternative view would be to appraise such a dance as simply a ceremonial with no conscious motivations supporting it. And without conscious motivations, functional analysis, in its earlier conception, would be irrelevant. But anthropologists and sociologists were unwilling to accept the notion that a cultural item could and would persist without serving the intended function. Like the Kosher rituals of the Jews, technologically unnecessary in an age of preservatives and refrigeration, the importance of ritualistic practices comes to reside in the function. Such practices served to maintain the solidarity and, hence, the viability of the group.

The application of latent-function analysis represents a significant step forward in the appraisal of institutional functions, and it is hoped that the application of this analysis will allow us to perceive aspects of the guidance function that will be both illuminating and instructive. It is also hoped that such analysis will point to directions for revision in operation and technique.

The emphasis of this chapter is upon the functions of education as these relate to guidance activities. The focus upon function is necessary in order to point up a concern with latent functions and dysfunctions. In order to talk about the latter two notions (latent functions and dysfunctions) we must describe educational goals such that the direct and indirect consequences of pursuing these goals can be described. Ultimately we turn to the functions of the guidance role and proceed with the same kind of analysis, in terms of latent functions and dysfunctions, that structures the first part of the chapter.

## THE PURPOSE OF LATENT-FUNCTION ANALYSIS

Robert Merton has specified several advantages that latent-function analysis has for the promulgation of sociological knowledge.[1] Not all these purposes are relevant to our interests in analyzing the guidance function, but at least two purposes are, and we shall consider these.

The first purpose of latent-function analysis that would concern a scholar looking at educational goals and functional activities is the idea that this approach clarifies the analysis of seemingly irrational social patterns. For example, several activities, beginning quite early in the school career of children, are directed toward developing an interest in pursuing some occupational goal. Despite clear evidence that most career choices are unrealistic before the high school years and are often unfortunate after that,[2] added to the fact that career decisions are class-linked for the middle classes and unreliable for the working classes, extensive guidance with related activities occurs to orient young students to specific occupations. Manifestly, the function of education and guidance in this endeavor would appear to be the accumulating of appropriate data upon which tentative career decisions may be made. These tentative decisions ordinarily contribute to ordering the course of study selection, avocational interests, and educational goals. The persistence of these guidance activities (they really cannot be called career or vocational activities because they occur much too early in the student's educational life) cannot be defended on the grounds of any validity criteria, as schools seldom attempt to research or evaluate the success or failure of such programs. But the school's function in this area, if we are to apply latent-function considerations to the problem, is not so much specific allocation to occupational roles as it is the instilling in the pupil of a commitment to perform such occupational tasks as will integrate him

---

1. Robert K. Merton, *Social Theory and Social Structure,* The Free Press, New York, 1956, pp. 60–72.
2. Donald Super, *Psychology of Careers,* Harper & Row, Publishers, New York, 1957.

into the economy on a citizenship basis. It then does not matter that the manifest motivations for the establishment of given activities are not clearly fulfilled, so long as the other, often more pervasive goals are being met. "Irrational patterns" may be too strong a way to describe the kind of activity discussed in this example, but as long as we may make the case that certain activities are ongoing as a guidance function either long after or in the absence of validation of their usefulness, the notion of a latent-function approach helps to order our understanding of the viability of those functional activities.

A second purpose discussed by Merton for the application of latent-function analysis is that such an approach precludes the substitution of moral judgments for scientific analysis. An excellent example of the kind of fallacious evaluations that are made of specific behavior patterns may be observed in a consideration of the specified issues of the Presidential election of 1964. The Goldwater campaign attempted to gain momentum on the issue of "moral decay" in the nation. There was no particular imputation that Lyndon Johnson was himself immoral in any way, but the campaign implied that Goldwater could do much to return the nation to a more traditional morality. Suppose that we were to focus upon this issue of moral decay and in some intelligent way evaluate as to their function, such behaviors as would fall into this category. We could begin by suggesting that while we accept the manifest function of activities such as gambling or prostitution to be based purely on the economic motivations of those persons controlling them, these activities are still morally "wrong" and in violation of either ethical or legal codes. This kind of analysis, however, does not help us to understand the existence of such behaviors insofar as they are apparently against the interests of the majority of the members of the society.

Let us examine the issue in another context. Within the confines of Catholic definitions of the responsibilities of marriage, prostitution and adultery are theoretically taboo. Nonetheless, within primarily Catholic countries such as France and Italy, these behaviors are common. If they were not, the traditional family system, held tightly together by the nonsanctioning of divorce, would perhaps explode into disruptive patterns similar to those in the United States. In this way, prostitution and adultery have the latent function of allowing marriages to continue in the traditional manner. This is one specific example of how latent-function analysis helps to explain behavior patterns. Along with the example from the 1964 election, it also shows how, if we wish to proceed scientifically to understand something, we are somewhat defeated if we attempt to evaluate it morally. What was called "moral decay" in that election may simply be a latent functional adaptation to changing social life.

The emergence of the delinquent gang, particularly those gangs composed of high school students, is a significant problem for the school, and if adjustive counseling is conceived of as being an important guidance activity, then these gang members could represent a large percentage of those with whom the counselor comes into contact. Theoretically, of course, adjustive counseling is held to be at the core of the guidance function. Operationally, we may presume that such counseling, at least in terms of quantity, is differentially available in different high schools. Perhaps, because of a larger range of perceived problems, those schools in communities where delinquent gangs are most likely to emerge should have well-trained counselors in greater quantity than schools in those communities where gangs do not develop. This is, however, not likely to be the case.

What is the function of the gang? It has, in most respects, the same function as nondelinquent peer groups. It provides both an area of independence and support for this independence. It provides a socialization function in areas that parents do not find easy, and predictably so, to handle. It serves as a recreational outlet. It provides information, clarification, and experience while students are implementing sex roles. Now, if this is the function of a group of peers and may be supported within normal friendship contexts, what becomes the special function of the delinquent gang? At this level of analysis, we begin with appropriate notions about the function of deviant behavior. If they steal, it is for the money. If they fight, it is to protect their "turf" or impinge on another. If they strike out against the establishment, it is to punish others or abstract ideas that they reject. In some senses, the behavior of the delinquent gang may be viewed from the perspective of a vendetta against a system that has betrayed the members of the gang. In other senses, the behavior is purely instrumental to concrete goals. In all, the delinquent gang is but one symptom of the "moral decay" about which well-meaning reformers speak.

Despite punishment, ostracism, failure, and limited rewards, the delinquent gang as a social phenomenon not only retains its membership today but proliferates in number, although not always in the same aggressive form as in the past. We may sometimes incline to judge delinquents' behavior in terms of a traditional ethical code, but this is not relevant to understanding the gang. Perhaps the best way of understanding what makes the gang a viable phenomenon is to analyze its function, employing the notion of latent functions in such a way that remedial techniques may be revealed and current operational mistakes avoided.

We might begin directly by suggesting that the latent function of delinquent gangs is to preserve the status egos of its members, not necessarily in competition with but as an alternative to satisfying the traditional expectations of contemporary industrial society. Ours is a performance- or achievement-oriented society. Integration into that society and mobility within it is highly correlated with an individual's capacity to compete successfully for the rewards. The capacity for competition is differentially distributed throughout the population. Without reference to the characteristics of those who are disadvantaged in the endowment of this capacity, it is sufficient to posit the fact that certain members are disadvantaged in this way. Ours is also a status-oriented society, and the manifest indicators of status are those rewards that accrue from meeting the rigorous expectations established by the industrial bureaucratic order. We have already discussed the achievement norms of the status society in our treatment of the Protestant Ethic. These are the values and expectations that make the system go, and status comes to be defined, actually, in terms of how well persons have lived up to the particular elaboration of the ethic in its unique institutional setting.

Within education there appears to be a unidimensional value system that establishes the prerequisites for status, although emphases will vary from school to school. The college-prep curriculum is more highly valued by the members of the system than the industrial-arts curriculum, as the former reveals a greater emphasis and realization of several of the core values of the Protestant Ethic: ambition, perseverance, industriousness, and high aspiration for personal fulfillment. As we have posited status as the crucial concept behind personal motivations in our system and as, presumably, most members of the adult world and just about all members of the nonadult society strive for it, we then have to see how the delinquent gang fulfills this function. Moreover, we would want to relate the values of the larger system to the values of the gang in such a way as to explain how status may be achieved in violation of the important values of the society.

Our conclusion should be becoming evident. Having failed in one system, certain persons require an alternative system, one that will confer status upon its members. But this explanation is still quite incomplete because a system requires a set of values around which status activities may be mobilized. We must therefore also explain how members who have failed in the general system may accept their need to move to an alternative system when they have already internalized the values of the original system. And this point particularly needs explaining because the values of the delinquent system are precisely the opposite of those of the general system. Here is where the notion of evaluation of self becomes an explanatory mechanism. Since preservation of the ego is important to those who have failed to achieve in the institutions' terms, rather than accept their failure they may preserve their egos by deciding that the goals were not worth anything in the first place. If school success is not valued, then school failure is not much of a failure. We must go one step further and identify the mechanism by which this rationalization of values becomes possible, and this takes us full cycle, exposing the latent function of the delinquent gang.

Once having decided upon an alternative system of values and a negation of the original values, the members of the gang must socially reinforce this negation. It becomes necessary for the members, first, to reward behavior in the new system so as to maintain it and, second, to act upon the new rationalized beliefs so intensively as to convince themselves that the beliefs are valid. The more the behavior violates the normative system, therefore, particularly in irrational ways that seem to serve no utilitarian purpose such as property destruction or unprovoked aggression, the greater the likelihood that the newly rationalized system is not sufficiently internalized. In time, however, delinquent behavior becomes established as the normative mode, and instrumental acts are systematically attempted. It is at this point that the gang begins to fragment into smaller groups with highly specific delinquent and, later, criminal purposes. The one original function, however, which we are using as an illustration of latent-function analysis, resides in the gang's capacity to support members through the transitional stages of shift from normative to delinquent modes. The gang's behavior is such that there is mutual reinforcement of behavior consistent with the new value structure.

## DYSFUNCTION

Our evaluation of whether or not we have achieved a stated goal is usually based on some observable criterion. Recidivism among criminals may be a criterion by which rehabilitative counseling may be evaluated. Pupil gain from pre-test to post-test may be a criterion for evaluating the success of teaching techniques.

Although education has traditionally applied very vague criteria to the limited amount of evaluation that occurs in schools, our concern is not with advancing the cause of more and better evaluation. We are only interested in proposing that the way we look upon educational functions be expanded to consider not only whether functions are being fulfilled but also the broad range of consequences, or perhaps even cost, of fulfilling these functions.

## DYSFUNCTIONS AND EDUCATIONAL GOALS

In analyzing educational tasks we have seen how the idea of latent functions expands our perspective. The notion of dysfunctional consequences provides a further analytical tool to aid our evaluative tasks. A dysfunction is an outcome detrimental to the unit of analysis, in our case, the school. The detrimental outcome occurs as a result of engaging in activities linked to the primary function. Some programs adopted to serve certain functions may have negative consequences for all members of the group, other programs may affect only part of the group in some negative way. Still other programs may have practically no dysfunctional consequences. We cannot understand any of these effects unless we are prepared to consider the dysfunctional dimension in evaluating our programs.

The guidance function is aimed at individualizing our whole approach to instruction, mental health, career mobility, and social maturity. The techniques involved derive logically from the function activities themselves. Our approach will be to consider separately each category and the techniques relevant to these categories. The techniques that we shall consider are those involving not only school counselors but those employed by all functionaries in the pursuance of these guidance-oriented goals. We must agree that the guidance activity requires a cooperative effort among all educational personnel, although we must admit in the beginning that certain dysfunctional consequences occur as a result of a lack of coordination involved in the task. For example, if individualizing academic instruction is one stated guidance goal, then the counselor's role is one of discovering the characteristics of individuals so that instruction may be directly related to these characteristics. If the activities of the counselor provide data that are misused or misinterpreted by teachers, the outcome is detrimental. The counselor may engage in several relevant activities. He may uncover techniques usually not available in schools for adducing important data on students; he may be required to translate these data in meaningful ways to parents and teachers so that instruction may be adapted; and he may further play the role of supporter or motivator of the student while the process is progressing. The potential for dysfunctional consequences is tied to the way these activities are incorporated into the overall program. Teachers must be willing and able to utilize data in individualizing instruction; specialists must be available to administer and interpret individual tests;

administrators must support the entire cooperative effort by coordinating the necessary interaction among teachers, specialists, and counselors.

## Instruction

Individualizing instruction is a meaningful idea in the abstract to most teachers. Operationally there are many difficulties. With larger groups than most teachers would like, the notion of individualizing may appear to be feasible only through operating with gross categories based upon their best understanding of the kinds of data on which individualizing proceeds. Teachers rely upon IQ scores in formulating instructional techniques; they are cognizant of socioeconomic and ethnic differences; they are aware of the role that the family plays in shaping many of the adaptations students make to school. If they should evaluate, even intuitively, the psychological, sociocultural, physiological, and educational data that are made available to them, they would find it excessively difficult to make really refined decisions about individualizing instruction. But it is a step in the right direction to assume that high IQ students learn in different ways and at different rates than low IQ students, that the same differences operate with poor and well-off, with majority and minority groups, and with students from presumably socially and emotionally stable homes and those from homes that are either physically or socially disorganized.

Although there is no invidious intent on the part of the teacher, students quickly perceive a differentiation occurring around instruction. Certain students are in one reading group and other students in another; one student is called upon to answer certain kinds of questions and another student other kinds; some students are given mechanical tasks and other students cognitive tasks or leadership tasks; some students are given more individual help than others and are asked to read other kinds of books in line with differentiated interests. These interests are ordinarily not only differentiated but also stratified. The whole process of attaching value to specific treatments of individuals enters into the sociometry of the group. From this point on, there may be dysfunctional consequences arising out of well-meaning classroom organization.

Before proceeding with an analysis of possible dysfunctions, we will answer a likely criticism of this discussion, which would be that other things than those we have mentioned are meant by "individualizing instruction." That may be, but the sociologist is only involved with observing behavior, with what appears to be happening in the classroom around certain functions. We may even admit that certain schools are organized efficiently enough to individualize instruction in line with the real intent of this notion. We are only concerned with suggesting a method of analysis, beginning with an evaluation of what is actually happening in classrooms, that will help us explore a more comprehensive range of consequences of educational practice than was possible without a consideration of dysfunctional consequences.

What, then, are the dysfunctional consequences that emerge out of attempts to individualize instruction? If evaluated differentiation of classroom members should occur, and there are many sociometric techniques to derive this, then several consequences are likely. First, there are variations of the halo effect in presuming a continuum of ongoing definitions of persons. At the far extreme is a definition of certain students as "problems" with all the emotional connotations that such a term has for teachers. The treatment of "problems" by teachers and students is considerably different from the treatment of "angels."

Second, there is the realization of the self-fulfilling prophecy. The definitions that others make of a person seep into his perception of himself. If he comes to define himself as a person who requires special help and attention, he will continue to require this help, denying the possibility that he can achieve in the same standard way that most other students achieve.

Finally, the most frequently conceived method for individualizing instruction is to work somehow through barriers to learning by attaching instructional techniques to student interests. We may presume that deep down every student is interested in something, but sometimes in digging around for these interests we latch on, in desperation, to some semblance of an interest far below the level of motivation. This approach is not only equivocal but blinds us to other approaches to student interest, and primarily to ways of creating such interest. More important, this process evolves into one technique of establishing an interest pattern from which teachers and ultimately counselors work to design a future for the child. This subject is more appropriately dealt with in the section on career mobility.

## Mental Health

Rather than worry about operationalizing the concept *mental health,* as we are not interested in raising empirical questions, we may proceed comfortably by suggesting a set of psychological states that would yield readily to scientific conceptualization if we were pushed to it. When persons talk about mental health, they ordinarily mean something close to what Maslow has called "self-actualization"[3] or what Allport meant in discussing his notion of "becoming."[4] Freud talked about the ability to work and love. Others whose concern is with breaking down generalized concepts talk about a necessary combination of indicators such as productivity, feelings of security, efficient perception of and comfortable relations with reality, feelings of making a contribution to a group, and, lately, the notions of creativity and autonomy.

It would not be difficult to raise the argument that guidance action directed toward the solution of this functional problem leads us, as a society, further away from this state than if the function were not presumed to be relevant to the guidance enterprise. If persons work for status and income only, if they love cautiously, if they are productive only as cogs in an industrial task, if they allow their actualization to be played out by actors in unrealistic media such as movies or television, if they feel no solidarity with the human family,

---

3. Abraham Maslow, *Toward a Psychology of Being,* D. Van Nostrand Co. Inc., Princeton, N.J., 1962.

4. Gordon Allport, *Becoming: Basic Considerations for a Psychology of Personality,* Yale University Press, New Haven, Conn., 1955.

if their creativity is withered on the vine of passivity and they need to be entertained, and if their mode is conformity, then all our concepts are myths and our function is something else that we do not readily admit.

What are our guidance techniques which are intended to produce this list of indicators of mental health or mental illness? Helping a student to understand his abilities in relation to his goals? This is a worthy task but is dysfunctional unless we somehow can contribute to the student's appreciation of the relativism of values of aspiration. Can we tell him that being a draftsman is as worthy a career as being an engineer in a world that negates this assumption?

We tell students that they are individuals with basic drives and needs, and we ask them what their drives and needs are so that they may inspect them and fulfill them. But having uncovered them, we are forced to couch our advice in such words of caution that their frustration may actually increase. They need to love and be loved, to touch and to be angry, to express their emotions, to feel a sense of independence. But what do we give them to provide these things? Expressive activities such as athletics and dance? Intellectualized comments about the human body, if even that? Sterile advice about responsibility when the need for independence is gnawing at them? Extracurricular activities that are highly supervised? Lectures on the goodness of other people? Perhaps the single most dysfunctional technique resides in the misuse of affect that is spilled out onto a group of small children by a mother surrogate who cannot possibly supply or even measure equally the amounts of affection that are distributed. This kind of affection breeds a dependency and spirit of sibling competition that persists into adulthood. The children learn their independent roles and the source of belonging in such a spurious manner that a vacuum is created and millions of them later marry and have children of their own for all the wrong reasons, reasons that frequently lead to resentment, confusion, and divorce.

There are in some schools courses, often taught by a part-time counselor, that go into such issues as love, marriage, and family life. But how do we live with idealized concepts such as *togetherness* when the basic issues of individuality have never been resolved? Where do students learn that opposites do not attract and that the dangers of family competition in every sphere of marriage, including competition for the affection of the children, are very real? The fact that discussion in such courses becomes restricted in the interests of happy community relations does not negate the value of such projects, but it does sabotage them to the extent that confusion is as great and perspective is as distorted after the interchange as before.

We attempt to engender productivity, a sense of making a contribution, to enhance feelings of self-worth, but do we retreat from the mold of patronizing certain attempts by maintaining our systems of esteem based upon a hierarchy of contributions? How do we resolve the stigma attached by members of the group to certain kinds of contributions that not only are assigned as low values but also define the contributing persons to the group?

Our principal techniques consist of accumulating reams of data, case-history data as well as psychometric, which we evaluate, and of then making some decision about psychological barriers to educational progress. This in itself may be dysfunctional insofar as it keeps the "problem" glued to some established criterion of satisfactory counseling that may be the source of the difficulty to begin with. If we begin with the assumption that good grades are desirable, and here we have a student with high potential whom we label an "underachiever" because he is not achieving good grades, then we presume that some deficiency resides in the person rather than in the system in which he is failing. Perhaps it is the system, its unidimensional standards and short-sightedness, that is the source of the difficulty, and given another system of approach and reward, the psychic block could be relieved. Here we may have reached an untenable Utopian impasse, for what does one propose as an alternative system? The extent to which the idea is Utopian may only be uncovered by a moratorium on fixed standards. The point is really one of questioning the degree to which we attach our conceptions of mental health to reasonable functioning within a system that for many is highly unreasonable.

We espouse innovation and creativity in students and provide an increasing variety of materials for their creative manipulation. What are we doing in the area of evaluating creativity so that special and individual arts may be pursued independently of some overriding generality that we use to assess creative persons? Do we seek creative persons or creative acts? And what does it say about our honest appreciation of these lofty goals of encouraging creativity when after forty-five minutes of finger painting we stress cleaning up and beginning the arithmetic lesson? Sometimes cleanliness may be incompatible with creativity, and those who have internalized this value would rather be clean than creative. Have we assessed the value of routinized scheduling as this may affect creativity? The dysfunctional outcomes of our abortive efforts are to practice creative behavior in an atmosphere that ordinarily sends students into unresolved ambivalences about their inclinations to be creative. These ambivalences, as we know, are typically resolved in the direction of living in a system that is well ordered, clean, and highly predictable, so that individual initiative is seldom called forth except in the area of doing more of what everybody else is doing.

Erich Fromm[5] and David Riesman[6] have characterized our society as a sick society, and if this is true, the mental health of which Maslow, Allport, Freud, Rogers, and others speak would not only be anomalous but dysfunctional in itself if one wished to live at peace with his fellows. They have proposed the notion of autonomy to suggest a compromise of the healthy man with his time and place. Any attempt on the school's part to produce an autonomous personality would involve a built-in consideration of how we may live harmoniously with ourselves and at the same time in a society that expects behaviors that conflict with this harmony. Without both, our attempts would be dysfunctional in the way suggested. Perhaps this is the stage we have achieved at best. Our best guidance-oriented functions may be accomplishing something in the area of developing a sense of responsibility to oneself, to be complete and fulfilled, to seek humanitarian goals, to discover our best creative talents, to work and love

---

5. David Riesman, *The Lonely Crowd,* Yale University Press, New Haven, Conn., 1961.

6. Erich Fromm, *Escape from Freedom,* Holt, Rinehart & Winston, Inc., New York, 1941.

with complete trust in our capacity to do both. Might this not be a case of sending a Christ or a Gandhi to be crucified in an alien world? Although goals and accomplishments may be dysfunctional to persons, they may yet be worthy, and this last discussion should exemplify the case. The guidance function may need to take cognizance of the fact that the job, so far, is incomplete if its purpose is to produce a healthy person. Ultimately, a generation of healthy graduates may build a world in which we need not escape from freedom. Until then, the function may require an extensive evaluation of the prerequisites of mental health and survival.

Finally, many of the dysfunctional consequences of guidance techniques used in reducing mental illness may be laid at the door of inadequate evaluation. The absence of a rigorous, disciplined approach to evaluating a person's progress has led to an ad hoc approach based partly on educational progress and partly on counselor intuition. The responsibility of the educational guidance counselor in the area of mental illness may be limited. To quote one source, the concern of counselors "is with clients in the normal range."[7] With this in mind, we may agree without any hindrance to our analysis of the problem. Mental illness, if we choose to define it as such, and it becomes our responsibility to do so, involves many of the student problems counselors face daily. There are in the "normal range." Problems of chronic anxiety, psychoneurosis, or psychosis will require referral, but mental illness must be considered a category that includes more problems than these. An extreme position suggested earlier is that the whole of society is sick.[8] The connotation here is that mental illness is any human condition that restricts persons from living satisfying, productive lives, given that the economic order does not by definition restrict this possibility, as in the case of the desolate millions in India.

Let us grant that we are seeking solutions to normal-range personal problems that restrict adequate educational functioning. If we presume that a student who increases his grade performance while

---

7. Milton Hahn and Malcolm MacClean, *Counseling Psychology,* McGraw-Hill Book Company, New York, 1955, p. 11.
8. Erich Fromm, *op. cit.*

undergoing counseling is an example of success, then we may be sacrificing the advantage that our contact with the student could have had over the long haul. For any methodologist recognizes the inadequacy of inferring success from a treatment based upon a circumstance that might have had many sources or causations. But we are so bogged down in our task, so overburdened with wholly inadequate pupil-counselor ratios, that we do not have the foresight to see how an absence of tested criteria restricts the development of the field, on the one hand, and blinds us to possible broader preventive techniques, on the other. The support of a mental-health function for guidance does not preclude a traditional one-to-one relationship, but if learning the adaptive modes to improve one's educational performance at one point in time is our guiding criterion, the disadvantaged student becomes forced into the same routinized educational mold that is so dysfunctional to the grander plan of generalized mental health in our society.

## Career Mobility

Career mobility begins early and is an interinstitutional process. The family, the church, and the peer group all help to set the motivational basis with which the school begins to define and to prepare students for fitting into occupational roles. It is logical, given the emphasis industrial societies place upon adaptive occupational functions, that the school has assumed certain responsibilities. This function for the school lies very close to the core of educational counseling. The focus upon personality development and minor neurotic problems is but a recent appendage to the guidance function. This function begins in elementary school when students are asked to devise a notebook about a given career and are advised by teachers to choose some career that interests them. This is a small, insignificant beginning perhaps, but when one looks at the total educational emphasis on this orientation, the dysfunctions become readily apparent.

A good place to begin this discussion is with the student looking at the outside world for which the school wishes to ready him. How does he see this world from his vantage point? He sees it populated by identifying labels: postman, milkman, lawyer, business man, doctor, teacher, and a mass of blue-collar workers. Later, he comes to enlarge his definition of occupational roles to include status. Much later, he begins to differentiate statuses within statuses, the surgeon from the general practitioner, the foreman from the assembly-line man. People for the most part are workers. This is industrial society's definition reduced to its smallest unit of perception, the young school child. The impersonal definitions of persons in an industrial society begin with large labels and proliferate into smaller ones. The difference between rural and urban society in this context is the number and inclusiveness of defining labels.

We have already discussed the notion of the dysfunctions of differentiation of the student population in another context. It is chiefly within the realm of differentiating for purposes of occupational allocation that the greatest dysfunctions occur. This is true not only for those who are assigned inferior status but also for many who are assigned superior status. In the middle of the twentieth century, the greatest dysfunctions might be attributed to those who have been assigned middle status in our ever widening concern for differentiation. Let us treat these three status categories separately, as different kinds of dysfunctions are involved.

**THE LOW STATUS STUDENT**

The North-Hatt Occupational Prestige Scale,[9] derived from a randomly sampled cross section of the American public, represents the valuations of occupations by these persons. The study involved 3,000 adults, who were asked to evaluate the prestige of ninety occupations during 1946. Since there was a considerable range of occupational types represented in the sample, the evaluation could not be said to reflect any class bias. We have evidence that an occupational rating system is part of the human consciousness, but we cannot be certain when the configuration of status, aspiration, and occupation begins to

---

9. Leonard Reissman, *Class in American Society,* The Free Press, New York, 1959, pp. 152–155.

solidify in the child's mind. It is almost certain, however, that these definitions are made by the time that the student begins to choose his educational curriculum in secondary schools. Since the dominant cultural goal in American society is status, measured by income and the social power that prestigeful occupations confer, we may infer that the dominant instrumental mode either centers around or is closely tied with occupations. Eugene Weinstein studied the process and fact of social stratification in the perceptions of elementary school children.[10] He varied the age and social-status sampling to trace developmentally the onset of definitions of adult status and to see if differences appeared between the children of different socioeconomic statuses. His findings indicated that as age and grade level increased, the criteria for evaluation broadened but that the one criterion all groups at each age level held in common was that of occupation. When asked for their criteria of status, the children make answers like the following: "Their jobs." "What does he do for a living?" "If he's a factory worker or something like that."[11] Some status differences appeared in the evaluation of occupations. Low status children tended to regard skilled occupations such as electrician and carpenter as being a fairly high status job while middle class students stuck primarily to the professions in designating their perceptions of high status occupations.

The dysfunctional consequences of encouraging low status children to consider skilled occupations as worthy of their aspirations is that many of these occupations are being replaced by automation. Certainly, as Weinstein's data indicate, evaluations are relative to the focus of perception, and it is in the maintenance of this relativism that the schools declare themselves willing to settle for different ceilings for different classes of students. This seems to be the commonsense educational solution to the problems of aspiration, but because the solutions are always ad hoc to begin with, a changing social structure such as ours may easily make ad hoc programs inappropriate. Unfortunately, the adaptive mode of both education and government

10. Eugene Weinstein, "Children's Conceptions of Adult Stratification," *Sociology and Social Research,* vol. 42, no. 4, 1958.
11. *Ibid.,* p. 279.

continues to be geared toward solving problems either as they appear or as continuing difficulties in the system suddenly become a platform for educational or political reformers. An obvious case in point is the current concern for the children of the disadvantaged; the forces of change in this area, however, are looking for bandaids rather than preventive inoculations.

Our major assumption underlying the analysis of dysfunctions for students who appear to be headed for the least prestigeful occupations is that their definition of themselves is pejorative and clearly affects motivation. Persons in a given social system typically rely upon others for self-definition, so that tentative self-assessments based upon individual evaluation of cultural goals and one's relation to them is reinforced by the behavior of others. The value of one's social context is substantially considered in David Nasatir's chapter of this book, Chapter 9. The presumption here might be that the important mechanism influencing the dropout is the fact of comparing himself to others around him. This certainly appears to be the problem in schools where students of varying abilities are differentiated from each other yet thrown into a context where invidious distinctions are constantly being made. This behavior of others, as much research has tended to demonstrate, takes the form of evolving clique structures and forcing into isolation those who do not have highly valued qualities, either familial, extracurricular, or purely academic.[12] For the low status student, esteem may be attained only through alternative systems such as those mentioned in the discussion of the formation of the delinquent gang. Other alternatives are to concentrate exclusively on extra-school relations and, for females, to orient themselves to a role that appears to be above invidious evaluations, that of housewife.

Low status is a burden to students, and like others with burdens, these students look for and gather with birds of a feather. This is dysfunctional because social mobility is often a function of associating with a peer group with heterogeneous qualities and aspirations. It is through integrated peer groups that the qualities of the best rub off

---

12. See Hollingshead, *Elmtown's Youth,* John Wiley & Sons, Inc., New York, 1949, and C. W. Gordon, *The Social System of the High School,* The Free Press, New York, 1957.

onto those who seem to lack these qualities. It is here that style and manner come through so that a person may adopt a certain pose that causes others to treat him in a desirable way. Despite certain dysfunctions of fraternities and sororities, which it is not necessary to describe here, the mobility function of this kind of interaction is useful.

The intrinsic value of certain occupational activities not highly valued in a status-seeking society becomes lost to those who have to engage in these activities. It is difficult to have pride in work for its own sake when the society sees pride only as a function of income and status. This is not only unfortunate for the role occupants but equally unfortunate for the population that has to rely upon their services. It is impossible to regain the pride of artisanship in a bureaucratized assembly-line society, but the school, as a vehicle of socialization, could instill a sense of pride in productive work if we could somehow find the mechanism that would allow us to dispel status differentials. One example of a possible procedure would be to build a bright new shiny industrial arts school, communicate the idea that students will only be accepted on a competitive basis, and never accept the idea that the school is to be used as a receptacle for those who cannot compete successfully in academic subjects. It is certain that a real concern about status images does considerable harm to the valuable goal of producing a labor force with pride in its capacities and service, particularly at the level of non-professional occupations.

One of the most serious mistakes, it would appear, that has been made in our efforts to accommodate the national need for trained scientists has been education's push to raise the standards of scientific achievement in the schools. This action logically increases the number of those who fail in the system even though the better students may be pushed to achieve more than in the past. A search for talent is certainly an important activity, but if the kind of talent required by the society is bought at the cost of degrading the performance of the marginal student, then the price is too high. An intelligent and purposeful plan should always accompany innovations, and this plan should concern itself not only with the manifest goals for which the plan was inaugurated, such as the raising of academic standards, but also with the consequences for those who do not meet the revised expectations. The problem of innovation in education is that we attempt to fit new ideas into old structures. If we could foresee the dysfunctional consequences of new ideas within traditional structures, we might see a way of reorganizing the structure. We could, for example, surrender our universalistic standards and single criteria and, instead, structure a set of curricula around standards and criteria that are not viewed as weaker or stronger, better or worse, but simply as different. This could be indicated when students of the same statuses have performed very differently on the same tasks and made dissimilar choices of activities and programs. This step might require an abandonment of traditional grading systems, which is already being tried experimentally in some places. However, even a nongraded school becomes a meaningless innovation unless it is logically tied to implementing specific goals or avoiding the dysfunctional consequences of traditional educational structures.

## THE MIDDLE STATUS STUDENT

The middle status student is the one who moves through the grades holding occupational aspirations similar to those of the students who will predictably have successful college careers. He does not, however, exhibit the ability that would place him in a position where access to universities is easy. He may be either an overachiever who, but for excessive motivation, would have fallen into the low status group, or he may be an underachiever who, but for lack of motivation, would have fallen into the high status group. Most of these students come from a background that expects from them a college degree and a career commensurate with this degree. With this background they ordinarily remain in the academic or college preparatory curriculum only to find, in a time of extreme competition for college entrance, all the obvious avenues closed. High school counselors spend much of their time finding colleges where such students may continue their education. These activities are a natural outgrowth of solving some of the dysfunctional consequences of the stratified status system that schools help to perpetuate.

Psychologically, these students are men in the middle. They can-

not attain the pinnacle of professionalism, and they have been socialized not to be able to accept an identification with vocational careers.
What can a guidance counselor do with them? Three avenues appear
typical. First, he may help them find a four-year college whose standards are such that access is possible and the likelihood of survival
high. Second, he may encourage them on to a four-year college with
the expectation, communicated in a mature way with available data,
that they will not survive the four years. Third, and this seems to be
the predominant contemporary mode, he may encourage them to enter junior colleges with the expectation that they will explore their
aspirations while not losing time toward a college degree. If they
prove themselves in the junior college, they may transfer easily to a
four-year institution. If they do not, they have simply extended their
high school education by two years and possibly attained valuable vocational training. Generally, the dysfunction of any of these plans
centers around the likelihood that many of these persons are chasing
status symbols rather than a productive life. By the time they are confronted with the reality of their abilities, they have already gone down
a long path and must retrace many steps. It is not likely, even though
they retrace their steps, that they will ever be able to completely accept a lower status career than that to which they were conditioned
to aspire.

The junior college in America is an interesting case of the way
educational organization responds in order to accommodate problems
that never should have arisen in the first place. Burton Clark[13] has
designated the activities of the junior college, in relation to our theme
of dysfunction, as the "cooling-out function." This function presumes
an emphasis on diminishing aspiration for students. It is conceived as
a two-year period during which many students are encouraged to consider, for instance, careers as technicians rather than electrical engineers. This is not to say that this is the only function of the junior
college. Many students are realistic, and for the lower status students
in the high school, the junior college is one of the best avenues for
social mobility available in our system.

---

13. Burton Clark, "The Cooling-Out Function in Higher Education," *American
Journal of Sociology,* vol. 65, May 1960, pp. 569–576.

The middle status student lives with a kind of marginality that forces him to attempt to adopt the characteristics of high status students while at the same time considering the realities he must live with if he does not make the grade. Counseling these students in junior and four-year colleges becomes an important function of higher education, and at times unavoidable mistakes made at the secondary level may be corrected. The question remains, however, as to how we may buttress our counseling efforts at the secondary level so that an excess of commitment, accompanied by dubious capacities to achieve commensurate with that commitment, be conscientiously checked before excessive alienation and psychologically harmful frustration develop.

## THE HIGH STATUS STUDENT

Those students who, through their high aspirations and adequate abilities, manage to achieve a high status position within the school are potential victims of a self- and other-designated determinism. They are told, and come to know through many tangible and intangible sources, that their futures are bright, that they will, through effort and perseverance, attain lofty goals in occupational areas highly valued by their society. Many of them, because of competition for college access and because schools require some kind of general career decision early in the student's secondary education, make decisions that are irreversible. It is often not until the middle of the college years, when students begin questioning the direction of their lives, that a disruption in direction takes place. Unless the disruption is significantly dramatic, the student ordinarily resolves the conflict by going on to finish what he has started. This industriousness is another value that usually accompanies ambition and status seeking in the psychology of high school students. For many of these high status students, the decision to continue is made simply because the cost attending a shift in curriculum appears to be too great a price to pay for a change of mind.

Others experience a similar disruption once career goals are attained, when the costs involved in a switch in career are even greater than for the student. At this point a family is often being maintained and economic comforts that were awaiting the completion of long academic training are being realized. Many college advisors are certainly aware of the vast numbers of persons who talk to them about planning a new career by taking the preparation very slowly and finishing after the children are "on their own."

The source of potential dysfunctions involving high status students lies in the inability of educators to control the consequences of the invidious distinctions that are made regarding choice of curriculum. The effect of peer-group expectations must influence many persons to sign up for an academic or college preparatory course of studies when their interests lie with commercial activities. The power of seeking and retaining group approval is strong and has been mentioned several times as an important concept in explaining educational dysfunctions. It is possible that members of a tightly knit clique choose not only a high school curriculum that will keep all together but also specific careers and specific schools in which to pursue advanced training. Despite the fact that we have made only slight advances in discovering ways to accomplish a best fit between individual personality and the social personalities of colleges, the mere fact that we are working toward this indicates that we recognize that different schools are best for different persons.

A male member of a high status peer group is unlikely to choose a career in teaching. This suggests that the invidious occupational distinctions that permeate the thinking of college-bound students reach beyond the considerations already discussed and involve distinctions regarding sex as well as college curricula. The dysfunctions of this form of structuring goals are well known to educationists who are concerned about the "feminization" of teaching.

## SOCIAL MATURITY

When cumulative records, or case records, were conceived as a necessary adjunct to the organization of a guidance function, there was very little rigorous training coordinated within the school by which teachers could assist counselors through documenting information that would be of use in the counseling venture. Most schools make some attempt to impress teachers with the importance and usefulness of this task. The writer has observed in over forty schools in an advanced educational system how deficient teacher comments are, however, in providing useful data for pupil guidance. One teacher was permitted, over a period of ten years, to discharge his responsibilities in this area with comments confined to "good," "O.K.," and "bad." The dysfunctions of cumulative folders themselves will be discussed in the last part of this chapter. The issue is being raised here only as a way of representing the definition most educators hold of social maturity. Any observer of these records will perceive a legion of descriptive comments like "socially immature" or "socially mature." In some cases these comments will be extended by such statements as "doesn't work well in groups," "keeps to himself," or "always takes an active leadership role in the group," the last representing an indicator of social maturity. Social maturity, in educational terms, appears to be strongly tied to the issue of being integrated into a group. Any resistance to this integration, either through withdrawal or aggression, presumably reflects social immaturity. The guidance function seems geared to help a student find his place in the educational society of students as a way of encouraging him ultimately to fit comfortably into the society at large. Certain definite assumptions underlie this goal and the techniques utilized to accomplish it. First, there is the assumption that the individual requires the fellowship of others to sustain him in his social life. Second, there is the belief that cooperative participation is the foundation of the democratic principle and that individuals will be rewarded personally in that participation. Thirdly, it is assumed that a feeling of belonging is conducive to the mental health of the individual. And fourth, there is the belief that a person in isolation cannot survive the social sanctions imposed by his fellows.

For the most part these assumptions are sound on logical grounds, as are all the goals of the individualized-education emphasis. They may be incorrect for some persons at certain times in their developmental life, but this is not a serious objection. Any function within a large institutional framework must proceed on the basis of generalizable principles such as those that guide the stated assumptions. As was the case with the other categories discussed, dysfunctional consequences occur as a result of functional implementations. It is conceivable that goals alien to American democratic ideals may have, under implementation, very positive consequences for members of the system. An exploited, apathetic population may be aroused to acts of purposeful democratic liberalism under the implementation of totalitarian goals, a major case in point being the American Revolution. What we do in terms of our adopted functions is essentially the mechanism by which dysfunctions occur. Any evaluation of the functions themselves, although legitimate in the sense of making judgments about goals that are or are not worthwhile, lies in the realm of philosophic inquiry. Sociological analysis is confined to the observations we may make about the behaviors of groups in an ongoing social system.

One function of the social group has been to socialize members as to appropriate modes of behavior and then to sustain the members in the enactment of these behaviors. The point at which persons who have been socialized adequately to normative expectations no longer need the sustenance and approval of significant peers differs for different types of persons. Some types may relinquish a strong affiliation early in their development. Others may never have the capacity to strike out for social independence and will consistently rely upon a supportive peer group for cues to behavior. Social independence is a condition of autonomy, a peaceful coexistence between persons and their social world. This condition is seldom one of open conflict, except in circumstances where personal commitment to independence in certain social areas is challenged. We have always preached standing up for our rights and principles, which is not necessarily inconsistent with expectations to live harmoniously with our fellows. In our time, however, we are finding it increasingly difficult not to operate as if these attitudes were inconsistent. In the name of harmonious group affiliation, we are pressing students into the mold of group living, perhaps damaging irreparably their capacities for autonomy. Symptoms of this reliance on group sustenance are seen not only in the conformity that has captured most of us but even in the conformity of those who seek deviant groups as escapes from traditional expectations.

Some of the norms of group identification are interesting to consider in the light of a discussion of dysfunctional consequences. To paraphrase as well as recite some typical slogans, we could have "don't be a rate buster," "my group right or wrong," "one for all and all for one." Put in this way, doctrinaire group affiliation leads not only to sustenance but also to restraint, perhaps even deference. Deferring one's individuality for the maintenance of the group may be functional to the ongoing system but may indeed be dysfunctional to the individual. To put the matter slightly differently, without requiring this deference neither the group nor the individuals are restrained. If, in our efforts to develop social maturity, we rely upon group affiliation to provide the servicing mechanism and do not consider the ways in which restraint may be avoided, we are simply solving one problem but engendering another. This may not necessarily be the case, but the considered effect of group affiliation upon different types of persons needs evaluation.

The second assumption that requires scrutiny is that persons receive rewards as a result of group participation. In practice, however, most members of groups do not participate in a contributing way, except as followers. In some senses it seems that the major function of a group is to provide an arena for certain individuals to assert their leadership qualities. It is only in a very ideal sense that groups are constructed in which each member finds a meaningful role. There are, after all, only so many roles for persons to play, unless we artificially divide the labor so that everybody does something. Most groups, in actuality, operate either in terms of a few leaders or contributors and many followers or in terms of individual initiative conducted in isolation. Few teachers have such adequate expertise in group dynamics that group members of a class may all gain a feeling that they have contributed meaningfully. If contribution becomes the criterion by which persons feel they are being evaluated, then the whole competitive system begins to operate so as to create an atmosphere in which students attempt to degrade the contribution of others so as to uplift the value of their own. A consequence of group participation may be a feeling of reward in group accomplishment such as we perceive on an athletic team, but on the whole the manipulation of groups leads to competition for leadership, alienation due to a feeling of meaninglessness when the threads of the group task are loosely woven, or powerlessness when the control of the group and its goals are in the hands of others.

It would seem, in a competitive society such as ours, that the best technique for mobilizing a cohesive and cooperative spirit is to define an enemy so that group activity brings the rewards of victory. This has dysfunctional consequences also. Unfortunately, the major consequence of group membership seems to be the creation of a flock conception of self, which, while maintaining a mechanism for conformity, may easily suppress inclinations for individuality. When counselors advise that students should be given a role to play within some kind of group activity as a way of developing social maturity, it is at best a random and overly generalized technique by which some persons find gratification and others a deeper feeling of resentment than when they were being left alone. The consequences of group membership are unpredictable for the individual.

The third assumption about the group is that a feeling of belonging is conducive to mental health. Mental health is presumed to mean the security that accrues from mutual support. There are at least two dangers inherent in this assumption, although, as with the other assumptions, the achievement of an ideal affiliation by which mental health goals are accomplished is desirable. The first danger is that the price for mutual support may be as detrimental to mental health as the value of support is good for it. Personal goals and needs are subordinated to the expectations of the group, and the self-actualization of which we spoke earlier is impossible without establishing a posture of autonomy that for most young people is almost impossible of realization, given the anxieties of identity in children and adolescents. The second danger is that the group defines for persons those activities that are acceptable. Any choices that are then apparent to the individual are only those subject to the range of behaviors acceptable to the group. While a person is looking for cues as to what is or is not acceptable, a state of continuing anxiety emerges centering around the dangers of making unacceptable choices. In David Riesman's terms, anxiety is the vehicle by which other-directed societies are locomoted.[14] In the sense of using anxiety to produce conformity, personal psychological difficulties such as doubt or guilt about one's own capacities are substituted for by the anxieties inherent in constantly maneuvering for group approval. In the long run, the probabilities of resolving individual problems are greater than those of resolving group-linked problems. Togetherness, in the sense and mode of normative conformity, seldom allows the kind of rebellion that most psychologists agree is necessary for the development of a self that enjoys the independence that is synonymous with maturity.

## MANIFEST FUNCTIONS, LATENT FUNCTIONS, AND DYSFUNCTIONS OF GUIDANCE ROLES

Having presented an overall evaluation of the functions and dysfunctions of the guidance enterprise in education, as these relate to the goals that have evolved through the maturing of the field, we can advance our analysis further by looking at the roles of the school counselor. Each role presumes a specific function, and we can look at these roles independently of the part each plays in the solution of some general guidance problem.

The composite ideal counselor plays many roles. At times, when funds to pay more than one salary are available, a division of labor may be achieved and certain roles differentiated. This does not affect our present analysis as we are considering the various roles separately. The important roles in any organization of a guidance program are the following:

1. Data collector.
2. Evaluator.
3. Record keeper.
4. Advisor-predictor.

---

14. D. Riesman, *op. cit.*

5. Disciplinarian.
6. Parent surrogate.
7. Integrator.

This list is certainly not exhaustive. It is, however, comprehensive enough to allow for an adequate examination of the counselor role in terms of function, which is our concern.

These categories may be treated conceptually as independent roles, although practice dictates that they are segments or dimensions of a single role. As specialization increases, and social history gives every indication that all occupational life embraces specialization, then these categories may soon be separated and combined into two or three functions that are logically related, such as data collector, tester, and evaluator. The following evaluation of the role of the counselor, to be precise, is a discussion of the functions of role segments. The notion of function assumes that some specific activity, in this case a role segment, is positively related to some system that is the structure by which goals are attained. The latent function of role segments refers to those outcomes not manifestly expressed as the purpose of the activity. In order to talk about outcomes, we cannot be restricted to a discussion of ideal purposes of each activity. An outcome is discovered by pausing from time to time to evaluate, as the discussion will lead us to points at which the consequences of a certain activity appear to be a function of violating either the intention or the techniques theoretically most desirable in the performance of the role segment.

## Data Collector

Four kinds of data appear to be relevant to the performance of the role of data collector. Insofar as this work is prescriptive, which is not its manifest purpose, a consideration of the categorization of relevant data may be helpful to the counselor. Any decisions made by school counselors regarding the welfare of students are presumably made with the best and maximum amount of data available. This principle applies in any decision-making process, as well as in any scientific or quasiscientific venture. The kind of problem always dictates the kind of data that is relevant. The counselor's problem suggests the relevance of (*a*) physiological, (*b*) psychological, (*c*) sociocultural, and (*d*) educational data.

Physiological data are any information about the physical properties of the counselee. These data are accumulated through physical examinations, health records, and intensive interviews with the student and his parents. Data on hearing, eyesight, weight, height, history of diseases, deformities, and coordination are examples of relevant physiological material.

Psychological data involve objective observations about individual behavior. This material is collected from a range of sources including observations made by the counselor. Psychometric materials that provide insight into feeling patterns—personality tests, including projective tests, and essays written or drawings made by the student in class—are useful means of collecting these data.

Sociocultural data involve material about the background of the student. His race, nationality, religion, family size, voluntary associations, community, parents' occupations, physical and social mobility patterns of the family, as well as any incidences of divorce or social disorganization within the family are examples.

Educational data are those facts about the student's progress in school, including all psychometric data at any time derived in order to place the student educationally. Grades, particularly grade patterns, scores on achievement tests, intelligence tests, occupational-interest inventories, participation in school activities, both curricular and extracurricular, and curriculum choice are examples of this kind of data.

Data collection that considers scientific objectivity and completeness a goal is the ideal manifest function when certain facts are pursued more extensively than others and consequently emphasized more. Schools may take cues for organization and persons may be fitted into school organization according to the kind of data considered most relevant. If sociocultural data predominate, as in the case of culturally deprived youth, then the role of the counselor becomes integrative. If psychological data predominate, perhaps because the counselor sees his role increased in professional stature through identification with the clinical professions, as was the case revealed by Cicourel and Kitsuse's work discussed in the next chapter, then the counselor's function may preclude resolution of certain kinds of problems through structured social organization. When physiological data are emphasized, the solution of student problems may lead to activities that increase the emphasis on health and physical education in the school so that all aggressive students may be given physical outlets and nervous students calmed by hot showers. The emphasis on educational data stabilizes the value and precision of educator judgments and test results, maintaining the system in its present form.

The process of data collection, as it occurs in most schools today, is almost in the form of an assumption or set of assumptions about what is important and what the school should do. It is a latent function only in the sense that it serves to maintain these assumptions in such a way that the available pupil personnel services continue in the ways most suitable to the capabilities of the present personnel.

*Evaluator*

Evaluation, as a role segment, involves clarifying the meaning of data by which counseling proceeds and judging the results of the counseling activity. Put more simply, what is the problem, and has the problem been solved or reduced as a result of the counseling process? One of the latent functions of evaluation, in the sense of interpretation of the problem, is that it frequently maintains the practice that is available, thereby restricting alternatives to those within the existing educational structure. That is, the interpretation of the problem is influenced by the facilities the school has available to deal with it. Frequently, such an interpretation is made with the ongoing needs of the system as the unit of analysis rather than the needs of the student. When constant classroom disruption is the situation that provokes a referral to the counselor, the extent to which the emphasis on the classroom influences interpretation of the problem becomes a key determinant of the consequent counseling activity. In this sense, the latent function of evaluating often becomes the retention of a mass-production educational philosophy, by which defects are sorted out, rather than the introduction of an integrative philosophy, by which defects are seen as legitimate educational responsibilities. Performance of the evaluator role segment often accords with the philosophy of the school rather than with that of the profession. What, for example, is the meaning of classroom disruption? Does meaning hinge upon maintenance of administrative organization or upon some professional ethos dealing with the meaning of his behavior to the student?

The whole question of meaning is crucial to our conception of evaluation. The word itself implies attaching value to something. When we ask what something means, such as a specific aggressive behavior or the results of an achievement test, we are implying that behavior and scores have a certain value that may be designated in terms of a cluster of values that represent the system. Actually, the criteria themselves by which the success of counseling is determined are generated out of the values of the institution. If a student raises his grade or ceases to disrupt the class, these behaviors are taken as indicative of successful counseling. Showing insight into one's problems or making realistic decisions, on the other hand, are difficult to measure, and such criteria for evaluation are influenced by professional considerations rather than the concerns of the system. The process of evaluation cannot proceed in a vacuum; therefore, the question of which values predominate and influence the meaning attached to behavior is a serious issue. It is the kind of issue that actually exposes the latent functions being serviced by the role segments in counseling, particularly that of the evaluator. The latent function of evaluation, then, appears to be that it maintains the important values of the school as an ongoing institution, whereas the manifest function is simply to interpret data and judge outcomes so that prognosis and evaluation of counseling may proceed in individual terms.

## Record Keeper

Securing and recording a body of facts about students has been, at best, a haphazard educational activity. At worst, it has been totally ignored. Accumulating records on students—we will not concern ourselves at this stage with their use—has typically been a charge of the classroom teacher. The role that counselors have played in this activity has been slight, except for records kept on students who have been in the counselor's office over a period of time regarding some specific problem. In some progressive systems well-trained counselors make a special effort to instruct and advise teachers in the techniques of record keeping. This is a special case.

Record keeping on individuals is a legitimate guidance activity, functional to the guidance goals of advising students and individualizing instruction. The latent function served by such an activity occurs when such records are utilized for administrative organization. This is not to suggest that administrative organization, per se, cannot be instrumental in achieving guidance goals. It is only when records are viewed as vehicles for avoiding threats to the control systems of schools that a latent definition may be applied. Many transfer students in the secondary schools, for example, cannot be given the lofty privilege of a fresh start. Records are used to define persons, place them on dimensions of achievement, citizenship, family economic status, ability level, aspiration level, and so on. What we are proposing, by way of inference, is that all students are gradually niched, typed, or classified and that this process leads to premature expectations on the part of teachers and administrators and a self-fulfilling prophecy on the part of students. Record keeping is a major controlling element in an institution that relies heavily on long-range organizational planning. In this sense, no student ever receives a fresh start after the first grade. It would be rather difficult for the institution to make their long-range plans without some predictive data to tell them how many special reading teachers, shop teachers, and remedial facilities, as well as college advising hours, it will be necessary to provide. Records follow students from grade to grade, and it is interesting to observe, as the writer has observed, how the comments of the third-grade teachers are almost identical with the comments of the second-grade teacher. Either students do not change or teachers believe what they read in the records to the extent that believing makes it so. This knowledge helps the teacher structure her expectations, and she structures her classroom in terms of these expectations. Again, the latent function of records is organization with an eye to routinization of activities and control. It simplifies a complex task, an activity presumably not always beneficial to individual students.

## Advisor-Predictor

Giving advice to students is or should be based upon intelligent predictions that a given direction will be suitable for a given individual. These predictions are based upon an analysis of relevant data and are mindful of the notion of probability. That is, when advice is proffered, it is usually couched in a framework of logical uncertainty to the effect that the advice is given as an educated guess about the meaning of the accumulated data. For example, if a student were advised that, on the basis of his scientific achievement, he should not go to medical school, the counselor would also state that failure in this venture is not guaranteed. It is simply a best guess. If a counselor is well trained, a best guess is a meaningful contribution to a counselee. The issue that we need to evaluate is the basis upon which a best guess or, more generally, advice itself is given.

The latent function of this role segment occurs when advice is given to preserve or legitimate a host of earlier educational decisions. This involves the unquestioned adoption of all the assumptions about students that the school has made in formulating its programs. One such assumption may be that society requires a range of competencies, that we need auto mechanics as well as space scientists. This assumption, however, involves positing another one, that because this range is required we must decide who is to fall into which category. Once categories are designated and long-range educational programs mapped, it becomes highly disruptive to both the student and the system to advise a reorganization of program. The role of an advisor may, in many cases, be enacted within a framework of limited possibilities. Advice to students becomes increasingly restricted with each educational step the student takes. The frame of reference of the counselor is the student's progress to date and his age. An eighteen-year-old senior cannot be advised to start over again in a new program. Schools are institutionalized passage rites, never going backward and forward, but always forward toward some kind of closure, even if this means dropping out of school.

Other assumptions that govern predictions are made of the basis of ascribed characteristics of students: that one student will succeed in college because his father is a doctor, that another will probably succeed in a manual trade because he has mechanical abilities and comes from an economically deprived family.

Most advice given by counselors in schools has to do with suggestions about how best to fit into the acceptable mold of the citizen student. This is predictive only in the sense that deviance or nonconformity will not be tolerated and disruptive acts will be punished. In this way, the advisor-predictor role segment operates latently, and often dysfunctionally, to control the amount of nonconformity that the institution can and will tolerate. The function is latent insofar as it preserves the regulations regarding deviance. It is dysfunctional insofar as all students cannot fit a common-denominator mold without cost to them in the development of individuality, spontaneity, and creativity.

We do not wish to suggest that it is undesirable to maintain the regulations that control behavior through giving the advice that it is wise to conform. Such advice is clearly realistic, and students who deviate will be adversely affected. But to argue that a manifest function of counseling is preserving the control elements in the school would meet strong objections from the profession. This is directly relevant to the consideration of our next category, the counselor as disciplinarian.

## Disciplinarian

There is often controversy in school guidance circles regarding the role of the counselor in discipline. Resolution of this controversy would evolve from the explicit definition of discipline, on the one hand, and of the role of the counselor, on the other. "Should" begins a question that may be relevant to those whose interests lie with expanding role definitions and responsibilities. It is irrelevant in a consideration of the consequences of what "is," which is the socio-logical rather than the practical concern. Looking at the range of possible definitions of the counselor's role as disciplinarian, we may assume that all counselors become involved with discipline cases in some way. The range in approach to discipline cases runs from clearly punitive decisions to an avoidance of the discipline problem itself and concentration on more general aspects of a student's personality. If discipline is regarded by the counselor as a clear-cut responsibility to reinforce the control elements, thereby aiding teachers to concentrate on content, then we might expect counselor-counselee interaction to be closer to the authoritarian-punitive end of the continuum. Making sure that a student does not repeat disruptive behavior may require short-term directive counseling, whereas a focus upon why the student felt compelled to be disruptive could require a longer-range nondirective approach that might have to expect re-currences of problem behavior.

Although we are faced with an empirical question about how most counselors actually do behave, let us accept the probability that many or even some take the position that considerable responsibility rests with them to alleviate the number of conflicts that teachers experience in the classroom. Then we would presume that in these cases, the learning experienced by the counselee, insofar as counseling involves learning, adds up to a consideration of the consequences of his behavior. This is certainly a legitimate outcome. The difficulty,

conceptually, is that he learns only about the institutional consequences. The manifest learning outcome would involve an evaluation
of consequences within an atmosphere of how change will effect him
positively, rather than how not changing will effect him negatively.
At least one counselor has perceived the role to be framed within a
reinforcement program in which the counselor decides the effectiveness of reinforcers.[15] A variation on this theme would involve, if we
wish to operate with the concept of reinforcement at all, a consideration of the relative value of negative versus positive reinforcers. That
is, it would involve deciding which disciplinary factors may be
described as positive reinforcers and which described as negative and
then making some analytical (if not empirical) assessment of the
effect of each. Students of elementary psychology are aware that rats
respond more effectively and permanently to positive reinforcements.
This does not mean we may generalize this to human behavior in
social contexts. It does mean, however, that the same question about
the comparative effectiveness of reinforcers is relevant to the discipline
role in educational guidance.

The clarification of consequences within a negative reinforcement
framework is merely an elaboration of the institutionalized control
theme of the school. The definition of the disciplinary role itself would
expose the extent to which this role segment is manifest or latent,
functional or dysfunctional. This would depend upon the activities
of the practitioners, that is, which set of school routines is maintained. If the goals of counseling are for improved adaptation on the
part of students rather than controlled conformity, the disciplinarian
role aims at a primarily manifest function. The opposite definition,
by which the disciplinary role seeks to operate as an extension of the
control function and does so, would involve a latent function.

Assuming a disciplinary role that connotes maintaining the control
elements of the system becomes in many ways dysfunctional to the
pursuance of professional guidance goals, in that the counselor becomes defined as an administrator of sorts and the openness and

15. P. E. Opstad, "The Role of the Counselor in Discipline," in *Readings in
Guidance,* Lester D. and A. Crow, David McKay Company, Inc., New York,
1962, pp. 137–140.

frankness of his interaction with the students becomes restricted. This would clearly be antithetical to the kind of atmosphere required for any honest attempts at helping students overcome their problems. This notion will be discussed further in Chapter 7.

## Parent Surrogate–Friend

The accepting, understanding parent figure in a cold impersonal bureaucratic system like the school represents a psychological oasis for many students. Although the function of parent surrogate–friend is conceived as a source of psychological and social support for students, the more crucial system-related function of this role segment is that the oasis provides a tension release necessary to the maintenance of normal routines. Relief and rehabilitation leaves in military life make it possible to fortify individuals psychologically so that they will return with greater acceptance to the rigorous routines and stress of that life. Many formal organizations also recognize that some form of griping board diminishes the steam that frustration builds upon and thereby reduces the likelihood of conflict within the organization. In this sense, the manifest function of making available to the student a friendly parent surrogate, although helpful to the individual student, serves the latent function of reducing internal conflict.

Cold impersonal interaction between members of the bureaucracy and the student population is one factor that contributes to the kind of stress and frustration that sometimes erupts into student rebellion. The Berkeley incidents of the past several years are the most glaring, although unrepresentative, examples. More typical are the frequent incidents of high school faddism that often disrupt the continuity of the school year. Long hair, boots, mini-skirts, Beatle suits and the like have, in all parts of the country, caused situations of publicized conflict between school authorities and student bodies. Students do not, for the most part, enjoy the anonymity of large bureaucracies like our urban and suburban high schools and most universities. And being unclear about how one does achieve a personal identity in an anonymous system, they latch onto any fad or issue that presents itself. This is not to say that many students do not persist in rebellious behavior because of a loyalty to a certain ideology. But the masses of students who engage in active rebellion are primarily those who are entranced by the opportunity to identify, to rise above the conformist personality.

Few university students would say that they received sufficient, adequate, and personalized advisement during their university careers. As do high school students, many college students latch onto instructors who take an interest in them and their work. In many cases teachers do fulfill this need. Latent-function analysis would reveal, from reviewing the kinds of behavior discussed here, that any system that does not provide this function is destined to experience opposition in maintaining the institutionalized routines by which the manifest goals are attained.

One other latent function of playing the role of parent surrogate has to do with maintaining a competition motivation as an important means of achieving task goals. The formal counselor does not produce this kind of motivation, but the guidance teacher does. The guidance view of students as feeling, needing, sensitive beings has influenced many teachers to adopt a philosophy of affect, of relating to students in a highly personalized, warm, and friendly manner. In many senses, the role is a mother role. This is pricipally true in the early elementary grades, but the styles and adaptive modes developed by pupils in these crucial years serve as deeply internalized motivations for school behavior. Helping young children overcome and live with the anxieties of childhood is the manifest function of the guidance segment of the teacher role. Using the competition for the affection and love of the parent surrogate as a motive for achievement and citizenship rewards is the latent function. The consequence of this competition for those who are not adequately endowed to compete successfully is the dysfunction of the kind of personalized interaction involved in this segment of the guidance role. Sibling rivalry would not necessarily be bad if losing out in the battle for love and affection were not a necessary consequence of losing a sibling struggle. As we discussed in an earlier part of this chapter, education does not yet know what to do with the losers. In this way, then, the fact of playing a parent-surrogate role, although functional to certain security goals, may be dysfunctional to students who in the long run will ultimately come up against an impersonal system that they will either continue to treat as a system of personalized rewards or to which they cannot relate because personalized rewards and affection are in no way visible.

## Integrator

In general, the integration function consists in finding everyone a comfortable place in an interactional system of peers and authorities. Sociologically, this is a relatedness function in which actors in a given system interact with others in terms of the prerequisites, restrictions, and status of their roles. The counselor, in playing out the prescriptions for this role segment may see the integration function as one in which he helps persons to fit in, and feel a sense of belonging, with the members of his system. This would appear, in terms of the definition of the counselor as to the expectations for his role, to be the manifest function of this particular segment. The latent function of integration, in the sociological sense, is the fitting in of persons into the larger task demands of the society. That is, society expects the school to instill commitments in students so that they will fit productively into an industrialized society. The school responds to this demand by finding for each student a role that he may identify as his own and thereby learn the expectations, requirements, and rewards of this identification. The fact that individual roles are positions within a complex network of roles implies that one not only learns his role but also the way in which his role relates to other roles. In this way the school pursues its socialization function with a minimum amount of confusion and disorganization. The dysfunctional consequences of this integrative behavior may occur when status distinctions invade the definition of a student's role in relation to others. The role of the student as follower, blackboard washer, industrial-arts major, or typist for the school paper may result in dysfunctional consequences for the school. The typist may be integrated into the effort of turning out the paper, but she knows the esteem attached to her role is not the same as that attached to the editor or sports writer. The counselor as integrator is engaging in a manifest function when he seeks to establish students in some position within the system so that they may relate to others in seeking personal and system goals. When the prestige elements of the different student roles are clear, however, and persons respond to less prestigious positions with aggression and refusal to participate in important activities, the counselor's integrative activities may also be perceived as dysfunctional. The consequences of status differentiation have been discussed substantially in the earlier part of the chapter. It is here that the major dysfunctional consequences of our attempts to integrate members into a system occur.

Integration of the members of any task group is crucial to the effectiveness of that group *vis-à-vis* their task. To the degree that the task goals are consummated, the institution preserves itself. It is this preservation that constitutes the latent function of integrative activities, whereas the individual growth of persons as a result of group membership, regardless of what facets of growth are considered, is the manifest function of integration.


## CONCLUSION

Sociologists have found the notion of function to be an invaluable handle in grasping the meaning of social systems and of how segments of the system fit into the larger institutional picture. And because function has become such an invaluable conceptual tool, it is only logical that theoretical expansion on this theme should have occurred. The useful elaborations of latent-function analysis and dysfunctions have grown out of this expansion. In this chapter, we have attempted to apply these ideas to the actual functions and activities specified and practiced by school guidance workers. In the process, we have revealed several alternative explanations for the persistence of ongoing activities. In general, this broadens our understanding of the guidance process beyond that which the traditional evaluative perspective can reveal. This is because the evaluation of guidance practices has been framed around practical questions suggested by a limited range of purposes. Functional analysis opens the inquiry by posing evaluative questions about the purposes that activities serve for the institution as well as for the individual.

The applied value of this kind of inquiry is meaningful only to the extent that pupil personnel workers are able to evaluate their roles in relation to other roles within the system. Once they understand this relationship, they will perceive the consequences of their activities upon the student, both now and in the future, upon the school, and ultimately upon the society. No one counselor needs to worry about the impact of his role enactments on so grand a scale, but generalized activities and functions do have effects that are predictable, and counselors should be aware of these.

# CHAPTER 5

# SOCIAL RESEARCH IN
# EDUCATIONAL GUIDANCE

DESPITE THE FACTS that educational research has greatly expanded with the support of Federal grants and that general sociological interest in educational phenomena is on the increase, research on the process and function of counseling and guidance has not taken a sociological turn. A few exceptions exist, and these will be discussed. However, many researchers, ordinarily not sociologists, have seen fit to include some simple social variables in studies relating to guidance and counseling.

In Chapter 3 we discussed the various levels of theory that are possible in a behavior discipline. We should emphasize here that the level of theory that is being employed is usually predictable on the basis of the amount of scholarly writing and research that has been developed within a given discipline. It is logical and correct that we should know some facts before studying concepts and that we should explore single concepts before attempting an analysis of the relationship between several concepts.

The stage of empirical inquiry into the social aspects of guidance and counseling has not progressed far beyond the beginning. The purposes of this chapter are to bring the reader up to date on what has been done and then to suggest logical variations on the already established themes. These suggestions will consider both the basic facts and concepts that appear to have been ignored as well as a more complex level at which further inquiry might proceed.

## REVIEW OF RESEARCH LITERATURE

As a logical outgrowth of general social concern for problems of the poor, particularly of urban Negroes and those generally labeled as "culturally disadvantaged," the most frequent social variables introduced into inquiries dealing with guidance have been socioeconomic status and race. Other social factors that have been studied and will be discussed are sex, religion, nonacademic characteristics of families, cultural differences, role identifications, role conflicts, and noneconomic qualities of student status.

Although this section is primarily devoted to the research that appears in the literature, particularly in guidance and counseling journals, a few position statements have appeared in the same places that supplement some of the perspectives already argued by the author. These should be noted, for although they do not in themselves constitute research, they do suggest a perspective for evaluating current research and directions for future investigations. These statements utilizing social perspectives in the analysis of guidance deserve presentation and comment, primarily because they are even more rare in the literature than research papers. This is particularly significant because opinion papers require very little effort, in comparison to research projects, to prepare. And considering the uniqueness of the perspective, one would suspect that many journal editors, interested in variety, would be eager to publish them. The truth is that few scholars are thinking about guidance in sociological terms, which is also to say, because sociology is primarily a research discipline, that papers offering directions for inquiry are currently as crucial to the stimulation of interest in the social-research opportunities in guidance as would be a successful project. Several commentaries will be briefly discussed. Each reveals a different perspective for viewing either the role or interactional dynamics of counselors and counseling. As such they are prescriptive of directions for empirical investigations.

The first important comment is that offered by Gilbert Wrenn.[1] He has expressed a concern that guidance, which emerged as a response to specific cultural change, has trapped the perspective of functionaries in the cultural dimensions that created it. He argues that continued changes in that culture would presumably affect the role of counselors in the school. How, for example, are technological innovations, the development of an economy and politics based upon subliminal propaganda as sophisticated in industry, the emergence of super cities, and the disappearance of old occupations and the creation of new ones, to influence changes in the role responsibilities of guidance counselors?

We have argued earlier that institutions change slowly and that roles, once stabilized, are resistant to innovation. Wrenn takes this one step further by suggesting the process utilized by role occupants to protect themselves against change.

Like Job of old we protest the inevitable, we argue about it. Even better than Job we protect ourselves from the disturbing reality of change by surrounding ourselves with a cocoon of pretended reality—a reality which is based upon the past and the known, by seeing that which is as though it would always be. This is "cultural encapsulation," an encapsulation within our world, within our culture and sub-culture, within a pretense that the present is enduring.[2]

To what extent does counseling suffer this cultural encapsulation? The exploration of this question requires, first, delving into working indicators of cultural changes that affect the counselor's role. This is at a fairly low theoretical level but is a crucial empirical job that can open the doors to explanatory hypotheses regarding the interaction of role with cultural change.

One question that might be raised here would center about the differential shift from a vocational or college-advisor role to a "professional," clinical one. The research of Cicourel and Kitsuse is the only major empirical attempt to explain this shift in terms of socio-

---

1. C. Gilbert Wrenn, "The Culturally Encapsulated Counselor," *Harvard Educational Review*, vol. 32, no. 4, Fall 1962, pp. 444–450.
2. *Ibid.*, p. 445.

logical variables.[3] This work will be discussed at greater length in the summary of research that follows the present section.

Wrenn suggests some specific encapsulations that could be prescriptive of the kind of research that would make a contribution to our socioeducational knowledge of the guidance process.

1. "The tendency to be surprised or even unbelieving regarding changes in truth."

It is here that we might tap the value systems of counselors, directing our inquiry specifically to those beliefs that we may argue are traditional, conservative, and perhaps dysfunctional. The virtue of work, of marriage, of maturity, and of a time to choose a vocation or an educational objective are some suggestions offered.

2. "Academic folklore."

The beliefs about the value of grades, of tests, of books, and of rewards for industriousness and productivity may in some ways be out of tune with changing cultural demands. A descriptive analysis of this folklore system among school counselors would be a basic increment to our understanding of the role in relation to cultural change.

3. "The assumption that the counselor may safely draw upon his own educational and vocational experience in counseling the student."

Educational and occupational change are two currents that help to shape the society in the direction culture wishes it to go. What is the actual incongruence between counselor conceptions of the educational and occupational world of today and some reliable indicators of reality? What, for example, are the best predictors of academic failure, past and present? Dr. Nasatir's work, presented in Chapter 9 of this book, is an important attempt to reveal the social contexts of academic failure. How, we might ask, once we are familiar with such work, does the counselor's conception of the effect of certain contexts relating to failure jell with contemporary realities? Those who are interested in pursuing research in guidance along the lines suggested here might easily apply, from Wrenn's discussion of the problem, other empirical questions that need answering.

Wrenn's concern about cultural encapsulation is reiterated in a

---

3. Aaron Cicourel and John Kitsuse, *The Educational Decision Makers*, Bobbs-Merrill Co., Inc., New York, 1963, pp. vii–178.

paper by D. E. Muir.[4] Muir argues that current social-science theory flatly rejects the notion that people are free to make independent decisions. This idea, if applied to school counselors, takes us back to the concern expressed throughout the book that the sociocultural environment, in relation to the social characteristics of counselors, provides the best explanatory potential for the counselors' conception of their role. Muir's view is that, in the face of evidence indicating this encapsulation, counselors continue to view themselves as capable of making independent decisions and of influencing the systems in which they operate. Operating in the abstruse world of intuition and insight, which in the stage of preprofessionalism constitutes an acceptable mode of decision making, counselors are hesitant about accepting the necessity of scientific prediction. All this is really saying is that a person exists in a sociocultural context. Given this fact, however, the more important question for theory and practice becomes "Under what conditions might the person understand why he makes certain decisions and how he makes them?" If sociology knew how people make decisions, the counselor who knew sociology could influence the system and would not have to depend on the sociological version of fatalism. It is one of the more important points of the book that knowing sociology could make a difference in the why and how of counseling decisions.

The degree to which a transitional shift from intuition to scientific prediction has occurred is an empirical question, answerable only through an intensive search into the methods counselors use for decision making. This takes us into the area of values on the one hand and, on the other, into a search for observable predictors of scientific modes of thinking and behaving.

As a response to the increased emphasis upon educational guidance, suggested by such indicators as the extensive support of the National Defense Educational Act, professionalism, according to Dan Lortie, emerges as an impinging concern. In an important statement[5]

---

4. D. E. Muir, "Implications of Contemporary Social Science for the Field of Guidance," *Personnel and Guidance Journal,* vol. 44, no. 6, pp. 581–585.

5. Dan C. Lortie, "Administrator, Advocate, or Therapist? Alternatives for Professionalization in School Counseling," *Harvard Educational Review,* Winter 1965, pp. 3–17.

Lortie addresses himself to speculations about how this professionalism might occur. Many empirical questions are suggested, and we will cull these from his exposition. As a sociologist looking at theoretical directions for professionalism, Lortie focuses first upon the extent of consensus upon the services to be provided by members of the profession. Without this consensus, he does not see the feasibility of emerging professionalism of any real sort in guidance and counseling. His review of the literature indicates that no such consensus exists.

Two other conditions are projected as prerequisites to professionalization—first, the development and diffusion of collective beliefs that would characterize members as a unique group and, second, a general patterning of interactive relationships both in and out of school. Let us look at these criteria separately and consider the possible research ramifications. It is here that we hope to be able to designate areas not only where research is possible but, in this case, where we may find necessary data on which to base decisions about professionalizing.

First, on the subject of collective beliefs, we point the reader to a consideration of what special, joint values of school counselors are not, as a total configuration, the same as the values of other occupational groups. What components of this configuration are derived from professional clinicians, what from psychometrics, what from student cultures and their various subcultures (i.e., the surfers, the gangs, the popularity crowd), what from school administration, and what from the general public expectations for the role of the counselor?

The importance of looking at and doing research into the question of professionalism takes us again into the area of decision making. The relevance of the kind and number of decisions that counselors make to the outcomes of the counseling interaction is obvious. Data on the variations that occur in student responses as they are related to levels of professionalism may help counselors develop a more scientific basis for methodology. Professionalism, independent of criteria needed to designate it, may be viewed in terms of conceptual sophistication apparent in the methodology of the occupation. The value of scientific rigor and conceptual sophistication in any body of methodological knowledge may be assessed, for instance, in the expectations people have from treatment by a medical doctor. Confidence in the expert in counseling interactions is a desirable operational goal, and this expertness and confidence would seem to be a logical consequence of professionalization.

Evidence from M. Lieberman[6] taken from profiles of interest inventories suggest that teachers are many different kinds of people; math teachers, for example, are more like mathematicians in the general range of interests than like most other teachers. He concludes that what is taught is a better indicator of commonalities than being a teacher.

Socialization to a profession, to a spirit of professionalism, has been the subject of considerable sociological inquiry. The medical student in particular has been the subject of intensive analysis.[7] The impact of empirical inquiry into the subject of occupational socialization has been to turn our attention away from differences and toward the infusion of a spirit of commonality (self-image) through the inculcation of a belief system as well as the provision of knowledge. The problem of generalizing anything in particular from Lieberman's data is that interest inventories are not belief systems. It may be that, although counselors are recruited from diverse teaching interests and areas, the socialization process has the desired outcome, which is a common belief system and common knowledge.

We know that most school counselors are recruited from the teaching ranks. To what extent do value systems, reflective of their particular teaching speciality, influence their beliefs about the role of counselor? We are hypothesizing differences in belief systems and that these belief systems have some consequence for role enactment. Both are empirical questions and require study. But if we assume that these hypothetical questions may be proven valid, then the barriers to professionalization, if a collective belief system is one criterion, are considerable. The solution would seem to lie in controling the situations

6. M. Lieberman, *Education as a Profession,* Prentice-Hall, Inc., Englewood Cliffs, N.J., 1958, pp. 219–221.

7. R. K. Merton, *The Student Physician, Introductory Studies in the Sociology of Medical Education,* Harvard Univ. Press, Cambridge, Mass., 1957. Also, H. Becker and G. Greer, "Student Culture in Medical School," *Harvard Educational Review,* vol. 28, 1958, pp. 70–80.

of training and admission so that all persons would receive a common socialization. M. Schlossberg[8] emphasizes this point in her discussion. One might suppose, by way of a preliminary hypothesis, that those teachers recruited to counseling from vocational fields will differ in their belief systems about the function of guidance from those who taught academic subjects to college-bound students. Other characteristics of teachers may supply data related to the content of their belief systems. One that could be crucial would be the extent to which the attainment of a teaching job constitutes personal upward mobility. Other factors would be the kinds of neighborhoods and the kinds of school administration to which a teacher is exposed and the kinds of informal interaction with students that transpired during the teaching segment of the counselor's career.

The second criterion mentioned by Lortie was the patterned relationships, both in and out of school, established by the counselor. What kinds of routinization of interaction with teachers, administrators, students, and other counselors has occurred? We would also want to look at the patterns of affiliation outside of school with occupational and nonoccupational voluntary associations. What patterns of interaction are established for routine contacts with parents, social workers, college admissions officers, welfare agencies, psychiatrists, and psychologists?

Lortie's task evolves into one of speculating about the various directions that professionalization in counseling might take. Conceiving that any professional enterprise must ultimately congeal around certain specific functions, he designates three cluster types: administrator, advocate, and therapist.

The relationship of counselors with other school personnel depends upon the cluster chosen as the definition of the type of role to be professionalized. If administrator is chosen, then one set of values and interaction patterns will arise, and the same is true for choosing advocate or therapist. The administrator will represent himself to colleagues and students in such a way that patterned expecta-

---

8. M. K. Schlossberg, "A Sociological Framework for Evaluating Guidance Education," *Personnel and Guidance Journal*, vol. 44, no. 6, pp. 581–585.

tions for behavior and interaction will incline toward the bureaucratic. As advocate, a person who allies himself with the student rather than with the bureaucratic machinery of the school, certain conflicts are certain to emerge unless, in time, the educational enterprise allows the formation of this kind of autonomy. Granting this eventuality, inter-action patterns would emerge around the definition of the counselor role as one of arbitration. In a sense, the counselor would represent the students' interests in the arrangement of programs and the con-ciliation of interpersonal problems on an individual basis. Students, argues Lortie, are consistently becoming embroiled in bureaucratic conflicts and require someone with knowledge of the system who can manipulate it to resolve these conflicts.

The therapist role, we would suspect, would be that most opposed by the majority of school administrators and board members. To legitimate this role would require an excessive investment on the part of the school district. Student-counselor ratios would have to decrease, and other functionaries would have to assume the excessive responsi-bilities of administration and vocational guidance. If, by some chance, the initiative of members of the counseling profession were to thrust them into this role administratively, the task of establishing attitudes necessary for successful counseling (i.e., trust on the part of the stu-dent-client) would require an analysis of ways to shape values within an institution.

Research into the prevailing belief systems and general social characteristics of counselors, as these relate to the development of pro-fessionalized routines, is an area that could yield data that would in-crease our knowledge of professionalization. It could, as well, con-tribute ideas about the applied tasks that education might undertake and increase the reliability of the current emphasis on specialization.

M. Schlossberg[9] suggests possible empirical adaptations of the Merton notions about medical socialization[10] to the training of guid-ance counselors. If, as Schlossberg suggests, professionalism is a process of adult socialization involving changes in self-concept and internalization of the professional role, we could begin our investiga-

9. Schlossberg, *op. cit.*
10. Merton, *op. cit.*

tions by testing out some assumptions about self-concept and internalization of roles on practicing counselors. From there we could probe into the behavioral objectives of counselor-training programs and evaluate the changes in concept about role and self that occur after and throughout the training period.

## Research on Socioeconomic Variables

The educational research in the area of socioeconomic variables more often than not takes the form of relating several dimensions of economic status, or two dimensions of race (white and non-white), to some criterion such as vocational choice, extent of counseling, type of counseling, evaluation of counselors, source of referrals, or delinquent behavior. We will review some representative studies.

Two studies, one by G. J. Pine[11] and the other by K. H. McDonald,[12] have demonstrated the relationship of socioeconomic status to two factors of important consequence to school counselors, delinquent behavior and motivation. Pine's conclusion is that those students who are downwardly mobile in the social structure are more likely to participate in delinquent behavior than those who are upwardly mobile. His most crucial finding is that socioeconomic aspiration is a better predictor of having behavior troubles in school than the student's present structural position. Similar findings by Weinberg and Skager[13] corroborated this notion when socioeconomic status and aspired status measured by curriculum choice were related to adjustive and career counseling. This study also supported the expectation that lower class students would be counseled more frequently for adjustment problems than middle class students.

Considerable research has established that in almost every area of academic work, the social status of the student is predictive of his

---

11. G. J. Pine, "Social Class, Social Mobility, and Delinquent Behavior," *Personnel and Guidance Journal,* vol. 43, no. 8, April 1955, pp. 770–774.

12. Keith H. McDonald, "The Relationship of Socio-economic Status to an Objective Measure of Motivation," *The Personnel and Guidance Journal,* vol. 42, no. 10, June 1964, pp. 997–1002.

13. Carl Weinberg and Rodney Skager, "Social Status and Guidance Involvement," *Personnel and Guidance Journal,* vol. 44, Feb. 1966, pp. 586–590.

performance. McDonald has suggested that socioeconomic status is not a factor in academic motivation, but this stands out as one of the few reports contradicting the accumulated evidence. If motivation bears any link to achievement, then this particular finding is thrown into doubt and methodological questions might be raised.

If we wish to talk about the relationship of socioeconomic status (SES) to motivation, we may call upon the published findings of Herbert Hyman,[14] James Davie,[15] Joseph Kahl,[16] and Bernard Rosen,[17] who all report conclusive differentials, based upon social class, in the educational aspirations and motivations of students. Earlier work done by W. Lloyd Warner[18] and A. B. Hollingshead[19] established that class position is highly predictive of the amount of academic success, regardless of how it is measured. Hollingshead described some of the first cases in the literature of the discriminatory basis of counselor-counselee interaction. The kind and quality of counseling offered at Elmtown High differed according to the position of the family in the class system of the community. Variations on this theme have so flooded the literature that the issue has achieved the status of a given. What still remains, however, and this may be the single most important dimension to-be pursued in future research, is to discover the mechanisms by which such differentiation occurs. With this knowledge, counselors may be able to control the forces that lead to ever-widening gaps between students of various economic backgrouds.

One study supported the expected interaction of SES and the

---

14. Herbert Hyman, "Value Systems of Different Classes: A Social Psychological Contribution to the Analyses of Stratification," in *Class, Status and Power,* ed. by R. Bendix and S. Lipset, The Free Press, New York, 1966, pp. 426–442.

15. James Davie, "Social Class Factors and School Attendance," *Harvard Educational Review,* vol. 23, 1953, pp. 168–174.

16. Joseph Kahl, "Educational and Occupational Aspirations of 'Common Man' Boys," *Harvard Educational Review,* vol. 23, 1953, pp. 186–203.

17. Bernard C. Rosen, "The Achievement Syndrome: A Psychocultural Dimension of Social Stratification," *American Sociological Review,* vol. 21, 1956, pp. 203–211.

18. W. L. Warner, R. Havighurst, and Martin Loeb, *Who Shall Be Educated,* Harper & Row, Publishers, New York, 1944.

19. A. B. Hollingshead, *Elmtown's Youth,* John Wiley & Sons, Inc., New York, 1955.

academic performance of students identified as "gifted."[20] SES was shown to be related to persistence in the gifted category as well as to being identified as gifted.

Studies conducted in interstitial, or culturally deprived, communities reveal data that would have applied value for counselors in such communities. At the same time, knowledge is being incremented about the characteristics of lower class children and their interaction with educational problems. One study conducted in such a community revealed that vocational choices were unrelated to occupational interest-inventory data and were unrealistic when compared to student ability level.[21] Another project in a similar community found that students did not see the counselor's role as adequate to their needs in the areas of vocational guidance, the discipline process, and the overall philosophy of guidance.[22] This suggests that counselors in these communities may need to vary their techniques so that they may be congruent with the perceptions of a lower socioeconomic group. At the level of higher education, one study reported that the SES of clients at a university counseling clinic was significantly lower than the SES level of a random selection of non-clients.[23]

University counseling centers are in many ways different from their counterparts at the secondary school level. The training of personnel differs in that many go through a training program in clinical psychology. No teaching experience is required, and most of the staff are familiar with research procedures. As a result, not only is research tolerated but it is encouraged. This is logical because many persons acting as counselors plan to derive a dissertation out of their setting. The relationship of the counseling center to the rest of the educational enterprise differs from the relationship between the two in public

20. Robert W. Schmeding, "Group Intelligence Test Scores of Gifted Children: Degree of Consistency and Factors Related to Consistency," *Personnel and Guidance Journal*, vol. 42, no. 10, June 1964, pp. 991–996.

21. R. A. Ruble, S. Caplan, and David Segal, "A Theory of Educational and Vocational Choice in Junior High School," *Personnel and Guidance Journal*, vol. 42, no. 2, Oct. 1963, pp. 129–134.

22. Ernest Spaights, "The Culturally Disadvantaged Evaluate a Guidance Program," *Guidance*, vol. 3, no. 2, Fall 1963, pp. 54–58.

23. Harry Lewis and Malcolm Robertson, "Socio-Economic Status and a University Psychological Clinic," *Journal of Counseling Psychology*, vol. 8, no. 3, Fall 1961, pp. 239–242.

schools in matters of both autonomy and ecology. The division of functions within large university complexes makes this possible. Research is needed to distinguish between the two kinds of counseling endeavors, as well as to relate the two on activities they share. We would like to answer such questions as "How do students who received career guidance in high school approach the college center, with what expectations and with what role definitions?" "How do the kinds of role conflicts that affect students in high school compare with those that occur in college?" These questions may be researched in two ways. Socioeconomic variables such as parents' occupation and education, family mobility, personal mobility, social aspirations, and institutional status may be held constant, or these same factors may be permitted to vary and be used as predictors of behavior related to referral and attitudes toward the counseling experience.

There is a great deal we still need to know about the interaction of socioeconomic variables and school counseling. We have made but a modest beginning. The effect of mobility upon the counselor's definition of his role, the extent to which he views attaining a counseling position as institutional mobility, his previous and past judgments of the shift in his power and autonomy are possible directions for future research. Ultimately, we need to know how social class influences the flow of interactional activities between student and counselor. A theory, based upon thorough evidence, of the variations in interaction between students and counselors, as these variations are related both to class and class definitions, made one of the other, would be a vital increment to our knowledge of social and institutional interaction.

### Guidance and Race

Linking racial characteristics to counseling behavior is a variation on the socioeconomic theme, but important differences exist. Definitions that two persons, counselor and counselee, make about each other utilizing socioeconomic cues may be quite different when racial components are varied. In sociological research we are aware that it is unwise for white interviewers to interview Negro subjects. In education we suspect that the results of individual testing may vary with Negro testers testing white children and white testers testing Negro children. An open-minded counselor may presume that a lower class white student can attain lofty aspirations with the help of ability and honest evaluation, whereas the same counselor, assessing vocational aspirations for a Negro child, may apply a different set of expectations based upon knowledge of the problems that Negroes encounter in their encounters with the American mobility structure. This is true for the unbiased counselor. What definitions would be made by one who has not freed himself of racial prejudices? Unlike psychiatrists, counselors seldom are required to undergo any intensive soul searching. And what about the expectations that Negro students may have for the performance of white counselors?

One study attempted to answer some of these questions. Although an insufficient sample was used upon which to generalize to Negro-white interaction in counseling questions, the results establish a condition that should influence others to replicate the study with larger samples. The study matched six Negro students with white counselors and six with Negro counselors. The students had approximately the same characteristics and problems. The conclusion was that the white counselors were unable to establish rapport or neutralize the counseling atmosphere. Those students who undertook counseling with a Negro counselor showed marked improvement in their attitude and behavior. The white counselors determined that inability to establish rapport was based upon (1) the counselor's lack of knowledge of the Negro's social and psychological patterns, (2) a stereotyped conception of the Negro, (3) the Negro's distrust of the white man, and (4) the inability of the counselor to determine when rapport was established.[24]

Another study seemed to indicate that the perceptions of Negro high school students of the kind of advice they received about attending college did not suggest discrimination. On the other hand, grade-point comparisons of those who had been advised to attend college suggested a tendency for counselors to be less willing to advise Negro

---

24. Waldo B. Phillips, "Counseling Negro Pupils: An Educational Dilemma," *The Journal of Negro Education*, vol. 29, no. 4, Fall 1960, pp. 504–507.

students with marginal grade averages to attempt college than their white counterparts.[25] Milliken, reporting on the evaluation of an NDEA guidance institute, found support for the hypothesis that prejudice was related to "effective" versus "non-effective" counseling.[26]

When counseling proceeds, as the ethos indicates it should, with the counselor in possession of as much data on the individual counselee as it is possible to have, the old questions of racial bias in measures of achievement, intelligence, or ability are raised. A large body of research supporting the racial or cultural bias of psychometric instruments need not be reiterated here. One summary of an extensive set of investigations still being conducted in Negro neighborhoods in New York should suffice. Deutch and Brown report on the intellectual differences of Negro and white first and fifth graders of different social classes with special emphasis on the lower class.[27] The IQ means for white children were significantly higher than those for Negro children at each level, the differences increasing as grade level increases. One of the foci of the project was the relationship between achievement on the tests and the presence of a father in the home. This was negative, and as more Negro children are fatherless than white children, one mechanism for explaining the observed differences may have been identified. A great deal more probing is required before all the factors that account for this difference are established.

Looking for some tendencies in the area of empathy, counselor regard, and the genuineness, concreteness, and depth of exploration, one study selected four counselors, one Negro and three white. The Negro counselor was totally inexperienced and the white counselors varied in experience. Eight Negro clients interacted with these four counselors. The conclusions showed a clear preference for the inexperienced Negro counselor. All counselees indicated that they would return to see the Negro counselor. None indicated that he would want

25. O. Pat Barney and Lurel D. Hall, "A Study in Discrimination," *Personnel and Guidance Journal*, vol. 43, no. 7, March 1965, pp. 707–709.

26. Robert L. Milliken, "Prejudice and Counseling Effectiveness," *Personnel and Guidance Journal*, vol. 43, no. 7, March 1965, pp. 710–712.

27. Martin Deutsch and Bert Brown, "Social Influences in Negro-White Intelligence Differences," *The Journal of Social Issues*, vol. 20, no. 2, April 1964, pp. 24–25.

to return to see the most experienced white counselor, a trained Ph.D. In general the "best" interaction, according to the criterion measures mentioned at the beginning of this paragraph, seemed to be occurring with the Negro counselor.[28]

It is just such data that counselors are forced to employ in making educational and vocational predictions for Negro students. One study showed that the instruments were as reliable in predicting student grades for Negroes as they were for whites,[29] but this represents no more than a restatement of what we already know, that race explains scores on predictive instruments as well as on the achievement such instruments predict. What is still required is the identification of the mechanisms that explain both. Hopefully some of the financial support being poured into explorations of this problem will yield reliable evidence about the nature of these social mechanisms.

There is still much data, easily accessible, that may aid counselors in making realistic assessments of the mobility structure for Negroes. One kind of data would be a statistical analysis of the proportion of Negroes entering various occupations. One survey of colleges of engineering revealed considerable increases yearly in the number of Negroes enrolled.[30] Data are available on other vocationally oriented college schools and departments and should be collected and organized. We need descriptive data on the evaluations of occupations by Negroes and explanatory data on the basis for these evaluations.

James Coleman[31] reports data on the distribution of counselor contact by race. He concludes that Negro pupils proportionally have a slightly greater access to counseling on a nationwide basis than do white pupils. His survey indicated a ratio of one counselor for every

28. George Banks, Bernard Berenson, and Robert Carkhuff, "The Effects of Counselor Race and Training Upon Counseling Process with Negro Clients in Initial Interviews," *Journal of Clinical Psychology,* vol. 23, no. 1, Jan. 1967, pp. 70–72.

29. J. Don Boney, "Predicting the Academic Achievement of Secondary School Negro Students," *The Personnel and Guidance Journal,* vol. 44, no. 7, March 1966, pp. 700–703.

30. Robert Kiehl, "Opportunities for Negroes in Engineering—A Second Report," *The Personnel and Guidance Journal,* vol. 42, no. 10, June 1964, pp. 1019–1020.

31. James S. Coleman et al., "Equality of Educational Opportunity," U.S. Government Printing Office, Washington, D.C., 1966, pp. 529–530.

97 Negro pupils and one for every 112 white pupils.[32] In only one geographic area, nonmetropolitan Northeast and Midwest, do white pupils have greater availability to counselors. Other data indicate that those counselors who are available to Negro students are mainly Negro counselors. In no geographical area are there ever more than 3 per cent Negro counselors available to white students.

These data are purely descriptive and no qualifications or interpretations are offered. Some speculations, however, seem necessary. First, it is likely that the kind of counseling, which was not controlled, would be more important data than the amount of contact. Negro students may be those who are assigned to counselors as discipline problems whereas white students may be receiving college advice. Second, data are reported indicating that the Negro counselors who were considered in the study had not attained, in comparison with the white group, as many master's degrees in guidance. This would suggest that white students are receiving more professional guidance and counseling than Negro students. The difference, however, was not great (white 72 per cent, Negro 65 per cent).

We need, more than anything else, a systematized methodology for investigating interracial interaction in counseling. We have to look at differential value systems, age and sex variations, role modes for minority-group members, and the structure of expectations for all educational personnel that may spill over into the counselor's office. If the conflicts and disjunctures that affect minority-group students may be alleviated by guidance action, we must further evaluate the context of the school, the realities of de facto segregation, and particularly de facto segregation within integrated schools. Social engineering may be the counselor's best tool, but research on the several variations of such engineering needs to be conducted. This would involve the problems of, first, establishing theoretically the mechanisms of interaction that affect attitude and, second, setting up experiments to be conducted in a climate amenable to the controlled manipulation of ethnic interaction.

---

32. This figure represents an estimate based upon a definition of a counselor as any person assigned to see students six or more hours per week. Full-time counselor–student ratios are, of course, much greater.

## Sex of Counselor

Within some contexts, the sex of the role occupant is not considered relevant to the performance of the role, unless, of course, physiological qualities are in some way necessary to the tasks required. Being a male or a female engineer, lawyer, accountant, or anesthesiologist (to remain within the boundaries of professional roles) presumably has little effect on the task performance. There are some social implications in the way sex influences job availability for these roles, and historical socialization explains the disinclination women experience in aspiring to certain roles. The counseling situation, however, has certain characteristics that may reveal knowledge about the unique contribution that sex may make in the explanation of special forms of social interaction.

Although the sex of the counselor would appear to be a relatively simple factor, not worth excessive investigation, the dynamics involved could be considerable. Are there, for example, variations based upon sex in the way in which students relate to the counselor?

One researcher, Frances Fuller, has provided us with data on several issues relevant to the question of sex. Some of her findings are ( 1 ) female counselees express significantly more feeling than male counselees regardless of the sex of the counselor, ( 2 ) male counselees express more feelings in the presence of male counselors than of female counselors, and ( 3 ) counselees who have no preference for the sex of the counselor express more feeling and progress from intake to counseling more often than counselees who express preference.[33] Fuller indicated further that both male and female students prefer a male counselor.[34] This may vary according to the age level of the counselee, may be affected by exposure, or may not affect the outcome of the counseling interaction. These are other things we would like to know. We would have use for data that expose the basis for these preferences. There are many routes to knowledge about

33. Frances F. Fuller, "Influence of Sex of Counselor and of Client on Client Expressions of Feeling," *Journal of Counseling Psychology,* vol. 10, no. 1, 1963, pp. 34–40.
34. *Ibid.*

the effect of sex in counseling, but few are being pursued. There is, in addition, room for the development of theories regarding the effect of sex in role interaction that could set forth propositions capable of being tested. The woman's role in American society has a distinct history that may be traced and out of which certain assumptions may emerge. The mother image may lead a theoretician into speculation about some roles in which women may achieve outstanding rapport with students (e.g., supportive counseling) and other roles that might produce differential distrust (e.g., college advising). There are certainly some problems that boys feel they can discuss more easily with men and some problems that girls can discuss more easily with women. It strikes one as somewhat disjunctive that in many junior and senior high schools, young girls going through a physiological process that considerably affects their social and academic behavior do not have a female counselor with whom to discuss this problem.

## The Family

Counselors are certainly aware that career decisions are in many ways influenced by the characteristics of the student's family. We have already discussed socioeconomic characteristics and recognize that career choices are in line with class position. Suppose we were, for purposes of analysis, to dissolve the socioeconomic evaluation of careers and consider briefly the way in which career decisions, linked to interest, are influenced by family experiences. Why, for example, should one child show considerable interest in an artistic career and another lean heavily toward a technical one? Anne Roe[35] has proposed a theory that links occupational pursuits and interests to experience in childhood. At least one study has tried to test the validity of this theory and found it lacking.[36] From the sociological perspective, we are concerned with the interaction patterns that serve as career influences. Motivation of career decisions, as Lieberman points out in

---

35. Anne Roe, *The Psychology of Occupations,* New York, John Wiley & Sons, Inc., 1956.

36. Douglas Hagen, "Careers and Family Atmosphere: An Empirical Test of Roe's Theory," *Journal of Counseling Psychology,* vol. 7, no. 4, 1960.

his analysis of the research conducted on motivations for becoming a teacher,[37] is an extremely tricky phenomenon, and much care must be exercised in the design and construction of instruments to tap relevant data. Nevertheless, we cannot avoid attacking a problem because the instrumentation is difficult. Advances in psychometric techniques and support for probing-interview approaches make the feasibility of accumulating reliable data a greater reality now than in the past.

Freudian psychology, upon which there appears to be increasing reliance by counselors in their drive to establish a more professional self-image, places a heavy weight on the family as the breeding ground for adaptations to social and psychological life. If occupations and career orientations in general derive from certain familial influences, we may raise the question of whether or not this fact provides a good or bad predictor of job satisfaction. Conflicts in college over identification with a particular occupational subculture might also be explained in these terms. We could design studies that would evaluate the relative effects of family versus nonfamily influence on vocational and educational choice.

One study that begins to get at some aspects of this problem looked at the way in which the family environment influenced the work-value orientation of females.[38] The study concluded that family influence increases as the socioeconomic status of the family increases, that females identify with the father's rather than the mother's idealized goals for her in high status homes, and that the greater the distance between the father's education and training and the mother's, the stronger will be this identification.

Certain cultural factors, independent of social class (although there are strong relationships) influence the kind of expectations that ethnic families have for their children and the kind of role dominance that exists in such families. Ethnicity is a consideration distinct from family insofar as we may make a case for the consequences of different ethnic adaptations to the American social structure. The socioeduca-

---

37. M. Lieberman, *op. cit., pp.* 214–218.
38. John F. Kinnane and Sister M. Margaret Bannon, "Perceived Parental Influence and Work-Value Orientation," *Personnel and Guidance Journal,* vol. 43, no. 3, 1964, pp. 273–279.

tional literature, however, concentrates mainly on the way in which the family operates to produce these different adaptations. Mc-Clelland,[39] as a good example, describes the way in which expecta-tions of mothers leads to the development of certain achievement attitudes in sons. He then extends this interactional conception to the case of the Jewish family and attempts to explain the high achieve-ment need of Jewish boys in this way.

Spanish-American families where mothers are dominant have been shown to be related to the achievement of girls and the nonachieve-ment of boys.[40] Jewish families have strong expectations for boys in terms of professional goals, as already noted, and this seems to have spilled over onto girls in recent years. The interaction of a non-academically successful male with his Jewish family may be predictive of certain kinds of anxiety neuroses with which counselors must deal. Research on the mechanisms of ethnic identification and school adapta-tion must proceed at a more complex theoretical level. We understand the context within which Jewish students succeed and Mexican-Americans fail, Japanese students do not disrupt classrooms in the way that many Negro students do. These regularities are a beginning. What family dynamics, however, help us understand the process by which such regularities exist?

### Aspiration and Ability

In this section we will look at the research of James Coleman[41] and its implication for future investigation. In his comprehensive in-vestigation of the role of the school in the process of establishing mechanisms for educational mobility, one analysis was made of the counseling function. This was done to see if counselors functioned to reduce the discrepancies that exist between aspiration and ability.

---

39. D. C. McClelland, *The Achieving Society,* The Free Press, New York, 1967.
40. Bernard Spilka and Lois Gill, "Some Non-Intellectual Correlates of Academic Achievement Among Spanish-American Students," *The School Coun-selor,* vol. 12, no. 4, May 1965, pp. 218–221.
41. James S. Coleman et al., *op. cit.*

The procedure was to compare the ability and aspirations of a group of students who had not seen a counselor or who had seen one only once with those of a group of students who had seen a counselor more than once during the previous year. The ability measure was a score on a reading comprehension test, and the measure of aspiration was the student's response to a question about his college plans for the coming year. The data were presented in such a way that the effect of race, sex, and social class could be observed. The results clearly indicated that seeing a counselor more than once reduces the discrepancy between ability and aspiration. In those specific cases where reversals were observed (situations in which a low discrepancy accompanied no counselor contact), it was found that fewer reversals occurred for females than for males, fewer for Negroes than for whites, and fewer for lower class than for middle class students. Upper and middle class white males showed the greatest number of reversals. The lower classes showed stronger correlations between contact and discrepancy than did the middle classes.

The class, race, and regional differentials in the context of school counseling suggested by the Coleman study[42] imply that counseling has not reached a stage of professionalization comparable to those professions in which training and evaluation are highly stable throughout training institutions. The key to the reduction of these differentials in task performance lies in three areas: the training procedure and curriculum, the stage of professionalism accomplished by the group, and the structural determinants within the school. We need research to expose the kinds of effects stabilization of training procedures would have, and we could vary simultaneously with training differentials the organizational styles within which counseling occurs. Given structure *A,* for example, a style that permits high autonomy to guidance functions, and training type *A,* some program sanctioned by the American Personnel and Guidance Association, are we likely to find more or less discrepancies in type and amount of counseling based upon SES and race, than with structure *B* and training type *B?* Several variations on this theme are possible. The work of Coleman

---

42. *Ibid.,* pp. 531–532.

and his colleagues has opened the door to a host of testable speculations about the factors associated with various results of school
counseling.

## Role and Professionalization

We have spoken at some length in other chapters about the
differentiation of functions that occurs in school counseling. There are
frequent situations in which counselors must decide which functions
are paramount in the responsibility hierarchy. There are certainly
times when counselors, performing one function, actually make a
major contribution in another functional area. While a counselor is
giving him advice about the availability to him of specific programs,
a given student may interpret this advice as indicating the counselor's
support and recognition of a competence about which he was unsure.
Vocational advice here, even if unheeded, becomes supportive therapy.

Most educational functionaries experience a period of doubt about
what is expected of them. This would apply, to make the general case,
when roles are recent additions to the bureaucratic division of labor.
The counselor's role would most likely be subject to frequent diffuse
expectations, and personal disorganization would result until the
counselor clarified for himself the routine expectations for his role
enactments. The lack of uniformity, across and within schools, of
expectations for the counselor's roles makes, as Lortie has already
suggested,[43] the professionalization of counseling difficult. At another
level of analysis, this situation may produce a series of role conflicts
about which we have little empirical data. Ultimately, we would like
to know how counselors typically resolve these conflicts. If, as in
Stouffer's study of role conflict in college students,[44] we discover that

---

43. Lortie, *op. cit.*

44. Samuel Stouffer, "An Analysis of Conflicting Social Norms," *American
Sociological Review*, vol. 14, 1956, pp. 707–717. Professor Stouffer arranged a
situation in which a student was given the responsibility of proctoring an examination for a professor. Given this situation, the student was asked how he
would react to a cheating student when he had been instructed by the professor
to turn in the name of any student found cheating. Three responses were possible:
Do nothing, warn the student, or turn his name in. The student as proctor was

certain conditions accompanying the conflict shift the direction of the resolution, we would want to be aware of these conditions and how they affect the decisions of those experiencing the conflict.

We would want to begin an analysis of the differential role perceptions of persons occupying pupil personnel positions with whatever descriptive data were available. One survey employed the distinction "generalist" versus "specialist." The generalist position is defined here as one in which the role is perceived as focusing upon a broad interpretation of task, emphasizing nonauthoritarian, student-centered counseling. The specialist position assumes a broad division of labor within which highly trained "experts" focus on limited areas such as testing, evaluation, or college advising. The study sought differences in perception from four types of persons involved in guidance activities: counselor-educators, guidance supervisors, counselors, and administrators. It was found that the counselor-educators identified with the specialist position more than any other group. The secondary school administrators perceived the role with a generalist framework more than any other group. As training increased, a tendency towards identification with the specialist appeared. The counselor group fell between the educators and administrators but did express sympathy for nonauthoritarian student-centered counseling. Those with the most training generally agreed that the counselor's role was not the same as that occupied by the clinical psychologist.[45]

Methodologically, there are basically two approaches to the problem of having persons evaluate the nature of a given position or role or the relationship of one role to the bureaucratic complex within which it is set. The first procedure is the one followed above, by which the investigator designates categories, defines them for persons, and has the persons react to these definitions. This procedure is similar to the early studies of stratification in which the researcher asked persons

---

playing two roles and confronted with a situation of conflict. The resolution was only really predictable if, as Stouffer points out, the relationship of the proctor to the cheating student could be determined. This makes sense. The proctor is not likely to turn in a fraternity brother but could be objective if the student were unknown to him.

45. Richard T. Knowles and Bruce Shertzer, "Attitudes Toward the School Counselor's Role," *Counselor Education and Supervision*, vol. v, no. 1, Fall 1965.

to identify their class from a specified list (working class, middle class and so on). The second approach, fundamentally a more reliable one, especially in the beginning stages of role formulation, is to present respondents with a fairly open-ended set of questions in which they are asked to specify the range of activities or responsibilities that they consider a legitimate expectation for the enactment of a given role. At the same time, the respondent is asked to specify as precisely as possible the meaning of each of these activities to him. Finally, he is asked to designate which activities he feels are not within the appropriate range of the counselor's responsibility. From these data, the investigator would collapse activities, combine categories, and emerge with a reliable set of indicators derived from the phenomenology of those involved.

Another approach to the same problem was through the vehicle of value orientations.[46] The focus of this study was upon how the degree of agreement between counselors and their administrators with regard to the values of each was related to role expectations for the counselor. Findings indicated no significant relationship between congruence of value orientation of counselors and their administrators and agreement of expectations. Other findings indicated that administrators had more traditional views of the role than did counselors and that male counselors and those between the ages of fifty-eight and sixty-seven were more traditional than female and younger counselors.

The point has been made earlier in this study that situational factors influence the kinds of role conflict experienced and the format that resolution takes. We would expect the same to be true for interpretations and satisfactions associated with role. At least one study provides supporting data. Counselors' opinions about their role and the way others related to it were studied in relation to conditions of isolation and nonisolation, that is, the degree to which counselors were set apart from general administrative functions and permitted to act in a somewhat autonomous capacity. Data were obtained from

46. Robert J. Nejedlo and Gail F. Farwell, "Value Orientations and School Counselor Role Expectations," *Counselor Education and Supervision*, vol. v, no. 2, Winter 1966, pp. 61–66.

twenty counselors operating in each circumstance. Isolated counselors reported higher satisfaction with their positions than nonisolated counselors and also perceived their faculties and administrators as more supportive of their role. At the same time, they reported that they read the professional literature and turned to fellow counselors less often than did their nonisolated counterparts.[47] This latter finding may indicate that the isolated group were more confident about decision making, a product of their autonomy, or it may suggest an overconfidence born of perceived noninterference. Hopefully the former interpretation pertains. A more probing analysis would be required to answer this question definitively.

Theory and research on the problems of role conflict, role stress or strain, and related concerns such as alienation and anomie have demonstrated the need for refinement of definitions and reclassification of phenomena. When we currently talk about role conflict, we employ such distinctions as role conflict in which a person owes allegiances to two or more institutions, in which there is a conflict in expectations between two members of the same institution, in which the same member holds conflicting expectations for the behavior of another, and in which the expectations of the institution are in conflict with a person's self-concept. Such distinctions should be considered when an investigation of counselor role conflict is embarked upon, for here, clearly, we have the probability of all types operating in some way. Unlike the church, where institutionalized socialization requires the clergy to internalize without challenge the prerequisites of his role, school counselors do not pass through a rigorous socialization period. And even when they do in a modified fashion, work in the field subjects them to the often conflicting expectations of other persons: administrators, students, and parents.

School counseling presents to the researcher a particularly fertile field for the study of role conflict. First, the role stands hierarchically between several others, which means expectations carry weights that are differentially evaluated by the role occupant. Second, counselors

---

47. Robert M. Wasson and R. Wray Strowig, "Professional Isolation and Counselor Role," *Personnel and Guidance Journal*, vol. 43, no. 5, Jan. 1965.

operate, depending upon setting, in different climates of autonomy, a situation highly conducive to stress or role conflict. Third, the functions and activities of counselors are diffusely defined in such a way that data on counselors would be generalizable to any roles in the stage of professional transition.

This transitional position explains the proliferation of types of training that qualifies a person to act in the capacity of school counselor. In some schools in some states, teachers may be shifted to counselor positions through arbitrary appointment by an administrator. Some schools permit counselors to operate while in the process of attaining certification; other schools require complete certification. Some situations find persons spending half their day as teacher and the other half as counselor. Some districts are highly organized around guidance functions and may contain specialized functions with clearly designated specialties. Some school districts may have a guidance director, a fact that establishes a bifurcation of hierarchies; in this situation the role cues may come either from the director or head counselor or from the principal or vice-principal. Each of these situations contains different elements that might reveal regularities in expectations and conflict. One study, looking at differentials between counselors who also teach and those who do not, found that teaching counselors have their highest effectiveness in the areas of vocational and educational problems, whereas nonteaching counselors are able to win confidence and trust more easily than their teaching counterparts.[48]

Buford Stefflre[49] raised the question as to whether or not any drive toward the professionalization of the counselor role would lead counseling away from the goals of the school and education in general and toward a completely isolated definition in which student personal problems would be considered independently of how these problems produce barriers to educational growth. There is some evidence to

48. Allen E. Ivey, "Role Conflict in Counseling: Its Effects on College Students' Attitudes," *Journal of Counseling Psychology*, vol. 9, no. 2, 1962, pp. 139–143.

49. Buford Stefflre, "What Price Professionalization?", *Personnel and Guidance Journal*, vol. 42, no. 7, March 1964, pp. 655–659.

suggest that Professor Stefflre's concern is legitimate. In what has probably been the best sociological approach to the study of the professionalization of school counseling, Cicourel and Kitsuse[50] attempted to discover the process by which social differentiation occurred in education and also the effects of increased professional image. Acknowledging the fact that students are differentiated into more or less favorable roles (in terms of occupational or educational statuses), Cicourel and Kitsuse sought to know how the different rates themselves occur.

The authors chose an upper middle class suburban high school in which the role of the counselor was deemed crucial to the college allocation of students. They found, to begin with, that parents knew little about entrance requirements but that 97 per cent of them assumed that their children would go to college. In this case, the counselor has the powerful responsibility of making decisions and helping others make decisions in a climate of upper middle class expectations. In the process of defining students, the counselors, the authors felt, "actively seek and probe for problems." These were problems that fall close to the domain of what we might consider psychiatric therapy. In some way, these probings and the definitions of students as having certain kinds of personal problems began to differentiate them in the minds of the counselors; the course of the counseling interviews was consequently affected, certainly in the college-planning area. What was demonstrated was that the assignment of students did not follow the traditional pattern based upon grades or standardized achievement tests. Although the extensive interviews with counselors did not reveal any concrete consensus about the precise goals or techniques, that is, they were not certain about what they were doing, what was observable was an intensification of a specialized bureaucratic function.

The importance of *The Educational Decision Makers* is that it has attempted to explain the process of differentiation rather than look only at the factors associated with different statuses. It is the next logical step beyond the kind of research conducted by Weinberg and

50. Cicourel and Kitsuse, *op. cit.*

Skager[51] and Coleman[52] in which social statics rather than social dynamics were explored.

The Weinberg and Skager study revealed that students' participation in the formal and semiformal (extracurricular activities) structures of high schools was positively related to the amount of vocational counseling received. In several types of high schools (small town, rural, metropolitan, parochial, Negro urban), those students who were most visible to members of the formal organization were given the benefit of excessive vocational counseling. At the same time, students who enjoyed low status within the social system of the school received proportionally less vocational counseling and more "adjustive" counseling. Knowledgeability regarding vocational careers was also related to this visibility.

These statics do suggest the kind of dynamics operating in the school, particularly within the guidance enterprise, and so should help to frame empirical questions to be asked in subsequent investigations. First, there is an indication that either students who are not active in the school's status programs are more psychologically maladjusted than those who are or that maladjustment is perceived by school functionaries as an absence of adequate socialization to the school's ethic for industriousness and participation. Second, the research suggests that those students who presumably will need vocational counseling most (because they seem to lack motivations valued by the school and predictive of educational success) receive it least. How are these decisions made, what assumptions underlie the phenomenology of those making the decisions that produce the discovered differences?

Finally, the kind of research expounded in Chapter 2, in which the author sought to reveal the important concepts that counselors use in diagnosing student problems, should be pursued in the ways suggested in that chapter. There is still room for research on the most fundamental problems of counseling, and if a simple descriptive or correlational design is the best we can manage at this time and only a low level of conceptualization is possible, this is a function of the

---

51. Carl Weinberg and Rodney Skager, "Social Status and Guidance Involvement," *Personnel and Guidance Journal,* Feb. 1966, pp. 586–590.

52. Coleman et al., *op. cit.*

state of knowledge about the sociological dimensions of guidance. At least we have examples of the different approaches that have been applied and the kind of contribution that each makes.

## PROPOSALS FOR FUTURE RESEARCH

We have concluded our review of the empirical investigations made on social aspects of educational guidance. Some suggestions for varying the approach to the studies reviewed have been made. What follows is a brief discussion of the kinds of research problems that should be provocative in producing further knowledge about the sociological dimensions of guidance.

### Recruitment and Mobility

What is the process by which persons are recruited to the counseling field? There are many factors that might be explored in this kind of analysis. Basically there are two approaches, the second of which is of greater interest to the sociologist. The first approach would be a variation on the theme supplied by Anne Roe in her consideration of the relevance of early life experience in explaining career orientations. We might ask such questions as "What early experiences did you have in advising others and how did you feel about playing this advisory role?" Here we might get into the dynamics of family living, looking particularly at the role of the child in relating to siblings. Certain psychological dynamics such as introspection or isolation could provide clues to this orientation. In a personal interview with the author, one counselor revealed that she had spent much of her life in isolation, both from family and significant peers. In this isolation, she felt that she had developed a permanent concern with problems of adjustment, and lacking others to provide her with help, she had turned this concern outward and begun early to seek for the source of others' problems. One way of compensating for not having others to advise her was to take the initiative and play this role herself.

Of significantly greater interest to sociologists is the problem of how the system itself produces both vertical and horizontal mobility. We know that more men who go into elementary education become principals than do women. Several factors might explain this, the fact that men regard teaching as a primary means of supporting a family whereas women frequently see their salaries as supplementary, the fact that education as a traditional institution perceives administration more as a male role than as a female one, and the fact that the kinds of activities required of administrators, particularly those dealing with finances and plant management, are possibly more desirable to men than to women.

A school, as a social system in which persons make a limited range of adaptations, has several avenues for mobility. One definition of mobility within teaching is to go from "difficult" schools to "easy" or "good" schools. This is the most common form of horizontal mobility, and it is based upon a general consensus of teachers as to what constitutes a desirable community in which to teach. Another form of mobility, which can be conceived as horizontal in one sense, because no income differentials are involved, but vertical in the sense of status differentials, would be to go from teaching a slow-learner class to a college- preparatory class, or to jump from teaching in a junior high school to a high school or from a high school to a junior college. The stratification system within a given school or system is one that designates a specific hierarchical arrangement based upon responsibility and remunerative rewards. Above the teaching position is a range of possibilities—master teacher, department head, counselor, vice-principal, principal, assistant superintendent, and superintendent.

In what way does the counselor's position relate to this hierarchy? At this stage of professional transition, attaining a counseling position is viewed more as a step upward in a single hierarchical arrangement than as a shift in function. Being a counselor is still a logical step on one's voyage to a principalship. On the other hand, since a shift in function does occur and primary functions are defined differently in different schools, the actual status of the counselor will vary. Nevertheless, there is general consensus that counselors do enjoy greater status than do teachers.

If status mobility should prove to be the dominant explanation for career mobility, then this bodes ill for the prospect of professionalization of the counseling role. If we could locate a school system in which assuming a counselor role precludes moving to a principalship, we could research the differentials in motivation, role definition, and activities associated with professionalization.

The time is probably not too distant when the prerequisites for becoming a counselor will not include teaching. In the writer's own state, California, it is possible to be certified as a school counselor without teaching experience. Our attitude toward the question of mobility would then shift our research questions regarding motivation away from considering it a step toward the administrative role, except as the guidance function itself inevitably becomes bureaucratized.

Status, of course, is not the only factor that explains mobility striving within an occupational area. Frequently, we may speculate, the important motivation is to escape what one had, rather than to achieve something else. Moving from the classroom to the counselor's office may for many be motivated by a sense of dissatisfaction with teaching. The pattern of flight from the classroom may take several forms, to industry or other occupations or business ventures, to the home for women, to administrative roles other than counseling, and to counseling. A description of these patterns would be a helpful increment to our knowledge about the recruitment aspects of counseling.

Research on the motivational factors associated with recruitment would ultimately involve the isolation of factors such as status or escapism and the investigation of the way these factors are associated with role performances such as counseling effectiveness, interaction with school personnel, and professionalization. Another direction for research on recruitment would involve a focus on mobility patterns associated with institutional organization rather than on individual motivations. What kinds of organizations, in this case school systems, may be associated with different counselor-recruitment patterns? Do rural schools differ from urban schools in this regard? Do suburban districts recruit and manage placements differently than urban districts? Where is the emphasis on recruitment from within the system and where from without?

## Roles and Role Conflict

We must begin exploratory work to discriminate the various components of the counselor role and the kinds of conflict that may be linked to these components. The role of counselor as administrator would not present research with the same dimensions of potential conflict as would that of counselor as therapist. As administrator, for example, the counselor would not be involved with expectations emanating from the clinician's ethos, for which clinical psychologists would provide a significant reference group.

Mobility could provide an important dimension for the study of role conflict. Persons who conceived of their role as a step up in a hierarchy of roles could be subjected to different kinds of conflict than persons who saw counseling as a definitive role unrelated to mobility within the institution. The kinds of conflict and the reference groups that play a part in contributing to conflicting expectations would be different under different mobility systems. How they would differ and the various influences accruing from participating in different institutional settings are questions that require exploration.

Role identification is another dimension that holds promise for exposing regularities in counselor behavior in relation to administrators, teachers, students, and other counselors. A student teacher, for example, is simply playing at a role, and her behavior may follow certain patterns devoid of any kind of innovation. Student teachers are not expected to innovate. They are expected (not as an ideal but as a perception of the requirements of significant others) to imitate, to learn the procedures, and to try out proven techniques so as to experience working with them. When the student teacher becomes a certified practicing teacher, she has increased her identification with the occupational group and begins to formulate, within prescribed limits, her own style. When she becomes a tenured teacher, she may again revise her techniques and explore innovative possibilities.

The counselor's identification with the role follows a similar procedure. There are many variations of role aggregates that are enacted while serving in different capacities. Teacher-counselor, grade counselor, general counselor, head counselor, counselor-director are separate roles controlling, we suspect, the level and intensity of identification. Another factor influencing identification with the role would be the cognate roles that counselors view as most relevant to their task. Looking once again at the Cicourel and Kitsuse study, we observe that counselors in upper middle class communities identified their task as similar to that performed by psychological clinicians, whereas lower class communities produced counselors who identified more with vocational advisors.[53] The kind of identification with the counselor role that occurs may hinge heavily upon the interaction patterns of the school. Certain patterns will vary on the basis of the number of full-time counselors and part-time counselors present in a given school. Those who find themselves to be the only persons occupying this role may identify with the administrative or teaching elements within the school.

The career pattern may be another determinant of identification. If a teacher has come up through the ranks, serving in the capacity of teacher in a given school for several years and then elevated into the counselor's chair, his identification is likely to be with the teachers. If he spent only a few years in teaching service, became a full-time resident student in a counselor-training program, and then assumed a position in a school in which he did not teach, a different identification might ensue. We should be able to predict, with some certainty, that someone who had not taught, had participated in a full-time training program, and had then become a school counselor would identify with other counselors whether or not another one served in the same capacity within his school. This is mentioned as a possibility because there are murmurs about the desirability of such a career pattern.

Role performance is, in many ways, influenced by the amount of control the public exerts over the activities of the school. Counselors serving a community in which heavy parental participation exists are bound to experience controls that influence their behavior; they will undertake, for instance, many public-relations activities. They may also

---

53. Cicourel and Kitsuse, *op. cit.*

find it difficult to assign a doctor or engineer's son to a vocational curriculum even when the ability and interest profiles suggest the desirability of such a program. In this circumstance, the counselor may find that many activities center around a cooperative activity with parents, and the limitations as well as contributions that are involved in such a circumstance are well understood by practicing counselors.

Finally, we lack information on how counselors view their role in relation to educational aims. That is, having designated a set of aims, using either the educational or other community influences as the source we may evaluate the part goal consensus, such as we might find in a suburban elementary school where traditional as well as newly trained teachers interact, plays in defining the objectives for the elementary counselor. Where highly institutionalized expectations of either a conservative (Catholic parochial) or radical (Montessori or Summerhill) nature may be discerned, the range for setting role objectives will be limited. Ultimately we would like some definitive model relating styles of role perceptions, expectations, or behavior to some classification system of educational objectives.

It is out of a newly established perspective in education that the role of the elementary school guidance counselor has emerged. It would be interesting to test speculations about the way in which this new belief system shapes role expectations. Persons are differentially socialized to innovate beliefs in education, and against these innovations looms the influence of the public trust, and against this is the force of cultural change. Out of this complex environment definitions for role performance emerge. How they emerge and how they become institutionalized are important problems for empirical study.

## Counseling and Computer Sciences

Work has been proceeding at Harvard, at the Systems Development Corporation in Los Angeles, and certainly at other places to evaluate the role that a computer system may play in aiding pupil personnel services in their various tasks. The time is far distant when the machine can substitute for a counselor in the direct confrontation of students with problems of emotional conflict. But other segments of the counselor's role may be amenable to the facilities of the computer sciences. We have suggested earlier (Chapter 3) that concern about talent loss has led social scientists to investigate the possibility of adapting machine technology to the task of reducing this loss. This adaptation might involve a data bank of those characteristics of students, aside from the traditional data of school grades and achievement tests, that would be useful in making predictions of academic mobility.

It has already been seen that the traditional data have failed to discriminate potential abilities for students of the lower social classes. But we are very much in the dark about the kinds of data and the kinds of systems required to utilize this data that would differentiate students on grounds other than those traditionally employed. We are very much at the exploratory stage. A good deal of initial work must go into formulating new profiles or models for the prediction of academic and vocational success. The dependency upon grades and aptitude tests as well as occupational-interest inventories has not been adequate to predict either success or satisfaction unless we redundantly assume that success defined by high school performance will predict success defined by college performance. We should specify other criteria of post-high school success that in turn would lead us more proficiently to an evaluation of the kinds of information we need to predict this success. We should be beyond the point where we accept a college degree as validation of our selection and allocation instruments.

What social goals *are* we willing to accept as valid indicators of our allocation techniques? Are assuming an occupational role, getting married, raising a family, and avoiding contact with the law the limits of our hopes for the results of a good education? We should be ready to specify other criteria more indicative of adjustment and adaptation to society. One such criterion might be innovation, which we could define in several ways. Perhaps we need to frame our new criteria for allocative success around the deficiencies we perceive in our society. Innovation might then be defined as active participation in programs designed to improve one's own condition, to move away from apathy. We may advise students to go on to college with the idea that they will successfully complete a program and take a professional job. Do our responsibilities culminate with this? What happens after the student assumes this job? Are we willing to accept the fact that his entire vocational focus thereafter is concerned with improving his status in the organization and making more money?

Innovation may involve a continuing motivation beyond the degree-receiving or job-taking stage, a motivation for lifelong learning and self-fulfillment in terms other than economic. If we were defining criteria consistent with some of the ideals of education, we would perhaps focus upon a form of open-mindedness, a flexibility that would not only reduce the amount of extragroup hostility and prejudice but would also mold a personality that is unafraid of new and different experiences, the kinds of experiences that open vistas for this notion of self-fulfillment.

We would also want to speculate upon the circumstance of job dissatisfaction, exposing the conditions that produce it, such as lack of autonomy, and self-estrangement in the sense that a person may be living with the reality that his capacities are being frustrated by the organization's definitions of his role. Organizations have a distinct effect upon the personalities of their employees. Some personalities may be affected less than others, some occupational organizations may absorb the person and redefine him more than others. Teaching, for example, is an occupation that shapes the teacher to the philosophy of the school. Individualists could be advised about the prospects of their experiencing self-role conflict. But to do this we would require more data on the personalities of those we intend to advise. This would be part of our data bank, assuming we discover systems to utilize this data.

We need to develop indicators of different types of motivations for attending or not attending college. For this purpose, we would utilize information on the characteristics of students associated with particular college choices before beginning counseling. We would want data on expectations for college or work experience as well as data on the characteristics of all types of colleges. A computer could quickly locate a list of colleges congruent with the data on personality, motivation, and expectations of students who wish to attend college. We could perform similar tasks with occupations. For our data system we would require as many characteristics of educational and occupational systems as we could logically expect to be related to student satisfaction and success. And we could use the traditional as well as the newer definitions of success.

Since parents play such an instrumental role, either directly or indirectly, in outlining a student's aspirations and expectations for his future self, we would want to collect as much information on the parents as possible, ultimately testing the relationship of parent-child congruency in values, expectations, and success, as measured in the several ways mentioned.

We would, further, want to include data on certain kinds of contexts within which students work efficiently, productively, or innovatively. Some secondary analysis of grade performance in high school related to classroom context, once we could designate contextual categories, would be helpful in advising students. For example, a student who had received two low grades in algebra in two courses is, as a rule, logically eliminated from allocation to engineering. We might discover, however, that this student does not do well in any context similar to the one provided by the algebra classes and that it was not the subject matter at all that caused the grade. The algebra classes may have been taught, in tone of interaction, quite differently from a class in literature, in which, let us say, the student did quite well. Let us assume that our contextual theory has merit. We could easily test it by supplying the student with two different environments in which to study algebra. There is a good deal of information on the effects of certain kinds of environments, produced by the leader or teacher, on achievement for certain kinds of students.[54] This work suggests the crucial effect that environmental context has for the learning of any kind of subject matter. If we are correct in this supposition, we might then say that if algebra had been taught in an environment similar to the one in which literature was taught and vice versa, the grades might have been reversed. If this is true, our

54. Stern, Stein, and Bloom, *Methods in Personality Assessment,* The Free Press, New York, 1956.

counseling is proceeding on the basis of grossly misinterpreted data.

In a recent study by Leonard Baird,[55] in which he explored factors associated with role stress in graduate students, he found that significant differentials obtained according to the area of study. Students in English experienced greater stress than students in chemistry; reduction of future conflict should and can be within the scope of guidance activities. One would suspect, in a preliminary interpretation of such a finding, that there is an interaction of personality and content that is predictive of greater or less amounts of experienced stress. Commitment may be another factor that would influence the results. Commitment may be measured by a number of indicators, some of which might be present during the last part of the high school years. Such data as hobbies or voluntary activities associated with a projected future could supply the counselor with material on which to base certain speculations about a career.

A number of factors, both independent, such as student personality measured in different ways, and interactional, such as the relationship between personality and context of achievement, have been specified. Many more factors that appear to be related to both standard and as yet undesignated criteria for successful allocation will be adduced. The individual counselor cannot possibly assemble a profile utilizing the complex network of data that hypothetically relate to student success, innovation, utilization of higher education, job satisfaction, and open mindedness. But a machine could, and unquestionably computers will be put to this use.

In a discussion of the research possibilities related to the guidance function of schools, our speculations would be incomplete without a consideration of the utilization of machine technology in facilitating this function. Many of our examples of the kinds of data to be incorporated have been taken from standard and emerging sociological notions, some of which have been discussed in greater detail in other sections of this book. The key to this presentation lies in the inter-

---

55. Leonard Baird, unpublished doctoral dissertation, University of California, Los Angeles, 1966.

action of psychological and social forces, and it is hoped that when a data system emerges to aid the guidance function of schools, these social forces will not be ignored.

## Allocation and Differentiation of Students

The most common and probably the most important area of sociological inquiry in counseling and guidance deals with the interaction between students and counselors.[56] It is here that the greater portion of the activity resides. We have discussed extensively various schemes for the analysis of some aspects of this interaction. We have talked about status allocation and differentiation based upon economic factors, cues for definition of the other person in a one-to-one situation, sources of expectations for role enactment in the interactional setting, and characteristics of students affecting type and amount of counseling. Research is urgently needed in all these areas. We need, for example, to apply our model of cues for definition of persons to an empirical test. We need to devise new classification systems for controls over the types of interaction, and we need to test them. We require data on the characteristics of students as these are related to their definitions of counselors, of the interaction, and of the meaning of allocation to educational and vocational paths.

We know that economic factors influence the use of guidance facilities and the kinds of interaction (college advising, disciplining, adjustive therapy) that transpire in the counseling office. But we cannot explain adequately the way in which these effects or relationships occur. We may know that a student is sent by the principal or vice-principal to the counselor's office because the student does not make a "satisfactory adjustment" to his class. How does the counselor then proceed? Is there a standard procedure, or does the source of referral influence what transpires? Is there something about the

---

56. In sociology the importance of interaction as the basic unit of analysis and inquiry is still being debated. The opposite view is that interaction is the playing out of larger, more abstract and deterministic forces.

student that influences the counselor to act in one way rather than another?

The process of allocating along socioeconomic lines occurred for many decades prior to the institutionalization of guidance services. The school, as a passive agent of society, has been transmitting persons with the same stability with which it has been transmitting the culture. The norms and values of the adult society are passed along in the school and classroom through a traditional network of rewards and punishments. The school does not innovate upon the traditional value systems, nor has it made serious strides in innovating in the area of pupil allocation to occupational roles. Upward mobility for children of the poor has remained a part of the American democratic ethos, but institutional arrangements for the realization of this goal have not appeared, except as temporary shows of political intent. Any real drive within education to make the dream of equal opportunities a reality would require structural changes in the school that only occur as a result of impinging public request.

In absolute terms, the democratization of opportunity in American schools has increased in recent times. Certainly intergenerational mobility is now accompanied by similar rates of intergenerational educational mobility. What is being suggested is that although mobility of persons in the social structure increases, the dominant pattern of mobility has never changed. This pattern is one of unequal opportunities and therefore we observe differential success rates. Violations of this pattern, in some senses, serve to illustrate the fact although channels are open through education, they are at the same time closed to those who are insufficiently endowed to make use of those channels.

We may theoretically conceive of a system of education that would preclude the possibility of differentiation along social-class lines, but this would of necessity infringe upon the rights of parents to motivate their children as they see fit. This is not part of the cultural value system and therefore could never be part of the organization of education.

We have been concerned throughout this discussion with gross levels of differentiation, based primarily on a stratification model. But differentiation occurs in other ways according to other than economic criteria, and these ways are equally important to our analysis. Sociology as well as guidance would benefit from knowledge about the basis of allocation emanating from an interactional framework such as the counseling situation. Let us assume that several middle class students, some male and some female, approach the counselor looking for an interchange that will help them formulate educational and career plans. Does the sex of the student influence the interaction, and if so in what way? The general question is what characteristics of students, holding economic background static, influence the counselor in the way he differentiates these students? We may also assume that ability level is the same for all students, refining even further the area that we wish to tap for differentiation. Are there mannerisms, language differentials, ways of presenting oneself (aggressive, shy, and so on) that influence the counselor, and in what way? Is responsiveness to suggestions important, determination to hold onto one track, the perception of personal liking? Here we lack much information, but the concern is relevant to our consideration of differentiation and allocation. It helps us to free ourselves conceptually from the bonds of traditional inquiry, bonds like the almost exclusive focus we have heretofore placed on racial and socioeconomic determinants.

Within the existing philosophic and social framework, the role of the school counselor cannot be an innovative one. He may be able to work isolated wonders, but this makes a small dent in the logistics of mobility. The counselor, as Wrenn[57] has suggested, is encapsulated by the culture that he has digested. He is further encapsulated by the structural system within which he works and to which he ordinarily confers his allegiance. He has become one more mechanism for fulfilling traditional functions. We have little in the way of evidence to suggest that his new function is achieving results different from the overall outcomes that would have occurred without him. What

---

57. Wrenn, *op. cit.*

important social difference has the counselor made? Administering to the wounds that children suffer at the hands of teachers and other students is but a patching-up task. A penetrating, comprehensive investigation into the role of the counselor in influencing the systems of passage would reveal the mechanisms that produce success as well as failure. If, for example, we could discover patterns of student-counselor interaction that produce a favorable role-model image in the mind of the student, this would be one small but important contribution.

More importantly, perhaps, we could discover techniques, unique to the counselor, that would provide motivation for adequate role performance and induce aspiration and commitment. Perhaps these techniques would be innovative, but for them to be so, certain structural changes within the social system of the school would be required. In what way may the counselor's role be prescriptive of these changes? It would be possible to investigate the kinds of institutional arrangements that are conducive to the counselor's adopting certain role segments that would allow him to change basic structural elements so that students would not always have to live in a world of status differentials.

What has been suggested in this last part of the chapter is a highly idealized level of research into the role of counseling in the process of the allocation and differentiation of students. Some pilot or experimental studies, requiring vast sums of money and elaborate cooperation and willingness to innovate, could be attempted. But our knowledge about simpler things, outlined in this chapter, should come first. This is how a body of empirical knowledge builds. The function of guidance is a diffuse conglomerate, but all things considered, for most students the counselor is among the most favored persons in the bureaucracy. There must be something about the role that produces this expressive sentiment. To know it, we must attack the phenomenology of students, for of all the roles within the school, the counselor's is most likely to break the barriers of restraint and repression that operate systemwide. There is a point at which the values and definitions of students are congruent with the organization, and it is here that innovation is possible. Administrators and teachers may be concerned about the welfare of every child, but the counselor is uniquely suited, by training and by circumstance, to discover the individual needs and ultimately, through individuals, the needs and values of groups. When we know more about the counselor and his role in the organization, we may be able to supply information about the mechanisms that will allow him to put his discoveries to use.

CHAPTER *6*

# THE EDUCATIONAL COUNSELING
# SITUATION AS A SOCIAL SYSTEM

IT IS IMPORTANT for educational theory that analytic probes into an educational process come from several directions, as no one approach may reveal sufficient data to provide a comprehensive understanding of the process. Teaching, for example, has been studied extensively by psychologists and social psychologists, to a lesser extent by sociologists, very slightly by anthropologists, and to varying degrees by historians, philosophers, and experts in comparative education. This multidimensional approach demonstrates the contribution that diverse academic disciplines may and do make to education. These contributions are, essentially, the main body of substantive knowledge that constitutes the field. Some educational phenomena are not explored as frequently as others by this multidiscipline technique. It has, in the past, been convenient to consider the counseling function almost exclusively a psychological experience. This chapter is an attempt to extend analytically the sociological focus on the counseling process emphasized recently by Cicourel and Kitsuse[1] and Lortie.[2] More specifically, it suggests the role that sociologists' analysis may

1. Cicourel and Kitsuse, *The Educational Decision Makers*, Bobbs-Merrill Co., Inc., Indianapolis, 1963, pp. vii–178.
2. Lortie, "Administrator, Advocate or Therapist?" *Harvard Educational Review*, Winter 1965, pp. 3–17.

play in contributing knowledge about the actual interaction process of counseling and guidance.

When the high school student walks into the school counselor's office, either voluntarily or because he has been summoned, he walks into a highly structured social situation. This social interaction is conditioned by potent forces not completely controlled or created by either of the two parties. We are beginning by considering two individuals, student and counselor, as a social group, and as a social group they are governed by conditions peculiar to any group. As such, they may be analyzed in the same way that social groups have always been analyzed by sociologists and social psychologists. They may be described in ways appropriate to the empirical and theoretical knowledge that has been contributed by these scientific disciplines, and certain predictions may be made about the outcomes of educational guidance based upon the accumulated knowledge of how social groups affect the adaptation of the individual actor within the group.

More important than emphasizing the social-group concept in the analysis of a one-to-one interaction is the notion that counseling has developed a culture, a patterned sequence of behavior that is familiar and traditional for participants. As a recurring process, counseling has developed a system of expectations that we may talk about in terms of norms, values, functions, structures, and other concepts that will help order our analysis.

The focus of this discussion rests on the analysis of how two individuals, interacting in formal role capacities, make decisions about how to proceed with each other. Rather than apply such psychological concepts as shaping, conditioning, reconditioning, ego, and defense mechanisms, to the analyses of the counseling process, it is the intention of this chapter to consider the usefulness of applying sociological concepts such as norms, sanctions, roles and role set, bureaucracy, social systems, and social function. Once we structure the counseling situation in sociological perspective, we may then proceed to order the counseling relationship in such a way as to attempt an explanation of how persons make decisions about counseling goals and ways of relating to each other. This approach will further expose reasonable ways of looking at and classifying outcomes of the counseling relationship. For example, we should be able to say, once terms are defined and relationships clarified, something like, "If counselors have an organizational role set, rather than a professional or personal role set, then the most likely outcome of the counseling process will be one of fitting the counselee to the organization, of allocating him rather than changing him." The meaning of this hypothesis should become clear as we proceed.

## THE SOCIAL STRUCTURE OF THE COUNSELING SITUATION

The definition of a social group may be arbitrary as to some of its components, but consensus would have it that a group is *an organization of two or more individuals united by ties of mutual dependence and by a system of shared behavioral standards (expectations) or norms.*

When one actor produces a response in another and when that response in turn conditions the behavior of the first, these individuals may be said to exhibit mutual dependence. They are not accidentally interacting or randomly brought together. They are interacting in a social context with implicit institutional goals governing the quality of this interaction. Whether in any particular case the counselee opposes the counselor's help or whether the counselor is inexperienced or inefficient in pursuing the goals of the conferences does not influence the analytical consideration that these two individuals are in a state of mutual dependence. Both cooperation and conflict are social and operate in a sociological context, because each kind of activity is marked by reciprocal stimulation and response.

The larger context of socialization within the school produces for all members a set of institutional standards that govern both behaviors and relationships. The dominant cultural theme that is important to relationships is cooperation. One cooperates with teachers, with administrators, with other students. These are the norms, whether or not they are present in behavior. This is equally true for the clinical situation, in which the tacit assumption of cooperation underlies the interaction even if subconscious or unconscious considerations make the relationship one of behavioral conflict.

Students learn behavioral standards early. Norms and their implicit, appropriate sanctions in educational settings are usually so conditioned in persons by the time they reach the high school age that students not only always know what they are, they also, more importantly for our context, know how to evaluate in short order the degree of flexibility of these standards under apparently different conditions. Moving from one teacher to another, from a mathematics class to a physical-education class, or from a subject matter orientation to a counseling one, students enter with a set of ground expectations. They recognize that there is some fluidity to the boundaries of their behavior and that the degree of flexibility is determined by the way the leader and follower structure each other's behavior. Even in a highly nondirective counseling session, both parties recognize both the expectations of the larger system within which they are to operate and to some degree the way the other will behave. If the student refuses categorically to play the career game, for example, or to cooperate with the counselor in expressing interests and attitudes such as eagerness to advance himself, then he knows that he forfeits at least partially some of the advantages of career guidance.

Two individuals operating in a highly bureaucratized setting such as the school recognize the differences in the role positions in terms of both function and status. A student's function is to study and earn decent grades, and he is low man on the status ladder. The counselor's function is to help students, and he stands, hierarchically, somewhere between the teacher and the administrator. Roles carry prerequisites and mutual expectations for persons who occupy these roles and for those with whom they interact. If a role becomes institutionalized as a tradition-bound set of expectations for performance, understood to some extent by all members of the system, then individuals who interact in such roles, as teacher and teacher, teacher and principal, student and teacher, and student and counselor, have some understanding of both how they are expected to behave in the situation and how the other is expected to behave.

The analytical approach pursued in this chapter is to treat the counseling situation as a social system with standard classifications of expectations acting upon it. By the word *standard*, it is being suggested that the same general categories of influence that shape the expectations and procedures of any social system are acting upon the counseling relationship. In centering attention upon the counseling relationship as a social system, the important consideration will be the sources, location, and flow of standards and expectations that cue both members of the relationship as to how to proceed in interaction with each other or with the many others present when group guidance sessions are the focus.

## AN INTERACTION SYSTEM

The counseling situation as a social system is composed of a complex of possible roles relating to fairly explicit functions. Implicit in the enactment of roles is an interactional context from which system decisions are derived. What are some of the basic components of this interaction? Homans talks about three important dimensions of behavior within a social-system context of which interaction is but one.[3] The other two that he sees as important components of social behavior are *activity* and *sentiment*. The outcome of participation in the counseling situation is influenced not only by the specific interactional climate but also by what each member has to do and how he feels about what he has to do and about the person with whom he is doing it. These components will be explicated further as the construction of the counseling situation as a social system is pursued.

Guiding the behavior of both participants in the counseling situation is a set of norms and values as well as sanctions. The sanctions support the normative basis of the behavior. These would be unique insofar as they are appropriate in one context and not another. A

---

3. George Homans, *The Human Group,* Harcourt, Brace & World, Inc., New York, 1950, pp. 33–40. Other analytic schemes such as those developed by R. Bales (*Interaction Process Analysis,* Addison Wesley, Cambridge, 1950) and Kurt Lewin (*Resolving Social Conflicts: Selected Papers on Group Dynamics,* Harper & Row, Publishers, New York, 1948) could also be applied to this discussion.

school sanction such as a grade maintains grade-getting behavior, but grade giving in the home would not support family norms of punctuality and cooperation. A teacher sanction such as detention may discourage deviance in the classroom, but a counselor would rely upon other sanctions appropriate to stimulating a student's desire to cooperate in solving his own problem. Counselor responses that are pleasing to a student may encourage his talking about himself. What has been referred to in the area of verbal learning as verbal conditioning is, utilizing a sociological perspective, a method of sanctioning a given behavior in such a way as to maintain or change it.

Some sanctions are more likely to maintain or change certain kinds of behavior than others. These sanctions become the dominant mechanisms for maintaining the system in equilibrium (e.g., universalism in school and particularism at home). The reverse of this, playing favorites at school and treating members of the family in the same way one would treat strangers, would produce an unstable social system if the system were an industrial one to begin with.

Some acts hypothetically used by counselors or teachers, such as hitting students or hugging them, are disruptive to the interaction because they are not part of the normative system framework; they must be supported by other structures in that system. The description of the social system of counseling requires a description of the sanction patterns. What the sanctions are, in terms of a research problem, may be assessed through the notion of expectability. When a certain behavior disrupts the interactions, we may be certain that this behavior is outside the normative system.

As is the case with most subinstitutions, the norms guiding interaction in the counseling situation are variations on the normative system of the larger institution. At the same time, the professional ethos, about which we will talk later in the chapter, contributes a set of expectations about how one responds. Such a Rogerian dictum as "be accepting" has evolved from an instrumental technique, which presumably affects outcomes, to the level of a counseling norm. Any consistent violation of this norm will ultimately lead to negative sanctions being applied by both colleagues and counselees. These negative sanctions will serve to exert pressure on the violating person to return to the acceptable manner of interacting.

To the extent that a normative system has evolved in counseling, the major factor in its emergence has been the attribution of certain expectations of counselors from the student's experience in the school. The question, "How am I to behave to avoid negative sanctions?" when a counseling session is being attempted with the student for the first time, is resolved by projecting from the familiar to the unfamiliar. We will deal with this in more detail in Chapter 7 in the discussion of stereotyping. Let it suffice here that this process explains the content of definitions about how to behave that become institutionalized in counseling in the schools.

Activity for a student consists largely of engaging in certain tasks, primarily contributing information, discussing problems, inspecting motivations and the like, with another person who holds an official position in the school's bureaucracy. This activity is undertaken in specific ways that are consistent with the student's perception of what he is supposed to do. He is, from the expectations of his role behavior as a student, expected to cooperate, contribute, work hard, and ultimately accept the wisdom of the person in the authority role. This may not be perceived by the counselor as the ideal purpose, but it is nonetheless a predictable norm that students come to hold about their behavior in any educational situation.

The counselor too engages in routinized activities to accomplish specific counseling goals. These activities—probing, supporting, providing information, explaining—are elements in the social system about which the two members have sentiments and in terms of which they interact. The context of sentiment may be either the activity or the interaction or both. According to Homans, sentiments are rules regarding the treatment of persons that influence patterns of interaction and the execution of activities. Rules about how one relates to others dictate, for example, whether or not a person will confide in another, particularly within a bureaucratic structure such as the school. The rules may vary according to circumstances and the characteristics of the persons who apply them. How they differ and under what conditions is a legitimate problem for sociological inquiry.

Knowledge about what rules persons use to define the counselor and explanations about the variations in definitions would be useful to the applied task. For example, if we knew more about the factors surrounding the interaction that students use to tell them to apply Rule 1 (e.g., be respectful and impersonal) rather than Rule 2 (e.g., be friendly and informal), we might be able to shape those factors to produce the definitions of the situation we seek.

At a very basic level of analysis, norms and values determine the kind of activity, sentiment and interaction that transpires in the system. Although traditional culture of that system influences the norms and values, a change in the economic structure, for example, usually changes the society's normative structures. Basic feelings are only relevant to this kind of analysis insofar as they become a regular part of the action system. Ordinarily, the sentiments that evolve and influence the system are those that are not highly idiosyncratic but are typical patterned reactions concerned with maintaining the equilibrium of the institutionalized activities. How do we feel about each other in terms of getting a task accomplished? Is the other helping or retarding the progress? Are we proceeding in ways acceptable to me? Are the goals we are seeking worthy? Being comfortable with the answers to these questions tends, on the whole, to maintain the institutionalized activities and preserve institutions.

In a discussion of interaction, the chief concept governing the progress of this analysis, the notion of norms, values, and sanctions is basic to our initial conceptualization. Building upon this, we next enter into a consideration of other factors that help to elaborate our conception of interaction. Patterns of interaction may be highly conditioned by normative and evaluative considerations, but some components of this dimension may be examined without reference to such considerations. Such a question as "Does frequency of interaction between counselor and counselee produce certain affective sentiments?" is important to our knowledge of the interactional process. We may ask the same question about intensity, duration, or even about the various tones of a counselor's voice. We may talk about the ecology of the interaction, where each sits, and how each moves. These factors acquire meaning by having the idea of norms applied to them. The way to observe what is expected and what is not is to see how students react to increasing the intensity of an interview or prolonging its duration. For example, what is the point at which the counselee becomes bored? If there is such a point, can we then discover some standard or regularity that governs one's definition of a "normal" duration? Experimental techniques in varying the ecology of the therapy or counseling situation are feasible and logical. Sitting behind a desk creates one atmosphere and, to exaggerate an example, sitting on the counselor's lap would create another. We are not concerned with proposing the advantages of any one technique about another. We are simply suggesting that the behavior of participants in counseling is ultimately conditioned, to varying degrees depending on the behavior, by normative considerations.

There are many contexts in which the dynamics of social role may help to order our conceptualization of the counseling situation as a social system. Role is the expectations for behavior of a given position within a social system. These expectations involve interaction in the sense that definitions evolve from interaction and also in the sense that a person's behavior is evaluated by himself on the basis of how he expects others to react to given role enactments. The role of counselee evolves in the same way all roles evolve, from an ongoing set of actions and reactions. What I can do, what I should do, what I must do, become stabilized through time by the role taker's perceptions of his behavior through the eyes of those others participating in his interaction system. Role conflicts emerge as a result of a person's being a member of several social groups simultaneously, often with variations in expectations. An examination of the various types of role conflict can reveal a great deal about the social dynamics of the counseling situation.

In a society described by David Riesman[4] as "other directed," role conflicts may be expected to exert more intensive pressure than in a society where the expectations of others are of less concern. The other-directed style is epitomized in bureaucratic life, of which the

---

4. David Riesman, *The Lonely Crowd,* Yale University Press, New Haven, Conn., 1963.

school represents one institutional form. The stronger the control exercised by the expectations of significant others, the greater is the possibility that role conflict will be experienced by members of institutions in which competing expectations exist. A student participates in at least three institutions that are important to him and to society. These are the school, the family, and the peer group. He is given, or he takes, several roles within each. In the school he is the learner, the conformist or deviant, the grade getter or failure, the teacher's pet or just one of the troops. In the home he is son, brother, dishwasher, or perhaps, in a more abstract sense, the vehicle for mobility within the family. In the peer group he is leader or follower, athlete, enforcer, friend, lover, or financier. The congruence of the value systems of each of these institutions over the kinds of roles that should be played, as well as the method of playing them, determines the possibility of conflict.

Another conceptual approach to the problem of roles and conflict is to evaluate the types of conflict that are theoretically possible in a given context. Sarbin discusses five possible types:[5] intersender, intrasender, inter-role, role overload, and self-role. How might each of these types of conflict be represented hypothetically in the counseling situation?

INTERSENDER CONFLICT

The teacher expects the counselor to rehabilitate the student and send him back to class a quieter child. The student expects to be understood in his clash with the teacher, to be given support for his behavior in the name of justice.

INTRASENDER CONFLICT

The counselor expects the student to pursue his interests and feelings honestly with respect to future goals. At the same time the student perceives that the counselor expects him to focus upon occupational goals that are commensurate with his abilities, but not with his interests.

---

5. This is also discussed in Robert Kahn, Donald Wolfe, Robert Quinn, J. Diedrick Snoek, and Robert Rosenthal, *Organizational Stress: Studies in Role Conflict and Ambiguity*, John Wiley & Sons, Inc., New York, 1964.

### INTER-ROLE CONFLICT

The counselor expects the student to open up, be frank and honest with the counselor. The peer group requires that the child treat members of the organization with distrust and contempt.

### ROLE-OVERLOAD CONFLICT

The counselor is expected to treat all students as individuals and to be thorough in the continuation of counseling sessions. He is the only counselor for 1,000 students. How does he choose the students that he will provide with the most time?

### SELF-ROLE CONFLICT

The principal expects the counselor to observe all the rules and ethics of traditional public relations. The counselor believes that the only way he can help a student is to encourage him to disavow his parents' expectations for him.

A comprehensive analysis of the roles and conflicts superimposed upon the counseling situation reveals regularities in role expectations in such a way that potential conflicts may be predicted independently of the knowledge of individual counselors and counselees. Such is the business of sociological inquiry, and once the dynamics of counseling in schools are demonstrated to be of legitimate concern, that is, potentially productive of our understanding of institutionalized behavior, considerable research activity will follow.

## INTERNAL AND EXTERNAL CUES

Two concepts that will be pursued throughout this chapter to provide insights into the principle dynamics of the analysis are what we shall refer to as the *external* and the *internal* directives of the counseling relationship. What these categories suggest, essentially, is that both the counselor and counselee, in order to know how to interact with one another, rely upon two chief sources of information. One, the external source, provides them with some antecedent basis for how one behaves in the role of a counselor or a counselee. The other, the internal source, influences the relationship to the extent that decisions are chiefly arrived at from the interplay of the two persons, how they strike one another, what definitions each makes about the character of the other, and particularly the degree to which the rules and expectations for the interaction are not formally conditioned by some outside force.

In the purely clinical counseling situation, the source of directives answering the question "How should I act?" is ordinarily a kind of external commitment to act on internal cues. That is, to the extent that some theory or school of psychological thought rigidly structures the interaction, even though that interaction may appear to be structured on an "anything goes" format, we still have our principle directives for interaction from what we would call an *external* source. An analysis of the psychiatric interview, applying the same concepts of internal and external directives, would require that within the same definition, different indicators would need to be adduced.

It would be logical to assume that agencies that provide clinical functions would be organized, to a much greater extent than would the school, around the foundations of the professional philosophy, particularly as therapy is the prime function. Although they are not being considered in the present analysis, independent clinicians would be most likely to appeal to professional referents. In educational counseling, however, the source of external authority for role performance lies within the bureaucratic definition of how members of the educational hierarchy are expected to behave. More specifically, the source most useful for our purposes is the pressure, real or perceived, that the two members of the counseling situation feel is being exerted on them to act in ways aimed primarily at solving school problems and accomplishing school goals.

## PROFESSIONAL DIRECTIVES

So far we have suggested that two systems, which we have referred to as the *external* and the *internal,* constitute the major dimensions of the institution of the school providing reference points for the decision making of persons involved in the guidance situation. For the counselor, however, a third structure is required, although it may seldom be consulted operationally. This structure is the professional ethos of that formal professional organization of which the role occupant is either formally or informally a member. Not all counselors belong to the American Personnel and Guidance Association, but those who are certified or credentialed to operate in the role of school counselor have ordinarily undergone formal training that has communicated this professional ethos.

Graduate students learn the norms of performing in many professional roles long before they actually are professionals. Merton and Kendall's[6] study of the medical-student subculture traces the process by which students learn those attributes and beliefs of physicians that have nothing to do with the actual skills. The same process operates in law schools and schools of engineering, and candidates for doctoral degrees in most academic disciplines informally pick up the professional beliefs of their significant professors. The extent to which this professional ethos continues to operate, however, is greatly influenced by whether or not one is a member of a formal organization and by the kind of organization of which he is a member. The insistence upon academic freedom in American universities has little parallel in the public schools. Its absence has permeated the structure of public education in general to the point where compliance with administrative power elements supercedes the consultation of professional referents. The guidance counselor, having moved through the organization as a prerequisite to his appointment as a counselor, has been subjected to organization power lines and has become conditioned to standardized responses, which he will seldom find possible to abandon once he assumes a new role within the organization. The degree to which professional structures provide clues for behavior within the public school context is probably minimal, but nonetheless it constitutes another source of reference that needs to be included in any comprehensive paradigm of cue structures for decision making in educational contexts.

---

6. Merton and Kendall, *The Student Physician: Introductory Study of the Sociology of Medical Education,* Harvard Univ. Press, Cambridge, Mass., 1957.

## LATENT REQUIREMENTS IN EDUCATION

Education is a diffuse and sometimes self-contradicting process. It can move both toward and away from preconceived goals. For example, if self-motivated free inquiry, or curiosity, is an educational goal, then providing material to stimulate interest (films, field trips, extensive library facilities) moves a student toward this goal. At the same time, ritualistic scheduling, classes interrupted by other classes, institutionalized silence, and routine physical mobility for students may be dysfunctional for the same stated goal. The dysfunctional consequences, in this case, would be the emergence of a machine conception of education and a squelching of motivation for curiosity, which often requires a situation in which individual initiative and choice may be exercised. The creation of a configuration of rituals may have dysfunctional consequences as a result of the combining of factors where, separately, these factors, such as institutionalized silence, may be conducive to the development of a spirit of free inquiry. To generalize this example in terms appropriate to our concerns, institutions such as schools, or subinstitutions such as guidance centers, develop a set of goals or beliefs about their function. But when an organization begins to function toward the achievement of some explicit goal, there is always the possibility of failure through the interference of some latent requirements of the system. This discussion represents a concise restatement of some of the considerations presented in Chapter 4.

Besides certain specific aims of education such as equal opportunities, skill training, open-mindedness, communicating bodies of basic knowledge, conditioning for acceptable social habits, and democratic living, there exists a number of hidden functions that the school serves that would never appear in any listing of school purposes. Some of these would be the maintenance of the status quo in the stratification order, conformity, segregation, job stability for school functionaries, nationalistic chauvinism, and community entertainment. Specifically, these conditions are functions that the school has adopted out of a sense of commitment to the real expectations of the community, rather than to the idealized slogans of the democratic ethos. Institutions are created to maintain the society in basically its current form. Schools are what the core public wants them to be. The cry that schools are not doing a good job is actually a meaningless proposition because large institutions do the job that the public basically wants done and "good" or "bad" is purely academic. It is more useful to talk in terms of specific functions and to provide accurate descriptions of these than to worry about ideal standards. The function of education is general, and the function of segregation, as a specific example, is to perpetuate the status quo in social relationships.

The latent functions of education often clearly interfere with the accomplishment of the manifest aims of education. Although evidence of all the latent functions in all schools would be difficult to accumulate, it appears that such functions permeate education. Rates of intergenerational educational mobility, proportions of Negroes in college-preparatory courses compared to whites, the "Super Americanism" surrounding daily activities and in student texts, and the resistance of teachers and administrators to change and to experimental programs are all reflections of what the community expects of the school. The success of the school in preserving these traditional expectations is reflected, at least in part, by its viability and increasing importance as a social institution. The regimentation of students, enforced "groupiness," or group participation, doing what the others are doing, and forcing children into a preconceived mold all express an attitude that may be observed in most schools today. The outcome is, of course, a tendency to see conformity as the best way to avoid rejection.

The appeal to a nationalistic commitment to democracy through the emotions rather than through reason may ultimately prove to be dysfunctional to the maintenance of the democratic way that schools manifestly embrace. Ritualistic flag saluting, the unrealistic worship of men who told the truth while cutting down cherry trees or walked many miles to return pennies, or would not give up the ship, the refusal to discuss other forms of government, the hate and invidious competition with other governments as a way of life, an attitude implicit in daily communications in the school, are all examples of this chauvinism. If appeal through the emotions is the only way that schools can communicate our national history and the necessity for democratic government, then there can be no guarantee against turning a whole nation against itself and little likelihood that what is implicitly undemocratic in our democracy, such as denying Negroes the ballot, will ever be intelligently abolished. Recent events have shown that there is conflict in this area.

The issue of the segregation, de facto and de jure, that occurs in schools, even against stated opposition to this as a principle, is a further example of the way in which educational goals are consistently undermined by latent functions.

And finally, the question of community entertainment, while not in itself a matter for grave concern, carries the danger of selecting participants, such as coaches, players, actors, and entertainers of all sorts, for purposes of putting on a good show for the public rather than for purposes of using these processes as learning situations for the students involved.

## MANIFEST AND LATENT REQUIREMENTS AS DIRECTIVES

It is in the general area of latent requirements, discussed here and in Chapter 4, that many of the cues of the *external* directives appear. Manifestly, a school counselor holds that the most important goal for his particular function is to help students overcome barriers to their educational progress. But this discussion suggests that we need to ask such questions as "To what extent does he compromise this purpose in trying to please his principal, in trying not to endanger community public relations, in allocating lower class students to lower class roles, and perhaps in not seeing school 'undesirables' with the same commitment as college-bound youngsters?"

To extend the distinction between *external* and *internal* systems, it may be suggested that an interaction predicated predominantly on preconceived directives of what a specific role involves, e.g., providing reams of college data, reprogramming a student out of one curriculum into another, or discovering why a student acts disrespectfully in Mrs. Jones's English class, is one in which the counselor operates on cues provided by the *external* system. On the other hand, if the counselor's conception of what his behavior will be is held in abeyance until cues for it emerge out of his interaction with the student, then the process is *internally* directed.

One explanation for the diffuse context of educational process may lie in the confusion that persists over the school's responsibility as an agency of socialization. Tacit in the working ethos of most teachers is the fact that they are in some way defenders of the public morality and reinforcers, through the application of educational sanctions (grades, detentions, and so on) of acceptable values of the Protestant Ethic. It would follow logically, then, that school counselors, socialized in the educational bureaucracy, lend themselves as enforcers of the ethic to the kind of sociological analysis proposed here more readily than do clinicians. We are, in a very large sense, attempting to make a conceptual distinction between both the manifest and latent expectations of the formal organization of the school and the requirements of the interaction between two persons in a professional relationship. The former variable, organization requirements, important to the analysis of the educational counseling relationship as a social system, would be largely absent in the clinical situation of private counseling, although, as has been suggested, some new indicators of an external control system might be derived.

If the school serves a socialization function, which it does, then all roles in the bureaucracy, we may suppose, assume some segment of that responsibility. There is, unquestionably, much duplication in function, but analytically and, ultimately, empirically, we should be able to demonstrate that some staff members, occupying traditional roles, react differently to the amount of credence and value that attach to external directives. We might even suggest that some persons occupying educational roles can clearly distinguish between the learning and socialization functions of the role better than others can. The concept of socialization is being applied here in the special connotation of emphasizing normative behavior as the school defines the norms.

For example, there is the instillation of values around industriousness, morality, cleanliness, punctuality, respectfulness, nonaggressiveness, and a host of other commonly accepted "virtues."

## CUES FOR BEHAVIOR

When we speak of cues that reveal system expectations, we are referring to those stimuli that provide us with directives about how to respond in any given social interaction. Individuals are expected, frequently required, to respond in specific ways while enacting a specific institutional role. If we are talking about requirements, then it is usually clear what the manifest administrative or control regulations are. When we think of expectations, however, there is some flexibility. We need to be concerned about the degrees of clarity of these expectations, about degrees of rigidity, and about the degrees of autonomy that persons possess that permit them to ignore certain expectations under specific conditions.

### Degrees of Clarity

Normative prescriptions for certain social roles are sometimes quite vague, sometimes absolutely clear. When a student seeks help from a school counselor under situations of extreme duress of anxiety, the counselor knows that he is expected to provide time for the student and is expected to do this by all members of the organization. Another situation, which would reflect diffuse and conflictual expectations would be one in which a student reveals that he is so furious with the physical-education teacher that he is going to get at him in some way, perhaps slash his automobile tires. What are the expectations for performance in the counselor role in this case, particularly when the student cannot be consoled or dissuaded? Should the counselor invoke administrative power to restrain him? Should he reveal this information to school authorities and particularly to the physical-education teacher? Should he remain silent, acknowledging that he has done all in his power to convince the student that his aggressive act will accomplish nothing, even though the student is certain that in his own terms it will? Or should he call in the parents and turn the problem over to them? Institutional expectations are usually understood as generalizations and frequently do not encompass all contingencies. To rephrase our focus slightly, we are concerned not so much with what counselors typically do when norms are unclear or incompatible, but with what the references are that they consult when they make decisions. Another goal would be to assess the regularities with which certain cues are regarded as crucial in decision making. This aspect is, in part, accounted for in the paradigm proposed later in the chapter.

## Degrees of Rigidity

Granting that expectations for role performance are clear, the question arises, "How necessary is it for persons to conform to these expectations?" The school administration may expect a counselor to explore the world of job opportunities, and students may expect him to be knowledgeable in this area, but negative sanctions for de-emphasizing this area and perhaps to concentrate on problems of adjustment are seldom applied. Giving teachers feedback on the development of guidance techniques and new roles they might play in the guidance process may be an expectation of the system, but teachers seldom apply negative sanctions to counselors who neglect this responsibility. On the other hand, the expectation for counselors to be in their offices regularly to perform their function and to contribute their time in administrative planning is quite rigid. Extensive "goldbricking" is severely criticized and punished. The rigidity of institutional expectations may ordinarily be evaluated by a consideration of the extent of negative or positive sanctions that accompany compliance or deviance.

## Degrees of Autonomy

Autonomy in this context refers to the degree to which individuals occupying bureaucratic positions are free to determine their own course of behavior, acknowledging the expectations but dismissing them when certain other commitments become paramount. This involves one's belief concerning the power that inheres in the role.

A given school or school district may have fairly clear responsibilities in the area of public relations. That is, each member of the organization recognizes his part in the total responsibility of not offending the public trust. In many cases the public trust may be manifestly interpreted as not offending the power figures of the community. This would be a common situation in small-town social systems. Under these conditions, it could and usually does happen that the sons of community leaders are given preferential treatment in the school and allocated to positions of high social status. A counselor may find himself faced with the conviction that certain low status students, in community terms, require his assistance more than do the children of the elite and that, in many cases, these children of the elite must receive communication, as must their parents, that they are not suited by intellect or personality for the status positions to which they aspire. To what extent, under these conditions, may the counselor follow the dictates of what he considers to be his professional responsibility and ignore the system expectations for preferential treatment? To answer this easily, we may consult the influence that community leaders can and do exercise to ensure compliance within their school. On the basis of our findings, we may predict the degree of autonomy that is probable in a given system. We may increase the efficiency of our prediction by also consulting the tolerance level of the administration itself. But for our purposes, this is not the important issue. Here we are chiefly concerned with the source of the decision to act autonomously, whenever such behavior occurs. For this we have to attack the host of referents employed and weighed, sometimes in spontaneous fashion, by the person making the decision.

We might have just as well applied our consideration of clarity, rigidity, and autonomy to the student role, and, for the most part, similar referents would have been employed. We have not yet established, however, any empirical regularities that would allow us to specify either the cues chosen or the conditions under which one cue has preeminence over another.

These have been some considerations relevant to our discussion, but an overview of our task would require that we understand that certain formal structures underlie the complexities within which individual decision making takes place. These would be the external and internal requirements of the system to which we have added, within certain professional roles, the dimension of a professional ideology, which in itself may mediate the expectations of the other two systems or even provide the sufficient cues for decision making. When we relate our three structural elements as cues to our three conditions of expectations (clarity, rigidity, and autonomy), the relationships of Table I emerge as likely.

### *Table I*

| Expectations | Important Cues |
|---|---|
| High clarity | External system |
| Moderate clarity | Professional system |
| Low clarity | Internal system |
| High rigidity | External system |
| Moderate rigidity | Professional system |
| Low rigidity | Internal system |
| High autonomy | Professional system |
| Moderate autonomy | Internal system |
| Low autonomy | External system |

This hypothetical paradigm is more descriptively definitional than predictive. What is being suggested is that when institutional expectations are very clear, the external system is more clearly before the decision-making eyes of the role occupant. When they are less clear, but not yet hidden, it would seem appropriate to rely upon professional cues. And when the expectations are entirely vague, it would seem appropriate to rely upon cues that emerge out of the current interaction and the definition that each participant has made of the other in terms of some mutual acceptance and influence. The same logic would apply to the question of rigidity.

With autonomy, we are dealing with another kind of relationship than the first two, but it is important to our overall purpose. It is being suggested that the greater the autonomy regarding compliance with expectations, the more likely it is that the professional ethos structures the cues for performance. Where autonomy becomes the concern of the counselor in a way that suggests a compromised or deferred commitment, the internal cues are likely to take over as a balance between a total commitment to the student or client and a total commitment to the administration and/or public. When the counselor regards his autonomy as low or deferred to a time when he can achieve more power, the external system would be expected to supply him with most of his cues for interaction.

The counselor unavoidably is perceived by students and colleagues as a member of the administrative team. The extent to which he acts like one, plays the role of a member of the bureaucracy, and is guided by external-system directives, rather than detaching himself in the interests of accommodating his responsibilities to the perceived expectations of the counselee, is an empirical question. A further empirical question more crucial to the analysis being suggested here would be, "Even if the counselor does respond to cues from the external system, do these cues direct his interaction in the task area,[7] (non-socialization goals) or in the ethical area?"[8] For the analysis of any social system, but specifically for the consideration of the educational-counseling situation, a paradigm for counselor role adaptation is proposed (see Table II).

### Table II—A Hypothetical Model of Teacher Role Adaptation

| External Goals | Mixed External-Internal Goals | Internal Goals |
|---|---|---|
| High Task Adaptation | Moderate Task Adaptation | Low Task Adaptation |
| High Ethical Socialization | Moderate Ethical Socialization | Low Ethical Socialization |

### External Goals

In the area of external goals, the counselor responds to institutional goals as directives for his interaction with the counselors. Concurrently the counselee is led into responding to the same directives.

---

7. Referred to as "adaptation."
8. Referred to as "socialization."

His problem, if the session is instigated because he has one, centers almost exclusively around where he is expected to fit into the institution or where he is heading educationally according to his performance to date.

The counselor asks himself, "What does my role in the bureaucracy require of me in relation to the counselee?" In effect, he is leading himself to find a solution that is adaptive in the Parsonian sense of solving functional problems relevant to the institution's roles in the society.[9] In terms of this functional area, if he is interacting with an eleventh-grade student, he recognizes that his role requires that the counselee become a twelfth-grade student. If the student is ready to drop out of school, his purpose is to keep him in. If the student has a high IQ and wants to work in the vocational-arts curriculum, his job is to convince him that society needs engineers. These examples represent a condition in which the counselor conceives of his function as being closely tied to the overall function of the school rather than to the *internal* state of the counselee.

In the limited amount of time that high school counselors see students, there is small opportunity to begin *tabula rasa* and explore the entire life history of the counselee, working through every stage of conflict in his life history, including the dynamics of his current life situation, and at the same time playing the role of ameliorator of behavior that is detrimental to the institution's drive for a peaceful equilibrium and the student's continuity in his educational progress. The counselor must decide to play one of three roles in the interest of stabilizing the function within the bureaucracy, and these roles represent the three areas of the model. First, he may decide that time and student need make it impossible for him to play nondirective therapist and that he has got to keep the flow of students moving toward predetermined ends. He must help them on the road to college or to an appropriate occupation; he must influence them to relinquish their deviant patterns in the interests of their survival; he must convince them that, rightly or wrongly, the Protestant Ethic and the

---

9. Talcott Parsons, "A Revised Analytical Approach to the Theory of Stratification," in *Class, Status and Power,* ed. by R. Bendix and S. Lipset, The Free Press, New York, pp. 110–111.

ethic of cooperation and respect present the most instrumental path to success in school and society.

## Internal Goals

Second, the counselor may decide almost nothing in advance. He may wait for his cues for performance to emerge out of the internal interaction, and he may be committed to interpreting his role not institutionally but interactionally. In other words, he will be convinced that socialization (as defined earlier) may be employed as a means but never as an end and that goals are never predetermined for any individual until that individual, with the counselor's help, clarifies these goals for himself.

## Mixed Goals

Third, the counselor may decide that, to some extent, he may play both roles, to satisfy the institution's expectations to perform an active, semiadministrative function in solving school problems and also to help in the solution of the individual's problems. Expediency, and this may operate randomly, depending on the way the counselor perceives his time schedule and perhaps even upon the particular interest he has in some students over others, may motivate him to socialize directively at one time and to search nonevaluatively for openings and cues at other times.

## Direction for Research into Role Adaptation

The paradigm for counselor role adaptation proposed earlier suggests some boundaries for research but also raises certain methodological questions. The principle issue revolves around the placement of counselors into the proposed categories. Self-identification may be too idealized, counselee identification may suffer from predisposed stereotyping, teacher identification may be inappropriate because they have no knowledge of the counselor's actual performance. Perhaps the best method for classification would be the congruence between the counselor's perception of his performance and the counselee's. If the focus of the research is on the adaptation of the student to the counseling experience, then the perceived structure of the interaction by the counselee is logically the best source. If we are considering an exploration into the area of role conflict on the other hand, then other modes of classification will certainly be required. Hopefully, investigations in this area will also yield data that will relate the counselor's perception of where he places himself to personality, career patterns, identifications (professional or voluntary associations), and characteristics such as sex, age, ethnicity, and years of experience in the schools. Ultimately, preliminary research into the usefulness of the proposed categories would be applied to questions of the effectiveness of the counseling relationship, specifically in terms of legitimate goals of both the institution and the individual involved in the interaction.

## CUES AND PERFORMANCE

Students take some of their cues for any new social situation, such as the counseling one must be for them if no transfer from other therapy-type situations is operating, from the way the leader presents himself and responds to their actions. Therefore, the dynamics of the social structuring of the counseling session sets the tone, the direction, and the limits of the responses. As such it may be the single most important condition for achieving counseling goals. Again, as stated earlier, this would be particularly true in any setting where norms, values, and sanctions are already conditioning the interaction patterns of individuals whose earlier associations with the institution, be it school or church, are not easily eradicated when the counseling interaction is with a member of the bureaucracy.

The degree to which persons performing in the same bureaucratic role hold the same socialization goals would explain the extent of institutional stability that is maintained in a social system such as schools or the army. The maintenance of any social stability within the institution of the school may be determined, then, by the amount of digression that the individual actors in leadership roles are able to engage in—digression, that is, from the expectation of the maintenance of those values that the school is charged with reinforcing. This is especially true in the area of allocation. The normative expectation for the school and functionaries within it is generally to provide, for the society at large, hordes of individuals who are not only skilled to play certain roles but committed to playing them. Parsons has made this same point in describing the school class as a social system.[10] If a counselor, for example, who is cued by this traditional expectation (external cues) comes to interact with a student whose main interest happens to be in the expressive arts, perhaps painting, then it is likely that this counselor will attempt to affect a compromise between the student's generalized desire to paint and the institution's generalized desire to produce a citizen who will contribute his talents to some more productive enterprise in society's terms. The externally motivated counselor, then, would certainly be unlikely to suggest or even accept the young artist's suggestion that maybe he should forget about school and go off somewhere and paint. The school as one of the socializing agencies of the society is too rational and economically concerned to permit a child to leave its charge without establishing in him an ace in the hole (again in society's terms) for productive performance in case his artistic aspiration does not pay off. A counselor who takes his cues at least in part from this rational and economically motivated system would feel pressured to suggest that the artistically motivated student consider seriously the way in which his interest could be tied to "productive" work, such as being an art teacher, a designer, or a decorator.

If we were to empirically derive a situation in which most school counselors fall into the internal category (which we could never hypothesize), then it is likely that we would be either discovering a

---

10. Talcott Parsons, "The School Class as a Social System," *Harvard Educational Review*, Fall 1959.

larger social trend that places the school in transition as an agency of socialization or revealing a breach in the dam. For example, we could ask the theoretical question, "Is the school maintaining its role as an agency of socialization or it is relieving itself to some extent or in some areas of this charge?" Institutional change is certainly highly predictable when roles within this institution become more autonomous and more professionally suggestive of function than committed to the public trust. If the school teacher or school counselor, through some professional growth and the establishment of some professional authority, has the confidence of this affiliation, it is then likely that he will operate considerably more in the *internal* category.

In summary, the utilization of this model of guidance counselor–counselee interaction, once empirically confirmed, may not only prove valuable in describing the social context of the interaction and the categories of goals pursued but may also explain the stage of social function of a given institution.

## GUIDANCE FUNCTIONS

In the previous chapters, we have discussed the specific functions of the counseling enterprise. These functions were classified in terms of activities or procedures required to accomplish certain goals. In a discussion of the counseling situation as a social system, we want to employ a different functional perspective, one that exposes general categories of functions that apply for every social system. In this way we may theorize generally about counseling as a class of behavior; this theorizing, in turn, permits us greater latitude in designating characteristics or conceptual variables for study. This is what we are trying to do throughout this book, and it is the immediate purpose of writing a chapter on counseling as a social system. There is little value in describing some interaction situation from a given perspective not commonly employed if our only purpose is description. If we were to show the ways in which qualities of counselors or teachers could be looked at in order to classify these functionaries as parent surrogates, we would still need to answer the question as to why this analogy was developed. If we could then show that many student behaviors logically followed from the fact that such an identification was made, our purpose would then purport to have explanatory value. This is the contention here, that revealing counseling as a social system has explanatory potential and that we may predict behavior or explain it in ways that would be impossible without applying a social-system perspective.

We have mentioned the work of Talcott Parsons several times in this chapter. His ideas on the ordering of social life have influenced much of the thinking about social systems and institutions, and his framework for the identification and elaboration of system functions will be used here. Because, according to Parsons,[11] all social systems involve fulfilling four general functions, we may expect that the counseling situation is so involved. These functions are *adaptive, goal attainment, integrative* and *pattern maintenance*. They are, in Parsons' sense, the pillars of viability. Only through providing for each of these functions can a social system survive. The characteristics of the society determine which functions will be dominant. For example, American society regards the adaptive function as preeminent and requires most of its important institutions to direct their energies toward activities related to economic efficiency. This means building capacities in persons by which they may be fitted into the technological, industrial society. Economics provides families, schools, and political organizations with a ready-made platform, that is, to build up the economy and motivate and fit persons into it.

## The Adaptive Function

An ongoing social system maintains itself through fulfilling those expectations held for it from various sources. Each system is assigned some specific task by the society, and subsystems are assigned segments of this task. The school's primary task is to provide competent personnel for the occupational structure. The guidance task is differentia-

---

11. Parsons, *ibid.*

tion of and support of persons on their way to fitting into this structure. The adaptive goal is centered around efficiency in producing persons who make decisions and perform in ways that justify the existence of the system of guidance and counseling. These persons, the students, choose curricula, colleges, and occupations and discover ways of avoiding barriers to their educational progress and employ them. Self-understanding, making peace with family and authority figures, and discovering interests and abilities are outcomes of the guidance process that aim at fitting persons who are either confused, obstructed, or have lost their way into the adaptive patterns of the institution. That is, these persons are helped along the road to economic efficiency or back onto it.

It is not an accident that guidance in schools makes its central task one of career counseling. This is the implicit responsibility of the institution in as much as the school is a logical partner to the adaptive demands of the economic order. Adaptation predominates in our society, and if the main function of the counselor is to career counsel, he too is adaptive. If he goes about changing students according to allocation decisions, he is adaptive for the school. Changing the orientation of school counselors, asking them to play the role of clinicians, would be to encourage activities incongruous with the dominant social purpose of the school. This is why school districts resist vigorously any attempt to shift the emphasis in counseling from a vocational to a clinical approach. Counselor educators have sometimes attempted to have state departments of education accept the credentialing of persons trained in counseling without these persons meeting the teaching requirement. To accept such a proposal would be to open the door to the gradual overhauling of the counseling function in the direction of an autonomous clinical program. School districts and guidance personnel in administrative state department posts see these attempts as potentially disruptive to the servicing of the grander function that we have called adaptive.

It is clear that the adaptive function does predominate, and it is equally important to note that this is consistent with the dominant functional goals of the society, which the institution would be expected to reflect.

## *The Goal-Attainment Function*

Parsons states that the goal-attainment function is represented by qualities of "system goal commitment" and "legitimation of unit goal commitment."[12] System goal commitment is, first, the allocation (as choices of goals) by authority, as in politics and elections; second, it is locomotion toward or away from these goals by the whole system, as in getting elected. If the counselor makes general decisions about the allocation of students to different goal areas, he is, for the school, performing a goal-attainment function.

For the most part, school counselors do not contribute to the selection of system goals but rather have the goals decided for them by administrative authorities. Ideally the role of the expert, in the case of the professional counselor, would be one of deciding goals that his professional skills are adequate to achieve. Deciding upon specific mental-health goals for the system so that these would then become legitimate purposes of the guidance function would be a goal-attainment function. The capacity of counselors to operationalize certain kinds of goals that usually pass unnoticed as vague desirabilities, such as "social adjustment" and "emotional maturity," should ultimately force school authorities to recognize the role that counselors can play in the system goal-attainment function.

The counselor is involved in the goal-attainment function only insofar as his role is part of the process of deciding what sort of school the school will be and of making it that kind of school. If adaptive goals are dictated by the general society, the role of the school, before beginning to mobilize its resources to solve the adaptive problem, must be of deciding what the machine is going to look like, that is, what kind of school will be most efficient. The fact that a guidance organization geared for career allocation appears to be the most necessary function of counseling is not usually the counselor's decision. If, however, the guidance office decided that mental-health goals were more desirable for industrial efficiency than technical and scientific skills, and if the guidance personnel played a role in reorganizing the

---

12. Parsons, *ibid.,* p. 110.

school to this end, then goal attainment would clearly be a paramount function of guidance.

Within the parameters of the guidance task itself, guidance personnel must make some decisions about the organization of their own enterprise. In this case, the goal-attainment function of the guidance system is served.

## The Integrative Function

The third type of standard (Integrative) does concern integration and may be called the system integrative. It defines expectations with respect to a unit's contribution to the maintenance of solidarity with other units in the system. The focus is on the quality of attitude, on positive action to be taken in the interest of inter-unit solidarity.[13]

Showing solidarity, exhibiting qualities of loyalty to the system and its goals, and showing positive affect toward other members of the system in the sense of all being participants in a common and mutually beneficial endeavor represent another function essential to the viability of a social system and of subunits within that system. A social system regards all actors within it as members of a team. Such membership involves a complex of obligations and rewards and of understanding expectations of one's role in relation to other roles. In this way, members are coordinated to accomplish system goals that are made explicit in the determination of the adaptive function and internalized in the goal-attainment function.

Counseling is attuned to the system of achieving goals to which members are committed and aids in this process by helping to fit individuals into the composite picture. Counselors want students to feel that they belong, in the sense of being part of the school team and of some specific academic group that makes its particular contribution to the total educational endeavor. Disruption of the activities of either the school or the group, not pulling one's weight, withdrawing or functioning in isolation from the whole are dysfunctional to the grand design. Integration is also accomplished in showing students that

---

13. *Ibid.,* p. 98.

they do not belong; this has the effect of either changing their behavior or solidifying the knowledge students have about their relative positions in the social system of the school or classroom. This knowledge, in turn, stabilizes the behavior of persons who stand in these different relations to the activities and goals of the school. Any time the counselor deals with socially defined deviants, he is working in the integrative area.

In the broader sense, counseling as a unit performs certain services that may be evaluated as integrative in the way they tie together teaching and administrative activities. Thus counseling helps achieve interunit solidarity. It aims toward sensitizing persons to the fact that they enjoy common membership in a system that has the best interests of all as its purpose.

Another dimension of the integrative function, actually the counterpart of achieving solidarity through the infusion of a sense of loyalty, is the reduction of conflict between the various units of the system. Counseling operates as the intermediary between the teacher and student roles, attempting to bring about a balance and harmony such that each may work with the other in a predetermined task. This is accomplished through the employment of a particularistic interaction, an interaction founded upon the unique qualities of persons. Particularism brings about independence of roles as well as cooperation. It is the particularistic approach that is the special quality of the counseling task; students are integrated in terms of special and unique abilities, rather than only differentiated along some unidimensional universalistic scale as often is the case in the classroom. The counseling task is to encourage students to appraise their singular qualities—their abilities, interests, background, and the like—and to fit themselves into some cooperative role within the school. The guidance orientation in group dynamics in the classroom operates according to the same principle. A single student may not be able to donate special information to a group report, but he may recognize that he, better than the other members, can present it graphically or artistically. The sanction norm for performance in this area is a kind of diffuse acceptance in the sense of allowing a large and unspecified number of qualities to bring approval rather, again, than some universalistic or highly specific set of behaviors.

## The Pattern-Maintenance Function

Sometimes referred to as the latency function, the pattern-maintenance function is involved with maintaining those performances that are required to serve the other three functions and with regulating any changes required in these performances. This requires a process of enculturation, an instillation of a set of values and routines for preserving these values through a meaningful set of sanctions to which members will predictably respond. The system organizes a reward and punishment system, the main sanction norm being that of esteem, that helps to maintain the activities involved in fulfilling the dominant functions. For example, should a student express an intention of dropping out of school, all those values regarding the importance of an education are brought to bear by all the members of the system, by the teacher, the counselor, the administrators, and many of his peers. Should he then decide to stay as a response to negative sanctioning or the uniform impingement of the values of the school culture, the response is approval, and he is admitted back into the cultural system. Guidance counseling is seriously engaged with this function. Students are encouraged to pursue goals that the system values, and an important technique for motivating students to join the race is to establish for them the belief that such goals are legitimate and worthy. For example, we infuse in students the belief that the logical conclusion of their schooling is a job. At the same time, we want them to commit themselves to perform in some work capacity, to want to do the job and want to do it well. This activity takes place first at the level of educational goals and ultimately at the level of vocational goals, once academic training becomes differentiated. The material, data, and advice about the occupational world and educational training required to achieve a position in some segment of it is made available to students without the issue ever being investigated of whether or not the goal to which such data will be applied is worthy.

The worth of system goals is an inviolable working assumption, and to the extent that an institution or a unit of that institution operates on this assumption, it is reinforced and mainained as an implicit function of the institution.

The assumptions perpetuated through counseling related to the goal-attainment functions would be

1. To work is necessary.
2. To work is good.
3. To complete an education is necessary.
4. To complete an education is good.
5. To dwell in academic studies is good.

It is on the basis of the internalization of these values that many students are allocated to roles that may be the most efficient for the maintenance of the social order but personally dysfunctional in ways that have been discussed in an earlier chapter.

The performance norm that dictates expectations for the pattern-maintenance function, according to Parsons, is "cultural responsibility." Patterns are maintained through the exhibition of this responsibility in members of the system. Many activities, appearing as reinforcing value activities, are centered around this function. Special activities in elementary school classrooms are constantly being repeated in several ways regarding the importance of industriousness, punctuality, ambition, and so on. Seldom a day goes by without some student or group of students providing the excuse for another lesson on proper school behavior. By the time the student achieves secondary school status, he has either internalized the norms or rejected them. But even if he has rejected them, he knows what they are and is responsive to the consequences of acting in terms of a competing set of values.

The counselor as disciplinarian plays a crucial role in supporting and rewarding with esteem the return of students to the cultural design. At the same time he will attempt to infuse a sense of responsibility in the student, sometimes in the name of responsibility to oneself despite the fact that the behavior would be the same whether it was to the self or to the institution.

Counseling serves as an aid to the system in clarifying the more complex dimensions of the culture in which the student is to survive as well as in assisting students to accept shifting patterns that present new performance expectations for new educational programs or techniques. The counselor, in most cases, becomes the spokesman for the wisdom of educational change, as well as tradition, supporting the introduction of certain progressive changes. He does this by incorporating the change components into the adaptive structure that, while new techniques are being employed (new programs, use of technology, psychological instruments) traditional adaptive goals are still valued and pursued.

In his most ideal role enactment, the counselor provides data to students that presumably permit them a free choice of behavior but within the framework of likely consequences for the choice of various alternatives. That is, the kinds of data (interest scores, performance scores, teacher evaluations) only have meaning within the framework of traditional cultural patterns. The counselor is saying, "This is what you need to know in order to make the kind of commitment that we have socialized you (by pattern maintenances) to want to make." Pattern maintenance is a very real function of counseling, and the form is one of latency insofar as the maintenance of the system is paramount and individual student needs are concommitant goals.

## CONCLUSION

We have considered the counseling organization of schools as a social and cultural system. We have argued that new perspectives that order educational phenomena are useful in exploring knowledge about such phenomena. We have utilized ideas developed around the concepts of role, function, norms, sanctions, and interaction patterns to present this point of view. Student interaction with counselors is a regular, patterned process, requiring increased specialization. Universities, whose responsibility it is to develop such specialties, must increase the body of knowledge to be taught to meet the demand for specialization for improving the guidance function. In order to increase any body of knowledge, it is essential first to develop models or conceptual schemes flowing from general ideas. The organization of these ideas, the development of theoretical foundations from which future practice will orginate, is the task of every student who intends to make counseling a career. The social demand for specialization, for the training and allocation of educational personnel who are better equipped to understand the specific process they will help implement, provides the impetus for an explosion of knowledge about these processes. Education has itself consistently relied upon the social and behavioral sciences for the backbone of its methodology, and insofar as these methodologies add up to a discipline of education, such a discipline owes much to the systematic theoretical and empirical inquiries of behavioral scientists who make educational institutions their laboratory. Educators who do not understand the relevance of social scientific inquiry to educational practice will balk at the designation of schools as laboratories for research. But these administrators will decrease in number as the new waves of specialists, armed with new and sound conceptions of the school and its role in society, replace their atheoretical predecessors.

The usefulness of conceptual schemes such as those presented here may be demonstrated only by the activities of those who learn them and go into the field to see what sense they make in attending to daily routines.

# CHAPTER 7

# THE ROLE OF SOCIAL TYPING IN COUNSELING INTERACTION

THE TERM *stereotyping,* through common usage, has developed an opprobrious connotation. While we think unevaluatively of typing as a method of classifying persons or objects, stereotyping appears to attach a stigma to objects and leads to making invidious distinctions. Viewing Negroes as lazy, the rich as idle, Jews as ambitious, teachers as supermoralists, and college professors as ivy-tower retreatists involves a process of identification that influences human interaction. The term *culturally disadvantaged* was originally employed to designate a theoretical population for the purposes of devising remedial education programs. The theoreticians and researchers who were devising plans and projects to identify certain characteristics related to school failure had no intention of providing the masses with a concept that would invoke invidious definitions. But this has occurred. Estelle Fuchs's account of the events leading to the protests at the Samuel Slater Elementary School in New York City is a case in point.[1] In the process of communicating his perception of the educational problems associated with teaching Negro and Puerto Rican students, the school principal incurred the wrath of the community. The community did not wish its children to be identified as disad-

---

1. Estelle Fuchs, *Pickets at the Gates,* The Free Press, New York, 1966.

vantaged, to be treated as a special type. They rebelled against what they believed was prejudicial stereotyping.

Typing of persons on a grand scale is a product of urbanization. Although race and nationality groups bore the burden of rigid stereotyping in a rural society, the number of categories that could yield to stereotyping was comparatively small. The mailman was Joe and the shopkeeper Fred. In modern industrial society, every occupational group has been typed by the masses, a consequence of their inability to make personal identification because of a lack of frequent personal interaction.

Patterned definitions do not occur unless they serve some important social or psychological function. With the typing of persons into gross categories, both functions obtain. Socially, typing or stereotyping serves the function of socializing persons about how to behave in an interaction situation that is unfamiliar. Once socialization has occurred, typing then becomes the recognition and application of a course of action that is learned. Most conversations at social gatherings begin with "What do you do?" The answer to this question then governs the context of the subsequent conversation. Knowing what a person does appears to tell us something about his politics, recreation, style of life, preferences in entertainment, voluntary associations, and tastes in literature. Of course our hunches about these attributes are frequently erroneous, but nonetheless we perceive a general framework from which to build probing questions. We are not likely to ask an auto mechanic whether or not he thinks Bergman is a better film director than Fellini or ask a librarian whether Alston should play LeFevre at short or third. If we know persons more intimately, we do not have these problems. But urban society contains too many interaction situations in which the persons are unfamiliar to permit us to forsake our typings. Moreover, typing is a way of establishing social images that regulate the behavior of persons in a society. Because typing is based on positive and negative (usually polar) formulations of major cultural goals, members of a society create ideal types so as to shape their own behavior cognitively along the lines of the positive ideal and away from the negative ideal. In this sense, typing is a form of social control.

Psychologically, the function of typing is the reduction of anxiety. Fears about the unknown or unfamiliar are such that we want as quick a reduction of this psychic insecurity as we can manage. Many primitive tribes introduce strangers to their young as being uncles or aunts, typings that quickly reduce the anxiety in the children.

Occupation is not the only source of stereotyping that is a product of urbanization. Age-based subcultures have emerged as a result of the abrogation of many of the responsibilities of the family. The peer group has come to represent, for most adolescents in particular, a significant reference group, and the fads that are typical of segments of this adolescent society are very amenable to typing. A male walking down the street with guitar in hand, long hair, and sandals calls forth quick stereotyping, and in some suburban communities, children would probably be called off the street.

If open-mindedness and intellectual flexibility are manifest educational goals, then we begin to observe paradoxical behavior, as a result of certain kinds of typing. Stereotyping is a special negative case of neutral typing. Typing as well as stereotyping occurs in all places and seems to be an absolute necessity to social life as we know it. Stereotyping is both a rural and urban phenomenon, occurring most brutally in primitive societies, where the same cues that provoke stereotyping in the United States (color, hair style, and so on) are often used. The difference between primitive and urban stereotyping is that, in the latter case, it can be done against the dictates of the system's own idealized normative order. We have evidence of considerable stereotyping of students on the part of educational personnel based on hair length, hair styles, language, make-up, skin color, styles of dress, and so on. A single symbol may turn a teacher's interest away from a student and may evoke generalized negative sanctioning that affects educational careers. Teachers have readily admitted their repulsion toward symbols associated with the lower class.[2]

---

2. Howard Becker, "Social Class Variation in Teacher Pupil Relationship," *Journal of Social Science*, vol. 25, 1952, p. 451.

These same symbols may effect the guidance process in similar ways. Hopefully, counselors are too sophisticated to stereotype a total personality on the basis of one characteristic or to generalize to a whole social group from the behavior observed in one member of that group. But there is a caution that needs to be articulated. Although we would like to allocate high school seniors who intend to go to college to colleges that suit their personalities, it would be a mistake to assume that one personality trait effectively designates the appropriate college. A male student who prefers long hair is not necessarily a Berkeley type, nor is the female violinist in the school orchestra best placed at a girls' private college. Unfortunately, the overburdened guidance office may be forced to make hasty advisements because of the limited time it can offer each student.

Social typing has become almost the exclusive basis for political choice. Awareness of this phenomena, augmented by the availability and necessity of television exposure, now sends each political candidate to his public-relations firm to work out a program designed to produce the most advantageous social typing. We have become increasingly aware that issues constitute a diminishing factor in the election of public officials. This phenomenon is demonstrated graphically by the fact that movie actors, capitalizing on their favorable movie image, have received winning margins.

Lawyers are sensitive to the stereotyping factor as it affects juries and would never allow a defendant to retain his beard in court. Teachers or counselors would salvage many students from punitive measures by teaching them to respond to their accusers with "I haven't done anything, sir," rather than "I ain't done nothin!"

Social typing is a process that, when analyzed, provides considerable insights into social regularities. It is, after all, the sociologist's job to discover these regularities in social life, and it would seem that many social categories are revealed by the kinds of typing that persons employ. Klapp's analysis is instructive in comprehending the functions of typing. Utilizing three basic types, the hero, the villain, and the fool, he suggests that these represent . . . "three basic dimensions of social control in any society. Heroes are praised, followed, set up as models and given a central part in dramas. Villains and fools are negative models, respectively, of evil to be feared and hated, and absurdity to be ridiculed. Heroes, villains, and fools represent three directions of deviation: (1) better than, (2) dangerous to, and (3) falling short of, norms applied to group members or status occupants."[3] Stereotypes, in Klapp's terms, are ways to

. . . hold people at a distance and portray outside groups in an inaccurate way. Stereotypes emphasize error while social types represent real roles being played; stereotypes refer to things outside one's social world, whereas social types refer to things with which one is familiar; stereotypes tend to be conceived as functionless or dysfunctional (or, if functional, serving prejudice and conflict mainly), whereas social types serve the structure of society at many points. People often talk as if they would like to be rid of stereotypes but it is hard to conceive of society without social types.[4]

Stereotyping and negative typing are the primary concepts that focus this discussion. Stereotyping will refer to those definitions that students make about educational personnel prior to interaction or out of experiences unrelated to the specific interaction, such as family socialization. Negative typing will refer to definitions of persons as a result of interaction. Stereotyping involves attributing to a total personality some extension of a single trait or attributing to a total group some characteristic or characteristics associated with one or a few members of that group. Negative typing involves the establishment of role models by which persons who exhibit opposite qualities from those of the role model are categorically negated. Role models, positive and negative, may change places as interaction with both occurs. The perception of persons about others in their environment is seldom neutral. For many persons, particularly children, definitions of others are usually very positive, in which case the person can do no wrong, or very negative, in which case he can do no right. The combination of typical modes of psychological functioning and social organization forces society to live with stereotypes and negative role

---

3. Orrin Klapp, *Heroes, Villains and Fools,* Prentice-Hall, Inc., Englewood Cliffs, N.J., 1962, pp. 16–17.
4. *Ibid.,* p. 16.

models. It is possible, however, through an understanding of the mechanisms that produce these regularities in human interaction, to reduce the effects of these kinds of definitions of others.

The reduction of negative effects of common social modes is accomplished through the institutional regulation of behavior. Organizational patterns are necessary, within institutions, to effect the kinds of desirable interaction that negative typing makes difficult. However, educational reorganization usually occurs as a result of some important cultural evolution and seldom as a result of internal evaluation of processes and dysfunctions. Guidance structures, however, may have a better opportunity to control educational innovation than other areas that have a more traditional set of definitions about their task. Some proposals about the way guidance may moderate the effects of stereotyping and negative role typing are offered toward the end of this chapter.

For our purposes, stereotyping is crucially involved in the process of making definitions about new roles from characteristics associated with old ones. The source of negative counselor stereotypes may be found in the definition of teachers, and the potential source of stereotyping of elementary guidance counselors may be discovered in the definitions we make about secondary counselors.

## ELEMENTARY GUIDANCE ROLES

As greater specialization around guidance functions shifts to an equally specialized emphasis on age-differentiated counseling, the elementary counselor will emerge bearing the same relationship to secondary counselors as elementary teachers bear to secondary teachers. The desirability of such a role is already established in most educational communities. Practicing elementary counselors are rare, but they are a reality in some school districts. The structure of elementary guidance is as yet defined in very limited ways. From the standpoint of someone interested in describing typical patterns, the conclusion would have to be that elementary guidance is what a few people in a few places do with little professional coordination of activities. These patterns are in no way so routinized on a national basis that a radical revision of contemporary structures would run up against the barriers of tradition.

Seldom in the evolution of educational systems have we had the opportunity to assess a role previous to its becoming institutionalized. As social demands on the resources of the school increase, as they will, and specialization becomes an ever more dominant mode of organization, other new roles will emerge. The evaluation of these roles must involve systematic consideration of possible dysfunctional occurrences such as stereotyping, if the ultimate functional problems, for which the role was established, are to be adequately served.

The assessment of a role that is identifiable only on paper or in scattered and random activties subscribing to a role definition is not, in itself, of sociological interest. The study of a formal organization and its response to system demands, however, is. How does an organization reformulate its structured activities in the process of adaptation to external requirements? Sources outside the institution, in this case the school, have certain expectations. These expectations constitute a set of requirements to which the school must comply if it is to remain a viable institution. It is this compliance and the reorganization required that are worthy of analysis. The applied value of this kind of analysis is that a set of theoretical propositions are available for inspection so that the consequences of alternative organizational tactics may be evaluated prior to instituting specific structures or activities.

Education has long suffered the criticism that it does not plan for the future. School administrators are bogged down with plant management and public-relations responsibilities. Teachers assume little initiative in pushing for a dominant voice in educational planning. Professionalization of teaching has not reached the point where it can define areas of influence. Top-level administrators are concerned with budget, recruitment, supervision, materials, and curriculum. The guidance function does not possess the autonomy on a national level, or the influence on most local levels, to dictate criteria for accreditation of its own members, much less for those who intend to assume a new and diffuse responsibility.

It is likely, therefore, because external demands are impinging, that elementary guidance will become routinized in different ways in different places and settle into an established role on the strength of the sheer recurrence of activities. And if institutional change is unlikely, the material in this chapter must be considered as completely theoretical work. The value in this case may lie only in the kind of insights that it provides for individual practitioners, particularly as some of these people may be able to move the mountain in small ways so as to be able to avoid some of the pitfalls that always accompany unplanned or poorly planned activities. If controled change on an institutional basis may be influenced by ideas, the advantages of this kind of analysis are considerable.

## ROLE LEARNING IN EDUCATION

Role learning, in any institutional context, involves a process of internalizing the expectations of significant others, ordinarily those involved in performing the same function as the role taker. These expectations become internal cues for behavior, instructing the person about how to act in fulfilling responsibilities. Education, like the family and economic organizations, has a tradition of having persons learn roles by observation, intuition, training, or specific instruction. Once a social or institutional role has been defined, the limits of authority and autonomy are also defined, and institutional sanctions emerge to preserve these definitions and expectations. The values around privileged communication, for example, are preserved by the isolation and sometimes manifest rebukes of persons who violate these values.

Teachers who may wish to permit gum chewing in class are restricted from exercising free initiative by the predictable response of other teachers who see the teaching role as denying this activity. Those who are willing to abide by their personal evaluation of what a role allows or does not allow are quickly appraised of their responsibilities by the activities of the informal society of colleagues. Education, in particular, appears to react strongly to the violation of routines by individual teachers because the same students who were given freedom in one class may wish to exercise it in another, causing a disruption of the institutional patterns.

Roles within complex organizations are ordinarily hierarchically arranged. Not only do different roles fulfill different functions, but they also contain varying degrees of authority. Expectations, as clusters, center upon separate roles, but some single expectations obtain across all roles within an institution. An example of this in the school would be that all role occupants are expected to value and support the normative system of the larger society. Regardless of one's superordinate or subordinate position, any evidence of attitudes or behavior that runs antithetical to this value system would be grounds for removal from the school system. Showing support of free love, atheism, or communism or questioning the vales of patriotism, cleanliness, industriousness, or punctuality would be to challenge the larger system, and the viability of the institution depends upon unilateral subscription to the social ethic that dominates all the major institutions of the society.

Role taking in education may influence the total behavior of the person or simply that segment of the behavior that is visible in the school. Stratification of roles carries an implicit differential in the extent to which out-of-role interaction commands adherence to the original role. The school superintendent may hesitate about taking a second drink at a social affair, but the teacher has greater autonomy out of the organizational setting. Ecological factors such as community size and the extent of social interaction within the community may further affect the degrees of autonomy that are possible. Greater or lesser autonomy may be a variable that influences the amount of typing or stereotyping possible in an institutional setting.

## STEREOTYPING AND THE SOCIAL ETHIC

Culture heroes are those persons whose mobility, current status, or both are covered with a garland of virtues because of their adherence to important cultural values. In our society these virtues are represented by loyalty to God, country, and family and the observance of a supermoralism. Also included is the achievement of some kind of success, usually accompanied by economic rewards. The socialization function of the school is to help internalize these values in its students to the extent that they will respect the values in others and strive to attain them. This function has its roots in the initial affiliation of the school with the church. Even after the divorce of the two institutions, the responsibility of influencing the moral character of students was retained by the school. Operationally the school has never lost this conception of its obligation, although the sources of its moral authority are diffuse. A school grade is often a combination of (*a*) the degree to which a student followed directions or leadership, (*b*) the amount of industriousness he displayed, (*c*) the way he met certain standards of language and communications, (*d*) the neatness and punctuality of his required work, (*e*) some diffuse but still applied evaluation of his moral worth, and, finally, (*f*) an evaluation of his achievement on some universalistic standards.

From the evaluative procedures employed by educators, certain definitions are made of these educators by the students. For those who fail to meet the criterion of success, a negative typing emerges that has extensive consequences for the behavior of students. For it is here that the villain appears, the negative role model whose pronouncements must be defined as unacceptable because the person himself is defined that way. There can be no truth from the mouth of someone who is condemned as a villain, be he a politician, philosopher, father, or teacher. A negative model is one who convinces you that classical music is undesirable by proclaiming its worth.

Many teachers are defined as well-meaning but impotent captives of a rigid system or, in Klapp's sense, fools. These persons are not to be believed either and do not command confidence. They are viewed with distrust by sensitive students who are not quite integrated into the institution because of their marginal success in presenting a well-socialized image. These students are aware of their marginality, recognize that they are typed by an impersonal bureaucracy, and usually know the traits that betray them. These may be skin color, language, occupational designations, curriculum, or a host of other attributes. A student in the industrial curriculum recognizes his inferior status in the social system of the school and recognizes further that less is expected of him in the way of achievement and more in the way of manners. He learns that he will be accepted if he conforms. When a person finds that he is a member of an out-group, he is quick to apply negative stereotypes to members of the in-group, whether these members are other students or teachers. If a person is a Shark, then he can tell you all about the Jets in glittering negative generalities. The surfers make a stereotype of the nonsurfers and vice versa. There is a dwindling middle ground in contemporary institutional life. The students who experience the greatest amount of negative typing apply the same perspective in return, and it is this group that the counseling function sees as its most challenging responsibility.

## THE GUIDANCE ROLE

Guidance is a recognized function of the educational bureaucracy, and the counselor occupies an institutionalized role. One counselor behaves much like another with varying degrees of competence, and is subject to varying and often unclear evaluative criteria. Roles are expectations for behavior within the institution, and it is not of relevant consequence that the occupants have varying amounts of training, different kinds of training, or varying degrees of educational experience. That is to say, factors of training and experience do not affect the analysis of the role as a descriptive task, that is, what counselors actually do. On the other hand, such factors may influence the kind of patterns that become institutionalized as a formal role. If counselors retained a strong professional affiliation and if accreditation was controled by this organization, then counseling skills and knowledge would be uniform across schools on a national basis, and the limits of responsibility would be set within schools. Once these limits were established, the patterns would become institutionalized in a predictable way, and a descriptive survey would reveal one kind of role behavior rather than another. Whether a counselor was first a teacher and whether he assumes his new role in the same school in which he served as a teacher are factors that could affect the definition and routinization of his role. Counselors almost categorically arise from the teaching ranks and frequently assume posts within the same school. This is often determined by the fact that administrators pick and choose from their faculties, assign a person to part-time counseling responsibilities, and then suggest that he take some counseling courses.

The problems involved here, in light of the discussion of stereotyping around the social ethic, are considerable. In the process of role taking as teacher, a person adopts the socialization responsibility inherent in his task. He becomes defined as a type and usually lives up to this definition because it is the clearest way to establish role stability. Moving from one role to another within an organization involves a reorganization of tasks and responsibilities in those areas that are unique to the different roles. But we have suggested that certain expectations cut across all bureaucratic roles, and it is with respect to these generalized expectations that the most serious stereotyping occurs. This is primarily true in the area of producing the "good" citizen. Role definitions are more susceptible to change when the tasks are clear, but the activities involved in stimulating citizenship are highly diffuse. Moreover, accepting this responsibility requires a decision on the part of the role occupant that it is within his province. Methodologies may develop around tasks that are manifest responsibilities, and these techniques may be evaluated in terms of standard criteria such as achievement or behavioral change. But with latent responsibilities, techniques do not inhere in the role; they are, rather, intuitive and expressive, in the sense of being toned with positive or negative personal affect. The stereotype of the teacher, and ultimately of all educational personnel, derives from those activities that are established to motivate and condition students to accept the values associated with success, not from the activities directly linked to the more formal cognitive tasks.

## THE PUBLIC IMAGE OF THE TEACHER

It is difficult to talk efficiently about role definitions of school counselors without an initial consideration of the environmental context of his task. Roles contain the element of status as well as of function, and the history of the status dimension in education bears heavily upon the evaluation of the definitions students make of school personnel. The school environment is one that has experienced a long history of status strains. Except for short periods of its history, the teaching role has suffered the burden of low public valuation. This stigma has also attached to administrative roles as a result of the fact that administrators were once teachers. The strains for status and authority have their roots in history and in the ongoing interaction of schools with their communities. Negative typing of teachers, insofar as this is one element in the definition of educational personnel, has accrued from a public image that is only partly a function of the behavior of teachers. More than from actual behavior, the definition of teachers has emerged out of a set of unrealistic expectations for this behavior on the part of the general public. Teachers have always been the servants of the public trust, and as servants they were always expected to meet a complex set of supermoralistic and often incompatible practical demands. The caricatured image of the supermoralist teacher has traditionally been one of a middle-aged spinster, her hair in a bun, wearing wire-rimmed glasses, calling for perfection in a highly imperfect world. As such, she was seen as ineffectual in the "real" world, contemptible for exhibiting moralistic affectations that offended the human quality in the public, and disturbing and discomfiting to others who felt required to play a stiff role in her presence.

An important source of status strain has also been the history of community pressures on the school to meet incompatible expectations in the area of educational goals. The school, as a traditional social institution, cannot change its educational policies as frivolously as the public can change its mind. Schools require systemwide consensus on policy. The community requires no such agrement. The school may be criticized because of too much progressive education or too little, too many punitive measures or too few, too strong an athletic emphasis or too weak, as resisting integration, or as favoring the slow learner and ignoring the exceptional student.

A third source of strain evolves out of the rationalization patterns of those who do not wish to pay a fair share in the support of public education. Rather than accept their lack of interest and their desire to hold onto every penny they have, they convince themselves that their lack of support is motivated by their recognition of the inadequacies of the system itself, that teachers do not deserve more money because they do not have the skills or ability to command it.

The public image of the teacher is not a particularly favorable one. Public evaluation of occupations has seen the teacher ranked at the bottom of the professional class.[5] The North-Hatt scale revealed a ranking for teaching of 36 in 90 possible evaluations. Standing above the teacher were such occupations as building contractor, army captain, airline pilot, and artist.

Willard Waller[6] perceived a clear teaching stereotype. Writing at a time when teachers worked in the community where they lived, an atypical situation in the urban society, he saw the teacher as self-consciously isolated by the community. He described social interaction in the presence of teachers as highly artificial and elegant. He described a situation in which teachers experienced difficulty in renting a room in a private residence. This was, as he interpreted it, because people did not wish to be restricted in their behavior, and the teacher would definitely be considered a restraining influence. He relates the following epigram that he believes to be a representative example of the way in which myths are perpetuated: "Teaching is the refuge of unsaleable men and unmarriageable women."[7] Such a myth may be a gross exaggeration, but as a belief system it serves to control and influence interaction.

Few conceive the modern teacher as representing the image revealed by Waller, but the image of any occupation usually retains some elements of its historical conception. To these elements other

---

5. C. C. North and P. K. Hatt, "Jobs and Occupations; A Popular Evaluation," *Opinion News,* National Opinion Research Center, Chicago, Sept. 1947, pp. 3–13.
6. Willard Waller, *The Sociology of Teaching,* Science Editions, John Wiley & Sons, Inc., New York, 1965, pp. 49–60.
7. *Ibid,* p. 61.

considerations are now added: the feminization of teaching, relatively low salaries, the impotence of teachers professionally, and the fact that teachers are responsive and sensitive to public pressure. One does not esteem a professional who allows himself to be told what to do by untrained members of the society. Parents perceive that it is their right and responsibility to watch over the education of their children. They believe that they may do this because the technology of teaching lacks the kind of complexity that would set teachers apart from their critics.

In a society that evaluates status through gross symbols, income represents a major criterion for prestige. A person's worth is counted in dollars and cents, and most teachers do not earn as much as many skilled workers. Therefore, because skill commands income, teachers presumably possess little skill. And since so few men become teachers, in comparison with the other professions, teaching is very often considered as something to be left to the professional aspirations of the weaker sex.

Most members of society have had the opportunity, as students, to observe the behavior of teachers. This, many believe, makes them qualified critics. The public has probably observed, on many occasions, the humiliation of teachers by administrators. Students are aware of the effect that parental interjection or even the threat of this interjection may have upon the freedom of the teacher in and out of the classroom. At times students may also have witnessed the way in which a teacher's frustration was expressed in inappropriate aggression toward themselves.

The counselor begins his career with the need to overcome the initial handicaps of the definition of himself as the servant of the public morality, a characteristic ascribed to teachers in general. His opportunity to create a more favorable image rests with his ability to communicate to the individual student, his colleagues in the school, and the community at large an aura of his own professional autonomy. Our analysis is not concerned with what he needs to do but with the play of social dynamics that affect the kind of typing that influences the one-to-one interaction of student and counselor.

## STEREOTYPING AND CHILD DEVELOPMENT

The social definitions of others that a child makes are usually a product of his identification with some significant reference group. And because reference groups change as the child ages, earlier stereotypes may change and new ones emerge or the older typings may become intense fixations.

Changes in social stereotypes are a function of more than shifting reference groups. They may also be linked to ecological and demographic change. The most resistant attitudes to school integration are found in geographical segments of the United States where the least intercultural interaction occurs. Intercultural interaction is related to the availability of transportation and comunication facilities that throw diverse cultural groups together on a continuing basis. There is little transcontinental traffic through Mississippi, Alabama, and Georgia. These states are not geographically conducive to either the intra- or the international mobility of persons. Because of this, we would expect the least change, with the passage of time, of childhood stereotypes in these states.

The diminution of the grossest form of stereotyping, friend or enemy, occurs with maturity, when the child can finally handle complex definitions and relate to abstractions. This is true with nations as well as individuals. Those islands, for example, such as Hawaii and Samoa, that have experienced intercultural contact will contain populations less susceptible to the friend-enemy dichotomy than primitive areas of the world, such as the Northern Philippines or sections of New Guinea, Australia, and Africa.

Piaget has distinguished levels of abstract thinking related to chronological development[8] and suggested a clear, linear relationship between physical maturation and abstract thinking. This intervention here, as Piaget states, is that of interaction. Maturation is a necessary but insufficient condition for abstract thinking. That is, maturation is a matter

---

8. Jean Piaget, *The Origins of Intelligence in Children,* International Universities Press, New York, 1952.

not only of learning the content of values but also of learning the form of interaction (peers vs. parents). This point is important to our later discussion of the interaction between the counselor and the elementary school child.

We now have two themes by which to order our thinking about the complexities of stereotyping: the way in which such typing is linked to reference groups, on the one hand, and maturation, on the other. The dynamics are complex and are such that one condition may work against the other to increase, decrease, or change stereotypes.

## REFERENCE GROUPS

The first significant reference group in the social life of the child is the family. It is here that his first definitions of others are made. In the beginning the grossest form of typing occurs—the child differentiates between those he knows intimately and trusts and all others whom he does not know and does not trust. Siblings, for example, despite much internal rivalry, possess a distinct cohesiveness upon which emotional support is given. The importance of this support from both siblings and parents is such that the child develops a set of attitudes congruent with the others so as not to endanger this necessary emotional support. Variations upon this theme are many; they are related to family size, position of child, age of child, parental constitution, sex of child and so on. Only children, for example, may be expected to branch out more quickly to other associations than children with many siblings. The constitution of the family unit influences the attitude of the child insofar as this attitude is partly a function of the role the child plays within the family. Bossard, in a study of sixty-four families has identified several dimensions of family role.[9]

1. Areas of responsibility. At least one, usually the oldest, is identified as the responsible child. Other terms applied to this role by parents

---

9. James Bossard, *The Sociology of Child Development*, Harper & Row, Publishers, New York, 1960, pp. 108–109.

were "dutiful, bossy, drudge, leader, helpful, martinet, and police-man."[10]

2. Areas of sociability or popularity.

3. Areas of social ambition. "Social butterfly" is often applied to this assumed role, usually to female siblings.

4. Areas of scholarship or studiousness.

5. Areas of isolation. These roles may be perceived as antisocial, secretive, and nonparticipating.

6. Areas of irresponsibility. These roles do not involve the isolation of physical presence so much as the rejection of responsibilities within the family that others accept.

7. Areas of illness. The "sickly one" would be a common designation; many of these learn to "utilize their illness to gain them special favors or to justify their failures."[11]

8. Areas of special favoritism. The spoiled child is a commonly designated role.

These role areas may evolve as a result of many complex dynamics, but some regularities are obvious and Bossard has supplied empirical data to substantiate the characteristics associated with the several roles. Order of birth and sex of sibling appear to be the best predictors of which role will emerge. Some of the research conducted by Bossard has suggested, for example, that oldest and only children, males and females, accept the greatest amount of responsibility and take leadership roles more frequently than other siblings. Youngest children, particularly males, appear to be the most erratic and undisciplined. A few other statements in the literature on sibling position are

1. Eldest children are more serious.[12]

2. Intermediate children are more restless and neurotic than the eldest.[13]

---

10. *Ibid.,* p. 108.

11. *Ibid.,* p. 109.

12. Edith Neiser, *The Eldest Child,* Harper & Row, Publishers, New York, 1957, pp. 32–37.

13. James Bossard, *The Large Family System,* University of Pennsylvania Press, Philadelphia, 1956.

3. Eldest and youngest children are more successful in the school adaptation than intermediate children.[14]

4. Intermediate males with one older and one younger brother have the largest incidence of recorded delinquent acts of all male positions.[15]

Roles are always accompanied by attitudes, rationalizations, or dispositions that can be logically linked to the nature of the role itself. Being socially ambitious requires the emergence of values supportive of those qualities that are predictive of social success, i.e., attractiveness, grooming, friendliness, and so on. Responsible roles associate with values of industriousness, order, and morality. Other roles have their appropriate value aggregates. These values, in turn, lay the framework for the dimensions within which social typing and stereotyping occur. Those most concerned with academic ambition will stereotype groups around their dispositions toward school. A certain type will appear to the student to be associated with disrespectful attitudes toward the teacher and the learning situation.

The selection by children of deviant roles within the family requires the emergence of rationalized values. This follows the same process as in the development of values supporting nondeviant roles. In these cases, negative typing will accrue to persons who restrict the deviant behavior or exhibit highly normative behavior. These persons become caricatures of such types as teacher's pet, spoil-sport, sissies, and tattle-tales.

The family is more than a set of differentiated roles, however. It is also a culture, a system of patterned beliefs that affect the behavior of the members. The culture of the family may be attached to special qualities of ethnicity, race, geography, occupation, and status within the community. Socialization of the children occurs within this kind of framework, and definitions of others occur in terms of those characteristics that constitute the culture of the family. Persons from families with cultural configurations other than one's own become typed and posi-

---

14. Irving W. Stout and Grace Langdon, "A Study of the Home Life of Well Adjusted Children in Three Areas of the United States, *Journal of Educational Sociology*, vol. 25, 1951, pp. 67–85.

15. Raymond F. Sletto, "Sibling Position and Juvenile Delinquency," *American Journal of Sociology*, vol. 39, 1933–34, pp. 657–669.

tively or negatively defined in terms of similarities or differences. Much of the conventional educational wisdom brought to bear on the problem of cultural disadvantagement coheres around the notion of values in conflict. What this appears to mean is that the families of certain segments of the society are antithetical to educational values. This, however, does not demonstrate conflict. The real conflict occurs as a result of the inability of the two institutions to accommodate whatever differences exist. The values themselves are not in conflict, they are simply somewhat different, at least in the beginning. They become polarized as the out-group attempts to build defense mechanisms around their egos as the in-group attacks them for their failure to exhibit qualities consistent with in-group expectations. This dynamic is of crucial significance in explaining the negative typing of school personnel by lower class students.

Community reference groups are but a slight variation on the family theme. Persons similar to the parents—friends, neighbors, relatives— appear in the child's environment and are defined in terms of the relationship they have to the parents. Since the values of the parents are internalized early, the values and behavior of those close to the parents are usually congruent with the expectations of the children. The community, as such, lends support to the socialization process occurring within the family. Out of this process a position is taken by the children relating to one of two modes of adaptation that are typical in the society. One position is conforming or bureaucratic, the other is instrumental or entrepreneurial. These two modes, which are buttressed by beliefs about social functioning, cut across ethnic, economic, racial, and geographic lines. One's definition of others and eventually the rigid stereotyping of others frequently center around one's loyalty to one or the other adaptive mode. If the conformist value is internalized, those who exhibit deviant characteristics, who attempt to innovate on the acceptable means for the attainment of desired goals, are negatively typed. The heroes of this culture are those who attain success through the standardized channels; the villains are those who achieve status or power through deviant means. The process is somewhat reversed if the instrumental mode is the end product of family socialization. If adult members of the family and their friends support the attitude that we live in a survival-of-the-fittest society and the person who succeeds is the one who is best equipped regardless of means, then the heroes are those who succeed. The villains are those who frustrate mobility (the law, the boss, sometimes the white man), and the fools are the plodders. In a very serious sense, educational personnel appear to students with the instrumental orientation as just this kind of fool. In this way it becomes even more foolish to the student to be preached to about ambition, industriousness, and the routine virtues of conformist living when the persons doing the preaching are defined as grossly unsuccessful themselves.

The occupation of the father is frequently what directs the orientation of the child to one of the two adaptive modes being discussed. Occupation, as we have said, is a recurring meaningful symbol in urban society. Those whose fathers are in occupations that require conformist behavior for mobility, salaried workers in civil service or industry, especially organization men, are ordinarily conditioned to value the bureaucratic mode. Those whose fathers are large or small businessmen in either the legitimate or illegitimate sense, frequently pick up, along with those who are outcasts of the economic system entirely, an instrumental orientation. That is, they define relationships as utilitarian to their economic mobility. In this way, the son of the successful businessman as well as the son of the family on relief may make the same definition of the teacher or counselor, a definition that frustrates the best efforts of the educational personnel.

It should be noted about the role of the family in the socialization of the young, as this defines the kind of social typing that will occur, that children frequently reject their parents. Because they reject their parents, usually for some psychodynamic reasons, they subsequently reject the social thinking of their parents. This is an intrafamilial example of typing; children extend their personal rejection of the parents to the entire conglomerate of values and beliefs espoused by the parents. The occupant of a negative role model is one who lends his stigma to everything he says or does. One extension of this theme would be to the way in which an entire generation may reject the values of their senior generation simply because they are the senior generation. Once negative typing occurs, the entire culture of those negatively typed becomes either stigmatized or suspect. Educators, who have to work across generations as they do, are confronted with this further obstacle to their task.

## Peer Reference Groups

Neighborhood agemates constitute the second influential reference group in the maturing child's environment. From the third to the ninth or tenth year, peer groups are loosely structured, sexually segregated, and highly fluid in their membership. Seldom do these peer groups reflect other than a configuration of parental attitudes. In the earlier years, the peer group is more accurately designated as a play group or a cluster of different play groups. After the eleventh or twelfth year, agemates begin to solidify their boundaries, define themselves as uniquely distinguishable from the adult subculture and from other peer groups. These groups become differentiated from others according to a number of social distinctions that they make about themselves and others. In preadolescence and then more intensively in adolescence, agemates form about two types of peer groups to which they pledge their allegiance, the clique and the gang.

The clique constitutes the reference group that holds values generally consistent with those positively sanctioned by the major institutions. Or at least these values are not negatively sanctioned. They may be such that the major institutions, such as the school, the core American family, and the legal structure, are basically neutral. If values of dress, music, fads, clothes, or entertainment that are exclusively the property of adolescents and the pursuit of these values come into conflict with the normal routines of the institution, then negative sanctions may appear. The adult society may disapprove of the Beatles and the proliferation of groups and music similar to that of the Beatles, but there is no attempt to muffle this expression. At the same time, when adolescent activities focused by a mutual interest in a contemporary musical form begin to expand so that the routines and expectations of the adult society are threatened, institutions may intervene. Schools have recently taken a stand on hair styles, clothing, and the congregation of students around controversial social and political issues.

The clique as it has been traditionally defined is ordinarily congruent with the core values of the general society. At the same time, many segments of the adolescent subculture are not, and the gap between them is widening. Social clubs may continue to represent the most common form of tolerated clique activity, but the ranks of those adolescents concerned with American foreign policy, civil rights, abuse by the legal authorities, sexual license, psychedelic drugs, and the "credibility gap" in all political and social life are swelling. It is now a significant case of "them" and "us," and when such a polarization occurs, gross caricatures, the one of the other, begin to appear. The typical deviant (we are not concerned with traditional deviant gangs but rather with a large segment of the nondelinquent adolescent subculture) is portrayed as unkempt, long-haired, bearded, extremist, addicted, immoral, and politically radical. The view from the other side is equally caricatured—the adult is rigid, punitive, dishonest, mercenary, unenlightened, imperialistic, abusive, and reactionary.

Between the adult and a large segment of the adolescent world is a great gulf, and each group coheres around a common distrust of the other. The one is the rebel, the other is the establishment. Most of the adolescents identified as radical are not actually radical, nor do most of the adults fit the stereotype of reactionary, paranoid, member of the establishment. The point is that when stereotyping occurs, reality seldom intervenes to moderate social interaction. Concerned as we are about the interaction of members of two distinct age-based subcultures within an institutional complex, it becomes important to designate the social dynamics that reveal the basis of conflict. This particular mode of stereotyping is one such dynamic.

## The Gang

Unlike the socially and politically alienated segment of the adolescent subculture, the gang has a longer and more stable history. It is a sociological designation that has called forth considerable writing and research, much of which has been reviewed in earlier sections of this book. The concept of the gang has been utilized to distinguish collectivities organized around activities that are deemed illegitimate by the larger society. These activities are traditionally illegitimate, such as theft, destruction of property, willful injury to others, and drug traffic. They are not the activities that characterize the contemporary "hippies." The gang is a form of social organization that imposes severe restrictions upon its members, and each gang operates in terms of its differences from the general society and from other gangs. This further distinguishes the gang from the "psychedelic deviants" who attempt to integrate themselves into the larger adolescent subculture by adopting common dress, manners, and interests. The gang depends upon conflict. Thrasher's early work on delinquent gangs emphasizes the notion of integration through conflict.[16]

An important characteristic of gangs is that the members must internalize the acceptance of illegitimate means to goal attainment as the best social adaptation for them. Means involve values, and as deviant values become part of the ethic of the gang member, conformist values become anathema, and persons espousing those values are envisioned as either villains or fools, that is, in negative role models. Institutions such as the school, which house persons, particularly those in authority, who are defined as negative models, are themselves negatively typed, providing a target for group aggression.

## *The School*

Along with the family and the peer group, the school operates to socialize the youth of the society. It reinforces the traditional values learned elsewhere and attempts to shape behaviors that are in conflict with it, or are unformed, to its expectations.

The student *vis-à-vis* other students, teachers, and administrators learns his role within the institution. Certain expectations are clear and specific. He learns the expectations of authority roles regarding his

---

16. Frederick Thrasher, *The Gang,* University of Chicago Press, Chicago, 1936.

academic participation in the system; he learns which citizenship behavior is rewarded and which punished. At times, however, when rewards and punishments evolve from different role sources, he is placed in a position of conflict. An example is the case of the class clown. As the tension-reducing element in the classroom, perhaps the focus of comic relief, this student will often receive the plaudits of his classmates and accept the criticism and downgrading of his teacher as an unfortunate price that he is willing to pay. As the result of a complex interaction of institutional sanctions and individual abilities, the student finds himself a role within the social system of the classroom. He may be leader, scholar, artist, athlete, pet, or clown. Whatever his role, he adopts a cluster of values supportive of it and devalues those expectations that are not supportive. From this focal point, he begins making definitions of other persons and other roles. These definitions are frequently exaggerated polarizations. To the scholar the athlete may be a bully, to the athlete the scholar a sissy, to the conformist the class disrupter a pest, and to the class disrupter the conformist a pet. This form of negative typing extends beyond peer relationships into the realm of authority relationships, and in this way imposes a special binding on the teacher's or counselor's attempt to establish the kind of cooperation that he seeks.

## MATURATION AND CLASS DISTINCTIONS

We have suggested that one perspective for viewing the source of certain forms of social typing would be to look at significant reference groups and the roles persons choose within these groups. A second perspective is the level of social and psychological maturation. Maturation has been discussed as a product of exposure to social and cultural differences, on the one hand and, on the other, the development of a capacity for abstract thinking. In combination, this is not necessarily a linear relationship. It is not suggested, for example, that prejudicial stereotyping begins at a given level and decreases commensurate with either exposure or the capacity for abstract reasoning.

The literature on class typing reveals increasing differentiation with maturation.[17] Middle class children have few reservations about inter-acting with lower class children in the primary grades, but a clear segregation of attitudes and behavior appears at about the same time that clearly defined cliques begin to emerge in the child's life.

We may draw one inference from a combined set of data regarding typing of children according to social class[18] that would suggest that teachers in the primary grades make more stereotypic judgements of students than do the students themselves. Many of the stereotypes made in educational settings involve the invidious evaluation of lower class educational behavior. Some of the descriptions provided by Becker[19] in his study of teacher appraisals of lower class students revealed that teachers perceived lower class children as delinquent in such areas as health, cleanliness, sexual behavior, and aggression. Designations of upper class types as "neurotic" or "spoiled" were also revealed.

Persons typically employ a set of defense mechanisms aimed toward rationalizing those personal characteristics that are criticized by others. One way to overcome a perceived handicap that one can do nothing about is to redefine the handicap in such a way that it is expressed as a valuable quality. Another mode of adaptation is to degrade the context within which the quality is negatively defined. Both tactics have been employed by lower class children to protect their egos in what becomes for many of them an alien environment.

Social classes evolve their own heroes and villains. Often the hero of one class or one segment of a class is defined as a villain by another class or segment. Deviant innovators like those who have achieved quick economic mobility through illegal rackets would be an example of a hero in one class; the successful businessman would be a hero in another. Education is currently the most prominent means for attaining or maintaining social status, and all strata of the society in the last third of the twentieth century are beginning to acknowledge this reality. To many it is a reality accepted grudgingly, because gross inequities

---

17. Celia Stendler, *Children of Brasstown,* Bureau of Educational Research and Service, University of Illinois, 1949, pp. 90–95.

18. Howard Becker, "Social Class Variation in Teacher-Pupil Relationships," *Journal of Educational Sociology,* vol. 25, 1952.

19. *Ibid.*

are felt to exist in the access to opportunities for this education. When different channels were available to different classes, it was difficult to focus praise or blame on the school or to be concerned, as we currently are, about the extent to which the school dispatches its responsibility to achieve the American dream of equal opportunities. In the nineteenth and first part of the twentieth centuries, social classes could be differentiated on the basis of the channels that they typically explored to achieve status mobility. We have already discussed the latent function of politics as providing, at one time, a channel for lower and working class members of then low status minority groups like the Irish and the Italians. Labor organizations advanced the cause of group mobility for many working class persons; small businesses could be built into large ones, and invention and individual initiative could catapult many into economically secure positions. In an age of industrial and governmental bureaucracy, the mechanisms for individual mobility have been narrowed to one—education. The modern politician, dependent as he is upon an image, can seldom rise from the rank and file of labor, and minority groups will ordinarily put forth their most educated representatives, those that will appear to be acceptable to the mass of American citizens.

Differentiation of students, although highly correlated with class position outside of the school, causes a status system within the school to evolve. The criteria for ranking students along this status ladder are several: academic performance, participation in highly valued extracurricular activities, curriculum, clique membership, personal and social appearance, and popularity, which may be a function of some combination of the former qualities. When the typing of persons appears in the system, it reflects the evaluation by pupils of those qualities that are used to stratify the members. Negative typing occurs as students perceive members of the bureaucracy rejecting the student's criteria and imposing and maintaining their own.

As young children mature into adolescents and peer groups gain in solidarity, social typing takes on an equivalently rigid quality. Student peer groups, usually homogeneous as to social class, begin to make the in- versus out-group definition of others that was not meaningful to younger children, who find it difficult to conceptualize such dichotomy on a broad social level. For lower class adolescents, the social definition of educational functionaries is frequently that of an enemy or a villain. Another step in the social maturation of these students must be effected before a helping relationship, unencumbered by typing barriers, may be fruitfully established.

## THE DEFINITION OF THE COUNSELOR

We have conceived of the school counselor as occupying a position within the bureaucracy that contains several functional prerequisites. Organizationally, the role is segmented into many role obligations. Which role segments are emphasized in any school situation depends upon the requirements of the administration, the expectations of other functionaries, and the counselor's abilities and training. From the standpoint of the counselee or prospective counselee, one subjective emotion relates the counselors to all other functionaries in his school experience. This is the feeling that in some way he is being judged or evaluated. To the child's mind, the counselor is an authority figure, and all authority figures are in some sense judges.

Students divide their institutional world into authority figures and peers. The younger the child, the less complex is his differentiation of each group. Children learn early the qualities that are evaluated. The youngest children are able to make only the grossest kind of definitions of the criteria for their own evaluation. These are usually those behaviors that are shaped in the home and relate more to being a "good" or "bad" child than to being a student. In the first years of school, the child again experiences a similar shaping of his behavior to conform with the ethical expectations of his teacher. As he progresses in school, he perceives little variation in ethical expectations, although specific academic expectations become explicit and in many cases relegate the ethical norms to a less prominent position in the classroom environment. But every new situation begins with the commonality of ethical expectations, as academic expectations vary with the teacher and the level of difficulty of the subject.

If ethical evaluations are perceived by students as regulating their interaction with persons viewed as authority representatives of the institution, the question we must raise to guide any remedial efforts is "How do we manipulate the environment so as to preclude a definition of the counselor as judge?" A judge or an evaluator is a prominent social typing in educational systems, and this evolves into a negative type or even a stereotype when students have experienced a succession of unsatisfactory evaluations. Although we might make a similar case for all educational roles, it would appear that the professional ethos of the counselor is the most disturbed by this kind of typing. The counselor perceives that he is functionally retarded in his task if he cannot communicate that he stands in exclusively a helping and nonjudging relationship to the counselee.

Several generalizations have been made about the context of the counselor-counselee interaction, indicating that typing is bound to occur. It has been suggested that this typing takes the form of students' defining counselors as members of the bureaucracy, authority figures, and ethical judges. If this is true, what, specifically, might be some representative thinking on the part of the students? We may propose several examples, simple formulations of the kind of thoughts students may have while interacting with the counselor.

"Does he really mean it when he tells me to speak freely?"

"Do I really have more ability than I've shown, or is this just another line to get me to work harder?"

"Will he treat me better if I tell him that I'm really interested in school, even if I'm not?"

"Doesn't he resent me for what I did to the teacher? Isn't he on their side?"

"If I tell him I'll change, will he give me a break?"

"Will he help me more if I tell him I'd like to go to college?"

The skilled counselor is usually capable of communicating to the student that preconceived notions about his role are erroneous. Obstacles to this communication decrease as counselors establish a high degree of autonomy within the school. But our concern is with the structure of the role, not with the varying degrees of individual counselor skill.

The present structure is such that most school counselors engage in administrative tasks. They are perceived as a member of the team whose responsibility it is to deter nonconformity, to group students, to investigate violations of school rules, to keep records, to speak with parents about student problems. The office of the counselor is usually in the administrative wing or section of the school, and students are usually referred to the counselor within a context of some deviant or disruptive behavior. In the past, when a violation of the rules was committed and discovered, some authority figure was called upon to administer judgment. Why should the counselor be perceived as playing a different role, especially when all the associations (context, office, records) are the same?

## STRUCTURAL INNOVATIONS FOR ELEMENTARY COUNSELING

We have suggested that students learn how to interact with other roles within the school by clustering various authority positions into one manageable unit. At the most general level of perception, there is the formal system and its concomitant values and expectations, on the one hand, and the informal system, the society of peers, on the other. We have indicated that the formal system has evolved sanctions appropriate to supporting two kinds of activities, academic and ethical. Typing of members of the formal system occurs in line with the definition of persons as representing some set of expectations around these two dimensions. Typing of members of the informal system by members of the formal entails a more involved process, because educational behaviors as well as antecedent factors such as race, class, and nationality are considered.

The basis of the social typing of members of the formal system lies in the relation members of the informal system bear to the academic and ethical expectations of the institution. This in turn is a function of the roles that members take within the system. These roles evolve from a complex set of conditions that we have considered in an earlier part of the chapter.

The extent to which members of the bureaucracy allow social typing to influence their definitions of students is a function of a combination of organizational and personal dynamics. On the organizational side, role responsibility, autonomy, the existence of a professional ethos, the size and ratio of the interacting unit (35 to 1, 10 to 1, 1 to 1), and several contextual variables such as the distribution of social and economic characteristics like social mobility, sex, marital status, age, race, training, years of educational experience, and feeling of commitment all could influence typing patterns.

The structure of educational systems is a complex network of interaction patterns predicated on the knowledge and evaluation of separate roles. Any attempt to restructure the system would involve ways of reshaping the institutionalized basis for knowing and evaluating these roles. We have summarized the traditional basis for defining role occupants by members of both the formal and the informal organization. The operational basis for making these definitions may be succinctly stated in a number of traditional assumptions:

1. Students may be differentiated on the basis of compliance with the ethical expectations of the institution.

2. Students may be differentiated on the basis of compliance with the academic expectations of the institution.

3. Members of the formal organization may be differentiated on the basis of authority to control the activities and behavior of students.

4. Student status is a function of achieved position in the system that is structured on a unidimensional value system.

5. The student-teacher relationship is a subordinate-superordinate relationship.

These assumptions involve a process of differentiation and allocation of students to stratified positions, according to an authority system, itself differentiated by authority, linked to a cluster of traditional values. These values are unidimensional insofar as there is little latitude to achieve status on other grounds than those internalized by the authorities of the system. This does not refer exclusively to patterns of conformity or deviance. Skills in mechanical tasks are less highly valued than skills in communication, although there is no consideration that exhibiting mechanical abilities is deviant.

The restructuring of traditional interaction patterns to reduce the dysfunctional consequences of social typing would require some method of dissolving these traditional assumptions and others as well that perpetuate differential evaluation along a limited criterion range. Evaluation itself does not produce a context in which invidious definitions are made. But evaluation in educational systems occurs in order to place persons in different status relationships to each other. This may be functional to the allocation goals and responsibilities of the school, but it is dysfunctional to the best intentions of guidance services. Position within the status system is the focus from which other positions are viewed and personally evaluated, hence the structural focus of social typing.

Changing the basis of social relationships within an institutional context is the kind of task that cannot be executed, without excessive conflict, by administrative decrees. Such decrees, if inconsistent with traditional expectations, are potentially disruptive. If teachers are ordered to operate exclusively within the realm of individual levels of attainment and individual needs, they may accept the philosophy as legitimate, but in the end the mechanisms that are available to them lead to a process of stratifying students. We cannot, for example, take the normative system of one institution and impose it upon another. The school ranks students in terms of ability, manners, intelligence, and aspiration. The family is expected to love and reward the children equally without reference to differences in ability or intelligence. The traditional structure of the school is not amenable to the incorporation of family values into its own value system because values lead to mechanisms for their implementation. In time, these mechanisms become institutionalized and are difficult to abrogate. It would be as difficult to require parents to relate to students in a familial manner. It is not being suggested that this would be desirable; it is only posed as an example of the problems involved in restructuring traditional interaction patterns.

Activities that have educational utility may be organized outside the immediate context of the school. As this has not been the procedure with high schools, the theoretical position being taken in the last part of this chapter is directed toward the emergence of guidance functions on the elementary school level.

There is evidence that guidance services are currently being made available to elementary school children. This is a phenomenon of recent times and therefore the organization of routines for elementary guidance has not yet reached the stage of anything approximating the institutionalization of services available in the secondary schools. It is still quite feasible to establish a pattern that could become prototypic for a nationwide system of elementary guidance services. From the standpoint of the guiding theme of this chapter, the structure of guidance activities needs to be evaluated from the perspective of the amount of stereotyping and negative typing that is likely to occur. Although we may look to the area of elementary guidance as the most manageable in the sense of facilitating proposals for structural organization, many of the considerations pursued in the following section are theoretically generalizable to all guidance services in educational settings.

Five factors will be considered as relevant to the kind of definitions children will make of the school counselor. These are

1. The career pattern of the counselor.
2. The physical location of the guidance service.
3. The autonomy of the guidance service.
4. The basis of counselor-counselee interaction.
5. The referral process.

## The Career Pattern of the Counselor

Persons within institutional settings are defined by others in terms of the roles they occupy. These persons respond to the definitions by taking on the qualities and dispositions ascribed to them. Social interaction is a process of learning and playing roles in terms of the expectations that are perceived within the institutional situation. It seems likely, for example, although it remains an interesting empirical question, that school administrators recruited from the ranks of industry would operate in different ways than those coming up through the teaching ranks.

The source of social typing in education may be found both in the association of the role with other similar roles and in a demonstration of the revelation of the attributes of one role in the performance of another. Because of students' limited ability to discriminate different role functions within a single context, the counselor may be perceived by them as simply another kind of teacher, or he may reveal himself to them as a type of teacher through a number of qualities assumed in the course of acting as a teacher. Avoidance of this perceived negative association on the part of students who experience unsatisfactory adaptation to the school would require some planned determination of suitable career patterns for school counselors. The current pattern of having counselors emerge from the teaching ranks must be viewed as problematic on the grounds of the residual effects stemming from previous role taking.

## The Physical Location of the Guidance Service

If there is some positive value in allowing school counselors to be viewed as separate from the mainstream of educational activities, for example as not intrinsically tied to the discipline function, then one logical means of achieving this end is physical detachment. Conducting guidance activities in the administrative wing of the school may be efficient for the administration and transferring of records, but for young students, who make their definitions of school functionaries on such gross criteria as the physical proximity of activities, such a location is potentially disruptive of guidance goals. Educational researchers who wish to interview students or teachers recognize the importance of the setting for producing an atmosphere of uninhibited discourse. The same consideration would seem to apply to the counseling function. If this assumption is correct, then the greater the physical detachment from the ongoing activities of the school, the better. A separate physical structure might be the best test of the hypothesis, and research into the general assumption being suggested is strongly warranted.

## The Autonomy of the Guidance Service

The performance of roles is highly determined by the expectations of superiors in the line of bureaucratic authority. Students may not make a concrete definition of the counselor as executing a set of orders that descend from above, but a conception of a counselor as possessing some autonomy could strengthen the amount of trust felt by a counselee. The counselor as student advocate commands greater student acceptance when he is viewed as possessing some independence from the main line of administrative expectations.

Autonomy may be conceived as a function of organizational possibilities, on the one hand, and of professional affiliation, on the other. The first may frequently be a product of the second. The term *organizational possibilities* refers to the alternative structures for the organization of guidance activities. Some school districts have established a direct line of authority for guidance workers within a multidimensional network of educational functions. A guidance worker assumes the major responsibility for allocation of personnel, rather than a principal or a committee of school principals. Counselors may be viewed as part of the school team, but the responsibilities are dictated from the guidance office rather than the principal's.

Variations in organization are directly related to the size and budget of a school district. Other variations occur in terms of whether or not districts are organized around a unified or centralized conception. These are the conditions for organization. Autonomy, as a working principle, grows out of these conditions, but viewed as an independent structure of counselor-counselee interaction, it shapes the definition held by students of the counselor and the guidance office.

We have discussed professionalism at some length in Chapter 5. A professional person communicates an image very different from one who owes his identification to an occupational group that enjoys a mediocre social status. The professional image accrues from a selection process that ensures the attraction and continuation of quality. This applies, of course, to teachers as well as to counselors. Doctors and lawyers may be negatively typed by many segments of the population, but whatever exists in these roles that is seen from within and without as worthy, which in turn encourages positive typing, may be perpetuated by the control the members exert over access to the profession. One of these quality factors is autonomy, born of an implicit confidence in the member's ability to perform his task. Autonomy, then, may be viewed as a structure for functioning that is in itself positively valued and also as a condition that recruits better trained and better qualified personnel, who in themselves perpetuate a positive image.

## The Basis of Counselor-Counselee Interaction

It would seem, from the professional ethos of counseling, that the focal point of the problem-solving interaction is the student, not the school. When, to the mind of the student, conversations seem to revolve around reduction of conflict within the school, definitions of the interaction then emerge from the child's adopted student roles. If the child is brought to a guidance center because one or both parents feel he is unmanageable in the home, definitions of this interaction and the helping clinician emerge from the child's family role. Negative typing occurs when the basis for the interaction seems to contain the same elements present in the institutional context. The helping persons appear to be an extension of the school or the family in the sense of representing the original elements of conflict. Counselors may make nonjudgmental approaches to educational difficulties, but as long as the basis of the interaction appears to the student to be these educational difficulties, he will adopt those defensive roles that rationalize or belittle his failure. This condition encourages not so much an uncooperative interaction as a standoff, that is, the kind of role positioning that was characteristic of the problem in the first place.

If it is important that the student see the counselor as someone who is completely dedicated to his welfare and only tangentially concerned with ameliorating school conflict, then the basis of interaction will have to communicate this. In the same sense that trust is given by a delinquent gang only when a group worker is ultimately revealed as independent of legal agencies, a student will trust the counselor only when he reveals a similar independence. Group workers need not condone delinquency in any sense to achieve this trust, nor would counselors need to assert a lack of concern about school deviation. But if they are to achieve trust, this concern cannot be the basis of the interaction.

## The Referral Process

The process of referring students for counseling help is usually a matter of overt bureaucratic policy. The student goes from classroom to guidance office or from standard classroom to social-adjustment classroom to guidance office or performs some variation of this referral pattern. The process is perceived by students as the organizational management of deviant patterns. This management operates to facilitate adaptive allocation goals simultaneously, by washing out social unsuitables from the funneling process. For college-bound students the referral process is functional, and the definition of counselors is positive because there is a perceived congruency in values and goals. When this congruency is not perceived, then the danger that the referral process will be perceived as bureaucratic maintenance of conformity is inherent.

Although many of the concerns that led to the institutionalization of guidance referrals may be the same, alternatives for facilitating the same goals should be considered. Other institutions provide workable models: some variation on the open-door confessional policy of the church (if we substitute talking over problems for confession), intake and inpatient-outpatient activities of psychiatric hospitals and mental-health clinics, sociometric techniques for organizing groups in group work centers. Some alternatives may also be explored in terms of persons usually not involved in the referral process, that is, friends, family, and members of the community viewed by the student as filling positive role models. These persons may not initiate the action but may be integrated into the overall process so that a reduction in negative typing of the last person in the referral chain, the counselor, is effected.

The possibilities of restructuring institutional activities to reduce the effect of negative typing are limited or increased by the amount of flexibility that a school system will tolerate. Inspection of the five areas in which organizational and professional action is required will suggest some inherent difficulties. Some of the theoretical suggestions would require a radical reorganization of the lines of authority and communication, and for this reason they may be applicable only in the formulation of an elementary guidance system, where institutionalized structures are not yet firmly implanted.

Experts do not seem to emerge out of education as a result of experience in the system. Expertise, as a quality surrounding members of a particular occupational group, is a mystique perpetuated by a kind of nonaffiliation. In education, the expert is usually the consultant or advisor, and the strength of his recommendations is predicated upon his nonaffiliation with the organization itself. It is a peculiar irony that in this particular circumstance trust is a function of unfamiliarity. The strength of a cooperative network of guidance services that involves teachers and administrators may depend upon the separation of these services from the official routines of the organization. On this basis, the mystique of the expert may be effective not only in drawing support from other school personnel but also in eliminating the traditional basis of stereotyping in schools. Elementary guidance counselors may have an opportunity to set a precedent that will point the way for revisionist conceptions of the role of the secondary counselor.

## CONCLUSION

School counseling is a growing and proliferating educational activity. Services are being extended where they existed before and into areas where they did not. Counseling skills and techniques are being refined, improved, and discovered. But the best-trained, best-equipped medical facility in the world is impotent in the face of community distrust of medical practices. In the same way, counselors and guidance services in general are still mainly helpful to those who trust and desire their help. Technical discoveries progress at a faster rate than the social structures that are organized to make use of them. Perhaps the most important element in the lag between structures and facilities is the fact of social typing. This chapter has sought to detail the characteristics and effects of social typing in such a way that the relationship between counseling and the definition of counselors could be viewed from a social perspective.

Some areas for structural innovation have been discussed. Others may occur to the reader and should be explored. The vast network of roles and functions can provide a decade of speculation and empirical inquiry into the problem of situation definition, counselor definition, and guidance outcomes.

Social typing is, of course, reciprocal. It is in operation at the beginning of an interaction and changes or intensifies as persons seek to fit others into preconceived molds. At the grossest level of typing, we begin with those who are viewed negatively, positively, or neutrally. Many shades intervene and many categories may be supplied within each classification. For example, there are many kinds of villains; some are specific enemies, some are dangerous, and others are ideologically ugly but operate out of our ken, like a Latin American dictator or a park mugger who really does not affect us if we stay uptown. The worst kind of villain in the educational setting is the one who judges a student and makes his life miserable. From the standpoint of the counselor, on the other hand, certain student types are defined as posing the greatest problem, or "challenge," and stereotypes about individual character traits may thus intrude into the counseling relationship. Certain student types are not only "trouble makers"; they also resist our humanitarian efforts to help them. Discounting our own inability to find the right solution, we intensify our stereotypes and reduce our personal frustration. Such is the way of social interaction between persons with incongruent values and definitions of each other's roles. This is a matter of social regularity rather than of social desirability. Understanding such regularities and their effects is the first major step toward reorganizing the structure of problematic social interactions in counseling and guidance.

# CHAPTER 8

# TOWARD RESEARCH ON GUIDANCE: A STUDY OF THE ELEMENTS OF SOCIAL INTERACTION

## WILLIAM LEWIS SPEIZMAN *and* PETER McHUGH

> Guidance as a term was always hard to define or even describe. It embraced so many dimensions of activities, including everything from keeping records to going on field trips with youth, that it was difficult to assess this activity in any precise manner. With the concern about the counseling process becoming paramount in the field, it is now possible to seek concrete research outcomes about human behavior as affected by guidance.[1]

IN OUR VIEW, Barclay exhibits an unwarranted optimism. He presumes that guidance has been adequately conceptualized and that rigorous measurement can therefore be practiced. By assuming that problems of conceptualization have been solved and that the era of rigorous measurement is at hand, Barclay concludes that we can rush into the gathering of information about the concrete outcomes of guidance. But, we ask, have these problems in fact been overcome? Have we adequately conceptualized and described the basic social activities and social processes that together constitute guidance? What *particular* and *observable* interactional activities are we referring to when we say, for example, that a counselor has employed a "nondirective" technique? What are the specific interactional processes we have in mind when we say an interview has taken place in a "permissive atmosphere"? Do we know the concrete behaviors of counselors and counselees to which these ideas refer?

---

1. James R. Barclay, "The Attack on Testing and Counselling: An Examination and Reappraisal," *Personnel and Guidance Journal,* Sept. 1964.

Before they can be rigorously measured, these and other guidance procedures must first be assigned to empirical referents in the actual events of interaction between counselor and counselee. A "permissive atmosphere" must, in other words, be explicitly linked to the behavior of participants in guidance *as they interact with one another.* But in order to accomplish this linkage, we do of course have to know something about interaction. We must provide ourselves with detailed behavioral descriptions of guidance *as* interaction, descriptions that we can then use as referents for these more specific guidance procedures. Unfortunately, such descriptions are not now available, and so the accomplishment of the linking operation in a principled and rigorous manner is still more an ideal than a reality. And it will remain an ideal until we have developed an account of the interactional features of guidance, an account such that any observer could agree that the interaction events to which our substantive procedures refer have in fact taken place.

We are suggesting that the various kinds of counseling, atmosphere, and so forth can never be tested and evaluated until they have been linked to constituent features of guidance interaction. Our immediate problem, then, is not to add to the bulk of substantive programs for guidance that are already available, but rather to develop an adequate description of the basic activities and processes within which guidance occurs. The aim of this chapter is to conceptualize the elements of social interaction that could subsequently be used to formulate a set of researchable questions about the basic, constituent processes of the phenomenon we know as guidance. Only after these questions have been answered will we possess the kinds of adequate descriptions that are the precondition to seeking Barclay's concrete outcomes.

In order to formulate such questions, we need a general framework for the analysis of social interaction. Such a framework would provide a way of organizing an inquiry into the constitutive activities and processes shared by all kinds of guidance interactions. The first part of the chapter will deal at length with the framework we have selected. We shall then turn to a discussion of the specific research

questions generated by the framework. Finally, we shall make some
general points about carrying out research based on these questions.
Before turning to the body of the chapter, however, we shall comment
on the nature of sociological knowledge and method.

The classical social theorists—Weber, Durkheim, Marx, and
Simmel—established the reality of society and the consequences of
its existence. The society with which they were concerned was not a
reified society—not a "state" or "nation" or some other territorial unit
—but rather an overarching social entity that may or may not be
coterminous with the territory of geography. For these men society is
the locus of *social* forces that channel human endeavor in one direction
or another; it is the totality of the modes-of-doing that both create and
constrain the activities of all members. Society is the supraindividual
body of modes of treating the environment, others, and oneself. As
Durkheim put it, society manifests itself in the lives of particular
individuals by determining their activities, while at the same time it
predates and outlasts the life term of particular individuals.

Thus, the goal of sociological inquiry became the depiction of
society and its socially enabling and constraining modes of behaving
in the world. It is inconceivable, for example, that we could even
think about, much less organize to attain, such notions as "helping,"
"providing with information," or "counseling," unless society provided
us with ideas about the nature of man—his flexibility, rigidity, and
capacity for change. Where, say, does the view that men can be
changed, and hence sent to school, come from? Certainly individuals
do not make it up separately as they go along. Life as we know it,
and guidance too, would be impossible without society. In this chapter we shall refer to the influence of society as the *normative order:*
the sum total of socially practiced and enforced ways in which men
in daily life act, react, and interact.

The way to begin describing the normative order of guidance
interaction is to construct or build a model of the actor participating in
guidance. A model is the sociologist's conception of the behavior of
real actors in the particular situation he is studying, in our case guidance actors. The model generates a set of puppets, as it were, that

are designed to act and interact the way real actors do. The constructed model is a description of behavior that reproduces the interaction scenes of real actors, in the sense that the puppets generated by the model could be dropped into a real-life situation and things would proceed pretty much as they had before the model was constructed. Thus we have a model of actors who can do no more than what we allow them to do, for it is not a complete portrait of every facet of real actors in all their situations (we will not, for example, go into any detail about their psychic make-up. The construction of these models of the guidance actor constitutes the goal of an inquiry into the constitutive social processes of guidance.

## ELEMENTS OF SOCIAL INTERACTION: THE CONCEPTUAL FRAMEWORK

We have said that the substantive interests of sociology are the socially enforced ways in which men act and interact. Our framework will reflect this interest in some detail and will serve to generate a set of researchable questions about the constitutive features of the actions and interactions of guidance. One of the most important elements of this framework is the distinction between social reality and physical reality.

### Social Reality vs. Physical Reality

There is a fundamental difference between social reality and physical reality. Physical reality means nothing to the trees, mountains, atoms, etc., that constitute it. Imagine how absurd it would be to assert that an atom has an interesting theory about its movements, or that a tree feels guilty about the bird's egg that fell from its nest. Social reality, on the other hand, does have meaning for the persons who constitute it—that is what is meant when sociologists talk about *actors*. Men have theories about themselves and the world around them. For men, it is not trivial that Lincoln lived in a log cabin—humble beginnings constitute a *reason* for success according to our traditional normative theories of movement through life. Parents do cry "What have we done?" as their children fall from the nest, and in so doing exemplify their normative theories of responsibility. Similarly, psychotherapeutic versions of behavior are among the most institutionalized of our common-sense theories about ourselves, and thus deserve detailed study with regard to their influence, independently or whether they are right or wrong. (It is perhaps obvious that guidance would make a good site for such a study.)

Men *react* to their experiences in the world, and it is their distinctive feature that these reactions are normatively conceptualized. Men not only respond, but conceive of these responses as "embarrassment," "good luck," "success," "underachievement," and so forth. Social reality, then, is meaningful to those who constitute it. The social world is a *constructed* world.

Let us explore a bit further what it means to say that social actors are constructing the world they live in. To them their world is not composed of discrete noises, flashes, dots, and movements, but rather of a series of identities (girls, homes, fools, dates,) that themselves form recognizable and recognized courses of social action (flirtations, places to leave, deviant amusement, etc.). These identities and patterns, moreover, are not "out there," independent of the actors but are constructed by the actors themselves.[2] This is what we mean when we say that social reality is interpreted by the objects constituting it. It is the actor who identifies from the vast array of goings-on at a public beach, say, the set of objects, "a group of fellows running along" or "a few boys running after another" or "a few boys chasing one another." Actors also turn these identities into *courses* of action. In the chase on the beach, the actor might see the course of action as "a friendly game" or "someone in trouble."

We are thus saying two related things when we say that the objects of study in the social sciences (social actors) are interpreting

---

2. Nor are they "in here"; there is more on this later in the chapter.

the subject matter of the social sciences (social reality). First, because so-called "objective" event (the chase) can be interpreted in more than one way (a game or trouble), there is no meaning inherent in the social world. Second, since these same actors do in fact "find" meanings in that world, *they must be imputing these meanings rather than just discovering them out there.*

These points are so obvious that they may seem trivial. They may be thought to highlight a distinction that makes no difference. Obvious though they may be, however, their implications are vast and crucial to the doing of social science. For *persons treat the world about them in terms of the constructions they have made of it.* This is the meaning of W. I. Thomas' famous theorem, "If men define situations as real, they are real in their consequences."[3] The "customer" who "turns out to be" a "thief," the "disciplinary problem" who turns out to be the "child with severe problems at home," the "Negro holding hands with the white woman" who "turns out to be" a "blind man being helped across the street," all these constructions represent transformations in actors' interpretations of situations that confront them, and all of them represent a potential change in the courses of treatment they would carry out in those situations. The meaning the actor imputes to his world, the environment he constructs, thus informs and determines the action he takes. Consequently, the social scientist, as opposed to the physical scientist, must include in his account a description of the world *as it is constructed by the actors he is studying.* What does it mean, for example, to say that a counselee is uncooperative? What kinds of constructed worlds does this rubric mask? And how do those worlds get imputed as a course of action throughout the counselee's association with the counselor?

There is an equally important methodological implication of the fact that social actors construct their own worlds. Whereas a physical scientist controls the definition of stimuli, the social scientist competes with his subjects for the "right" to define them. Many examples of this competition exist in the social sciences, from the sociologist

3. W. I. Thomas with Dorothy S. Thomas, *The Child in America,* Alfred A. Knopf, Inc., New York, 1928, p. 574.

doing interviews for a sample survey who was thrown out of a house because he was thought to be a socialist to the respondent who identified the occupation of nuclear physicist as a cathartic. None is better known than the famous Western Electric researches carried out in the late nineteen twenties and early thirties by a group of sociologists, anthropologists, and social psychologists. These men had set out to study the effects of physical conditions of work on production. One of these conditions was the intensity of light in the work area. As the light was increased, they found the expected parallel increase in production by the work crew. Then they reduced the amount of light. Each period of reduced light was accompanied by a further *increase* in production; as they continued to reduce the light to a point below its original level, so that it was approximately equal to the light of a full moon on a clear night, they discovered that production continued to rise. Clearly, these researchers had inadequately taken into account the meanings constructed by the workers, in this case that they would define *any* research as a collaboration and any collaboration as an incentive to work. The intensity of light thus having been ignored by those being studied, it became an empty hypothesis for explaining worker behavior.[4]

Because our data are gathered by interacting with the subjects, and because their definitions of these interactions are variable, data gathered from these subjects may not be comparable. This is true whether one studies fertility rates, gross national products, or guidance, whether one uses sample surveys, laboratory experiments, or participant observation. Men do construct the worlds in which they live, and to describe social life the sociologist must take these constructions into account.

Given these premises, we must now set out some usable theory of how men construct their worlds and how these constructions determine their behaviors. We must outline our framework more systematically in order that it may be used to account for the sense-making activities of actors in guidance situations.

---

4. For a discussion of the Western Electric researches, see John Madge, *The Origins of Scientific Sociology*, The Free Press, New York, 1962.

## Constructing the World

### THE INVOKING OF RULES OF INTERPRETATION

Actors impute meanings to situations, and thereby construct their worlds, by invoking what we shall call a "rule of interpretation." The rule of interpretation is constituted by a set of normative assumptions about the situation. These assumptions include all the details that depict the history and prospects, both near and far, of the immediate events with which the actor is involved. The rule of interpretation provides the actor with an *assumed* knowledge of what has gone before and what will ensue in the situation he confronts. We can, for example, survive in a strange city only because we assume that it will be comparable to other places where we have been. And a guidance counselor does not need to have lived with a particular student in order to identify and differentiate him from other students.

It is through this assumed knowledge that an actor makes sense of events in his immediate present. Note, for example, how a student's file provides the counselor with a set of assumptions that get played out on their first direct meeting with one another. Another simple but accessible example of this is when a movie scene is mistaken as "the real thing." In a recent film by Vittorio de Sica, Peter Sellers plays the role of an Italian thief named the "Fox." At one point, the Fox returns home after escaping from prison only to be told that in his absence his young sister has "taken to the streets." Sellers rushes to the Via Veneto just in time to observe an evil-looking foreigner propositioning his sister. He then runs into the scene and begins beating the man, entreating his sister to forsake this new life and return home. Apparently, the Fox assumed that "taken to the streets" meant that his sister had turned to prostitution. He constructed the scene on the street as an attempt by the foreigner to purchase his sister's services. But actually his sister had "taken to the streets" only to obtain a job, in this case with a film company. And the scene he observed was just that—a scene in a movie. Moments after Sellers intercedes he is besieged by cameramen, technicians, and the director, who inform him he has just ruined a great scene. The Fox made sense of the particular events in the scene by assuming a knowledge of what was going on. He "understood" why his sister wore the high-hemmed dress with a precipitous neckline; he "understood" why the foreigner was showing his sister his wallet, and so forth. He invoked a rule of interpretation constituted by a set of assumptions as to what prostitution was, and what is likely to happen when prostitutes and gentlemen solicit.

In this illustration it is easy to observe how the rule of interpretation supplies events with meaning. The process in the film is essentially the same as that engaged in by the common-sense actors. In the most routine of situations, the common-sense actor "finds out what is going on" by assuming knowledge of the nature of events in which he is participating. The man on the street who is stopped by another fellow with a diminutive "Uh, excuse me" views the encounter as a probable request for information (e.g., "Where is the nearest subway entrance?") only because he invokes a rule whose constitutive assumptions about the other fellow's past and the impending course of their brief interaction renders the address sensible *as* a "probable request for information." If from the outset the man on the street invoked a rule assuming a different past and future, say a robbery attempt, then the very same opening sentence would be interpreted completely differently, say as a delaying tactic or a sizing up. Thus the actor assigns meaning by imputing a past and a future to the present, an imputation he assumes to be correct and adequate enough to carry him through them an events arise and disappear.[5]

## THE PRESUMPTION OF OBJECTIVITY

The actor further presumes of this world he constructs by imputation that it is an objective world, that it is "out there." He acts as if his constructions were things apart from himself, as if they were perceptions rather than imputations. The actor presumes of his constructed world not only that it is objective but also that it is made up of general and repetitive pasts and futures that he has only to

---

5. For a detailed investigation of this point see Peter McHugh, *Defining the Situation,* Bobbs-Merrill Co., Inc., Indianapolis, 1968.

"identify." Having presupposed the patterned nature of an objective world the actor can easily assume that a rule that adequately guided his assignment of meaning before will be adequate to his present situation.

Perhaps this can most easily be seen by a consideration of surprise. Needless to say, no one could ever be surprised if he had not assumed that what *would* occur was something other than what *actually* occurred. The bride left waiting at the church may be humiliated, but she is also surprised, for she had learned that the common-sense probabilities of absent grooms are exceedingly low. And one can here further see presupposed objectivity in what follows upon the groom's absence. The bride's wedding party, perhaps even the groom's, will begin to assign to the groom responsibility for the current abominable state of affairs and will expect to gain support from others in so doing. They will suppose that the bride has been wronged, that others will naturally see it this way, and that they could see it this way by merely having had it recited for them. Actors turn to the imputations and actions of others in the world for support of their imputations, and in this sense they see their versions of things as objective and not their own fancies. Only by assuming such objectivity, for example, could we have developed the categories of behavior labeled "psychotic"; the psychotic is one who seems precisely not to abide by our notions of the objectivity of things. Another example of presupposed objectivity is secrets. Think for a moment of your deepest and darkest secret and why you conceal it. You probably hide it because you expect some humiliating or punishing response from others should it come out in the open. As a violation of some precept, it will bring a response from others, and to anticipate such a response is to suppose that the rule is not idiosyncratic, that your secret behavior can instead be matched against the standards of society and of those around you. The most private matters come to be private by being compared to public, that is, presumed-to-be-objective, standards.

A final illustration of the presumed objectivity of the constructed world may be seen if we investigate the common-sense actor's notion of fact. A fact to the actor is any circumstance that he uses as grounds for his action. Facts are the events that he treats as "reasons" for behaving the way he does. In other words, facts are those assumptions of the actor that are *treated* by him as being objectively true beyond all doubt. For example, the discovery of early Viking voyages to North America in no way changes the validity of the statement that to generations it was a *fact* that Christopher Columbus discovered America.

## THE PRESUMPTION OF TYPICALITY

Not only is the constructed world known to the actor as objective, it is known to him as "typical." "The outer world is not experienced as an arrangement of individual unique objects, dispersed in space and time, but as 'mountains,' 'trees,' 'animals,' 'fellow-men.' "[6] The actor's knowledge of the features of his situation is knowledge of those features as manifesting typical properties of *classes* of objects and events. *The actor presumes that his assumptions about what is going on in his situations are correct until further notice, thereby providing him with an understanding of objects and events as typically possessing the properties of objects and events so understood in the past.* Having invoked a rule of interpretation and assessed the meaning of the situation, the actor has, in our terms, *typified* the situation, i.e., has constructed it.

## THE CONSTRUCTED WORLD IS BOTH SHARED
## AND VARIABLE

One consequence of the whole process of construction is that if different rules of interpretation are invoked in the same situation, different meanings will be assigned in that situation. This is an empirical corollary to the principle that meaning is not intrinsic to situations; being imputed, it is variable.

In a class in field-research methods at Columbia University, an exercise was carried out that exemplifies the differential application of rules of interpretation and the variable meaning that ensues. Students

---

6. Alfred Schutz, "Common-Sense and Scientific Interpretation of Human Action," *The Collected Papers*, vol. 1, Martinus Nijhoff, The Hague, 1962, pp. 7–8.

were asked to judge which of three suicide notes were "real," i.e., notes actually left by persons who had committed suicide, and which were "simulated," i.e., notes written by students in a social-psychology experiment who had neither planned nor attempted suicide. The students were told to use the following procedure in judging the notes. First, they were given two sample notes, one labeled "Real Suicide Note" and the other "Simulated Suicide Note," and asked to look at them before reading the three other notes to be judged. Second, they were instructed to formulate from the two sample notes a set of criteria for judging which of the three test notes were real and which were false. Finally, they were instructed to apply their criteria to the test notes.

In the exercise we were asking the students to generate a set of assumptions about the nature of real suicide notes that became a rule of interpretation for assigning meaning to the three test notes, in this case the alternative meanings of "real" and "simulated." Reproduced below is the second test note, followed by the written statements of two students. (The criterion is given first in the student statements, and then a passage from the test note that the student chose as the concrete behavior that "stands for" that criterion.)

## Test Note Number Two

Dear Nicole,
  I have been forced into a position where I feel my life is not worth continuing.
  Friday I lost the job I have held for the last seven years. When I told Evelyn she packed her bags and left me. For six years she has been living with me, not for me but for my money.
  Nicole, please take care of Hilary for me. I'm leaving and I don't want Evelyn to have her.
  I have nothing to live for, so I am checking out dear sister.

My love to you,<br>Paul

*Student A wrote the following:*
  Test Note Two: Real suicide note
      Criterion *a*: It is addressed to loved one. "Dear Nicole."
      Criterion *b*: It shows concern for future—here for his child.

Criterion c: It sets out an adequate explanation of cause. "I've been forced into a position where I feel my life is not worth continuing. Friday I lost the job I have held for the past seven years. When I told Evelyn she packed her bags and left me. For six years she has been living with me, not for me but for my money." And "I have nothing left to live for, so I am checking out dear sister."

Criterion d: It shows concern that other will not feel guilty: blame attributed to his wife (no concrete behavior given).

Criterion e: It makes reference to his love. "Dear Sister." "My love to you."

*Student* B *wrote the following:*

Test Note Two: Simulated suicide note

Criterion a: It is longer [than the other test notes].

Criterion b: It states a specific problem. Lost job, Evelyn left.

Criterion c: Its style. This feature of letter is problematic, and therefore difficult to judge.

Criterion d: It is repetitious and repeats idea that life is not worth living. "I'm leaving." "I'm checking out."

Criterion e: It shows no self-blame.

Criterion f: It makes no apologies.

Criterion g: It does look ahead. "Take care of Hilary." But this is minimal.

Criterion h: It shows some expression of emotion, but minimal.

These students thus assigned different meanings to the very same test note. Student A concluded that it was real, student B that it was simulated. Looking at the criteria they used, we see that they generated a total of thirteen different criteria of judgment (adequate explanation of cause, length of letter, concern with the future, and so on.) Student A used three criteria (a, d, and e) that were unmentioned by student B; student B used six criteria (a, c, d, e, f, g) not mentioned by student A. Student A's criterion b ("concern for future") seems close if not identical to student B's criterion g (" does look ahead"). Also, student A's criterion c ("adequate explanation of cause") can be construed as similar to student B's criterion b ("states a specific problem").

We know two things about these performances. First, the two students assigned different meanings to the notes, and second, they assigned these meanings by incorporating essentially different criteria or rules. We may conclude that the difference in judgment as to the nature of the note is due to the difference in the rules applied to the note.

Now it might be argued that we need not conclude that the difference in rule yielded the difference in meaning assigned, and so there could be other explanations for the divergence in the note's meaning. One such alternative is that something in the letters themselves determined student judgments. Some evidence on this issue was gained in the exercise. The students were told that "One or more of the test notes is real and one or more of these notes is simulated," and thus were led to believe that they would have to find at least one of the three notes to be real and at least one to be simulated. All twenty-four of the students who completed the exercise did in fact choose at least one note as false and one as real. Table I presents the aggregated choices of the twenty-four students.

**Table I—Number of Choices for Each Note as Real or Simulated**

|  |  | Chosen as Real | Chosen as Simulated |  |
|---|---|---|---|---|
| Test Note | 1 | 15 | 9 |  |
|  | 2 | 9 | 15 |  |
|  | 3 | 11 | 13 |  |
| TOTAL CHOICES |  | 35 | 37 | 72 |
|  | % | (47.2) | (52.8) |  |

By choosing at least one of these notes as real and one as simulated, the maximum skewness of total choices could have been two to one (two thirds of the choices going for either real or simulated). As it turned out, however, 35 of the 72 choices were for real and 37 for simulated. If choices had been assigned by tossing a coin, their distribution would have approximated 36 real and 36 simulated. The actual outcome of the exercise departed from a coin-tossing distribution by only one choice. There was, in other words, an almost perfectly random use of the available choices. It is clear that if the notes themselves were determining the choice, the distribution of real and simulated would have paralleled the two-to-one distribution much more closely. We conclude from this random distribution of choices that the letters were not the sources of the meanings assigned to them, and that they indeed reflect the social construction of objects.[7]

We have discussed in a general way the manner in which common-sense actors make sense of their worlds by invoking a rule of interpretation. We shall now go into greater detail about just *how* a rule of interpretation is invoked in assigning meaning by explicating several points, including (*a*) what it means to say that the actor presumes his assumptions to be correct "until further notice," and (*b*) the way objects and events in the situation may influence the assembly of a meaning, even though they are not the single source of that meaning. The bride does assume until further notice that the groom will show up. But she will recognize the fact when he does not. In this case the recognized event "absent groom" is the further notice that can play a part in the transformation of meaning ("Will I be a bride?") by calling the original assumption ("I will be married today") into question. It is this interplay between the assumption as a rule of interpretation and the events which collide with and transform it that we must next depict.

## HOW A RULE OF INTERPRETATION IS INVOKED

The common-sense actor is a witness to a set of occurrences in his here and now—to the trees, mountains, brides, absent grooms,

---

7. A second criticism might be made of this exercise, viz., that too few labeled notes were made available to students in developing their judgment criteria. It might be argued that with more sample notes the students would have made better, more accurate choices. By "better" would be meant that students would more frequently have chosen as real the note written by a person who committed suicide and as simulated the note(s) written by a person who had not. That students would have established other criteria, given more notes with which to work, however, in no way precludes the possibility that, again, as criteria varied from student to student so would their imputations. Second, to say that other criteria would have increased the students' accuracy is simply to accept the present argument. If, with new criteria, the students had more frequently chosen as real the suicidal person's note and as simulated the nonsuicidal person's note, then the accuracy itself becomes a function of the criteria.

real suicides and the like that are recognizable to him. We have said that to make sense of these occurrences, he must impute to them a past and a future. But in order to do this—in order to make sense of the present—he may have to *wait* until some part of the future reveals itself. In other words, his sense of the present will be made tentatively, while he awaits the outcome of that present. In Garfinkel's terms, the "actual witnessed appearances" of the present are assigned the status of "events of conduct" in terms of future developments with regard to those appearances.[8] In the illustration of the man stopped on the street, the sense he makes of the initial "Uh, excuse me" may depend on what subsequently takes place, say whether the fellow pulls a gun or asks for information. The individual occurrences in the situation are thus specific behavioral "documents" of the overarching meaning of the situation which the actor is assembling. At first the groom may only be late. Then, as the recognized event of a lengthy passage of time occurs, the bride may entertain and document various alternatives: an automobile accident, a misunderstanding about the date of the wedding, or, heaven forfend, a change of heart. She may proceed as if one of these might be true or as if all are equally likely, but in any case she will have to proceed from the church as if only the future can tell, and her dealings with those at the church will reflect this awaiting of a future that will illuminate what is now going on. Events are "recognized" by the actor, and it is in terms of these recognitions that he assembles and transforms the overall meaning of interaction. The recognized event of a pulled gun is the man's basis of deciding he is "being held up," of an absent groom that she is being "stood up."

The initial typification is the interactional expression of what Schutz refers to as a case of "unquestioned, though at any time questionable"[9] common-sense knowledge of the world. That is, the actor accepts his rule of interpretation and the meaning he assigns

---

8. Our discussion here will closely follow Harold Garfinkel, "Common-Sense Knowledge of Social Structures: The Documentary Method of Interpretation," in *Theories of the Mind*, ed. by Jordon Scher, The Free Press, New York, 1962.
9. Schutz, *op. cit.*, p. 7.

as correct until further notice. He will alter the meaning he has assigned only if the recognized events in his situation call into question the rule of interpretation. For example, let us assume our man on the street has taken the statement "Uh, excuse me" as a request for information, an imputation documented for him by the fellow's next act, which is to ask where he can find the Main Street bus. Our man will interpret subsequent actions of the fellow as just further evidence of the pattern he has assumed, and make sense of succeeding events in the interaction by treating them simply as further documentation of the underlying pattern of asking for information. He interprets the fellow's looking around as an attempt to find the places given in the directions on how to get to the bus. *Now* our fellow pulls his gun. Given the man's common stock of knowledge at hand, we will assume this is a recognized act. It is recognized, but not as just asking for information—it is the act of a robber. In light of this development the man will reinterpret the situation; he will invoke a new rule of interpretation, in this case the rule governing robberies and what happens in them, and take a different course of action than he would have taken if he had continued to make sense of what was going on in terms of the rule governing information requests.[10] He might still stand there but the meaning of this act, the way he conceives of it, will be quite different than if he had remained only to clarify his instructions.

Thus, the rule of interpretation is invoked by the actor waiting for future results to unfold in order to make sense of the present. Once it is invoked, the actor then uses this rule to make sense of the situation by converting particular "witnessed appearances" into documents of the underlying pattern he has assumed. This pattern or rule will continue until he can no longer use it to make sense of what is going on (why *would* a friendly stranger asking information pull a gun and demand money?). Berger and Luckmann refer to this

---

10. He may still "feel" the man wanted information, but now it is information desired for a completely different reason, viz., the getaway. The information request is thus still a recognized event, but the event has new meaning; it isn't that the man has asked for the bus in order to go somewhere, but to get away from somewhere.

potential challenge by recognized events as the "contradiction of the pattern."[11] According to Garfinkel, "the underlying pattern is derived from its individual documentary evidences, and the individual documentary evidences, in their turn, are interpreted on the basis of 'what is known' about the underlying pattern. Each is used to elaborate the other."[12]

## Constructed Worlds and Courses of Action

We have alluded in passing to some of the points that we shall make explicitly in this section of the chapter. We will move now from our discussion of how imputations are assigned to a discussion of the way in which these imputations informs and determine the actor's courses of action.

We have already cited W. I. Thomas' theorem, "If men define their situations as real, they are real in their consequences." To this we will add Weber's statement in the opening pages of his *The Theory of Economic and Social Organiaztion.*

In "action" is included all human behavior when and in so far as the acting individual attaches a subjective meaning to it. . . . Action is social in so far as, by virtue of the subjective meaning attached to it by the acting individual (or individuals), it takes account of the behavior of others and is thereby *oriented in its course.*[13] (Italics added.)

Both the Thomas and Weber passages refer to the manner in which the actor's construction of his situation affects the action he takes. *The common-sense actor is oriented to the construction he has made of the objects and events about him, and he takes account of that construction in assembling a course of action. He acts in the situation as if it were what he supposes it to be.* It is likely that the construction "being robbed" will be accompanied by rather different action than "being asked directions."

---

11. Peter Berger and Thomas Luckmann, *The Social Construction of Reality: A Treatise in the Sociology of Knowledge,* Doubleday & Company, Inc., Garden City, New York, 1966.

12. Garfinkel, *op. cit.,* pp. 691–692.

13. Max Weber, *The Theory of Social and Economic Organization,* The Free Press, New York, 1964, p. 88.

This view of the determination of action implies at least two consequences. First, if an actor changes his construction, so will his action change. Correlatively, if two actors construct the same situation in different ways—if they invoke different rules of interpretation and thus impute different pasts and futures—they will act in different ways in that situation. These differences include not only what they actually do but also what they expect will be the moment-to-moment events that will serve as documents of the underlying construction. Second, this view quite obviously implies that one way to adequately describe an episode of social behavior is to give an account of the activity of imputing meaning. We can study social life by detailing actors' constructions of their situations, constructions to which they will be oriented in carrying out their courses of action.

An exercise using the man-on-the-street situation already referred to provides an illustration and some demonstration of the points we have just made. One of the authors appeared before a class in sociology at Columbia University and asked the students to assist him in carrying out an exercise. They were told that the experimenter would describe a situation to them and that he would take the part of one of the persons in that situation. Each of the students was asked to take the part of the other person in the situation and to write down what the experimenter requested of them. The experimenter then described the situation:

You are just leaving the campus at about two o'clock in the afternoon; you are finished with classes and are leisurely walking home. As you approach the end of Campus Walk at Broadway and 116th Street, you notice a well-dressed man, holding a book in his hand and looking around in a somewhat bewildered manner.

The experimenter then said, "The man approaches you and says, 'Uh, excuse me.'" The students were asked to "write down what your response would be." After a short pause they were asked to "write down why you made that response; state your reasons for your response—the assumptions you made." After the students had been allowed sufficient time to follow these instructions, they were asked to "write down what you expect to happen next; what do you expect that I as the man will do or say?" Again they were allowed a brief period for writing and then they were asked to "write down your reasons for this expectation." Each of these instructions was made in order to elicit a specific piece of information. The first ("write down your response") was to ascertain what course of action the student would take. The second ("write down why you made that response") was to get at the construction the student had made of the situation. The third ("write down what you expect to happen next") was to elicit what the student conceived to be the future events "naturally" following from and as a document of the rule of interpretation he had invoked. The final request ("write down your reasons for this expectation") was intended to obtain an elaboration of the student's construction of the situation, as well as the relationship between this construction and the future events he had envisioned.

In the course of the exercise, the experimenter read four lines in his role as the man on the street:

1. The man approaches you and says "Uh, excuse me."
2. All right, now the man says, "Could you tell me where Hamilton Library is?"
3. All right, now the man says, "But they told me Hamilton Library."
4. "I want to get some information about the next summer session."

After each of those lines was read, the students were asked to write down the same four pieces of information—response, reasons for response, expectation for future, reasons for future expectations. Finally they were asked,

5. In the light of the entire conversation as you know it, write down anything you would like to have done differently—any comments or questions you would like to have made—at any point earlier in the conversation. Write down your reasons for these changes and specify which of my comments your change refers to.

The five lines read by the experimenter demand some further comment. As far as we know, there is no Hamilton Library at Columbia University. Instead there is a Hamilton Hall, which houses classrooms and the offices of several of the departments of Columbia College. Further, there are two libraries on the campus: Butler Library, which houses the University Library, and Low Library, which houses the administrative offices of the university. Thus, so far as we know, the second and third comments made by the experimenter referred to nonexistent buildings.

Following are two student protocols. Each is divided into five sections. The five sections refer to what the student wrote down after each of the experimenter's four comments as the man on the street and after the final question about changes. In each section is the response and reason, followed by the future expectation and its reason.

### STUDENT I

1. "The man approaches you and says, 'Uh, excuse me.'"
   Response: I'd stop and wait until he said something else.
   Reason: Because he might be a stranger and seeking directions of some sort.
   Future expectation: I think you'd ask me something.
   Expectation reason: Because I know of no other *logical* move for him to make other than ask a question of direction. (Italics in original.)

2. "Could you tell me where Hamilton Library is?"
   Response: I'm sorry but I'm not familiar with the buildings.
   Reason: Because I've only been here (in N. Y.) two weeks, and I don't know where it is.
   Future expectation: He'd say "thank you" and leave.
   Expectation reason: (None given.)

3. "But they told me Hamilton Library."
   Response: But I'm not familiar with New York. Maybe I can find someone who knows where it is.
   Reason: Because it is quite possible I wouldn't know where it is but someone else would.
   Future expectation: I think he'd wait for me to find someone.
   Expectation reason: Because maybe he'd believe someone else.

4. "I want to get some information about the next summer session."
   Response: Maybe he (you) could find what you want in Low Memorial Library.
   Reason: Because it handles all summer school materials, I think.

Future expectation: I think he'd ask for directions how to get there. I'd refer him to the college walk where he is and point out the building for him.

Expectation reason: (Not given.)

5. Would the student like to have done anything differently?
Response: None.[14]

STUDENT II

1. "The man approaches you and says, "Uh, excuse me."
Response: Look up.
Reason: Because I was approached and wanted to make certain he was speaking to me.
Future expectation: He will ask directions to one of the buildings on campus.
Expectation reason: Because this often happens.

2. "Could you tell me where Hamilton Library is?"
Response: There is no Hamilton Library. Do you mean Butler Library or Low Library or Hamilton Hall?
Reason: Because he is obviously confused about the buildings.
Future expectation: He will look through some papers to try and find out which building he wants.
Expectation reason: Because he has forgotten.

3. "But they told me Hamilton Library."
Response: They were wrong. Do you want a library or a classroom? What type of building are you looking for and why?
Reason: Because he is still confused.
Future expectation: He will say he is looking for a library.
Expectation reason: Because this is more likely than not. Most people not familiar with the campus are not looking for classroom buildings.

4. "I want to get some information about the next session of summer school."
Response: You want Philosophy Hall. That's where the summer session office is. (Direct him.)
Reason: Because this is the case.
Future expectation: He will thank me and leave. I will leave.
Expectation reason: (Not given.)

---

14. If students did not wish to make changes, they were told to write "No" or "None."

5. Would the student like to have done anything differently?
    Response: If he had said he was looking for summer session registration and not the library I would have told him where to go at that time.
    Reason: (Not given.)

These protocols demonstrate some of the points we have been discussing. In the first section, both students exhibit the "until further notice" feature when they say they would await a further act by the person who has addressed them. At the same time they begin developing an initial construction in their expectation that the fellow will ask for some kind of information regarding the location of a building or some other physical site. The students' initial constructions of this situation are quite similar. Student I has written that the fellow "might be . . . seeking directions," and that he expects to be asked a question, since he "knows no logical move . . . other than to ask a question of direction." This student has invoked a rule of interpretation governing information-request situations. Student II likewise states that "I was approached and wanted to make certain that the man was speaking to me"; the fellow "will ask directions to one of the buildings on campus, because this often happens." This student too has invoked the rule governing information requests.

It is also interesting that these students use the phrases "*logical*" and "this often happens." These terms suggest that because the student presumes the invoked rule to be "correct," because he considers it an objective assessment of what is going on, certain things *must* happen subsequently. Once the situation has been typified, the actor's stock of knowledge of such situations is *taken for granted as objective knowledge,* and therefore he presumes to know with almost absolute certainty what will ensue. There is no ontological reason that the experimenter's next comment could not have been "All right, now the man pulls a gun and says, 'Give me your money.'" Nor is there perfect certainty that something like this could not actually have occurred in a real-life situation. But the students do not act on these possibilities. One real outcome of the initial student typifications is that they remain to carry on the interaction and expect the other fellow to remain. Notice finally, in this first exchange, that both student actors have imputed a set of nonmalicious motives to the fellow.

We can see in the students' responses to the second statement ("Could you tell me where Hamilton Library is?") that their constructions of the situation begin to diverge. Student I assumes that the building mentioned (Hamilton Library) does exist, that he does not know its location, and that someone more familiar with the campus will know where it is. Student II, on the other hand, assumes that the building does not exist, that the fellow is "confused" and that the fellow must try and figure out the location he desires, since "he has forgotten" which building he wants to find. Let us point out again that so far as we know there is no Hamilton Library. But this does not imply that student II was not also making an assumption when he based his actions on this same construction; a "fact" is simply a construction of the world that is assumed to be objectively true beyond doubt. Therefore, student II also assumed that his knowledge of the campus was correct (i.e., factually true).

Notice the responses and expectations of the two students that follow this second statement. The first student tells the fellow that he is "sorry but I'm not familiar with the buildings"; he also expects that the fellow will say "thank you" and leave. This student, given his construction of the situation, concludes that his response to the second statement constitutes a terminating event in the interaction. With the utterance of his second remark, student I conceives that the interaction will necessarily come to an end, there being nothing in the rule of interpretation that would permit the activity to continue. Student II, on the other hand, says, "There is no Hamilton Library," and asks, "Do you mean Butler Library or Low Library or Hamilton Hall?" This student expects that the interaction will continue, that it makes sense for the fellow and himself to remain on the scene: "He will look through some papers to try and find out which building he wants." *Given the orientation to the different meanings they have assigned to the situation and the utterances within it, these two actors now begin to engage in different actions and expect that different subsequent courses of interaction will ensue.*

After the third statement, "But they told me Hamilton Library," we see that each student retains his construction of the situation. Student I continues to assume that the fellow is correct in stating that there is a Hamilton Library and that someone else can tell him where it is. Further, student I makes sense of the fellow's persistence (his failure to leave as expected) by assuming that the fellow does not "believe" what he has told him. (This imputation of disbelief we infer from student I's comment that "maybe he'd believe someone else.") On the other hand, student II assumes that the fellow "is still confused" and continues his attempt to find out what he is actually looking for. Student II does something else that is interesting in this response; he attempts to find out in more general terms what the fellow is seeking. Student II begins to search for the "reason" the fellow is at Columbia ("What type of building are you looking for *and why?*" (Italics added.) He is searching for what Schutz calls a common-sense motive, a search that is one of the most general in everyday social life. By finding out what it is a person *wants* to do, the actor can assign a future to that person and thus to the interaction he is having with him. It is in terms of this future, including the imputation of a motive that others are attempting to bring to realization, that the actor constructs his meaning and thus his course of action.

In the next section, the fellow explicitly states as his purpose in the interaction "to get some information about the next session of summer school." With this, the responses of the two students converge again; they both tell the fellow where he can obtain the information he is seeking. Once the fellow's purpose or motive was known to them, the students could more easily evaluate what the interaction was about; they could clarify past exchanges and ready future ones. *Given explicit knowledge of his purposes,* the students could, in the interactional sense, more easily provide the information he desired.

Student II later suggests this when he asserts, "If he had said he was looking for summer session registration and not the library I would have told him where to go *at that time.*" (Italics added.) The in-order-to motive of the fellow, his purpose, became the basis for final construction of the situation, the final response, and the conclusion by both students that the interaction would end. (This is explicit in student II's comment, "He will thank me and leave." In student I's case it must be inferred from the fact that he lists no further comments by the fellow.[15]

We might summarize this analysis by saying that insofar as both students construed the situation in the same way (by assuming it was a request for information rather than, say, a mugging episode), they carried out similar if not identical courses of action. Insofar as they diverged in their constructions of the situation, they carried out different courses of action. Student I's assumption that the fellow was correct about the existence of the building led him to seek someone who could tell the fellow where it was; student II's assumption that the fellow was confused led him to try and discover what building the fellow really wanted. Similarly, the students conceived of the interaction as having reached a conclusion at different times when their constructions diverged and at the same time when their constructions converged. Thus, one way of adequately describing the generation of episodes of social interaction is to give a thorough account of the work of imputing meaning in the situation.

We have already begun to fill in the picture of social interaction by relating constructions to actions. We will now complete that picture by putting together all the currents we have discussed, and then move on to the development of a set of questions about interaction in the guidance situation.

## Social Interaction: The Meeting of Worlds of Imputation

We have discussed some basic social processes that generate and maintain episodes of social action. We shall now present an account of how these processes operate in situations of social interaction.

By social interaction we mean any circumstance in which actors construct and treat one another and themselves according to normatively governed rules of interpretation. This definition closely follows

---

15. Though it is possible that Student I is uncertain, since one of his expectations about termination of the interaction has already been violated.

Weber's idea of social relationship: "The term social relationship will be used to denote the behavior of a plurality of actors in so far as, in its meaningful content, the action of each takes account of the others and is oriented in these terms."[16] This definition is broad enough to include instances of interaction in which the participating actors are not in the physical presence of one another. For example, given our definition, the interaction between a researcher applying for a grant and the review board passing on his proposal would be an instance of social interaction. This would be so because, in writing his proposal, the researcher would be attending to their desires, likes, and dislikes in his construction of the review board; and, in judging the proposal, the review board would be attending to his experience and competence in their construction of the researcher. Our definition of social interaction also includes what many authors have referred to as "face-to-face" interaction, in which participants are in the physical presence of one another. The participants in an episode of social interaction may be viewed as carriers, for they bring certain things with them when they enter the interaction. What they carry can be discussed under three convenient headings: (a) projects, (b) initial constructions, and (c) a stock of knowledge.

Projects are the actor's purposes in the interaction, and they may be either mundane or quite special. A student may enter an interaction with a guidance counselor in order to obtain the name of the advisor to a club or to obtain permission to transfer from a vocational course to a college-preparatory course. Further, the projects of interactants may or may not be complementary. They may or may not be simultaneously attainable in the interaction. For example, if a student seeks to obtain the counselor's recommendation for admission to a prestige college, while at the same time the counselor seeks to "aid the student in realizing" that he is not "Big Three" material, it is difficult to conceive how these two projects might simultaneously be accomplished. Finally, we might point out that each participant not only brings a project with him to the interaction but also brings a conception of what would constitute the accomplishment of that project. Imagine

16. Weber, *op. cit.*, p. 118.

that both the counselor and counselee have the purpose of transferring the student from a vocational to a college-preparatory course. The student might conceive of this project and its accomplishment in terms of being placed in an advanced section of the college-preparatory course. The counselor, on the other hand, might conceive of it in terms of placing the student in a mathematics-improvement course, which would require him to take further work in arithmetic before entering the algebra class. These conceptions of (*a*) the project and (*b*) its accomplishment are important because they provide the actors with their sense of what the ending of the interaction will look like. In the illustration just mentioned, the guidance counselor may well take his granting of permission to transfer to the improvement section as the last act in the encounter. The student, on the other hand, may consider this act a premature conclusion that halts things in midstream. The plurality of actors' projects brought to the encounter will be a first element that informs and determines the shape of the ensuing interaction.

The actor also brings to the interaction what we will call an "initial construction" of the situation. He comes to the interaction having invoked a rule of interpretation, in terms of which he imputes pasts and futures to the interaction itself and to the other actors he will confront; thereby he constructs for himself a set of expectations about what will occur in the course of the encounter. In accord with the rule he has invoked, the actor envisions *in advance* what the purposes of the other actors will be, what they will do to accomplish their purposes, and why they will do these things. The actor then treats these expectations as a set of *conditions* under which he must work to accomplish his own ends; having treated his initial construction in this way, the actor plans his strategies for the accomplishment of his purposes.

In constructing the interaction in advance and planning his strategies in the encounter, the actor attends in particular to the other actors' constructions of him. That is, the actor assumes that as he is making assumptions about the other actors in the interaction, so are they making assumptions about him. He sees them, and assumes that they see him, as a certain type of person with certain types of motives and seeking certain types of goals. And, just as he will treat them in terms of the construction he has made of them, so does he assume that they will treat him in terms of their construction of him. Since all participants in the interaction are engaging in these activities, there emerges what might be called a process of "double imputation." That is, in each actor's construction of the other actors there is included a conception of their construction of him. This double imputation—an imputation of an imputation, so to speak—finds expression when recognized events in the behavior of others seem to contradict our imputation of their construction of us. This may be seen when we make such startled responses as, "What do you take me for?" and "Who, me?" Statements such as these occur when the behavioral displays of others lead us to recognize that we have not been taken for exactly what we had intended. When upon finishing a formal dinner we are told, "Don't drink that—it is for your fingers," we might suddenly realize that our host has not seen us as what we had thought, and respond with some (more subtle) variety of "What do you take me for?" Thus, the actor builds a version of the other actors' constructions of him, and he assumes that they will treat him in terms of those constructions.

As we have mentioned, it is in terms of his initial constructions that the actor plans his strategies in the interaction. By strategies we mean those actions conceived of by the actor prior to their execution as helping to realize his purposes. These strategies include the whole spectrum of behavioral displays—utterances, movements, gestures, etc. They are intended by the actor to evoke from others treatments favorable to the accomplishment of his purposes. Strategies are designed to generate a construction of the actor by others that will lead them to treat him in the manner he desires. Thus, throughout the interaction the actor is constantly assembling behavioral displays that will maintain a relationship favorable to the accomplishment of his purposes. And it is most important to note that although the actor's substantive purpose may vary in and among interactions, what we can call his "relational goals" (i.e., treatment by others favorable to the accomplishment of his purposes whatever they may be) will always be pursued. Whether at home or at work, with a friend or an enemy, in good times or bad, actors are involved in social interaction and are pursuing their relational or "impression management" goals.[17]

The behavioral displays that an actor will incorporate in his relational strategies are formulated in terms of the stock of knowledge he carries with him to the interaction. The actor's interpretation and treatment of his world are based on what Schutz refers to as "a stock of previous experiences of [the world, the actor's] own and those handed down to [him] by [his] parents and teachers."[18] These "previous experiences" include situations, objects (including other actors), and events (including courses of action, his own and others'). This stock of previous experiences is not, however, simply "raw data," not an ungeneralized trace of discrete and idiosyncratic events (these are more appropriately called "memories"). It is, rather, a stock of previous experiences that are *conceptualized* by the actor in at least two ways and thus made useable in the present. First, as we have already suggested, the actor conceptualizes his experience of discrete situations, objects, and events as being typical kinds of things. He conceptualizes, for example, his encounter with Officer Jones not only in terms of what it is like to be pulled over for speeding by Officer Jones but also in terms of what it is like to be "stopped by a cop" for "any reason." The actor conceives of his story that his speedometer was broken not just in terms of "what you tell Jonesy" but also in terms of "the things one does to beat a ticket." Thus the actor conceives of his previous experiences with particular situations, objects, and events in terms of the *classes* to which those concrete things he has encountered belong. The actor stopped by Officer Jones would say in the future, "Isn't that just like a cop!" as easily as he would say, "Isn't that just like Jones!"

The second way in which the actor conceptualizes his previous experiences has to do with his assessment of the typical effectiveness of his own and others' past courses of action. Statements such as, "You can't buck city hall," "Some guys just will never learn," and "What's the use?" all reflect actors' assessments of the typical effec-

---

17. Erving Goffman, *The Presentation of Self in Everyday Life*, Doubleday & Company, Inc., Garden City, New York, 1959, *passim*.
18. Schutz, *op. cit.*, p. 7.

tiveness of particular types of actions. When he makes such a statement, the actor is saying, in effect, "I, as well as others, have found
that if we attempt to affect something done by politicians, there is a
very low probability that our efforts will meet with success." Taken
together, these conceptualizations of past experience constitute the
stock of knowledge an actor carries to an interaction. By using his
stock of knowledge in coordination with his interpretation of the
situation and his construction of the others involved, the actor
organizes certain typically effective actions as the behavioral displays
that are intended to manage others' impressions of him.

In summary, actors bring to an interaction what we have chosen
to call their "worlds of imputation." The episodes and outcomes of
interaction are nothing more than social transactions between the
imputational worlds that actors carry with them. Another way of
saying this is to note that in sociological analysis the actor *becomes*
his imputational world, for he is no more nor less than the set of
purposes, accomplishment conditions, constructions, stocks of knowledge, and strategies that he carries with him.

This becomes apparent once the interaction begins and the actors
initiate their documentary work and assemble their behavioral displays.
Now action is truly reciprocal, the constructions and courses of action
of one actor becoming contingent upon those of the other actors and
vice versa. The actor's rule of interpretation makes sense of the other
actors and their activities, recognized events maintain that sense or,
when they contradict it, force the actor to reinterpret what is going
on. Constructions are made and altered; impressions are managed
and remanaged. It is the mutual flow of these activities that constitutes the content of a social interaction.

But the basic processes of sense making, sense affecting, project
selection, and the assembly of behavioral displays are not the idiosyncratic acts of asocial individuals. They are rather the expressions
of normatively governed *relationships* between interdependent actors
and are thus the foundation and basic feature of the socially practiced
and socially enforced activities of daily life.[19] These processes are

---

19. Consequently, they are no more "in here" than "out there."

what Garfinkel calls "the *socially standardized* and standardizing, 'seen but unnoticed,' background features of everyday scenes."[20] Therefore it is these processes whose concrete embodiments must be described in order to give an adequate account of guidance interaction; and it is just such a description that remains a precondition for choosing between various substantive theories of guidance.

## SOME QUESTIONS FOR RESEARCH ON INTERACTION IN THE GUIDANCE SITUATION

In this section, we shall formulate some guidance research questions reflecting our general conceptualization of social interaction. We hope that answers to these queries will provide empirical descriptions of guidance as social interaction. Many concepts are thrown about in present discussions of guidance counseling, including such notions as non-directive counseling and eclectic counseling. But, as we stated at the beginning of this chapter, it is difficult to assign empirical referents to these and other such general terms. This difficulty is recognized by Gilbert D. Moore in his introduction to a recent volume on guidance research in high schools: "The objectives of counseling and guidance activities are easy to couch in general terms, but they are often difficult to express in concise and meaningful descriptive . . . behavioral terms."[21]

Answers to the questions we shall pose would provide us with the type of fundamental information we need in order to found our knowledge of the social processes of guidance. They would allow us to express, in the concise terms that Moore demands, the aims and procedures of guidance. We will phrase them in terms of one-to-one, face-to-face interaction between counselor and counselee in a counseling situation, making little explicit reference to interactions between

20. Harold Garfinkel, "Studies of the Routine Grounds of Everyday Activities," *Social Problems*. Winter 1964. (Italics added.) See also Garfinkel's *Studies in Ethnomethodology*, Prentice-Hall, Inc., Englewood Cliffs, N.J., 1967.
21. Association for Counselor Education and Supervision, Experimental Designs Committee, *Research Guidelines for High School Counselors*, College Entrance Examination Board, New York, 1966, p. vii.

the counselor and his coparticipants in a group counseling situation, to his interaction with parents, or to his relations with school and college personnel. But, although we will not focus on these kinds of interactions, our questions could be used to explore them by a simple substitution of terms. For example, the question, "What constructions of the counselor's purposes does the counselee bring to the interaction?" can be read as, "What construction of the counselor's purposes does the parent (teacher, groups of students, etc.) bring to the interaction?" Also, we will couch our presentation primarily in terms of counseling interactions per se. Although this is only one of the possible purposes of counselor-counselee interaction, it is the one that presently arouses greatest interest. What we have to say, of course, could easily be applied to interactions dealing with information services, testing services, placement services, and so forth.

1. What are the interactional activities of counselor and counselee prior to their actual confrontation?
This question refers to the way in which counselor and counselee go about setting up, or generating, interview situations. We might ask, for example, what sources of information about the interview and one another are available to the participants and, most important for guidance as interaction, how they make use of this information. What records does the school keep on each student and which of these documents does the counselor use? (Not which should he use, but which *does* he use?) Then, how does the counselor interpret the records he does use—what remarks, say, does he take as evidence that the student "should be seen"?

With regard to counselees, what do "all students know" about counselors and counseling in their high school? How does the student attend to this information pool, what does he listen to and what does he not? What "problems" does the student construct as being issues to be taken up with his counselor rather than with his friends or teachers? Will a student take a conflict with another student to his counselor, his friends, or his teacher?

Finally we might ask what relationship, if any, exists between the way in which the counselor and counselee conceive of "problems" as warranting an interview, on the one hand, and the substance of their initial purposes and constructions in the interaction, on the other.

2. What are the projects that counselor and counselee bring to the interaction?

This question refers to the purposes that the counselor and counselee bring to the interaction and to their conceptions of what would constitute the accomplishment of those purposes. One or both of the parties may conceive of a concrete outcome that they want to see generated in the interaction. For example, the counselor may seek information about the student's medical history, or he may want to talk to the student about the many fights in which he has been involved. The counselee may seek such specific things as information about college admission and summer employment, or he may attempt to get advice about a problem he is having with his parents. Needless to say, participants can seek negative outcomes as well. The counselee may know by the third interview that the counselor is going to reassign him from the academic to the vocational group, and he may attempt to block such a move.

On the other hand, the counselor or counselee may come to the interaction with an open purpose. That is, they may come into the interaction only for the purpose of discovering "why I was called in" or "why Robert asked to see me."

In answering this question we would also want to discover what counselor and counselee envision as the fulfillment of their purposes. What kinds of things does the counselee mean when he says that he wants advice—what kinds of counselor activities does he presuppose in this term? What, for the counselor, would constitute talking over a problem and what would, for him, constitute avoiding the issue? The answers to these questions would provide us with some idea of how the counselor and counselee conceive of themselves as participants in the guidance interaction. They would also provide us with the specific behaviors that are expected to be the documents of these conceptions, that is, with the actor's version of his own intentions.

3. What is the initial construction that the counselor and counselee bring to the interaction?

This question refers to the counselor's and counselee's initial construction of the whole situation, including the other actor, within which projects are to be played out. An answer would depict the expectations that the parties hold for the interaction at its outset. We would want to know such things as how counselor and counselee construct the purposes of one another, and their conceptions of how the other's purposes will impede or facilitate the accomplishment of their own ends. Further, we would want to know how the counselor and counselee construct the other's construction of themselves. What, in other words, do they see at the outset that the other "will take me for"? Does the counselor, for example, conceive of the counselee's construction of him as "just someone else who doesn't understand" or as "someone who can really help"?

These constructions will affect the participants' initial assembly of behavioral displays and the effects of these displays. What acts, as displays, does the counselee conceive as "letting the counselor know how I really feel"? Answers to these questions would provide us with a description of the construction of the interaction by the participants at the outset as well as their opening moves. The direction of the interaction depends upon this initial construction and, in turn, upon the stock of knowledge that counselor and counselee bring to their encounter.

4. What is the nature of the stock of knowledge that counselor and counselee bring to the interaction?

This question refers to counselor's and counselee's background information as to what *could* occur in the interaction, and how such contingencies are to be dealt with in terms of their projects. A stock of knowledge may include specific items concerning the particular individuals involved, for example, what Mr. Jones will do "if I start crying *again*." In this example "again" refers to a counselee's *concrete* past experience with his counselor as a *particular person* who reacts in *particular* and regular ways. The stock of knowledge also includes general typifications of potential interaction scenes. The counselor may wonder, for example, "what will happen if I tell this student, *as I have told others,* that his problems in school stem from his fear of his father." Here the counselor invokes his (and his teachers' and colleagues') *general* past experience with the *type* of person known as "student" who reacts in typically regular ways. It is the social interplay of typifications and particulars that organizes an interaction in a regular and, hence, describable way.

These first questions have dealt with the participants in guidance interaction as "carriers." We have suggested a few bits of information necessary to describe counselor and counselee at their point of entry into the interaction. It should now be clear that the content and congruence of these initial worlds of imputation are problematic and thus need empirical research. We hardly know what these worlds are empirically, much less whether they are uniform between counselors, counselees, and the various kinds of schools that comprise our educational system. To gain information on these matters would be to gain knowledge of how guidance interactions start and thus of what is likely to develop as they proceed. As the interaction unfolds, the counselor and counselee begin their impression management and documentary work, and research would here be formulated in terms of what they do together.

5. What are the general and specific impression-management techniques employed by counselor and counselee?

As the interaction proceeds, what are the general and specific things that counselor and counselee actually do in order to influence the imputations of the other? We can take an example of this impression-management work from a text book used in the training of guidance personnel.[22] A general project for the counselor in the interaction and its associated behavioral display is suggested in the following:

. . . create a permissive atmosphere so that the counselee feels free to express his feelings without fear of criticism or censorship. Take the attitude that the interview is a cooperative relationship.[23]

---

22. In using this material, we do not mean to imply that it gives an apt picture of real guidance interaction, nor that its behavioral accounts are adequate for our purposes. We use these examples only to provide concrete illustrations of our points.

23. J. Anthony Humphreys et al., *Guidance Services,* Science Research Associates, Chicago, 1960, p. 172.

In this passage, the implicit project seems to be to engender *in the counselee* the impression, or construction, that the situation is an open one in which he may do as he pleases in expressing his problem. The display that is intended to engender this construction in the counselee is to manifest the attitude that the interview is a "cooperative relationship." The behavioral referents of a cooperative relationship remain undetailed, however, and this is a crucial omission. To take another example, the project of a counselee might be to "convince him that I can do the work in college prep," a project the student intends to accomplish by a statement such as, "In junior high I did all right gradewise."

The general techniques used by each participant to influence the other—their conceptions of effective and ineffective displays, and the activity of changing the other's rule of interpretation or purpose—would be explored in answering this question.

6. What are the ways in which counselor and counselee go about making sense of the displays of one another?

Here we refer to the ways counselor and counselee engage in documentary work, how they interpret the specific behavioral displays of one another. In the course of the interaction the participants will go about making sense of specific actions engaged in by the other; they will, in other words, assign meaning to the behavioral displays they witness by typifying them in terms of the rule of interpretation they have invoked. If the student's aptitude scores are high and his grade-point average is low, the counselor might conceive of him from the outset as an "underachiever." In the course of the interaction, the counselor might see the student's sighs and silences as representing "disinterest" and "disaffection" from his school work. He might make sense of these as typical displays made meaningful by the "underachievement" rule of interpretation. The counselor would, in other words, make sense of these displays (assign them a reason) by construing them to be manifestations of the underlying pattern he has already "discovered" in his examination of the student's record. On the other hand, similar displays might be interpreted by the counselor as demonstrating that the student is "not just" an underachiever but rather "a young girl with a deeper problem."

Answers to this question would thus tell us something about the way in which counselors and counselees regularly go about making sense of the concrete behavior of the other during the interaction. They would include the process of documenting underlying patterns as well as recognized further-notice acts that provide transformations of those patterns.

7. What do counselor and counselee take as possible outcomes of their interactions?

This question refers to (a) potential closing moves that counselor and counselee treat as available to themselves and to each other; (b) their conceptions of the other's reactions to their closing moves and the techniques they would have to employ to gain acceptance of these moves as terminating events; (c) Their conceptions of what will follow upon the closing of their face-to-face interaction (a trip to a social worker, a visit with the principal). This information would provide further knowledge of how different types of interactional "results" are generated during the interaction itself—for example, how counselor and counselee go about engineering in a concerted way a referral to a psychiatrist.

These seven questions provide the beginnings of an inquiry into the constitutive features of guidance interaction. They are in no way an exhaustive catalogue of the information bits that should be gathered, nor are they necessarily a final or optimum formulation of a set of questions to be researched. We could, for example, elaborate our questions on the initial purpose of counselor and counselee (and their subsequent modifications of that purpose) to include a specific treatment of the complementarity of projects. And we might reformulate the counselor's section of Question 4 in terms of his conceptions of therapeutic treatment, using this as a prime category of impression-management techniques. None of these possibilities has been ruled out.

The outcome of our research would be a model of the actors and interactions that we collectively refer to as "guidance counseling." Before concluding the chapter, we will comment briefly on research design, as the outcomes of our questions require certain contexts of observation.

## DESIGNING RESEARCH ON GUIDANCE INTERACTION

In this section, we shall suggest three fundamental methodological and technical considerations that would be involved in carrying out the kind of research we have discussed.

First, we must attend to what Schutz calls the "taken-for-granted" feature of common-sense processes and activities: It is generally true that invoking a rule of interpretation, selecting a project, assembling behavioral displays, and engaging in documentary work are not *considered* processes by the actor.[24] This may best be made clear by analogy. Most people know how to walk, as evidenced by the fact that most people do walk. However, these same people would be hard pressed to state verbally just what they do in walking. This task becomes still more difficult if we add as a condition that their account must be complete enough to that someone could learn to walk simply by following their verbal instructions. Now it is surely correct that people also go about assigning meaning, selecting projects, and so on. As with walking, this is evidenced by the fact that they actually engage in these activities. But to say this is so is not simultaneously to claim that these people could give an account of their activities *that would be adequate for transforming another person into what they are—a doer of what they do.* Yet such a set of instructions for transforming another is precisely what we have in mind when we speak of constructing models of the counselors and counselees we would be studying. Thus, the information we need in order to found our knowledge of guidance cannot be gained simply by "talking to people." Assuredly they would have something to say about what they are doing, but so would the walker. Because the actors we study take the processes we are interested in completely for granted, it is

---

24. Thus, we are not positing psychological rationalism and all its pitfalls.

difficult for them to give us anything but an interpreted and therefore partial version of what they are doing. The problem with common-sense accounts is that, being taken for granted, they conceal themselves and thus are inadequate as the sole basis for making a counselor of a layman. In our terms, such accounts will not themselves provide the necessary empirical referents of a conceptualization of guidance interaction. Before suggesting a way of dealing with this problem of taken-for-grantedness, let us turn to the second methodological consideration, the normative goverance of the activities we have been discussing.

We have already suggested that the extent to which the sense-making and action-assembly processes are normatively governed is an empirical question, and we have pointed out that by "normatively governed" we mean those activities whose appropriate enactment is socially enforced. Though normatively governed, however, actors can and do deviate from norms. But, because they are normatively governed, their deviations will bring a response both from others and, often, from themselves. Thus, to the extent that the processes we have discussed are normatively governed, their miscarriage by an actor will get him the "characteristic reaction we term punishment,"[25] or sanction. In addition, normative governance, as we have defined it, means "socially practiced." This implies that normatively governed activities are, by nature of being sanctioned, self-perpetuating and recurring in the interactions we wish to study. This implication of normative governance overcomes what might appear to be a subjective orientation of our framework. To the extent that meaning, imputation, and the rest are not idiosyncratic activities but rather are normatively governed processes, we may anticipate less than an infinite number of models of the actors we would study. There would be fewer models than people and thus an eradication of subjectivism. Given a particular society and hence a particular normative order, the activities of members can vary only in limited and particular ways.

Getting back to the problem of taken-for-grantedness, this prob-

---

25. Emile Durkheim, *The Division of Labor in Society*, The Free Press, New York, 1964, p. 70.

lem can be managed by our using our knowledge of the nature of normatively governed activities in the following way. If a certain mode of acting is normatively governed, then we assume that any actor who does not comport himself in the prescribed way will be the object of sanction. He may, for example, simply be "set straight" about what he should have done, or he may be threatened or injured for his misconduct.[26]

These considerations aid us in dealing with taken-for-grantedness, because we can check our influences as to what the normatively governed processes are by observing when actors sanction one another or when they sanction a researcher for making "an absurd suggestion." Take the "setting straight" process. When norms are broken, an actor often articulates the proper (i.e., normatively prescribed) meaning that should have been imputed in the situation and the proper action that should have been taken. Conformity to the norm is taken for granted and thus difficult to observe. But by observing the application of sanctions and by attending to the utterances designed by actors to "set one another straight," the researcher provides himself with a tool for overcoming the taken-for-granted nature of the processes he wishes to study.

A final methodological consideration, mentioned in the early part of this chapter, is the competition for rights to define stimuli in social-science research. In designing such research, we must be aware that what we call "data" or "findings" are not simply a one-party product. They are not the outcome of the activities of subjects alone or of the researcher alone. In one way or another the researcher affects the material he gathers as he carries out his inquiry. The principles of interaction that govern the confrontations of counselors and counselees also govern the confrontations of researchers and subjects. The researcher's construction of the subject informs and determines his treatment of the subject. In turn, this treatment by the researcher is used by the subject in constructing and treating the researcher (e.g.,

---

26. This notion of sanctioning applies equally to the participants in an interaction and to a researcher who is studying that interaction. The researcher may be sanctioned for violating his rights as either researcher or participant, and this may make a tremendous difference in the kind of data he elicits.

in constructing "what he wants to know"). It is difficult to imagine an interaction in which such construction does not take place, and so the issue is not how to eliminate bias. It is rather how to give an adequate and explicit account of the *researcher-subject interaction* so as to provide a context in which to evaluate the meaning of the subject-subject interaction we refer to as data. Bias, in the sense that it is an imputation, is an inevitable characteristic of any social relation, including the one between researcher and subject.

In summary, social research must be designed to deal with the concealed and taken-for-granted nature of common-sense activity. This can be accomplished by selecting research sites in which some kind of setting-straight behavior occurs. Finally, the fact that imputation is a regular feature of common-sense activity makes it imperative that the researcher know not only how his subjects conceive of one another but how they conceive of him as well. Otherwise, he will be unable to isolate his effects from those of his subjects.

## CONCLUSION

We have attempted to outline a plan for overcoming the problems that stand in the way of our quest for knowledge about guidance. Until research answers to questions such as ours have been obtained, until we can give adequate accounts of the constituent features of guidance, we will remain trapped in the vague testimonial state of the "walker." We will be unable to provide students of guidance with an agenda of actual, concrete activities that will methodically generate the component outcomes of guidance programs. Not until models of the common-sense worlds of guidance actors have been constructed can we begin to carry out the research that will firmly ground our knowledge of guidance.

# CHAPTER 9

# THE SOCIAL CONTEXT OF ACADEMIC FAILURE*

*DAVID NASATIR*

WHEN EQUALITY of opportunity prevails, success in competition is the natural result of ability and effort; hence—in the American Dream, at least—it is to the better man that success eventually comes. Failure in such a situation is interpreted as a weakness of the individual, and thought is rarely given to the social arrangements that define and produce the failure.

Such a belief is perhaps especially prevalent in the United States, with its strong heritage from the Puritan days when success was widely accepted as an indicator of virtue, and where even today there is constant reiteration of the theme that equal opportunity is the natural state of our society. Yet no matter how rapidly the economy may expand, no matter how rapidly the society may change, there is never room at the top for everyone. Despite the contrary expectations of the American Dream, failure is a common phenomenon, and failure is the central concern of this chapter.

Success and failure are, of course, terms that are difficult to define. Few activities in American life provide such a clear indicator of failure, however, as can be found in the classroom. This is especially

---

\* The material in this chapter has been adapted from David Nasatir, *College Dropouts: Social Sources of Academic Failure,* Jossey-Bass, Inc., San Francisco, 1968.

true at the college level. Increasing demand for highly trained workers and a rising level of education generally have produced a demand for universal higher education previously unknown. In conjunction with the growth of the American population, it is increasingly common to find young men and women entering institutions of higher learning; it is even more common to find them aspiring to do so. With an increase in the absolute number of students has come an increase in the number of failures as well. During the prewar years of 1933 to 1937, for example, an average of 347,000 youths entered college each year. A similar period after the war, 1947 to 1951, was characterized by an average annual enrollment of freshmen amounting to some 581,000. During this time, although the proportion of students not graduating in four years had dropped from about 51 per cent to 44 per cent, the absolute number of individuals experiencing such failure climbed to an average of over a quarter of a million (256,000) per year.[1] The memory of academic failure is common, therefore, to millions of Americans. If present trends continue, it will be common to millions more.

Regardless of personal costs, failure has many social costs as well. Since premature withdrawal causes institutions to operate at less than full capacity, legislators, trustees, and school administrators have become concerned. They have turned to social scientists for help, and the advice received has been, largely, on two subjects: selection and counseling. This division also reflects, implicitly, the twin foci of this chapter, i.e., the influence on academic failure of properties associated with the daily existence of students as well as those more appropriately considered as antecedent to the university experience.

Aid is frequently sought for the development of an admission policy that will increase the efficiency of school plants by reducing the number of failures and withdrawals. As the drive to offer educational opportunities for everyone broadens, the pressures upon university and college facilities becomes more intense. Administrators are faced with the problem of making a selection from the abundance of

---

1. Data adapted from *U.S. Office of Education Biennial Surveys of Education*, U.S. Government Printing Office, Washington.

applicants, and the most readily defensible basis for discriminating is an estimate of eventual success or failure in academic life. This has been done, by and large, by looking for some clue in the applicant's personality or his background that would predict his outcome at an institution of higher education. But, like all attempts to predict human behavior, predictions of failure are far from perfect.

Despite elaborate attempts to screen students prior to admission, academic failure and voluntary withdrawal continue to be pressing problems for college administrators. Among one half million freshmen in American colleges and universities in 1954, withdrawals prior to graduation amounted to almost 60 per cent.[2] And, according to W. Max Wise,

The proportion of entering freshmen who stay to graduate in the college of their first enrollment has apparently remained remarkably stable over the past twenty years. . . .[3]

Such stability is even more remarkable when it is remembered that this has also been a period of increasing enrollment, improving selection techniques, and constant broadening of the counseling, testing, and guidance programs for those students actually admitted. Failure is a persistent as well as a common phenomenon.[4]

Of course, failure does not occur with the same frequency in all settings; some schools are renowned for their difficulty whereas others are notoriously easy. But, as will be shown later, the rate of failure within institutions is quite stable, and the differences between them persist over long periods. It is this very stability that suggests that failure rates are worthy of study and that they may be, at least in part, the consequence of a distinct set of conditions, conditions that

---

2. Robert E. Iffert, *Retention and Withdrawal of College Students,* U.S. Department of Health, Education and Welfare, Office of Education Bulletin 1958, No. 1, U.S. Government Printing Office, Washington, 1957, p. 17.

3. W. Max Wise, *They Come for the Best of Reasons: College Students Today,* prepared for the Commission on the College Student of the American Council of Education, Washington, 1958, p. 15.

4. It will be shown later that failures constitute the majority of premature withdrawals.

augment or diminish the proportion of failures in a group despite changes in the composition of the student body or the availability of counselors. This chapter is an attempt to contribute to the understanding of academic failure by identifying some of these conditions.

In order to foster this analysis, it is necessary to employ traditional analytic concepts in new ways. An attempt to do this is made in the following section where a consideration is given to the maner in which the informal life led by students in combination with their peers may influence academic failure. But, as a knowledge of group life alone is not sufficient to explain failure, consideration is also given to qualities of individuals that may be related to failure. By combining these approaches to the problem, a series of specific hypotheses is generated.

## A SOCIAL THEORY OF FAILURE

There is . . . in a cohesive and animated society, a constant interchange of ideas and feelings from all to each and each to all, something like a mutual moral support, which instead of throwing the individual on his own resources, leads him to share in the collective energy and supports his own energy when his is exhausted.[5]

Durkheim's conception of group life, as represented in this quotation from *Suicide,* suggests two variables for the analysis of group influences upon individual behavior:

1. The collective energy of the group.
2. The ability of the individual to share in that collective energy.

Two additional factors must also be considered, however, in order to study academic failure:

3. The goals toward which the collective energy of the group is directed.
4. The resources of the individual himself.

---

5. Emile Durkheim, *Suicide,* trans. by John A. Spaulding and George Simpson, The Free Press, New York, 1951, p. 210.

Three kinds of variables have been identified here: those dealing only with properties of groups (1 and 3), that unique to the individual (4), and that treating the relation of the individual to the group (2).

When we review the literature of academic failure, we observe that the major emphasis of existing research has been upon the last of these considerations. Most studies of failure have sought its source solely in the characteristics of individuals. It is intended that this chapter will introduce the consideration of additional dimensions to the work of future investigators.

We turn first to those variables characteristic of groups rather than individuals. A distinction has been made between collective energy and collective goals. It is clear that both factors must be considered simultaneously in the study of failure, as a high level of effort devoted to anti-academic goals may produce a failure rate similar to that occurring when academic goals are present but only slight effort is expended in their pursuit. Nevertheless, as an heuristic device, these factors will be treated separately during this discussion.

The collective energy of a group is distinct from the average energy of all the individuals in the group. It would be possible, for example, to have a group of energetic individualists, each pursuing his own interests, with little interaction and no mutual support. It would also be possible to have a group of individuals each of whom had relatively little energy but was deeply involved with the lives of his fellows. The group as a whole might be as vital as the first group was energyless, even though the individual members of the first group were possessed of great (but uncoordinated) vitality. The second group would draw upon the vitality of its members in such a way as to focus it and coordinate it and, in so doing, provide a source of energy distinct from the sum of the individual energies involved. Collective energy is an integral and irreducible quality of the group itself. It is, however, analogous to the energy of an individual, diffuse but potentially available for a variety of purposes. Some part of that energy must be devoted to maintaining the group itself, of course, and to that extent it is unavailable for other uses. The collective energy must be distributed, therefore, among a variety of tasks such as the pursuit of academic goals at the group level as well as supporting members who are pursuing such goals at the individual level.

Talcott Parsons has suggested that individuals face repeatedly the dilemma of choosing between behavior directly beneficial to themselves but harmful in some way to their group or subordinating private interests for the sake of the collective good.[6] Each group must have, therefore, a set of norms prescribing the manner for resolving such conflicts when they arise in a variety of specific situations. Thus the normative system of every group may be located on a continuum ranging from self-orientation (by which it is felt that individuals *should* pursue their own interests in specified situations of conflict between those interests and the interests of the group) to collectivity orientation (by which, in specified areas of behavior, the interests of the group should be served above all). The collective energy of the group is enhanced or diminished by the norms that the group generates to resolve this dilemma. Where a strong collectivity orientation prevails, a cohesive group exists which permits "the constant interchange of ideas and feelings . . . [and] mutual moral support" of which Durkheim spoke.

Energy devoted to fostering group solidarity and assuring that the problems of the group are solved may be called "cohesive energy," and groups to be studied may thus be classified as more or less cohesive. It is maintained that group cohesion itself, even though it may take away energy from individual scholarly work, has certain positive contributions both to the general and to the specifically academic well-being of individual students.

The picture the individual has of himself, his inadequacies and his strengths, is shaped in large measure by his informal associations. The informal life of the residence group, for example, provides the opportunity for the individual to perform many roles and come to be known by other group members as a total person rather than simply a fellow student, and to be treated as such. Out of primary group situations like this, the individual may draw psychological as well

6. Talcott Parsons and Edward A. Shils, eds., *Toward a General Theory of Action,* Harvard University Press, Cambridge, Mass. 1954, pp. 80–81, p. 248.

as technical support for performing his academic work. To the extent that diffuse moral support is helpful in the adequate performance of the student role, its absence should be noticeable by an *increase* in the failure rate.

Not all individuals need such support to the same degree, of course, and it is partly for this reason the resources of the individual himself are explicitly considered later on in this chapter. For some youths, the important references for their self-image and self-esteem are not to be found among collegiate peers. They are, in Riesman's term, "inner directed."[7] They may choose social isolation precisely in order to devote more of their time and energy to those activities (like studying) for which they do not need the informal support of others and which do not call upon them to invest some of their own resources in maintaining the group.

For many others, however, the lack of integration into a group may be a peculiar handicap in that they cannot obtain those informal supports to the ego necessary to raise the level of self-esteem. Such individuals may fulfill in their actions a self-image of inadequacy. They may forego devices and activities that they feel will benefit them little because of their own ineptitude and, by foregoing, thereby damn themselves to the more difficult task of going it alone. Students of this type may find that leaving school is a technique whereby they can break off from a situation in which their self-esteem suffers in order to reestablish relations with scholarly life in a more hospitable atmosphere. The anonymity provided by changing from one school to another is often enough to allow such students to start anew in their quest for knowledge and/or a degree. Withdrawal from school may also solidify the amorphous role in which late adolescents find themselves. By leaving school, either withdrawing or flunking out, the air is cleared, tension is reduced, and some sort of fresh start can be undertaken.

Some support for this notion is gained when it is noted that not all failures and withdrawals are lost to higher education. Many of

7. David Riesman, with Nathan Glazer and Ruel Denny, *The Lonely Crowd: A Study of the Changing American Character,* Doubleday Anchor Books, Garden City, New York, 1955, pp. 29–32.

them delay completion of their degrees or go elsewhere to finish their work. According to Robert E. Iffert, 41.5 per cent of those who drop out of school do so without leaving any record of transfer, but 12.0 per cent do transfer to other institutions.[8]

A first, tentative hypothesis may be presented now, in light of the discussion of the informal supports available to individuals in highly cohesive groups. All other things being equal, the rate of failure may be expected to diminish with increased group cohesion.

All other things are never equal, however, so let us now turn to some of the additional factors to be considered in the study of academic failure. It will be recalled that in addition to variables characteristic of groups, the first part of this chapter suggested the necessity of considering the manner in which individuals were related to groups of differing character.

Whereas high cohesion per se may provide informal supports to Ego and thereby aid in the reduction of failures, an inability to tap the benefits of a cohesive group may produce the opposite effect. Thus the student may be driven to some act that is tantamount to withdrawal in order to remove himself from the situation. Feelings of emotional deprivation should be more pronounced for those on the border of highly integrated groups than for members of groups in which there is little or no integration. Merton[9] has discussed in great detail this mechanism producing such feelings of relative deprivation.

When the individual sees the benefits of group membership close at hand, and yet these benefits are denied him, the benefits are relatively more important in creating a sense of deprivation than if those benefits were unknown to him in the first place. Thus, the re-

---

8. Robert E. Iffert, *op. cit.,* p. 18.

Iffert goes on to say that of the remaining students about whom data exists, 11.2 per cent were still in attendance after four years at their original institutions, but had not yet graduated. It must be remembered in the interpretation of these figures, however, that many students followed careers that may have placed them in more than one category. Iffert goes on to estimate that, at the maximum, about 60 per cent of the students entering college will eventually graduate.

9. Robert K. Merton and A. S. Kitt, "Contributions to the Theory of Reference Group Behavior," in *Continuities in Social Research,* The Free Press, New York, 1950.

lation that the individual bears to his group or groups is related to feelings of positive personal worth that are, in turn, often related to adequate academic performance.

A second tentative hypothesis may be stated now by considering the manner in which failure is affected by the relation of the individual to the group. As a condition for the reduction of failures stemming from the collective energy available to members of a cohesive group, individuals must be able to tap that energy, they must be integrated into the group in some way. But, under certain conditions, integration into a cohesive group may also promote failure. Therefore, before stating this hypothesis in final form, it is necessary to consider a second property of groups—the goals toward which their collective energy is focused.

An excessive involvement with the concerns of the group, its continued existence, and the problems facing the group as a whole may in fact, be deleterious. Where individuals feel strongly obliged to serve group interests, even above their own, an important step may be taken on the road to failure. By devoting all their energies to solving the problems of the group (in addition to maintaining the group's academic standing), individual members may perpetuate the group but become academic failures in the process. This type of situation is analogous to that of "altruistic suicide" as described by Durkheim. Here, however, it is the overidentified and overcommitted student who fails in the university because of his excessive involvement in group life. Thus conditions favorable to the perpetuation of the group may, in fact, be reflected in an increase (up to some limit) of the rate of individual failures within that group. In contrast, groups characterized by the primacy of a self-orientation norm (i.e., noncohesive groups) may have difficulty in perpetuating themselves as groups even though there is no formal removal from the university due to academic failure of the individual members.

Postponing for the moment any consideration of the qualities of the individual student, it is possible to note how integration into some cohesive group may actually foster failure because of the goals of the group itself. Among some groups, for example, we might even expect to encounter an analog to what Durkheim called "obligatory" altruistic suicide. Although no data are available, it might be expected that there would be a high rate of obligatory altruistic failure among committed members of groups such as the Free Speech Movement at Berkeley. A part of the ideology of such a group insists that the grades and grading system as they are now presented are illegitimate in many respects. Devotion to the cause of reform may be shown symbolically by harvesting the fruits of academic reprisals; hence, failure and withdrawal are positively valued. Students become heroes of a sort by visibly sacrificing themselves for the good of the movement.

Similar events may be seen in the actions of some college youths who jeopardize their academic standing for the greater glory of their reference group. By doing the outstanding feats of staying away from the library or participating in twenty-four-hour ping pong matches or decorating floats for parades at a time when exams are also pressing upon them, these students are committing a kind of altruistic failure. It is possible, of course, that commitment to the group may also have the opposite effect. Membership in the honor society, for example, may require outstanding academic performance. It is unnecessary to elaborate upon the significance of group norms in this respect.

The examples cited here are extremes, of course, and no group with a voluntary membership could exist for long in the university setting with a normative system permitting complete self-indulgence, nor could a group persist that demanded total obligation to the group above all else—even in the single, restricted area of academic behavior. Complete self-orientation would mean the end of the group. Important functions (such as recruitment and socialization of new members) would be neglected. Yet an all-encompassing concern with the problems of the group would, in the university at least, also require attention to individual performance. Groups in which academic performance of the members falls too low are in danger of losing their legitimacy. To the extent they are recognized in some way by the university, they are subject to university sanctions for inadequate academic performance of too many individual members.

It is clear, however, that some consideration must be given the degree to which a group focuses its energy upon the activity of getting good grades for its members. If groups might be classified, in some manner, as being more or less concerned with grade-getting activities, it would be possible to restate the hypothesis presented earlier in the following, less tentative form. Integration into cohesive groups with an emphasis upon grade-getting activities will be associated with a lower rate of failure than where any one or all of the above factors are missing. But even this formulation ignores one of the factors set forth at the beginning of this chapter: the resources of the individual himself.

Early in the discussion it was suggested that not all individuals need or desire the support to be obtained from group membership. They were labeled as inner-directed at that time, but such a label is really too narrow. Not only are some students inner-directed rather than other-directed, some are brighter than others, some more sophisticated, others are more mature, and so on. Clearly, such differences may be taken into account when studying failure, and the bulk of published research on this subject is focused upon them exclusively. In order to complete the formulation of the hypothesis being developed here, therefore, it is necessary to consider the role played by individual differences in the production of failure.

As mentioned before, not all students need the informal supports of group life, and, perhaps, some are uniquely suited to resisting its pitfalls as well. The impact of the group upon the individual should be most apparent, therefore, in cases in which there is a relatively high potential for failure anyway.

For individuals close to the borderline, even a slight shift in academic performance will be reflected in failure. It is possible then, to formulate the previous hypothesis in the following manner:

Among those students prone to failure by virtue of their individual qualities, the rate of failure will be reduced where they are integrated into cohesive groups in which academic activities constitute an element of the group's collective goal.

The first difficulty encountered in attempting to carry out the testing of this hypothesis is identifying a population for study. Just what, in fact, are the groups referred to and where do they exist? If it is possible to identify such groups, what sampling strategy should be employed to assure variation on the two dimensions cited, cohesion and academic orientation? Even if it is possible to get a sample of such groups, what would be the strategy for obtaining individuals prone to failure who were members of such groups and members with varying degrees of involvement or integration at that? A sample that did not provide variation on all of these dimensions simultaneously would be inadequate for testing the hypothesis. In order to answer some of these questions, the following section is devoted to a review of the work of previous researchers in the field.

## REVIEW OF THE LITERATURE

Within the past ten years alone, at least 135 studies, reports, articles, books, and dissertations dealing with academic failure and withdrawal have appeared. Although only a few of these have dealt with college students, those that do tend to utilize the same general approaches to the problem as those that treat the secondary school student. A brief examination of these approaches will be helpful in clarifying both theoretical and methodological aspects of the problem.

The studies can be classified in many ways. Some simply report rates of failure for different institutions or for different kinds of students, whereas others attempt to explain the processes whereby an individual comes to withdraw or fail. Many studies do a little of both, describing the situation in some particular setting and presenting an analysis of possible causes as well. But whether the works are descriptive, analytical, or mixed, they still display certain systematic differences.

The theoretical orientation of the research provides a most important basis for the classification of studies, and a great deal can be gained from an examination of the assumptions underlying these works. Thus, a first division may be made between the purely psychological and the purely sociological approaches. A good example of the former, characterized by its emphasis upon the characteristics of individuals, is the work of L. E. Boyer, "Admission Tests as Criteria for Success in College."[10] Although presented as a descriptive study (of a special sort) there is an implicit explanation presented as well: failures are due to the inept screening of applicants. The tautology is clear, of course, because, by definition, those who leave early were improperly admitted in the first place. It is presumed in this study (and others like it) that it is possible to identify the potential failure on the basis of indicators such as his family background or his responses to tests. If the proper indicators can be discovered, perfect predictions will result and there will be no more failure.[11] Although there is some merit in this idea, it ignores the variety of situations that may develop in the college experience. It is presumed that factors antecedent to the moment of testing allow one to predict behavior in unknown situations yet to occur. To the extent that it is possible to make such predictions, therefore, they should be made in this study, but it is also necessary to explain the situation in which such predictions fail.

On the other hand, there is research such as that conducted by Robert Iffert,[12] which is of a more sociological orientation. In his excellent work, *Retention and Withdrawal of College Students,* he has organized his data in terms of the type of institutions being studied. Thus, data appear for the failure rate in public versus privately controlled institutions; these latter, in turn, are divided among church-related and independent schools. Tabulations are also made by year and by major. Within these contexts, Iffert also provides tabulations for men and for women, home location in relation to college, college housing and activities. Studies of this sort, which may be labeled "vital-statistics" studies, pay only minimal attention to factors that

---

10. L. E. Boyer and J. E. Koken, "Admission Tests as Criteria for Success in College," *Journal of Education Research,* Dec. 1956, pp. 313–315.

11. See for example, Emma W. Bragg, "A Study of Student Withdrawal at W.U.," *Journal for Applied Psychology,* vol. 47, 1956.

The long dominance of educational research by educational psychology has produced many studies of this type, the "psychological correlates" study. Success or failure of an individual is related only to his individual attributes in such work, and little attention is paid to his milieu in which failure does or does not occur.

12. Iffert, *op. cit.*

might predict success or failure. But they do make a strong attempt to determine differences in failure rates. The basis for discriminating among contexts, however, is limited to differences that are recognized administratively; other means of classifying contexts are simply not employed.

A variation on the above approach is frequently carried out by collegiate registrars. An attempt is made to determine the characteristics of all failures and relate these to the administrative units in which they are located. Thus comparisons will be made by academic major or residence, for year in school and sex. While such studies do, indeed, relate individual and contextual data, they often do so by falling victim to what has been called "the fallacy of ecological correlation,"[13] for the logic by which one concludes that the relation between variables in an aggregate population hold for the units of that population is often faulty. Although it is possible for departments with a high proportion of women to have a lower proportion of failures, it does not follow that women have a lower probability of failure than do men in any given department.

Although an additional approach, which may be identified as "developmental-social-psychological," combines features of the above orientations, it is worth considering in its own right. From this point of view, the social life of the child is thought to encourage or inhibit the development of innate characteristics such as creativity or intelligence as well as to give rise to socially determined ones such as a need for achievement or an authoritarian personality. Through social interaction, it is maintained, the child learns to organize his approach to the world. Thus the early years of family life mold the student into a sensitive, complex, but relatively unchangeable creature. It is usually assumed that the process of personality formation terminates some time before adult status is reached. There are, of course, many systematic elements involved in the socialization process—patterns common to large sectors of the society.[14] These differences and similari-

13. W. S. Robinson, "Ecological Correlations and the Behavior of Individuals," *American Sociological Review,* vol. 15, June 1950, pp. 351–357.
14. For a concise but clear introduction see Frederic Elkin, *The Child and Society: The Process of Socialization,* Random House Studies in Sociology, no. 19, Random House, Inc., New York, 1962.

ties are often tied closely to such factors as social class, religion, and race.[15] But the basic argument here is that no matter what the process by which it is formed, a given personality type will call forth a specific (predictable) response to events. With a knowledge of personality type, then, it is possible to gain an understanding of a specific failure in a given situation (after the fact) and correct matters by matching personality types with environments hospitable to them. Little is mentioned, however, of just how the nature of the environment is identified. For a good general view of such work, see G. W. Durflinger.[16]

As an example of how this approach is used in the study of failure, let us consider reaction and rebellion against adult authority. Reaction and rebellion are considered by many to be a necessary part of the maturation process. By the time a child is old enough for college, his basic personality structure is well established and so are the patterns developed for reacting to authority. Thus failure may be viewed as resulting from rebellion against authority figures in general (as represented by the faculty) or as rebellion against parental desires for college attendance. Such an interpretation has, in fact, been made by Dana Farnsworth of Harvard University.[17] He suggests that failure may even be prevented by identification of the student personality type followed by proper guidance into a sympathetic collegiate environment. No suggestions are made, however, on how to identify the qualities of such possible environments.

Implicit in work of this type, however, is a recognition of the importance of environments. Most studies focus upon entire organizations (schools, colleges) or upon administrative divisions within such

---

15. Allison Davis and Robert J. Havighurst, *"Social Class and Color Differences in Child Rearing"* in *Personality in Nature, Society, and Culture,* ed. by Clyde V. Kluckhohn and Henry A. Murray, Alfred A. Knopf, Inc., New York, 1948.

16. G. W. Durflinger, "The Prediction of College Success: A Summary of Recent Findings," *Journal of the American Association of College Registrars,* vol. 19, 1943.

17. Dana L. Farnsworth, M.D., "Some Non-Academic Causes of Success and Failure in College Students," *College Admissions,* vol. 2, College Entrance Examination Board, New York, 1955.

organizations (classes, majors, residence arrangements). It is assumed implicitly that the differences that are important to the understanding of failure are related in some manner to the administrative distinctions. The manner in which they might be related or even the nature of the differences is never made explicit, however, nor are any attempts made to quantify the nature of these supposed differences. The consequence of this strategy is to attribute to an unspecified source the causes of variation in failure rates. Yet it is clear, intuitively as well as theoretically, that there are differences among these groups. The problem remains of how to identify and classify those differences.

There can be no denial of the influence upon daily life of events long past. Habits, tastes, opinions, prejudices, and skills are all formed over a long period. An individual comes to share with others the meanings attributed to specific acts or objectives only through social interaction, and he maintains his picture of the world through a never-ending process of reality testing. It is, in fact, this very characteristic that dooms to failure attempts to predict human behavior solely in terms of social attributes at birth, specific attitudes at some specific time, or knowledge only of the characteristics of a person's environment. The process whereby a person comes to behave in a specific manner is highly dependent upon his interactions with the phenomenal world around him, especially the actual and anticipated behavior of the others with whom he interacts.

Thus, the individual actions which make up the behavioral patterns of groups are taken into account by the individual members of the society even though the patterns themselves may not be consciously perceived. Individuals tend to act in a way that acknowledges the reality of such patterns for their own daily lives. An exclusive focus upon the unique history of an individual is insufficient, as is a focus that excludes all but the present; it is necessary to understand the reality in which the individual is acting in terms of the history he brings to it.

The brief review of studies presented here reveals two major points. First, there appears to be a relative neglect of sociological and institutional approaches to the problem of academic failure even though repeated references are made to the impact of differing environments upon students. Consequently, the theoretical apparatus so useful for the analysis of recurring patterns in social life has rarely been employed in the investigation of failure. Second, the multiplicity of psychologically oriented studies has produced a large number of correlations between diverse attributes of individuals and later success or failure in college. These works do provide an extensive list of variables that have been tested and retested and demonstrated to have some stable empirical relationship with failure.

## FAILURE RATES AS PROPERTIES OF GROUPS

Unlike jail and the army, universities are difficult to enter but easy to leave. For the 12,667 students studied by Robert Iffert, "the rate of graduation in regular progression from the institution of first registration was 39.5 per cent."[18] The *majority* of students who enroll in American colleges and universities do not graduate from them at the end of four years! Only 40 to 50 per cent of the students who register as freshmen at the Berkeley Campus of the University of California can be expected ever to receive their first degree from that institution.[19] Moreover, by graduation about 20 per cent of Berkeley's graduates have withdrawn and returned at least once during their undergraduate career.[20] Between 14 and 18 per cent of the graduates who withdraw did so at least twice.[21] The situation at Berkeley is not

18. Robert E. Iffert, *Retention and Withdrawal of College Students,* U.S. Department of Health, Education and Welfare, Office of Education Bulletin 1958, no. 1, U.S. Government Printing Office, Washington, 1957, p. 17.

19. Stated in private communication with the author by Sidney Susslow, administrative analyst for the registrar at the University of California, Berkeley.

20. *June 1957 Graduating Class, University of California at Berkeley: A Statistical Survey,* Office of the Registrar, University of California, Berkeley, May 1958, p. 6. (Mimeographed.)

21. Data are not widely available for failures and voluntary withdrawals separately, but, according to the registrar's files at Berkeley, of the students who had entered in the fall of 1959 and left by the spring of 1961, 52 per cent had

markedly different from the situation at other large public universities;[22] withdrawal is a common phenomenon.

Many factors operate upon an individual to bring about his withdrawal whether voluntary or involuntary: finances, health, marriage, and disenchantment, to name only a few. However, when year after year the majority of potential graduates leaves prematurely, systematic as well as idiosyncratic factors would appear to be in operation. This section discusses some of the possible sources of such systematic behavior.

Like every subgroup, the college population is affected by the great changes and developments that take place in society as a whole. Wars, depressions, and other upheavals are reflected in enrollments and in withdrawals. The data presented in Tables I and II demonstrate some of these effects. Although there are many deficiencies in the data, they may be considered at least as a rough indicator of the rate of withdrawal over the years. These figures were computed from a rather complete enumeration of institutions made by the United States Office of Education each fall. Because of the manner in which the data were gathered, there is no distinction made between withdrawals from one institution and those same withdrawals who have entered another. As a consequence, it may not be too accurate a representation

---

been dismissed. Although there are important differences between dismissal and withdrawal, the manner in which the social context operates to affect the two rates is presumed to be comparable, as failures constitute such a large portion of those who leave school prematurely. Therefore, in this section, no distinction is made between these two phenomena.

22. Iffert, *op. cit.,* Table 8, p. 16. The grand total graduating in four years is 39.5 per cent.

See also *A Profile of an Entering Class at Wayne State University: The First Ten Years of Those Entering in September 1949,* Office of Divisional Studies, Division of Admission and Records, March 1962, p. 3. (Mimeographed.) Twenty-four percent of the total high school group graduated by the end of the fourth year, 35 per cent by the end of the fifth year, and 46 per cent by the end of the tenth year.

See also the "Retention Studies" of the Pennsylvania State University, Table 3–50 "Analysis Made in Fall, 1953, of the Status of all Students On and Off Campus Who Were Admitted as Freshmen in Fall, 1950" (December 1954, mimeographed). It is stated that 46.5 per cent of the students who entered in 1951 were registered in 1953.

of the actual level of permanent withdrawals from higher education. But if the proportion of intrainstitutional transfers is presumed to remain fixed, or relatively constant over the years, then the figures show at least the relative increase and decrease in withdrawal rates.

**Table I—Number of Students Enrolled for the First Time in U.S. Colleges and Universities, 1932–1952, and Number of First Degrees Granted During Even Years 1934–1952 with Interpolated Estimate of Odd Years 1935–1955 and Percentage Difference Between First-time College Students and Degrees Granted Four Years Later**

| First-time College Students | | First Degree Granted | | Interpolated Estimate of First Degree | | Per cent Withdrawing from Higher Education |
|---|---|---|---|---|---|---|
| 1951 | 529,950 | 1952 | 331,924* | 1955 | 387,401* | 45.8 |
| 1949 | 594,126 | 1951 | 384,352* | 1953 | 304,857* | 48.7 |
| 1947 | 619,232 | 1950 | 432,058 | 1951 | 384,352* | 38.0 |
| 1945 | 474,859 | 1948 | 271,019 | 1949 | 351,538 | 26.0 |
| 1943 | 314,311 | 1946 | 136,174 | 1947 | 203,597 | 35.1 |
| 1941 | 379,070 | 1944 | 125,863 | 1945 | 131,019 | 65.4 |
| 1939 | 417,539 | 1942 | 185,346 | 1943 | 155,605 | 62.7 |
| 1937 | 367,983 | 1940 | 186,500 | 1941 | 185,923 | 49.4 |
| 1935 | 366,734 | 1938 | 169,943 | 1939 | 175,722 | 52.1 |
| 1933 | 307,690 | 1936 | 143,125 | 1937 | 154,043 | 49.8 |
| 1931 | 336,997 | 1934 | 136,156 | 1935 | 139,641 | 58.6 |

* Data from U.S. Office of Education Biennial Surveys of Education. After 1951, the number of first-degree candidates was given annually instead of biennially. Except for the starred (*) figures, the estimate of first-degree population for odd years was derived by interpolation from the even year data given in the second column.

During the early thirties, with the Great Depression affecting all spheres of American life, the withdrawal rate was high. As the New Deal prosperity began to be felt, this rate began to drop. The economic factor of college attendance and withdrawal always plays a vital role, of course, but the growth of scholarship funds, both private and governmental, has given independence to many of the financially marginal. The war years showed another great rise in dropout figures, unquestionably due to the ravages of the draft. The returning veterans and the GI Bill brought a sharp postwar decrease in withdrawals. As seen in Table II, almost 98 per cent of all the men who enrolled in the nation's colleges and universities in 1944–45 went on to graduate from the institution of first registration four years later. The lowered attendance figure during the early forties and its inflation after the war suggest the postponement of college for many. This postponement only caused a temporary distortion; the average dropout rate from 1945 to 1949 was 42.2 per cent. The 97.5 per cent figure has never been approached at any other time for which data is available. The percentage of students withdrawing increased once again with the onslaught of the Korean War and once again dipped with the veterans' return. The limited character of this war attenuated somewhat its impact upon college graduations and withdrawals.

Although wars seem to affect only the males, or at least affect their withdrawal rate in the most pronounced fashion, all students are affected by the economy. With the continued growth of the American economy, the proportion of college-age youths enrolled for degree credit has increased steadily.[23] The push for college has broadened to sectors previously uninterested or unable to become involved in such activities. What is surprising, however, is the stability to be found in the proportion of students withdrawing.[24]

Reexamining the data presented in Table II, we see that the standard deviation for the distribution of the percentage of students withdrawing each year from 1947 to 1958 is 2.75 as compared to a figure one and one-half times as large (4.18) for the percentage of 18 to 21 year olds enrolled in college during those years. When the recent increasing effort to prevent withdrawal by means of placement tests, special counseling efforts, and increased financial aid is noted, this stability is even more surprising. The withdrawal process, although affected by the larger developments in society, represents a unique social phenomenon directly affecting over a million students each year.

Although a consistently large minority of American college students withdraw from schools, it would be erroneous to conclude that all

23. *Opening Enrollment in Higher Education, 1960: Analytic Report,* U.S. Office of Education, Division of Educational Statistics, Washington, 1960, p. 12. See also Table 1 of this chapter.

24. W. Max Wise, *op. cit.*

"The proportion of entering freshmen who stay to graduation in the college of first enrollment has apparently remained remarkably stable over the past twenty years, with slightly higher percentages than formerly now graduating from the colleges in which they enroll as freshmen."

*Table II—Number of Bachelor's and First-professional Degrees Conferred Each Academic Year, 1947–48 to 1958–59, and Ratio to Resident First-time Degree Credit Enrollment Four Years Earlier, and Percentage Withdrawing, by Sex: Aggregate United States\**

| Year | NUMBER OF FIRST-LEVEL DEGREES CONFERRED | | | PER CENT OF FIRST-TIME ENROLLMENT IN THE FALL FOUR YEARS EARLIER | | | Total Per Cent Withdrawal |
|------|-------|-------|-------|-------|------|-------|------|
| | Total | Men | Women | Total | Men | Women | |
| 1958–59 | 385,151 | 254,868 | 130,283 | 55.3 | 59.1 | 49.1 | 44.7 |
| 1957–58 | 365,748 | 242,948 | 122,800 | 56.3 | 61.0 | 48.8 | 43.7 |
| 1956–57 | 340,347 | 222,738 | 117,609 | 58.6 | 63.9 | 50.7 | 41.4 |
| 1955–56 | 311,298 | 199,571 | 111,727 | 58.0 | 61.7 | 52.4 | 42.0 |
| 1954–55 | 287,401 | 183,602 | 103,799 | 60.9 | 65.5 | 54.1 | 39.1 |
| 1953–54 | 292,880 | 187,500 | 105,380 | 56.7 | 58.6 | 53.5 | 43.3 |
| 1952–53 | 304,857 | 200,820 | 104,037 | 54.6 | 56.2 | 51.9 | 45.4 |
| 1951–52 | 331,924 | 227,029 | 104,895 | 58.4 | 61.4 | 52.8 | 41.6 |
| 1950–51 | 384,352 | 279,343 | 105,009 | 64.8 | 69.8 | 54.4 | 35.2 |
| 1949–50 | 433,734 | 329,819 | 103,915 | 62.3 | 66.0 | 52.8 | 37.7 |
| 1948–49 | 366,698 | 364,333 | 102,476 | 76.7 | 97.5 | 49.6 | 23.3 |
| 1947–48 | 272,311 | 176,146 | 96,165 | 69.0 | 82.5 | 53.1 | 31.0 |

\* Adapted from Wayne E. Tolliver, *Earned Degrees Conferred, 1958–59*, U.S. Department of Health, Education and Welfare, Office of Education, OE–54013 Circular No. 636, U.S. GPO, 1961, Table 1, page 2.

schools have a high rate of failure. There is in fact a great deal of diversity. The Commission on Human Resources and Advanced Training reported in 1953 that in forty-one institutions the percentage of

*Table III—Percentage of Freshmen Who Discontinued College at Institution of First Attendance, by Period of Attendance, 1950\**

| Period of Attendance | 1950 Freshman |
|----------------------|---------------|
| Not beyond first year | 27.3% |
| Beyond first year, but not more than two years | 15.0% |
| Beyond second year, but not more than three years | 6.0% |
| Entered fourth year, but not graduated | 7.3% |
| Graduated in four years | 44.4% |

\* Adapted from W. Max Wise, *They Come for the Best of Reasons: College Students Today*, prepared by the Commission on the College Student of the American Council of Education, Washington, D.C., 1958, p. 15.

entering freshmen who graduate varied from about 15 to 85 per cent with a mean of 52 per cent.[25] This variation may in some measure be explained by differences in the policies of the institutions them-

25. *School and Society*, vol. 78, July 25, 1953, p. 27.

selves. Large public universities may be required to accept almost all applicants. Where age and residence rather than academic promise are the admission criteria, high withdrawal rates due to academic failure are common. In elite private colleges many adaptations are made to prevent withdrawal of the highly select clientele. Iffert notes that the survival rate in public universities is 33 per cent compared to a rate of 48 per cent for private universities, and that the rate for independent private schools is 49.6 per cent compared to 43.7 per cent for church-related schools.[26]

Letters were sent to some twenty-five degree-granting institutions listed in Volume 3 of the 1961 United States Office of Education *Education Directory*. School officials were asked for the proportion of students withdrawing each year from their institution. This data is presented in Table IV.

Even within types of schools a great deal of variation still exists. Table IV shows that two of the private women's colleges in a sample

**Table IV—Percentage of Students Withdrawing from Selected Sample of Colleges and Universities by Year, 1954–1961\***

| School | 54–55 | 55–56 | 56–57 | 57–58 | 58–59 | 59–60 | 60–61 | 61–62 |
|---|---|---|---|---|---|---|---|---|
| 1 | 20 | | | | | | | |
| 2 | | 11 | 11 | 11 | 11 | 10 | 10 | |
| 3 | 5 | 8 | 7 | 4 | 7 | | | |
| 4 | | | | | 19 | | | 16 |
| 5 | 6 | 8 | 11 | 12 | 9 | 7 | 9 | 9 |
| 6 | 25 | 19 | 19 | 20 | 16 | 15 | 14 | |
| 7 | 29 | 22 | 21 | 21 | 20 | 16 | 15 | 15 |
| 8 | 4 | | | | | | | |
| 9 | 4 | 5 | 4 | 6 | 6 | 8 | 6 | 6 |
| 10 | | 9 | | 8 | 8 | 8 | 7 | |
| 11 | 4 | | | | | | | |
| 12 | | | | | | | 5 | 6 |
| 13 | | | | 6 | 8 | 7 | 4 | 5 |
| 14 | | | | | | | | 14 |
| 15 | | | | | 12 | 14 | 14 | 11 |
| 16 | | 9 | 10 | 12 | 13 | 13 | 12 | 11 |
| 17 | 9 | 8 | 8 | 9 | 8 | 9 | 8 | |
| 18 | | | | | | 9 | 10 | |
| 19 | 10 | 8 | 12 | 13 | 5 | 4 | 6 | |
| 20 | | | | | | | 24 | 22 |

\* Data obtained from representatives of the administration of each institution.

---

26. Iffert, *op. cit.*, Table 8, p. 16.

of American colleges and universities gave such divergent figures as 95 per cent (3) and 85 per cent (7) when describing the proportion of their students who survive four years and graduate at that time. A similar comparison of two elite men's colleges shows a survival rate of 80 per cent for (1) and 94 per cent for (9).

Fluctuations in the general rate of withdrawal have been related to large-scale upheavals in American society, such as war and depression. The preceding section has attempted to demonstrate the differences to be observed among various institutions due, presumably, to differences in institutional policies and recruitment. We turn now to an attempt to establish the stable and enduring character of these differences in rates in an attempt to learn more about the sources of such stable differences.

**Table V—Differences Between Percentage of Students Withdrawing from Selected Institutions and National Aggregate of Percentage Withdrawing by Years, 1954–1959**

| School | 54–55 | 55–56 | 56–57 | 57–58 | 58–59 | Range |
|--------|-------|-------|-------|-------|-------|-------|
| 1 | 35 | 37 | 37 | 37 | 38 | 3 |
| 2 | 34 | 34 | 35 | 40 | 36 | 6 |
| 3 | 19 | 22 | 21 | 24 | 25 | 6 |
| 4 | | 31 | 31 | 33 | 34 | 3 |
| 5 | 36 | 39 | 38 | 40 | 41 | 6 |
| 6 | 14 | 23 | 22 | 23 | 34 | 20 |
| 7 | | | | | 26 | |
| 8 | | | 32 | 36 | 37 | 4 |
| 9 | 10 | 20 | 20 | 23 | 25 | 15 |
| 10 | 36 | 38 | 38 | 40 | 41 | 6 |

Although the specific rates of withdrawal are quite different for different institutions, these rates are quite stable at any given institution. This is especially true when fluctuations in the rates for any given school are examined in light of national trends during that same period. In Table V, the differences between the individual withdrawal rate for each school and the rate of the nation as a whole is reported for each year in which data were obtainable. Here it can be seen that the range of variation of these differences is less than 21 per cent for all schools, and the average of these variations is less than 10 per cent.

Within an institutional context, however, many of the general characteristics of the withdrawal rate of that institution are modified. Thus, the withdrawal rate for women is roughly the same as that for men in general, but lower than the men's rate in technical schools and much lower in teachers' colleges, albeit higher than in the technical schools.[27] The withdrawal rate for dormitory residents is higher than for fraternity residents.[28] Thus it seems clear that although withdrawal is a phenomenon variable from setting to setting, it is relatively stable in any given context.

One very likely reason for failure, of course, is the cumulative character of academic demands. Earlier courses provide the foundation for later ones; simple introductions are followed by increasingly difficult studies. It might be expected, then, that a similar pattern of failure and withdrawal would be characteristic of all schools regardless of the absolute level of failures encountered. This is indeed the case. The pattern encountered, however, does not suggest an increasing

### Table VI—Percentage of 12,667 Students Continuing in Attendance at Institutions of First Enrollment by Years*

| Not Beyond First Registration Period | Beyond First Registration, Not More Than One Year | Beyond One Year, Not More Than Two Years | Beyond Two Years, Not More Than Three Years | Entered Fourth Year Not Graduated | Graduated 1954 | Others |
|---|---|---|---|---|---|---|
| 10.7 | 16.6 | 15.0 | 6.0 | 7.3 | 39.5 | 4.9 |

* Adapted from Iffert, *op. cit.*, Table 8, p. 16.
According to the registrar at Berkeley, "50 per cent of the 696 undergraduates dismissed in the Spring were just completing their first year" and "45 per cent of all the students who withdrew during Fall, 1957, had completed no semesters of work at the University. These students, except for the few who withdrew repeatedly, and completed no work, were new students at the University."

rate of academic failure over time as the exigencies of the school situation increase. On the contrary as illustrated in Tables VI and VII, most failures and withdrawals occur at the beginning of the college career and then taper off. And, as can be seen in Table VIII, this is an old and stable pattern.

Despite the variations in level to be seen from campus to campus and the characteristic rates for special subgroups on a campus, the pattern of withdrawal rates for any given group of entering students

---

27. Iffert, *op. cit.*, Table 8, p. 16.
28. *Ibid.*, Table 42, p. 76.

remains quite similar for all schools.[29] Table IX shows the percentage of various classes withdrawing.[30]

### Table VII—Semesters Completed and Class Standing of the Withdrawals. Percentage Withdrawing by Number of Semesters Completed (Undergraduates Only)*

NUMBER OF SEMESTERS COMPLETED

|  | 0 | 1 | 2 | 3 | 4 | 5 | 6 | 7 | 8 | 9 | 10 | 11 | 12 | 13 | 14 | 15 | | |
|---|---|---|---|---|---|---|---|---|---|---|---|---|---|---|---|---|---|---|
| Fall 1957 | 41 | 8 | 19 | 6 | 11 | 4 | 6 | 1 | 1 | 1 | 1 | — | — | — | — | — | 100% | (537) |
| Spring 1958 | 19 | 32 | 9 | 13 | 5 | 10 | 4 | 3 | 2 | 3 | 4 | — | — | — | — | — | 100% | (297) |

* Adapted from "Withdrawals and Dismissals of 1957–58, University of California at Berkely: A Statistical Study," Office of the Registrar, University of California, Berkeley, June 1960, p. 62 (Mimeographed.)

The relation between week of withdrawal and number of semesters completed at the university is shown for Fall, 1957, and for Spring, 1958, in Table 7. In general, there is a steady decline with slight peaks at the weeks most closely associated with examinations. This is more pronounced for those who have completed no semesters in the Fall of 1957 and one semester during the Spring of 1958. It would appear that the pressures most clearly associated with formal academic requirements take their toll quite early. For those who survive into late years at the university, this relation tends to disappear, and the dropout rate is quite steady throughout the year—indicating nonacademic reasons for withdrawal. The mean is approximately 6.6 per cent of the withdrawals per week.

The common explanatory factors have small impact upon this pattern of stability. It is similar for men and women, rural and urban, regardless of residence or major.[31] Once again there is the suggestion of a process characteristic of the social structure reflected in the failure rates.

---

29. W. Max Wise, *op. cit.*, p. 16.

"Of those who drop out of the college of first registration, slightly more than half do so during or at the end of their freshman year. Almost equal proportions of men and women stay until graduation: the dropout patterns of men and women through the first four years of college are similar, with the exception that the sophomore year tends to be a terminal period of enrollment for more women than men. . . . Studies of continuation in college do not suggest that dropouts occur exclusively among the less gifted students, since, of those enrolled who are in the upper 20 per cent of indicated ability, only about half stay until graduation. Studies of persistence in college indicate that, of the students who ranked in the top fifth of their high school classes, 43 per cent stay to graduation from college; of those ranking in the next fifth, 30 per cent stay to graduation; of the middle fifth, 19 per cent stay; of the next lowest fifth, 10 per cent; and of the bottom fifth, 4 per cent."

30. Data are from responses to the request for information cited earlier.

31. Iffert, *op. cit.*, Chap. 6.

## Table VIII—Percentages of Freshmen Who Discontinued College at Institution of First Attendance, by Period of Attendance and by Sex, 1931 and 1950*

| Period of Attendance | 1931 FRESHMEN (%) | | | 1950 FRESHMEN (%) | | |
|---|---|---|---|---|---|---|
| | Total | Men | Women | Total | Men | Women |
| Not beyond first year | 33.8 | 34.0 | 33.5 | 27.3 | 27.4 | 27.0 |
| Beyond first year, not more than two years | 16.7 | 15.9 | 18.2 | 15.0 | 12.2 | 19.1 |
| Beyond second year, not more than three years | 7.7 | 8.1 | 6.7 | 6.0 | 6.3 | 5.6 |
| Entered fourth year, not graduated | 3.9 | 4.6 | 2.4 | 7.3 | 9.8 | 3.7 |
| Graduated in four years | 37.9 | 37.4 | 39.2 | 44.4 | 44.3 | 44.6 |

Sources: For Class of 1954, see Robert E. Iffert, op. cit., p. 16. For Class of 1935 see John H. McNeeley, College Student Mortality, Government Printing Office, Washington, 1938.
* W. Max Wise, op. cit., p. 15.

## Table IX—Percentage of Students Withdrawing from Selected Institutions of Higher Education by Year in School, 1940–1941 to 1960–1961

| College | Year | 1st | 2nd | 3rd | 4th |
|---|---|---|---|---|---|
| 1 | 1940–41 | 20 | 23 | 7 | 0 |
| | 1941–42 | 23 | 15 | 7 | 0 |
| | 1942–43 | 18 | 11 | 2 | 0 |
| | 1943–44 | 18 | 19 | 6 | 0 |
| | 1944–45 | 19 | 13 | 1 | 1 |
| | 1945–46 | 17 | 16 | 2 | 0 |
| | 1946–47 | 16 | 15 | 5 | 0 |
| | 1947–48 | 20 | 18 | 3 | 1 |
| | 1948–49 | 15 | 16 | 5 | 0 |
| | 1949–50 | 21 | 18 | 8 | 0 |
| | 1950–51 | 19 | 15 | 7 | 0 |
| | 1951–52 | 21 | 18 | 5 | −1 |
| | 1952–53 | 18 | 19 | 3 | −6 |
| | 1953–54 | 11 | 17 | 4 | 3 |
| | 1954–55 | 10 | 17 | 6 | −4 |
| | 1955–56 | 12 | 21 | 5 | −3 |
| | 1956–57 | 16 | 18 | 3 | −1 |
| | 1957–58 | 15 | 19 | 4 | −1 |
| | 1958–59 | 15 | 20 | 5 | 2 |
| | 1959–60 | 13 | 20 | | |
| | 1960–61 | 9 | | | |
| 2 | 1949 | 13 | 17 | 2 | 2 |
| | 1950 | 11 | 20 | 9 | |
| | 1951 | 15 | 14 | 12 | 1 |
| | 1952 | 7 | 20 | 3 | 1 |
| | 1953 | 6 | 11 | 4 | 1 |
| | 1954 | 8 | 15 | 7 | 1 |
| | 1955 | 10 | 10 | 5 | 1 |
| | 1956 | 9 | 5 | 4 | 1 |
| | 1957 | 5 | 13 | 4 | 2 |
| | 1958 | 8 | 7 | 5 | 1 |
| 3 | 1957 | 8 | 10 | 5 | 5 |

Failure and withdrawal, then, may be considered relatively stable phenomena when viewed as characteristics of large groups. Attention has been drawn to the stability of failure rates as distinct from the unpredictable nature of individual failure. Such stability suggests that failure rates reflect, in some way, the quality of life within those groups. This is what might have been expected on the basis of the previous discussion based upon Durkheim's description of group life.

## STUDENT SUBCULTURES

As mentioned before, there is relatively little theoretical work available to guide in the identification of academic contexts, to assess their character, and to evaluate the nature of the impact that they exert upon the lives of the students in them. Theodore Newcomb's early work at Bennington[32] is useful in this regard for its demonstration of the general effects of life in a rather homogeneous college atmosphere, and his more recent work[33] demonstrates empirically how small groups—residence groups in this case—operate to socialize the newcomer to the values of a subculture and maintain the distinctive character of subcultures over long periods. C. Robert Pace[34] has used a questionnaire to obtain a picture of the "press" or atmosphere of an entire school. In private conversation he has indicated that he plans further work to compare differences in the press as perceived by members of different groups within the institution. These techniques, although reaffirming the value differences existing among subgroups and providing a device for describing existing differences, do not, however, provide a framework for categorizing those differences in a systematic way.

Martin Trow and Burton R. Clark[35] have produced a fourfold

---

32. Theodore M. Newcomb, *Personality and Social Change,* Dryden Press, New York, 1943.

33. Theodore M. Newcomb, *The Acquaintance Process,* Holt, Rinehart & Winston, Inc., New York 1961.

34. C. R. Pace, *The Influence of Academic and Student Sub-cultures in College and University Environments,* U.S. Office of Education, Cooperative Research Project 1083, June, 1964.

35. B. R. Clark and M. Trow, "Determinants of College Student Sub-cultures," Center for the Study of Higher Education, University of California, Berkeley, 1960. (Mimeographed.)

scheme of student orientations. These types are characterized by their attitudes in favor or against "school spirit," social activities, an independent dimension of study, and intellectual activities. It is implied, although not demonstrated, that these individual orientations reflect in some way specific subcultures to be found on a college campus. David Riesman and Christopher Jencks[36] suggest that subcultural value systems and specific campus groups may be related. In characterizing subcultures at Harvard (and suggesting their more general occurrence), they emphasize the role of different residence groups, or houses, and the various clubs in maintaining differences in the normative structures of these subcultures. Hence, existing information points repeatedly to living groups and clubs as being central factors in the maintenance of differences in subcultures, although such groups are, by no means, coterminous with the subcultures themselves.[37]

Although formal group membership may not coincide with subcultures on the campus, there is at least one argument to suggest that a sample of subcultures can be obtained by taking a sample based on formal group membership.

There is a growing body of research demonstrating the importance of propinquity in the development of friendship patterns.[38] Friendships usually develop within groups rather than across barriers to social interactions and among people who engage in common activities rather than among those who are rarely in contact. At the University of California, some living groups are almost a mile from others and separated by the campus, shopping districts, and busy thoroughfares. Within some large buildings such as dormitories or sororities there are also barriers to interaction, apparently, as informants state that close friendships tend to develop along a floor rather than between floors.

---

36. D. Riesman and C. Jencks, "Patterns of Residential Education, A Case Study of Harvard," quoted in *The American College: A Psychological and Social Interpretation of the Higher Learning,* ed. by R. N. Sanford, John Wiley & Sons, Inc., New York, 1962.

37. Rebecca Vreeland and Charles Bidwell, "Organizational Effects on Student Attitudes: A Study of the Harvard Houses," *Sociology of Education,* vol. 38, no. 3, Spring 1965, p. 234.

38. Theodore Newcomb, *op. cit.*

It is reasonable to assume, then, that the friendship group of the entering freshman will develop among those with whom he has the opportunity to interact in the most casual, spontaneous, and informal manner—his roommates and close neighbors within the living group. For the new student especially, the focus of much of the informal part of life is with friends and associates in the informal atmosphere of the residence. It is here, in conditions that foster the breakdown of social distance and encourage the spontaneous interaction of "whole persons," that a good part of the student's day is spent. It is in such a setting that he takes on the fullest character of individuality and uniqueness in contrast to his standardized role of student in the lecture hall. Residence groups appear to have more of the qualities of primary groups than do academic majors. It is to the informal residence group that the student most often looks for support and praise, and it is here that he develops his image of the nature of everyday life at the university. It is in casual association with friends that he learns the meaning attributed to various kinds of acts and the symbols of status of the educated man. And it is here that he learns the sanctions for deviation from group norms.

We can assume that formal groups such as residence groups and clubs provide the nexus between the individual and campus subcultures. They are, at the same time, carriers of the subcultures and the contexts of the students' primary-group interactions. Important traditions of campus life such as spring sing or intramural competitions are cast in the form of group, not individual, participation. Thus we may sample the content of subcultures by sampling formal groups. This procedure should provide information about norms regarding academic endeavor as well as the degree of social cohesion experienced in the informal settings of everyday life.

## CONCLUSION

This chapter has been an attempt to delineate the major dimensions of a theory of academic failure focusing upon contexts of social interaction within university settings. It has presented a summary of much of the important work that has attempted to identify factors associated with student success and failure in college. Academic failure is viewed from the way in which social environments, in various combinations and perceived in separate ways, can influence individual adaptations. At the same time the phenomenon of failure is presented as a group response to differential academic climates, maintaining statistical regularities over time within given institutions.

These ideas have been tested empirically and the results may be found in *College Dropouts: Social Sources of Academic Failure*.[39] What is important about the present task is that it clarifies for the reader, students of educational institutions, and potential and practicing school counselors some of the social dynamics of university life. It should sensitize these persons to look for social as well as individual explanations for academic failure. Social contexts, within which students pursue academic goals, must be considered as relevant factors in the diagnosis and prediction of academic success.

---

39. Nasatir, *op. cit.*

# INDEX

# INDEX

Status (*cont.*)
  suburbanization, 34–36
  urban renewal, 34
Status concept, 92
Stefflre, Buford, 216–17
Stein, Morris, 130n, 227n
Stendler, Celia, 295n
Stereotyping, 270–74
  child development and, 285–94
  by class, 295–97
  guidance and, 280–81, 284
  maturation and, 294–97
  social ethic and, 278–81
  by students of counselors and
    teachers, 274–75, 279–81,
    283–84, 297, 299, 302–3
Stern, G., 130n, 277n
Stokes, Donald, 121n
Stouffer, Samuel, 123, 143, 145,
  212n
Stout, Irving W., 288n
Strowig, R. Wray, 215n
"Student Culture in Medical School"
  (Becker and Greer), 196n
*Student Physician, The* (Merton and
  Kendall), 196n, 246n
Student rebellion, 99–101, 106, 126,
  292
  effect of on school policy, 134–35
  influence of on academic failure,
    361, 366
  interaction with bureaucracy as
    cause of, 185–86
Studies in Ethnomethodology (Gar-
  finkel), 341, 341n
"Studies of the Routine Grounds of
  Everyday Activities" (Gar-
  finkel), 341n
"Study in Discrimination, A" (Bar-
  ney and Hall), 204n
Study of College Peer Groups, The
  (ed. Newcomb and Wilson),
  128n
"Study of Student Withdrawal at
  W.U., A" (Bragg), 364n
"Study of the Home Life of Well
  Adjusted Children in Three

Areas of the United States,
  A" (Stout and Langdon),
  288n
Subcultures, *see* Peer groups
*Suicide* (Durkheim), 68
"Suicide" (Gibbs), 121n
Sumner, William Graham, 5, 21, 41
Super, Donald, 148n
Supreme Court (U.S.), 49
Survey Research Center (Berkeley,
  Calif.), 13
Systems Development Corporation,
  224

"Teacher Alienation" (Lamb, Mc-
  Hugh and Weinberg), 129n
Teachers
  education of, 6–7
  public image of, 281–84
Technology, 27, 42–46
  automation and, 43–45
  educational, 46
Testing, 146
*Theories of Personality* (Hall and
  Lindzey), 95n
"Theory of Educational and Voca-
  tional Choice in Junior High
  School, A" (Ruble et al.),
  201n
*Theory of Social and Economic
  Organization, The* (Weber),
  327n
*They Come for the Best of Reasons*
  (Wise), 354n
Thomas Dorothy S., 315n
Thomas, W. I., 315, 327
Thorndike, Edward, 41, 119
Thrasher, Frederick, 293
*Toward a General Theory of Action*
  (Parsons and Shils), 357n
*Toward a Psychology of Being*
  (Maslow), 157n
Trow, M., 128–29, 130, 378n
*Two Cultures, The,* (Snow), 60n
Typing of students, 300, 308–9
  dysfunctions of, 301